TEACHING ENGLISH LEARNERS IN INCLUSIVE CLASSROOMS

Third Edition

TEACHING ENGLISH LEARNERS IN INCLUSIVE CLASSROOMS

By

ELVA DURAN, PH.D.

California State University
Sacramento, California

With a Foreword by

Bruce Ostertag, ED.D.

With an Introduction by

Lou Brown, PH.D.

CHARLES C THOMAS · PUBLISHER, LTD.
Springfield · Illinois · U.S.A.

KH

Published and Distributed Throughout the World by

CHARLES C THOMAS • PUBLISHER, LTD.
2600 South First Street
Springfield, Illinois 62704

©2006 by CHARLES C THOMAS • PUBLISHER, LTD.

ISBN 10 0-398-07674-X (hard) ISBN 13 978-0-398-07674-0 (hard)
ISBN 10 0-398-07675-8 (paper) ISBN 13 978-0-398-07675-7 (paper)

Library of Congress Catalog Card Number: 2006044624

Printed in the United States of America
CR-R-3

Library of Congress Cataloging-in-Publication Data
Durán, Elva.
    Teaching English learners in inclusive classrooms / by Elva
Duran ; with a forward by Bruce Ostertag ; with an introduction by
Lou Brown. -- 3rd ed.
        p. cm.
    Rev. ed. of: Teaching students with moderate/severe disabilities,
including autism.
    Includes bibliographical references and index.
    ISBN 0-398-07674-X -- ISBN 0-398-07675-8 (pbk.)
    1. Children with disabilities--Education--United States. 2. Linguistic
minorities--Education--United States. 3. Inclusive education--United
States. 4. Multicultural education--United States. I. Durán, Elva.
Teaching students with moderate/severe disabilities, including
autism. II. Title.

LC4031.D84 2006
371.91--dc22   2006044624

8/25/08

CONTRIBUTORS

Lou Brown, Ph.D. is Professor Emeritus at the University of Wisconsin at Madison. He is world renown and is famous for his work devoted to persons with severe intellectual disabilities. He has published extensively and is internationally and nationally known for his advocacy work in educating persons with severe disabilities in the world of school, work, and the community. He is one of the founders of TASH, (The Association of Persons with Severe Disabilities).

EunMi Cho, Ed.D. is an Assistant Professor at California State University, Sacramento, Department of Special Education, Rehabilitation, and School Psychology. She is Coordinator of a Special Education Internship Program that is a collaboration between CSUS and Sacramento City Unified School District. Her areas of expertise include social studies methods, multiculturalism, and special education methods in social studies. She has also done extensive work with Korean families. She is fluent in English and Korean.

Vivian I. Correa, Ph.D. is a Professor and the Associate Dean of the Graduate School at the University of Florida. Dr. Correa received her Ph.D. in Early Childhood Special Education and Visual Disabilities from George Peabody College of Vanderbilt University in 1982. She taught at Texas Tech University from 1982 to 1985 and has been at the University of Florida since 1985. Dr. Correa has extensive experience providing training in the area of children with multiple disabilities and their families. She has worked with children and their families in a variety of PreK/primary programs since 1975. Dr. Correa is a native of Puerto Rico and has done extensive work with Latino children and their families.

Beverly E. Cross, Ph.D. is a Associate Professor of curriculum theory and urban education at the University of Wisconsin-Milwaukee in the Department of Curriculum and Instruction. She conducts research in the areas of teacher diversity, urban education, multicultural and antiracist education, and curriculum theory. Her research has appeared in such journals as the *Journal of Curriculum and Supervision, Educational Leadership, International Journal of Educational Reform,* and *The Urban Review.*

Elva Durán, Ph.D. is a Professor of Special Education in the Department of Special Education Rehabilitation, and School Psychology at California State University, Sacramento. She graduated from the University of Oregon and received her doctorate in special education with an emphasis in learning disabilities and reading. She has been a reading specialist, elementary, middle school and special education teacher in Guam and in El Paso, Texas. She has published, *Systematic Instruction in Reading for Spanish-Speaking Students, Teaching Students with Moderate/Severe Disabilities, Including Autism Strategies for Second Language Learners in Inclusive Settings Second Edition,* co-authored *Leamos Español K-2 Spanish Reading* program, has co-authored *ACCESS* curriculum for sixth, seventh, and eighth graders who are English learners and has published numerous articles in special education and English learners. Her areas of interest are English learners, culturally and linguistically diverse students, language and literacy and methods in English language development, and special education. She is fluent in English and Spanish.

Paula M. Gardner, Ed.D. is a Professor of Special Education in the Department of Special Education, Rehabilitation, and School Psychology at California State University, Sacramento. She is the Coordinator of Student Teaching placements in her department. She has been a teacher of students with mild/moderate disabilities and has done extensive work in the California districts helping the schools fully include students with moderate/severe disabilities in general education classes. She has become a leader in the field and throughout California with her advocacy inclusion work for persons with moderate and severe disabilities. She teaches positive behavior support classes at CSUS.

Rachael A. Gonzáles, Ed.D. is an Associate Professor of Special Education in the Department of Special Education, Rehabilitation, and School Psychology at California State University, Sacramento. She is coprincipal investigator in a grant collaboration with Monument Corridor in northern California. She is also Coordinator of the California State University and northern California teacher preparation program in special education. She teaches classes in English learners and special education, Level II credentialing courses in special education, and has developed a collaborative certification for teacher candidates who work with students with emotional disturbance. This is a collaborative effort between school districts and CSUS. Her research interests include, English learners, culturally and diverse students in special education, methods in emotional disorders, and mental health. She is fluent in Spanish and English and has participated jointly with northern California teachers in traveling through Cuba to study educational systems and classroom learning environments.

Chris Hagie, Ph.D. is an Associate Professor in the Department of Special Education at San Jose State University in California. She is the Coordinator of the Collaborative Intern Program at SJSU. She was a special education teacher and mentor for over twenty years and continues to provide consultation to school districts. Her research interests and topics of scholarly activities include the preparation of and optimal support for new teachers, effective discussion group practices in we-based courses, and instructional strategies for students with emotional disorders and moderate to severe disabilities.

Ming-Gon John Lian, Ed.D. is Director of the Centre for Advancement in Special Education Faculty Education, University of Hong Kong. He is a member of the TASH Board (The Association for Persons with Severe Disabilities). He has been a professor of special education at Illinois State University and is well-known for his contributions to the Asian American community and has published numerous articles and chapters in books in the area of Asian American students with severe disabilities. He is a national and international leader in his field.

Porfirio M. Loeza, Ph.D., is Assistant Professor of Language and Literacy in the Department of Teacher Education at California State

University, Sacramento. Dr. Loeza has been a bilingual leader teacher in California for over ten years. His teaching experience reaches across all grade levels. He completed his doctoral program in Language and Literacy and Culture at the University of California at Berkeley. While at Berkeley, he was coadvised and mentored by the linguist Lily Wong Fillmore and Eugene Garcia. Dr. Garcia chaired his dissertation research committee. His dissertation research centers on the examination of the literacy practices associated with the *"retablo"* in Mexican votive art. (A "retablo" is a small oil painting, usually made on tin, and most often made by popular or untrained artists from the provinces of Mexico). Despite his move from K-12 to the university, he continues to keep abreast of the changing trends in the schools. He regularly visits classrooms and frequently provides a guest lesson in the K-12 setting. He is fluent in English and Spanish.

Elba Maldonado-Colón, Ed.D. is the Professor, Coordinator of the Mild/Moderate Disabilities Program and Chair, Department of Special Education at San Jose State University in California. She is a leader in Spanish and English language and literacy development for monolingual and bilingual students, particularly English learners. She has numerous publications and presentations on culturally and linguistically diverse children/youth. She has taught courses in language development, language arts, reading, assessment, working with culturally and linguistically diverse families, curriculum and methods to facilitate and promote English language development, and promoting adolescent literacy (with focus on comprehension). She is fluent in English and Spanish.

Bruce A. Ostertag, Ed.D. is a Professor and Department Chair of the Department of Special Education, Rehabilitation, and School Psychology. He has developed model and combined programs in multiple subject and special education. He teaches courses in technology, assessment, education of the exceptional child, and methods courses in special education. His research interests include technology and assessment information for students in mild/moderate disabilities. He is well-respected by his colleagues and peers. He has also completed extensive credentialing work for the Commission on Teacher Credentialing in California.

Dr. Hyun-Sook Park, Ph.D. is a Professor of Special Education at San Jose State University in California. She is the Coordinator of the

Teacher Preparation in Moderate/Severe Disabilities. She has done extensive research in the area of social skill relationships, transition, friendships of students with moderate/severe disabilities and has also published extensively in each of these areas. She teaches assessment, methods and master's classes in the area of moderate/severe disabilities. She is the coprincipal investigator of a national grant in a transition and collaborative effort between San Jose State University and Sacramento and San Jose Unified School Districts. She has been coeditor for *Research and Practice for Persons with Severe Disabilities* and has been coprincipal investigator in several national grants. She is an international and national leader in her area of educating persons with moderate/severe disabilities. She is fluent in English and Korean.

Joyce Targaguila-Harth, M.Ed. is a doctoral candidate in the Department of Special Education at the University of Florida. She is specializing in early childhood special education and TESOL. She received her M.Ed. in specific learning disabilities from the University of Florida in 1977. She has worked with culturally and linguistically diverse students and their families in a variety of settings since 1991. She has served as a parent educator for Early Start and Even Start Programs and has had extensive experience providing training in the areas of bilingual special education, early childhood development, TESOL, and learning disabilities. Her areas of expertise and research include early childhood special education, bilingual special education, learning disabilities, working with families from diverse backgrounds and early literacy development. She is a native of Puerto Rico and is fluent in English, Spanish, and Portuguese.

I dedicate this book to **Dr. Kenneth Wiesner, M.D.** for all the years he has kept me well and for always being there for me. I have been Dr. Wiesner's patient for more than ten years and I can honestly say I have never had a more dedicated doctor take care of me with all my health needs and concerns. Dr. Wiesner is, first of all, a most dedicated doctor who cares deeply about his patients. He works late hours and is there at Sacramento Rheumatology Consultants at 6:00 a.m. to see many patients. I am one of those fortunate patients who are there with questions, concerns, and health issues early and late, and at other times to seek his wisdom, knowledge, and good common sense in treating me as his patient. I have been able to teach, enjoy my work, and have the ability to be a professor because he helps me daily. I appreciate all he has done and continues to do for me as his patient. Thank you, Dr. Wiesner for what you do for me and your patients on a daily basis. I could not have written this book without your help and guidance in assisting me to stay well through all these years!

I dedicate this book to **Dr. Bruce Ostertag, Ed.D.** for being a great friend, colleague, and for his support while I have been a professor at California State University, Sacramento. Bruce has always been there for me from the day I arrived on campus many years ago. He has unselfishly lent me course materials, given me advice, and when I was in need of his help during a difficult time in my life, there he was for me, ready to assist with each of my concerns. He did not leave my side and helped me as I walked a difficult path. He gives of his time and support unselfishly to so many and I am truly grateful for all he does and continues to do for me daily. Bruce, thank you for all the years you have been such a great friend and colleague. Thank you for all you have assisted me with for so long. You have been, and continue to be, a great friend and colleague!

FOREWORD

Once again, Professor Elva Durán has made an invaluable contribution to the betterment of children's learning with this newly revised text, *Teaching English Language Learners in Inclusive Education*. In her continuing efforts to speak of this topic, Dr. Durán's text updates and expands upon issues of great concern to those working with students who are English language learners as well as having special learning challenges. Given the unacceptable school dropout rates of these students, this book provides practical tools and strategies for educators to approach the unique learning needs of these students.

This text draws upon the most current laws and research in the interconnected fields of bilingual and multicultural education, language and literacy, and special needs. Additionally, Dr. Durán draws upon her extensive experiences via classroom teaching, university-level instruction, and textbook writing in these fields to present a highly useful compendium of ideas. Further, Dr. Durán has also coauthored two full curriculum programs: *Leamos Español-Beginning Systematic Instruction for Spanish-Speaking Students* and *Access-Middle School Curriculum for English Language Learners to Access Content-Sheltered Instruction*. The revised edition of this text also utilizes many of the functional strategies formulated in these unique curriculum programs.

The range of chapters exemplifies the width and breadth of this material. A sampling of these chapters include topics such as functional language and other language intervention strategies; transition; adolescent students with autism and other spectrum disorders; multiple disorders; issues related to Latino students; and issues related to African American and Asian American students. In addition to this revised material, two new areas are also addressed: literacy instruction for English learners and sheltered content instruction in social studies. Many of these chapters look at the use of direct instructional approaches that have proven to be successful strategies in addressing these educational areas.

In short, teachers and teacher trainers will find this clear, well-written text to be an invaluable resource in addressing the needs of myriad and unique students.

Bruce A. Ostertag

PREFACE

The uniqueness of this new and revised text edition can be seen in each of the chapters which have been completely rewritten to include new information on IDEA, No Child Left Behind, content standards, and research related to teaching English learners who are fully-included and may also have mild-moderate, and severe disabilities. There are new chapters in literacy development, sheltered content instruction, assessment, transition, inclusion, language development, and new information included in the chapters related to Asian, Latino, and African American students, and there is an entirely new chapter written on families. It has taken the coauthors between two and some two and a half years to finish writing their new chapters that have been included in the third and entirely new edition of *Teaching English Learners in Inclusive Classrooms*. The hard work that each coauthor did to complete their chapters is evident as teacher candidates and parents will read this new edition to help them teach all children.

The additional uniqueness of this revised edition can also be seen in the chapter titles and their contents. There is no other text to the knowledge of this author that gives such complete information on how to educate all children and youth and those who have mild-moderate-to-severe disabilities and are also English learners. The other unique quality of the new edition is that the majority of the coauthors are culturally and linguistically diverse, may speak more than one language, and have extensive background and experience in working with all learners in special and general education classrooms.

Additionally, each of the coauthors has extensive experience they have carefully woven in their chapters in also working with the teacher candidates and the children whom they teach. Thus, the chapters will reflect research-based practices as well as practical information for all children.

Elva Durán, Ph.D.

INTRODUCTION

LOU BROWN

For many years I have been informed and inspired by passionate and sustained commitments of Elva Durán to children whose first language was not an American version of English. Several years ago I agreed to write an introduction to a book she was planning. In January, 2003 I retired from the School of Education at the University of Wisconsin. Subsequently, I was consumed by three projects. First, several students and colleagues had been asking me to write some of the stories I often tell in lectures and presentations. I did (Brown, 2005a). Second, with the assistance of Professors Leonard Burrello and Pat Rogan of the University of Indiana, I recorded many of the stories and related information on three video discs (Brown, 2005b). Third, my Madison colleagues Kim Kessler and Betsy Shiraga of Community Work Services, Inc. and I produced a report of fifty individuals with significant intellectual and other disabilities who functioned in integrated work settings from four to twenty-four years after exiting public schools (Brown, Shiraga, & Kessler, 2006).

In October, 2005 Elva requested the promised introduction. I could not think of much to write that was not presented in the documents and video discs. Thus, I took editorial license in the form of copying elements of them for inclusion here. I am not sure this is proper. Indeed, some would probably say I plagiarized myself. Nevertheless, I think the elements are directly relevant to the plight of children whose second language is a USA version of English, who are not thriving in school and who are unlikely to be successful matriculants at community colleges, vocational/technical schools and universities.

Some who survive the birth process this year will be more disabled than any who did so before. Individuals with disabilities who enter and exit schools now are outliving their parents. As they age, many are presenting more longitudinal, complicated and expensive difficulties than chronological age peers.

When George W. Bush became President, he established an advisory group to address the issue of excellence in special education. In 2001, after over one year of comprehensive study, his group reported that approximately 70 percent of all persons with disabilities in the United States between the ages of eighteen and sixty-four were unemployed or grossly underemployed. Subsequently, his committee for people with intellectual disabilities reported that 90 percent of the approximately nine million adults in the United States so labeled were unemployed (PCID, 2004). A task force established by the governor of Florida reported that approximately 85 percent of all adult Floridians considered to have developmental disabilities and/or cerebral palsy were unemployed (Salomone & Garcia, 2004). Historically, individuals with disabilities whose first verbal language was not English have been represented in special education programs. It is quite likely that they are also overrepresented in unemployment statistics.

Some adults with disabilities have functioned productively in integrated work settings for centuries and each year increasing numbers do so in more communities around the world. Nevertheless, the post-school outcomes realized by the vast majority are tragically unacceptable and wasteful of hopes, dreams, lives and increasingly scarce tax dollars. Far too many exit school and are unnecessarily confined to segregated workshops, activity centers, enclaves or mobile work crews or stay at home all day with family members and/or others who are paid to be with them.

HOW TO KEEP UNEMPLOYMENT RATES HIGH

There are casual relationships between the nature of the special education and related services provided and the post-vocational failures of citizens with disabilities. If we wanted to maintain or increase these post-school failure rates, some of the actions we should continue are listed below.

• Maintain the myopic and dysfunctional views that diplomas and standardized academic achievement test scores are meaningful educational outcomes.

- Reduce curricular options to only academic courses that emphasize complex, abstract, grade level and verbally-laden content.
- Arrange for increasing numbers of students to receive special education and related services.
- Confine students with disabilities to special education schools and classes or place them in incomprehensible regular education classes glued to paraprofessionals.
- Provide instruction only on school grounds.
- Minimize parent involvement in school policies and practices.
- Transport students to schools that are far away from their homes in special vehicles.
- Hire many teachers with emergency credentials.
- Teach to developmental rather than chronological age.
- Do away with social promotion.
- Make it legal to quit school at age ten.
- Establish special schools for those who do not pass high school entrance tests. Keep them there until they either pass them or drop out. Almost all will drop out soon.
- Resist all changes in service delivery models, in-service and pre-service training programs, funding priorities, curriculum development strategies, and collaboration between special and regular educators.
- Refuse to perform any action that is not clearly required by the management labor contract. Indeed, demand overtime pay for each minute past the times specified in the contract.

If you are alive and function with disabilities, you must be somewhere. Where should you be? You must be with someone. Who should you be with? You must be doing something. What should you be doing? You should be in respected environments with individuals without disabilities doing what they do because an integrated life is inherently better than one that is segregated. We must do all that is reasonable to prevent anyone from experiencing a life that is segregated, nonproductive, sterile, unnecessarily dependant and costly. Conversely, we must do what is reasonable to prepare and arrange for all citizens to live, work and play enjoyably and productively in a safe, stimulating and diverse integrated society.

Vocational preparation refers to a student with disabilities being provided the actual experiences, skills, work ethics, attitudes, values and other phenomena needed to perform real work in integrated non-school settings and activities in accordance with the minimally acceptable standards of employers for at least minimum wages and employer-provided benefits at the point of exit from school. If a student with disabilities is likely to realize this standard by experiencing traditional service delivery models, curricula and instructional practices, use them. However, if the manifested progress of a student is not likely to result in realizing the "real work in the real world at the point of school exit," standard, alternative and supplementary experiences must be provided.

Authentic assessment refers to school personnel putting a student in real-life settings and activities and determining meaningful discrepancies between his/her expressed repertoire and the actual requirements of minimally acceptable functioning. Authentic instruction refers to teaching that which is actually needed to participate meaningfully in important real-life settings and activities. Authentic assessment and instruction are extremely valuable for persons with significant learning disabilities for several reasons. First, instruction in real-life settings and activities minimizes reliance upon generalization, and transfer of training skills that cannot be depended upon with reasonable confidence and safety. Second, valuable resources are dispensed only on teaching that which is actually needed for minimally acceptably functioning in important real-life settings and activities. Third, the actual materials, performance criteria, distractions, etc. experienced in the real world are accounted for in the instructional process.

HOW TO INCREASE EMPLOYMENT RATES

What can we do to prepare more students with disabilities to function effectively in the real world of work at the point of school exit? Individualized school exit portfolios are offered as reasonable alternatives and/or supplements to diplomas, grades, Carnegie units, courses, credits and/or scores on academic achievement tests. What should be in a school exit portfolio?

- Video records of at least four successful experiences in real jobs.
- Employer testimonials of competence.

- Verification that the student is working at least twenty hours per week in a job that pays at least minimum wage and offers employer-provided benefits at school exit.
- Evidence that the student and his/her family are connected to the persons and agencies that will provide support after school exit.
- Evidence of good work ethics, reliability, timeliness, and respect for the property rights of others.
- Evidence of reasonable physical status and appearance.
- Reasonable functional money and tool-use repertoires.
- Meaningful reading, math and communication skills.
- Minimally acceptable social and leisure competencies.
- Appropriate travel, lunch and break time skills.
- Clear descriptions of individual learning and performance characteristics.
- Valid knowledge of successful accommodations to disability manifestations.

If existing service delivery models are not resulting in preferred and realizable outcomes, what are the alternatives? Three of many are presented below.

Restructuring High Schools. Restructuring high schools refers to making changes in existing service delivery models, curriculum development strategies, personnel preparation programs and resource priorities so that students with disabilities can be provided with the preparatory experiences necessary to function effectively in real jobs that pay at least minimum wages and include employer-provided benefits at school exit. Some, but clearly not all, of the changes necessary to realize this important outcome follow. When a student enters high school, authentic vocational and related assessment and instruction should begin. During the first year, one-half day per week should be devoted to learning to function in real nonschool vocational and related settings and activities. Subsequently, the amounts of time spent learning to function efficiently in individually appropriate nonschool vocational and related settings and activities should be increased. If a student is enrolled in school after age eighteen, all instruction should be provided in integrated, respected and individually appropriate nonschool settings and activities. In short, integrated school should be faded out and integrated community should be faded in.

When students are not receiving authentic vocational and related instruction, they should be provided individually appropriate experiences in regular education classes. If individually appropriate educational experiences in integrated classes cannot be generated, the amounts of time spent in important nonschool settings and activities should be increased. Special education classes, resource rooms and other segregated settings should be avoided if humanly possible, so should arranging for a paraprofessional to sit with a student in math, science, history, and literature classes when the curricula are absurdly complex, incomprehensible and not meaningfully related to acceptable post-school functioning.

Students with disabilities should be given the opportunities and assistance needed to function in a wide array of individually appropriate and integrated school-sponsored extracurricular activities. If private therapy is individually appropriate, so be it. Whenever reasonable, which is in most instances, speech, language, physical, occupational and other therapies should be provided in integrated environments and activities.

The Buyout Option. Assume school personnel will not provide authentic instruction in individually meaningful nonschool contexts because they cannot figure out how to reallocate personnel so as to provide reasonable coverage; it is too expensive; insurance rates might increase; teachers, therapists, paraprofessionals and other instructional personnel do not want to leave school grounds during school times because it is too cold or too hot out; professionals who spend one hundred and eighty minutes per day commuting to and from work in heavy traffic need to rest during school hours; if teachers cannot get back to the school in the contracted time, taxpayers must pay time and a half for overtime; school personnel cannot manage the students in nonschool settings; or teachers are too old for that or were not trained to do it. In short, assume students with disabilities are in need of authentic assessment and instruction, but cannot receive it from school professionals. In such instances, school officials can purchase the needed services from private vendors with school-administered tax dollars. That is, they can exercise the "Buyout Option" (Owens Johnson et al., 2002).

The Finishing School. Assume school administrators will not allow the provision of individually appropriate instructional services in integrated and respected nonschool settings and activities by school personnel during school days and times and/or that teachers cannot, or will not provide it. Assume further that students with disabilities are unemployed when they graduate with diploma, drop out, or otherwise exit school. Is it too late? No. Is there no feasible option? Yes, the finishing school. The finishing school is essentially the offering of a second chance to learn that which should have been taught during the first passage through school. Thus, in a finishing school a student will learn the actual skills needed to be successful at a particular job; to get to and from work; to manage money earned; to act appropriately in public places; to maintain reasonable health; to manifest reasonable work ethics and to learn from compassionate feedback. The finishing school transcends language, racism, social promotion, sexism, tracking, dead-end jobs, academic achievement test scores, exit tests and the other reasons authentic vocational assessment and instruction were not provided during the first tour through school. The objectives and instructional strategies are clear: To teach that which is actually necessary for an individual to become a productive member of society. Failure, unemployment, involvement in criminal justice systems and producing children that cannot be supported are not in the curriculum and are not acceptable outcomes. This, of course begs the question, "If these are the right things to do the second time, why did we not do them the first time?"

REFERENCES

Brown, L. (2005a). Video discs. *Lou Brown Unplugged: A lifetime of experiences advocating for individuals with disabilities, their family members and the professionals who serve them.* Bloomington, IN: The Forum on Education at Indiana University. For information contact, http://www.forumoneducation.org or call 1-812-855-5090.

Brown, L. (2005b). *The stories of Lou Brown.* Manuscript available online from http://www.forumoneducation.org. Bloomington, IN: The Forum on Education at Indiana University.

Brown, L., Shiraga, B., & Kessler, K. (2006, January, in press). *A quest for ordinary life: The integrated vocational functioning of fifty workers with significant disabilities.* Manuscript available online from http://www.education.wisc.edu/rpse/faculty/lbrown.

Owens-Johnson, L., Brown, L., Temple, J., McKeown, B., Ross, C., & Jorgensen, J. (2002). The buyout option for students with significant disabilities during the transition years. In W. Sailor (Ed.), *Whole school success and inclusive education: Building partnerships for learning, achievement and accountability* (pp. 106-120). New York: Teachers College Press.

The President's Committee for People with Intellectual Disabilities. (2004). *A roadmap to personal and economic freedom for people with intellectual disabilities in the 21st century.* Washington, DC: U.S. Department of Health and Human Services.

Salomone, D., & Garcia, J. (2004, April 2). New Panel to assist disabled. *Orlando Sentinel,* (p. B1).

ACKNOWLEDGMENTS

The author wishes to thank the following people for helping her finish this book and for providing support, encouragement, and hope that this revised text would be completed.

The author first of all thanks from the depths of her heart each of her coauthors who worked so hard for so long to complete each of their revised, and in the majority of cases, completely new chapters. I am truly grateful to each of you because you had teaching, research to complete, coordination to do, and above all, many of you had families and significant others and many other responsibilities at work and yet you finished all of your chapters. I am eternally grateful to each of you!

I would like to thank Dr. Michael Lewis and Dr. Bruce Ostertag for being true colleagues, friends, and supporters in the years I have been a professor at California State University, Sacramento.

I would like to thank Dr. John Shefelbine, my colleague and friend, for taking time to talk about reading and our work at California State University, Sacramento.

I thank Dr. Kenneth Wiesner who is my medical doctor and is always there for me when I am ill or have questions about my health. No matter how busy you are you take time for me and your many patients. Thank you for your dedication and for keeping me well through the years.

I want to further thank my sister, Fina Lucero, who is constantly there for me each day to listen to me talk about my teaching, my work, my stresses and joys and is truly an inspiration to me in all that I do always! What would I do without you?

I want to also thank my colleagues Dr. Rachael Gonzáles and Dr. Hyun-Sook Park for always being there for me to talk about our work, our chapters, and the beautiful work that we do daily teaching our college students.

I would additionally like to thank Ms. Diana Vega who so patiently formatted this entire manuscript. Diana is bright, detail oriented, and has been a joy to work with on this project.

I want to thank my nephew, Robert Lucero, who often took care of my two Lhasa Apsos, Harmony and Weasley, so that I could finish my work on this textbook.

Additionally, I want to thank Dr. Bob Yack, D.V.M. and Dr. Tara Taylor, D.V.M. for assisting me with Weasley's and Harmony's medical needs. Thank you both for giving me peace of mind when it comes to my pets and their well-being.

Finally, I would like to thank Dr. Ruth Waugh, Dr. Doug Carnine, and Dr. Lou Brown for being inspirations to me for many years. I have learned so much from each of you through the years! Thank you from the depths of my heart for being the greatest teachers anyone could ever hope to have.

CONTENTS

TEACHING ENGLISH LEARNERS IN INCLUSIVE CLASSROOMS

Chapter 1

CREATING INCLUSIVE SCHOOLS FOR ALL LEARNERS

PAULA M. GARDNER

INCLUSIVE EDUCATION AND EDUCATIONAL REFORM

Historically, students with disabilities have been the recipients of educational practices based on restrictive and exclusionary values, often under the pretext of "what is best for them." Beginning in the mid-nineteenth century, children with the most significant disabilities were placed in residential institutions often receiving little to no education (Bybee, Ennis, & Zigler, 1990). It was not uncommon for this population of children to spend their entire life in a residential institution (Scheerenberger, 1983). There existed an assumption that children with significant disabilities needed protection from a world in which they did not fit in and in which they could not survive. Early in the twentieth century, attempts to educate those once thought "uneducable" were made (Kauffman & Hallahan, 1992). Classes and/or supports for children with moderate and severe disabilities remained rare, however. There were few federal laws in support of education and services for children with disabilities. As a result, children with disabilities were routinely excluded from our nation's schools. However, as the political and moral climate began to change in the 1950s and 1960s, a shift began to occur. Concerned advocacy groups pushed to move children and adults out of the institutions and in to the community. Schools and classes for children with disabilities were being opened all over the country, first in church basements and community centers and later in school districts. Yet, more than a decade later, programs for students with moderate and severe disabilities continued to reflect the practice of segregated classrooms and schools and continued denied opportunities for integration within the community (Brown et al., 1989). Over the past twenty years, however, legislation, case law, a climate of social justice in our culture, and research validated practices has led to an intensified debate regarding the context in which students with moderate and severe disabilities should receive their education. More and more educators are questioning the practice of responding to student diversity by creating separate special programs and/or classrooms, instead asserting the need to create an educational system grounded in democratic principles and the constructs of social justice (Gartner & Lipsky, 1987; Skrtic, 1991; Stainback, Stainback, & Bunch, 1989). These values are embodied in the practice of educating children with moderate and severe disabilities in supportive mainstream schools and classrooms. This practice, known as inclusion, advocates that children with disabilities be educated in age-appropriate general education classrooms located in schools that they would attend if they did not have a disability. For many general and special educators, an inclusive service delivery model represents significant change. The concept, although arguably simple to understand, is often complex in implementation. Addressing and overcoming obstacles or challenges to implementation recurrently requires an overall restructuring effort. A shift from labeling and sorting children with disabilities, focusing on their capability rather than their incapability requires a transformation of educational policies and practices. Many teachers, all over the world, have and are experiencing this transformation, discovering that children with moderate and severe disabilities can learn alongside their nondisabled peers. Teachers all over the world are witnessing academic growth never thought plausible, communication skills never thought possible, and friendships never thought probable. As a result of these positive outcomes, more and more schools are embracing inclusion as their vision for all of the children they serve (Fisher, Sax, & Grove, 2000). And yet, despite the great advancements that have been made in the past fifty years, much work remains to be done if schools are to effectively address the educational needs of students with moderate and severe disabilities in the general education classroom. For schools to effectively nurture those educators committed to including children with ethnic, cultural, linguistic, sexual, gender, ability, and socioeconomic differences they must first seek to understand what history has taught us. In the words of American philosopher George Santayana (1863–1952), "Those who do not remember the past are condemned to repeat it" (1995).

THE CIVIL RIGHTS MOVEMENT

Legislation has played a major role in the history of special education services for children with moderate and severe disabilities. In fact, much of the progress in meeting the needs of children with significant disabilities can be attributed in large part to court cases and the passage of a landmark federal law. The history of educating children with disabilities in the United States is analogous to that of other groups in our society that have been excluded or separated based on characteristics perceived to be "different." One of the greatest influences on those with disabilities was the Civil Rights Movement. The *Brown v. Board of Education* (1954) decision was the first case to address the issue of racial desegregation of schools (Turnbull, 1993). As Chief Justice Earl Warren ruled in the 1954 decision, separateness in education is inherently unequal. The Brown decision recognized "that if black children were educated separately, even in facilities 'equal' to those of white children, their treatment was inherently unequal because of the stigma attached to being educated separately and the deprivation of interaction with children of other backgrounds" (Rothstein, 1990). The application of the principles set forth in the Brown decision provided advocates of the disabled with the vehicle to address equal educational opportunities for children with disabilities. *Brown v. Board of Education* was a major impetus behind impending "right to education" cases (Turnbull, 1993).

LEGISLATION

Beginning in the 1960s and early 1970s legislation and litigation were used to ensure that the civil and educational rights of children with disabilities were preserved. At that time, however, no federal programs existed that addressed the needs and interests of people with mental retardation. In response to this void and as a result of widespread attention "right to education" court cases were receiving, President John F. Kennedy and Vice President Hubert Humphrey established the 1961 President's Committee on Mental Retardation. This committee was created to advise President Kennedy on how the federal government could best meet the needs of this neglected population through comprehensive state planning programs (Turnbull, 1993). In 1966, Congress established the Bureau of Education for the Handicapped Act, with the goal of providing leadership in special education programming (Turnbull, 1993).

By 1971, the principles set forth in the *Brown v. Board of Education* decision became a legal theory for two landmark decisions. These two court decisions cleared the way for reforming the way America would educate children with disabilities in the future (Marozas & May, 1988). *The Pennsylvania Association for Retarded Children (PARC) v. Commonwealth of Pennsylvania* and *Mills v. D.C. Board of Education* ruled that children with disabilities have the right of access to public education. According to the plaintiffs in the PARC case, the State of Pennsylvania failed to provide access to a free, appropriate education for children with mental retardation. The court found that due to the fact that the State promised to educate all of its children, it cannot deny any child access to an education. The court ruled that the presumption should be made that

> . . . among the alternative programs of education and training required by statute to be available, placement in a regular public school class is preferable to placement in a special public school class and placement in a special public school class is preferable to placement in any other type of program of education and training. (*PARC v. Commonwealth of Pennsylvania*)

In the *Mills v. Board of Education* case, 1972, seven children with learning and behavioral difficulties were denied an education as a result of the district's refusal to continue paying for their education, citing their inability to afford to provide the type and extent of services the children needed as the reason. These two cases found that "denial of education to children with disabilities and denial of due process in so doing violates the fourteenth amendment to the Constitution, which provides that the states may not deprive anyone of 'life, liberty, or property, without due process of law' nor deny anyone equal protection of the laws" (Rothstein, 1990, p.12). These cases not only affirmed the right to education for children with disabilities, but also the right to be educated in the *least restrictive environment* (Turnbull, 1993). Soon after, Congress established federal aid to those states that provided full educational opportunities to all children with disabilities (P.L. 93-380). Congress acknowledged that Public Law 93-380 was only to serve an interim until Congress could enact legislation that would mandate free and appropriate public education for all children with disabilities (Hallahan & Kauffman, 1994). What followed was the 1975 passage of Public Law 94-142, The Education for All Handicapped Children Act, a landmark statute in special education that has since undergone numerous amendments. The purpose of P.L. 94-142 was to assure that children with disabilities have available to them (1) a free appropriate public education (FAPE) which emphasizes special education and related services designed to meet their unique needs; (2) procedural safeguards and due process for both the children with disabilities and their parents or guardians; (3) assistance from states and localities to provide for the education of all children with disabilities; and (4) education in the least restrictive environment.

Before the date of enactment of the Education for All Handicapped Children Act (EAHCA) of 1975, the educational needs of millions of children with disabilities were not being fully met because:

1. the children did not receive appropriate educational services;
2. the children were excluded entirely from the public school system and from being educated with their peers;
3. undiagnosed disabilities prevented the children from having a successful educational experience; or
4. a lack of adequate resources within the public school system forced families to find services outside the public school system (Rothstein, 1990).

Currently, all fifty states provide educational services and supports to students with disabilities, agreeing to meet specific minimum requirements established by the Act.

THE INDIVIDUALS WITH DISABILITIES EDUCATION ACT

For more than thirty years, the guiding principles of Public Law 94-142, the Education of the Handicapped Act of 1975, has guided the education of children and youth with disabilities. A 1990 amendment renamed the law the Individuals with Disabilities Education Act (IDEA). The law underwent a major revision and was reauthorized in 1997 as P.L. 101-476, Individuals with Disabilities Education Act, IDEA. The law, which originally focused on process and compliance issues and creating and improving programs for children with disabilities, now included significant changes regarding educational opportunities for students with disabilities. In addition, it established important safeguards that ensured the provision of a free, appropriate public education to students with special needs and placed a high priority on student results and achievement. On December 3, 2004, President George W. Bush signed the Individuals with Disabilities Education Improvement Act of 2004, which again reauthorized the Individuals with Disabilities Education Act (IDEA). The new law preserves the basic structure and civil rights guarantees of IDEA. Additionally, Congress made the following declaration;

> Disability is a natural part of the human experience and in no way diminishes the right of individuals to participate in or contribute to society. Improving educational results for children with disabilities is an essential element of our national policy of ensuring equality of opportunity, full participation, independent living, and economic self-sufficiency for individuals with disabilities. (20 U.S.C., sec.1400[c] [1])

The Individuals with Disabilities Education Improvement Act of 2004 also aligns IDEA closely to the 2002 No Child Left Behind Act (NCLB), including important reforms to ensure equity, accountability and excellence in education for children with disabilities.

In addition to IDEA, which deals respectively with education and training for employment, two other important related federal laws support and protect the rights of individuals with disabilities. However, these two laws provide a broader definition of disabilities. The two federal laws which prohibit discrimination based on disability are Section 504 of the Rehabilitation Act of 1973 which bars discrimination against individuals with disabilities in public schools and any other federally supported programs and the Americans with Disabilities Act (ADA) of 1990 which ensures access for individuals with disabilities in all aspects of life, including education, the workplace, transportation, and telecommunications (Turnbull, Turnbull, et al., 2000;

Yell, 1998). The federal regulations for Section 504 state: "No qualified person with a disability(ies) shall, on the basis of this disability, be excluded from participation in, be denied the benefits of, or otherwise be subjected to discrimination under any program or activity which receives or benefits from federal financial assistance" (34 C.F.R., § 104.4).

IDEA, Section 504 and ADA address the deep roots of discrimination that continues to prevent individuals with disabilities, including our children, from successfully accessing and participating in all aspects of school and the community. "By allowing persons with disabilities to become full citizens in not only their opportunities but also in the hearts and minds of everyone in the community, [IDEA], Section 504 and the ADA will become a community standard rather than a needed protection" (Harris, 1996).

EDUCATION REFORM EFFORTS: AMERICA 2000: THE EDUCATE AMERICA ACT AND NO CHILD LEFT BEHIND

Disability laws like Section 504, ADA, and IDEA constitute an audacious and ambitious social agenda. However, the United States government has long been engaged in comprehensive school restructuring and reform efforts that continue even through the present. The impetus behind the move to reform schools is based on the desire to improve student outcomes. Reports pointing to the low achievement levels of American's youth compared with those of other industrialized nations have resulted in a call for higher standards and greater accountability (Fuhrman, 1994). In 1989, in response to these criticisms, former President George Bush embraced school reform by announcing America 2000: Educate America Act (U.S. Department of Education, 1994). This bipartisan reform effort provided monetary resources to states to assist in developing and implementing comprehensive educational reform. It has been described as "the beginning of a new era in school and education reform—a revolutionary, all inclusive plan to change every aspect of our education system, while at the same time aligning its individual parts with one another" (p. 1). America 2000 had four central themes: (1) better and more accountable schools for today; (2) a new generation of schools for tomorrow;

Table I
AMERICA 2000: EDUCATE AMERICA ACT

Goal 1:	By the year 2000, all children in America will start school ready to learn.
Goal 2:	By the year 2000, the high school graduation rate will increase to at least 90 percent.
Goal 3:	By the year 2000, American students will leave grades four, eight, and twelve having demonstrated competency in challenging subject matter, including English, mathematics, science, history, and geography; and every school in America will ensure that all students learn to use their minds well, so that they may be prepared for responsible citizenship, further learning, and productive employment in our economy.
Goal 4:	By the year 2000, U.S. students will be first in the world in science and mathematic achievement.
Goal 5:	By the year 2000, every adult American will be literate and will possess the knowledge and skills necessary to compete in a global economy and exercise the rights and responsibilities of citizenship.
Goal 6:	By the year 2000, every school in America will be free of drugs, violence, and the unauthorized presence of firearms and alcohol and will offer a disciplined environment conducive to learning.
Goal 7:	By the year 2000, the nation's teaching force will have access to programs for the continued improvement of their professional skills and the opportunity to acquire the knowledge and skills needed to instruct and prepare all American students for the next century.
Goal 8:	By the year 2000, every school will promote partnerships that will increase parental involvement and participation in promoting the social, emotional, and academic growth of children.

(3) becoming a nation of students; and (4) making our communities places where learning happens (U.S. Department of Education, 1994). The Goals 2000: Educate America Act (P.L. 103-227) was signed into law on March 31, 1994. Public Law 103-227 included six goals developed by President Bush and two additional goals established by the Clinton administration (refer to Table I).

Although the language of Goals 2000 specifically addresses the needs of "all children," many have questioned whether the legislation and terms "all children" includes students with disabilities. The legislation is, however, clear in the bill's definition of "all children" to include not only typical learners, but also those who are from diverse cultural and ethnic backgrounds, limited English proficient, disadvantaged, and those students with disabilities.

> The terms "all students" and "all children" mean students or children from a broad range of backgrounds and circumstances, including disadvantaged students and children with diverse racial, ethnic, and cultural background, American Indians, Alaska Natives, Native Hawaiians, students or children with disabilities, students or children with limited English proficiency, school-aged students or children, and academically talented students and children. (P.L. 103-227)

The Office of Special Education and Rehabilitative Services (OSER) also identified key program features of the America 2000 initiative. One of the most important features with relation to inclusion was as follows: "All students, including those with disabilities, are a valued part of the school community and contribute unique talents and perspectives to the school. All students must be ensured equal opportunities to access activities, materials, equipment, and classrooms throughout the entire building" (Smith, Hunter, & Schrag, 1991). Additional features of inclusive educational practices identified in Feature #2 of the America 2000 initiative are as follows:

PRACTICE 1:   Schools should provide opportunities for students to have shared experiences by offering extra-curriculum activities to promote a sense of belonging and to teach students how to relate to and communicate with peers.

PRACTICE 2:   Peer advocate and peer tutoring programs are examples of educational strategies that equip students with the skills involving empathy and problem solving, and that foster mutual understanding and respect.

PRACTICE 3:   School programs should promote social supports and friendships among students with disabilities and their nondisabled peers. Strategies include forming circles of friends and recruiting intact student cliques from social networks. (Smith, Hunter, & Schrag, 1991)

Quality education for all children, including those with disabilities, was the goal of America 2000 and the goal of The Elementary and Secondary Education Act (ESEA), renamed "No Child Left Behind Act of 2001" (NCLB). The current No Child Left Behind debate is not a new one, however. Both America 2000 and NCLB were designed to promote educational systems that increase implementation strategies that foster improved outcomes in inclusive communities. The No Child Left Behind Act has expanded the federal role in education and set requirements in place that affect every public school in America. NCLB establishes high standards, accountability for all, and the belief that all children can learn, regardless of their background or ability. This law, although venerable is seriously flawed and underfunded. And while general and special educators alike have expressed concerns about whether these reform movements adequately address the unique needs of students with disabilities and those with other special needs, both support the collaborative ethic inherent in inclusion.

LEAST RESTRICTIVE ENVIRONMENT

Not long after the passage of P.L. 94-142, educators and parents of children with moderate and severe disabilities began to question the effectiveness of separating their children from their nondisabled peers. They argued that a separate education, with little to no access to typically developing peers prevented them from being a part of the larger school community. And thus, the concept of inclusion was launched. A multiplicity of terms has been used to describe and advance inclusive practices. The practice of educating students with disabilities in general education classrooms is based on the principle of least restrictive environment (LRE), a provision that has been included in the federal laws for thirty years. However, some educators interpret least restrictive environment, formerly known as the mainstreaming or integration principle, to mean being educated in the least restrictive environment with the appropriate supports and services. For children birth to three years of age, the appropriate setting would be the child's "natural environment" and for all other children three to twenty-one, education alongside their nondisabled peers (Etscheidt & Bartlett, 1999). Whereas others interpret LRE to mean being educated in a environment most like the general education setting, but not necessarily the general education classroom. The goal of educating children in the least restrictive environment is the practice of providing students with disabilities the opportunity for interaction with and social acceptance by students without disabilities (Stainback & Stainback, 1986a, 1986b).

Specifically, the Individuals with Disabilities Act of 2004 (IDEA) reflects the legal intention to educate students with disabilities in the general education environment by mandating:

> to the maximum extent appropriate, children with disabilities, including children in public or private institutions or other care facilities, are educated with children who are not disabled, and that special classes, separate schooling, or other removal of children with disabilities from the regular educational environment occurs only when the nature or severity of the disability is such that education in regular classes with the use of supplementary aids and services cannot be achieved satisfactorily. (Rothstein, 1990, pp. 317-318)

Nowhere in the IDEA statute or regulations however, is the term "inclusion" used. The IDEA statute and implementing regulations emphasize the requirement to educate children with disabilities in general education classes with their nondisabled peers: "While the Act and regulations recognize that IEP teams must make individualized decisions about the special education . . . IDEA's strong preference that, to the maximum extent appropriate, children with disabilities be educated in regular classes with their nondisabled peers with appropriate supplementary aids and services" (US CODE, 2005). Consequently, schools must consider the general education classroom in the school the student would attend if not disabled as the first placement option before a more restrictive placement is considered. Accordingly, building and cultivating collaborative, supportive, and respectful relationships among general and special educators in order to address the unique needs of children with disabilities must be viewed as a high priority.

Educating children with disabilities has long been advocated as a shared responsibility between general and special educators (Wang, Walberg, & Reynolds, 1992, Fuchs & Fuchs, 1994). Collaboration is based on a belief in the value of shared decision making. Fuchs and Fuchs suppose, "Now is the time for inventive pragmatists, not extremists on the right or the left. Now is the time for leadership that recognizes the need for change; appreciates the importance of consensus building; looks at general education with a sense of what is possible; respects special education's traditions and values and the law that undergirds them; and seeks to strengthen the mainstream, as well as other educational options that can provide more intensive services, to enhance the learning and loves of all children" (p. 305). Yet, despite the considerable progress that has been made concerning the education of children with disabilities, educators still have differing opinions on how to define, interpret, and implement the education of children with disabilities in the least restrictive environment. Though laudable, the interpretation of and placement in the least restrictive environment continues to generate complex and controversial debates.

In view of the fact that services and supports for students with disabilities continue to evolve, educators often raise the question about the relationship of IDEA's least restrictive environment requirements to inclusion. A report by the U.S. Department of Education cited that in 1999–2000 approximately forty-seven percent of all school-age students with disabilities received at least seventy-nine percent of their education in general education classrooms (U.S. Department of Education, 2001). However, this percentile largely addresses those students with mild disabilities. The percentage of children with moderate and severe disabilities being educated in general education classrooms for most of the day although improving is less then twelve percent. The practice of being educated primarily in classrooms apart from their nondisabled peers continues to be prevalent.

EDUCATION REFORM EFFORTS: THE REGULAR EDUCATION INITIATIVE

During the 1980s, the relationship between general and special education gained the national attention of educators, researchers, policymakers, and advocates. Educational literature began to focus on the merger of general and special education services (Schloss, 1992). Debates about whether children with disabilities should receive their education in the general education classroom were occurring all over the country. The concept of least restrictive environment and how it should be interpreted was once again at the heart of the discussion. What emerged from this highly controversial issue of least restrictive environment and integration was the political, economic, and sociological issue of reconceptualizing the goals of special education through reform efforts such as the Regular Education Initiative (REI) and inclusion. Both the Regular Education Initiative and inclusion have been described as full access to a restructured mainstream for all students with, respectively, mild and severe disabilities (Skrtic, 1991). These two reform proposals are still being debated. In 1986, through speeches and articles, Madeleine Will, then Assistant Secretary of the U.S. Department of Education, suggested that the "dual system" of educating students with disabilities presumes that students with learning problems cannot receive an appropriate education in the general education classroom and, therefore, must be educated in separate remedial programs, such as a resource room or special class. This is referred to as the "pull-out approach" (Will, 1986b). As a high-ranking government official, Will argued that the "pull-out" approach is driven by "conceptual fallacy; that poor performance in learning can be understood solely in terms of deficiencies in the student rather than deficiencies in the learning environment" (Will, 1986b, p. 13). This approach would require educators to always "create a new educational environment" (Will, 1986b, p. 14). Will argued that the REI is a commitment to search for ways to serve as many children as possible in the regular classroom by encouraging special education and other special programs to form a partnership with regular education. Will stated, "The objective of the partnership for special education and the other special programs is to use their knowledge and expertise to support regular education in educating children with learning problems" (Will, 1986b, p. 23). In the same year, Will cited several problem areas affecting the current special education service delivery model:

1. Special education services are fragmented into numerous categorical programs.
2. Special education and regular education are a dual system of education where the responsibility for students with disabilities is passed to the special education professional.
3. Special education students in segregated programs are often stigmatized by their chronological aged peers.
4. Eligibility criteria are often so rigid that disputes between parents and schools develop and impact negatively on the student's education. (Will, 1986a, p. 412)

Proponents of the REI (Davis, 1989; Gartner & Lipsky, 1987, 1989; Reynolds & Wang, 1981; Spon-Shevin, 1988; Stainback & Stainback, 1984, 1986, 1987, 1988, 1989, 1990; Wang, Reynolds, & Walberg, 1986, 1987, 1988, 1992) called for "a dissolution of the present dual system in our public school system, to be replaced by a unitary educational system, which, if carefully designed and implemented, would allow for a more effective and appropriate education for all students" (Davis, 1989, p. 440). Stainback, Stainback, and Bunch (1989) suggested that, while education is "technically a subsystem of regular education, the United States has in effect created a separate system for educating students with disabilities. The operation of separate systems has a number of disadvantages, including: (a) the instructional needs of students do not warrant the operation of a dual system; (b) maintaining a dual system is inefficient; and (c) the dual system fosters an inappropriate and unfair attitude about the education of students classified as having disabilities" (p. 15). Proponents of the REI also maintained that separating and segregating students with disabilities from their nondisabled peers resulted in stigmatization (Biklen & Zollers, 1986; Gartner & Lipsky, 1987; Lilly, 1988; Reynolds, Wang, & Walberg, 1987; Stainback & Stainback, 1984; Stainback, Stainback, & Forest, 1989; & Wang & Birch, 1984).

A critic of the Regular Education Initiative, Kauffman (1989) argued that the negative effects of labeling a student with disabilities have been overestimated and that "the nonlabeling issue is exploitable for its public relations value . . . [and] is also consistent with the Reagan-Bush administration's approach to equity issues, which relies on the surface appeal of nondiscrimination without analysis of the deeper meanings for individuals with a history of disadvantage" (p. 265). While Hallahan, Kauffman, and Lloyd (1988) challenged that the REI was not based on research, but the opinions presented in an early paper by Margaret Wang and Maynard Reynolds (1981), Will argued otherwise. Will (1986b) stated that the REI was based on empirical research outlined in studies on the inadequacies of special education service delivery models (i.e., Heller, Holtzman, & Messick, 1982; Hobbs, 1975, 1980; Wang et al., 1981). Writers commonly identified as critics of the REI (Gerber, 1988; Hallahan & Kauffman, 1994; Keogh, 1988) advocated for a more cautious approach to the restructuring of general and special education programs. A major argument was that the REI was "consistent with the Reagan-Bush policy objectives of reducing federal influence and expenditures for education, which has resulted in federal declining support for programs designed to ensure equity in education of the disadvantaged and handicapped" (Kauffman, 1989, p. 256). Others questioned general educators' willingness the educate students with disabilities (Singer, 1988). Singer asked, "What leads special educators to believe that regular educators are willing to take back responsibility for special needs children?" (p. 416). Additionally, critics of the REI cautioned against the dissolution of the current dual educational system (Byrnes, 1990; Kauffman & Hallahan, 1990). Byrnes stated, "Without clear proof that the REI is more beneficial to these children, whose current rights are hard-won, how can a teacher, principal, or special education administrator tell a parent that the old way is no longer good and that REI is better? What evidence will we bring to a court?" (p. 348). While proponents contend the REI was based on empirical research, opponents characterized the United States Office of Special Education and Rehabilitative Services (OSERS) policy statement as a political proposal grounded in ideology.

EDUCATION REFORM EFFORTS: INCLUSIVE EDUCATION

Will's (1986b) advocacy to educate students with learning problems, including "those who are learning slowly, those with behavioral problems, those who may be educationally disadvantaged, those who have mild specific learning disabilities and emotional problems" (p. 1) in the general education classroom (i.e., the Regular Education Initiative) was soon expanded to include children with moderate and severe disabilities in the general education classroom. Full inclusion, inclusion, inclusive schooling, and inclusive education are terms that have emerged to describe this practice. Inclusion represents a statement of public policy that affects the fields of both general and special education. Inclusion refers to the practice of educating all children in neighborhood classrooms and schools (Lipsky & Gartner, 1989a, 1989b). "Inclusion asserts that each student living within the boundaries of a particular school should be included in all aspects in life at that school" (Alper & Ryndak, 1992, p. 374). Inclusion is a policy of placing students with disabilities "in a regular education classroom for the entire day. The necessary support services to ensure an appropriate education come to the student in the regular class setting" (Hardman, Drew, Egan, & Wolf, 1993, p. 485). Inclusion has been "heralded as critical for social, educational, legal, and philosophical reasons" (Hanline & Fox, 1993). Sailor (1991) outlined the basic components of most inclusion models as:

1. All students attend the school to which they go if they had no disability.
2. A natural proportion (i.e., representative of the school district at large) of students with disabilities occurs at any school site.
3. A zero-reject philosophy exists so that typically no student would be excluded on the basis of type or extent of disability.
4. School and general education placements are age and grade appropriate, with no self-contained special education classes operative at the school site.
5. Cooperative learning and peer instructional methods receive significant use in general instructional practice at the school site.
6. Special education supports are provided within the context of the general education class and in other integrated environments. (p. 10)

Debate surrounding the issue of moving from an exclusive educational system toward one where all students are included, where the primary placement of the child is in a general education classroom, where the necessary support services (i.e., special education teacher, paraprofessionals, curriculum materials, and technology aids) to ensure that an appropriate education comes to the student in the general class setting, and continues to be at the forefront of educational concern. And, while many educators support the principles of inclusion, inclusive practices and access to general education varies widely depending on state and local policies.

Just as litigation helped pave the way for the deinstitutionalization of individuals with disabilities, lawsuits established a legal basis for inclusive education, as exemplified in the *Sacramento City Unified School District v. Rachael Holland* case. A decision by the Ninth Circuit Court of Appeals in the 1992 Holland case, affirmed a child with moderate disabilities' right to an inclusive school program. The court found that the Sacramento City Unified School District had not demonstrated that Rachael, an eight-year-old girl with moderate disabilities, could not benefit from placement in the general education classroom and supported the testimony of significant nonacademic benefits a child with a disability may receive from interaction with nondisabled peers. The court's decision reflects the fundamental purpose of the Individuals with Disabilities Education Act's integration requirement (Holland, Civ. S-90-1171-DFL). According to the late Disability Rights Education and Defense Fund (DREDF) Director and attorney, Diane Lipton (Lipton, 1994):

> The decision of the Ninth Circuit is a momentous victory for children with disabilities across the nation. The Holland case follows in the tradition of *Brown*

v. Board of Education. It signals the end to a system that automatically excludes children with disabilities from the regular public school classroom and relegates them to segregated 'handicapped only' classes and schools.

In support of the decision, the Justice Department, on behalf of the Office of Special Education in the United States Department of Education, filed an amicus brief. On June 13, 1994, the United States Supreme Court affirmed the court's decision refusing to hear the school district's appeal, leaving the Ninth Circuit landmark decision intact. The Assistant Secretary of the Office of Special Education and Rehabilitative Services, Judith Heumann also provided a federal level perspective. In 1994, Judith Heumann declared:

> We need to give a clear message that people with disabilities are capable and should be integrated into the world. We do not advocate a "one size fits all" approach in making decisions about where disabled students should be educated. Educational placement decisions for students with disabilities are made at the local level and must be based on the needs of the individual student. Any other approach is not consistent with the Individuals with Disabilities Act (IDEA) and should not be confused with effective educational practices for inclusive classrooms. While there may be some children who would not be appropriately served full time in the regular education classroom, these children represent only a small number of children with disabilities.
>
> We believe that the regular classroom, with the necessary supports in place, is where most students should be. . . . Both teachers and disabled students may need supports in the classroom to make inclusion work. . . . But the necessary supports depend on the individual student and teacher needs.
>
> The United States Department of Education's mission is to ensure equal access to education and to promote excellence throughout the nation. Inclusion is consistent wit this mission and is an essential component of current school reform initiatives. Consistent with the Individuals with Disabilities Act (IDEA), the regular education classroom in the neighborhood schools must become part of the broader educational reform agenda in this nation. . . . We must share our respective experiences and expertise to design an American educational system that promotes equity and excellence for all of the nation's students. (p. 1)

Despite the fact that educators and parents of both typically developing and special needs children will most likely continue to question the benefits of educating children with disabilities in integrated settings, it is not a passing fad. This practice will continue to impact educators at the state and local level. Norm Kunc (2000), disability advocate and educator, calls on all educators and parents to prevent exclusion and segregation from occurring and to move beyond benevolence in support of inclusion.

STUDENT PLACEMENT

Despite school reform efforts such as the Regular Education Initiative, inclusion, America 2000, and No Child Left Behind, large gaps continue to exist between the policy and practice of educating children in the least restrictive environment. State and local agencies continue to prescribe educational placements based on a restrictive continuum. A continuum of services implies districts offer a range of different educational placement options ranging from the most restrictive, full-time residential school, to the least restrictive, the general education classroom. The continuum of services model (Deno, 1970), although intended to provide a variety of service options based on the individual skills and needs of a student, helped to create a system of lock-stepped placements based on disability labels. As a result, students with moderate and severe disabilities were routinely placed in self-contained special education classrooms of students with similar disabilities. And, despite the fact that IDEA mandates that a students' placement in settings other than the general education classroom as the least restrictive environment must be specifically justified, the practice of separating and educating children based on an identified disability continues all too often today. Consequently, placements in general education classrooms have eluded the majority of children with moderate and severe disabilities (Kode, 2002). The more common service delivery model is one where students are placed in a resource or self-contained special education classroom with limited opportunity for integration with their nondisabled peers.

Advocates of inclusion prefer to view the continuum of service model as one that is fluid, providing all students with disabilities the opportunity to be educated in the least restrictive environment, the general education classroom. In this way, the presumption of inclusion can be challenged only if and when documentation supports that the student with disabilities cannot benefit from being educated with his/her typically developing peers even after being provided with supplementary aids and services. Only then can the decision to provide specialized services and supports outside of the general education classroom, in a more restrictive placement on the continuum, be recommended.

CLASSROOM SUPPORTS AND INSTRUCTIONAL STRATEGIES

The literature clearly articulates the "why" of inclusion, but the "how to" many find confusing and somewhat elusive. First and foremost, for students with moderate and severe disabilities to be successfully included in the general education classroom, administrators, general and special education teachers, staff and parents must demonstrate a strong commitment to the education of all children. The principles necessary for building successful inclusive school communities involves careful planning and support. Figure 1 represents principles necessary for building an effective learning environment where all children are valued members of the school community. These principles and resulting recommendations are based on extensive research from several authorities (Gartner & Lipsky, 1987; Halvorsen & Sailor, 1990; Hunt & Goetz, 1997; O'Brien, Forest, Snow & Hasbury, 1989; Stainback & Stainback, 1990). They include:

1. Visionary leadership and a vision or mission statement that reflects a shared commitment to educating all children.
2. A strong sense of community involvement in the education of all children.
3. A commitment to the study and celebration of diversity.
4. Curricula adaptation and effective instructional practices.
5. Support services for staff and students.
6. An understanding of changing roles and responsibilities among both general and special educators.
7. High standards and expectations.
8. Collaboration and cooperation.
9. A partnership with families.

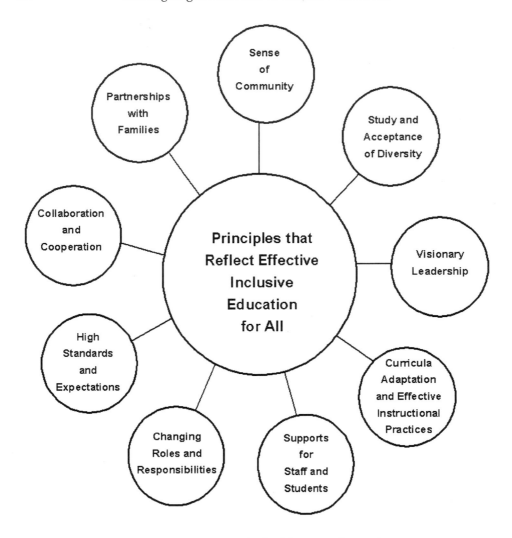

Figure 1. Represents principles necessary for building an effective learning environment where all children are valued members of the school community.

In schools such as Mariemont Elementary in Sacramento, California, neighborhood students with disabilities are included in every aspect of the school community. This has been established through careful planning, encouragement, and the belief that all children bring unique needs and gifts to the educational community. This planning includes various steps of preparation in order to provide successful inclusive opportunities. These steps include:

Step 1: Identifying the supportive educational team;

Step 2: Getting to know the student, including identifying the strengths and areas of need;

Step 3: Developing educational goals based on both parent and teacher(s) desired outcomes;

Step 4: Identifying necessary support services;

Step 5: Developing a daily schedule of activities, peer tutoring and or peer buddy programs;

Step 6: Establishing a regularly scheduled time for general and special education teacher collaboration;

Step 7: Establishing a regularly scheduled time for parent/teacher collaboration;

Step 8: Establishing a plan for ongoing evaluation of the student's needs and accomplishments;

Step 9: Providing for personal and professional development opportunities.

Successful inclusion involves the participation of all children in all aspects of the school life. The following section further elaborates on several of these principles. In addition, other specific strategies for successfully building inclusive communities have been addressed.

BECOMING A TEACHER FOR ALL STUDENTS

Preparing teachers for the inclusion of children with significant disabilities in the general education classroom is an issue of great importance. In order for inclusion to be a positive, meaningful experience for all children, the general education teacher must become a confident and comfortable facilitator of learning and support opportunities. Educators who have been trained and are equipped with the breadth and depth of skills and strategies necessary for addressing the needs of a diverse student population experience greater success and satisfaction than those who have not received training (Soodak, Podell, & Lehman, 1998). Those who have not received the necessary training often feel overwhelmed and ill-prepared whereas those trained have reported numerous benefits, both personally and professionally (Scott, Vitale, & Masten, 1998). In Gardner's (1994) study on exemplary inclusive general education teachers, teachers anecdotally shared such feelings as, "I wasn't sure if I was doing the right things...but then I began to watch how the other children were reacting . . . it all seemed so natural." Another teacher commented, "I was so nervous in the beginning . . . it's hard to believe . . . he is such a joy," and "I was spending so much time worrying and planning about how to make her fit in that I forgot to just let her be a kid." One teacher summarized her feelings by anecdotally stating, "By supporting her academic needs and social interactions I helped all the children . . . it's a win, win situation." School districts can support the acquisition of effective skills and strategies by providing opportunities for general and special education teachers to collaborate and by providing ongoing staff development. By doing so, districts demonstrate a clear commitment to building successful and supported inclusive learning communities for all children.

COLLABORATIVE CONSULTATION

Today, the practice of teaching in isolation is given little credence. General and special education teachers alike must regularly interact and collaborate if successful inclusive educational communities are to become a reality. Through collaborative consultation, both the general and special educator is given the opportunity to share their expertise and skills. Consequently, collaboration refers to how individuals work together not necessarily what they do. They assume shared responsibility and equal authority for the students with disabilities. Two major assumptions of effective collaboration consultation in the schools are (Idol & West, 1991):

1. Educational collaboration as an adult-to-adult interactive process can be expected to have an indirect impact on student outcomes; thus, the process of educational collaboration among adult team members typically yields changes in teams member attitudes, skills, knowledge, and/or behaviors first, followed by changes in student and/or organizational outcomes.
2. Educational collaboration may be used as problem solving; thus, it can be an effective tool for proactive strategic planning or reactive, but efficient, problem solving in any organizational structure in the school environment (p. 72).

Friend (2005) contends that a collaborative relationship requires effort on everyone's part. They identified the following key characteristics of effective collaboration:

• Collaboration is deliberate and voluntary
• Collaboration is based on parity
• Collaboration requires a shared goal
• Collaboration includes shared responsibility for key decisions
• Collaboration includes shared accountability for outcomes
• Collaboration is based on shared resources
• Collaboration is emergent

Research supports that collaborative consultation is a proactive approach to meeting the needs of the students with disabilities in general education settings. When implemented properly, the general and special education collaborative approach of providing services to students with disabilities based on a common vision, shared decision making, and mutual respect, should result in valid inclusive practices.

PROMOTING, UNDERSTANDING, AND CELEBRATING INDIVIDUAL DIFFERENCES

Classroom teachers can promote an acceptance and understanding of differences by creating an environment of positive supports. These supports are based on the principles for constructing and supporting successful inclusive school communities (see Figure 1) as well as considerations for equitable opportunities (Figure 2). These principles and considerations emphasize the fundamental role general education teachers' play in the education of children with disabilities. One such role is that of an interpreter. This is not meant in the usual context of interpreting for students with hearing impairments, but rather one where the teacher serves to elucidate the needs and desires of a student, the communicative intent of a behavior, and/or physical and health-related issues facing the child with disabilities. In this capacity, the general education teacher serves as a valuable source of meaningful information for typically developing students, instructional support personnel, teachers, administrators, and parents. For example, an ex-

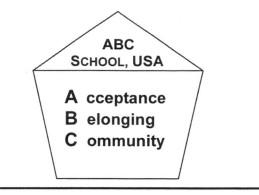

Inclusion Considerations

1.   **Fair is not the same—Fair is *getting what you need*.**

2.   **Special Education is not a *room* or *building*.**

3.   **Students with disabilities are not the *only* students that present diverse needs that require individual accommodations.**

Figure 2. Inclusive considerations for equitable opportunities. Presentation by Paula Gardner. Adapted from BTSA Sacramento, California.

emplary inclusive general education teacher could be observed answering specific student questions similar to the following. "Will Mary fall down if we don't hold onto her?" or "Why is she so wobbly?" or "When she screeches like that does that mean she is excited?" Interpretive support might resemble, "When Matt covers his ears like that he is telling you something very important . . . you are speaking too fast and/or to loud for him," or "What Anthony is trying to tell you is that he wants to be the first to roll the dice." Interpretive support often leads to an increased understanding of the differences, needs, feelings and behaviors of the students with disabilities. Consequently, typically developing students can be heard making such statements as "I hate when people speak all at one time or too loud at me, too" and

"Pammy can hold on to me if she wants to." The type of interpretive support just described helps to facilitate a better understanding of a child with disabilities' uniqueness, strengths and needs. Robert Barth (1990), a Harvard Professor described the value of uniqueness and diversity in a statement:

> I would prefer my children to be in a school in which differences are looked for, attended to, and celebrated as good news, as opportunities for learning. The question with which so many school people are preoccupied is, "What are the limits of diversity beyond which behavior is unacceptable?" But the question I would like to see asked more often is, "How can we make conscious, deliberate use of difference in social class, gender, age, ability, race, and interest resources for learning?" Differences hold great opportunities for learning. Differences offer a free, abundant, and renewable resource. I would like to see our compulsion for eliminating differences to improve schools. What is important about people–and about school–is what is different, not what is the same. (pp. 514-515)

Today's schools and classrooms represent great diversity. Educators, administrators, and support personnel in effective inclusive schools demonstrate a strong commitment to and appreciation for the richness that student diversity adds to the school community.

SHARING THE LEARNING ENVIRONMENT

Advocates of inclusion have long been concerned about the isolation those children educated in separate classrooms and/or schools have and are experiencing. Students with disabilities need to be included in the general education classroom physically, instructionally, and socially if successful peer interaction and acceptance is to take place. Unfortunately, the all too frequent practice of separating and educating children with disabilities in schools different from the neighborhood children has resulted in little to no opportunity to build relationships. Familiarity and/or prior social interactions make an important contribution to the frequency of social interactions. In a review of play behavior, Rubin, Fein, and Vandenberg (1983) reported that children tend to select and interact when in the company of a familiar peer. Doyle, Connolly, and Rivest (1989) reported similar results in an earlier study. Another study investigating social interactions between students with and without disabilities in inclusive classrooms found that these interactions were a valued source of personal growth for students without disabilities (Staub, Spaulding, Peck, Gallacci, & Schwartz, 1996). This finding supports Peck, Donaldson, and Pezzoli's descriptive study (1990), which investigated twenty-one typically developing high school perceptions of the benefits received from developing relationships with peers who had moderate or severe disabilities. Results of the study indicate that the relationship established between those students with and without disabilities resulted in improvements in self concept (e.g., "I felt good about myself"), growth in social cognition (e.g., "They have feelings too, and they need to have the same things we do, and they feel the same things we do"), increased tolerance of other people (e.g., "I've treated my own friends better . . . I haven't been as cold to people"), reduced fear of human difference (e.g., "You get to meet a whole range of people—so you're not afraid of the unknown anymore"), development of personal principles (e.g., "If there is something personal between us then they're just going to be my friend, no matter what other people say"), and interpersonal acceptance and friendship (e.g., "I felt like I could just be myself and have fun"). Social competence has been linked to general developmental progress, cognitive development, communicative competence, and academic success (Guralnick, 1986; Strain & Odom, 1986). The extent of benefits and/or personal satisfaction received from such interactions is an important question to address in future research.

Whereas sharing the physical learning environment alongside their classmates without disabilities in their neighborhood school is a start, it is not enough. Other critical steps are necessary when addressing a student's academic needs and social relationships. Additional strategies teachers employ to promote successful inclusive learning environments include instructional support, facilitation of peer interaction and acceptance, the creation of cooperative learning activities, technological support, flexible collaborative planning time for general and special education teachers, and curricular infusion, adaptation and/or modification (Smith, Polloway, Patton, & Dowdy, 1995).

BUILDING PEER RELATIONSHIPS

The first factor for promoting positive interactions among children with and without disabilities is access to and opportunities for interaction. Research has found that teachers play a significant and critical role in facilitating strategies that address the social interactions of children (Gardner, 1994; Hunt, Alwell, & Farron-Davis, 1996; McEvoy, Shores, Wehby, Johnson, & Fox, 1990). In a study by Gardner, general education teacher behaviors and strategies that facilitated positive social interactions between students with severe disabilities and their nondisabled peers in an inclusive classroom were examined. This study revealed thirteen teachers' different behaviors and/or strategies that were used to facilitate positive social interactions. In each of the observed inclusive classrooms, the teacher manipulated specific strategies that preceded the occurrence of a social interaction between the children with and without disabilities. These behaviors included:

1. *praising/complimenting* students for desired behaviors and/or approximations toward a desired social behavior of both the student with a disability and his/her nondisabled peers;
2. providing *verbal prompts* to help students perform a desired behavior;
3. *modeling* appropriate social interaction skills;
4. *questioning* students during an activity and/or interaction in an attempt to promote generalization of skills;
5. providing *close proximity nonverbal facilitation* to reinforce or promote an affiliation;
6. *eliciting peer support* as a means to recruit natural communities of reinforcement;
7. providing *choices of* what and with whom the child with the disability would like to play;
8. demonstrating *affection/warmth* toward the student with a disability;
9. *pointing out contributions* made by the student and/or providing an opportunity for the student to *assume a leadership* role within the classroom;
10. *initiating conversation* in order to lead peers to recognize the value of the student as a valued member of the classroom community;

11. constructing opportunities to engage in *cooperative activities* designed to promote peer relationships;
12. providing *physical assistance* when necessary, in order to provide better access to and support during a social interaction; and
13. using *gesture prompts* as a means to facilitate and/or maintain positive social interactions.

Soderhan and Whiren (1985) support the premise that initiating conversation and monitoring teacher-child interaction, may actually lead to increased social interactions among peers. Other frequently observed teacher behaviors such as teacher prompt, praise, modeling, and peer support are all well-documented and supported evidence-based strategies. It should be noted, however, that at times, typically developing peers might appear to ignore or respond to students with disabilities in a neutral manner. A teacher may initially view this as an undesirable and unacceptable outcome. However, the reality that student social relationships might not occur spontaneously or without facilitation does not mean that inclusion has failed. All children, at different points in their lives, experience both positive and negative social interactions, neutral interactions, and/or children who appear to ignore or tolerate them. In essence, these interactions, or lack thereof, indicate that every child, even those with disabilities, has the right to be provided the opportunity to experience the full continuum of possible social interactions. It also means that teachers have a significant responsibility to develop and implement strategies to maximize opportunities for face to face interactions, nurture friendships, and provide positive role models.

The results of Gardner's study support Gottlieb's (1981) suggestion that mere placement in a general education classroom alone is not sufficient to provide for increased social interactions between students with and without disabilities. Specific teacher behaviors to facilitate social interactions are important factors in stimulating social interaction. Research by Turnbull, Pereira, and Blue-Banning (2000) confirms the earlier research of Gottlieb and Gardner finding that if teachers encourage and facilitate the participation of students with and without disabilities' in both curricular and extracurricular activities, friendships are more likely to develop.

CIRCLE OF FRIENDS–CIRCLE OF SUPPORT

In many inclusive classrooms, teachers use a more formalized strategy to increase social interactions between students with and without disabilities. The strategy used in many countries throughout the world is called *Circle of Friends* or *Circle of Support*, built on the underlying philosophy of interdependence (Forest, Pierpoint, & O'Brien, 1996; O'Brien, Forest, Snow, & Hasbury, 1989; Perske & Perske, 1988). "A circle of friends is something that many of us take for granted unless we do not have one. A circle of friends provides us with a network of support of family and friends. A circle of friends is available when one needs loving advice, and to provide support when it is needed" (Perske & Perske, 1988). In this approach, the teacher asks for student volunteers to participate in a circle of friends activity. While this intervention almost guarantees substantial contact between children with and without disabilities, the teacher still assumes a pivotal role in the facilitation of interactions. The activity, in its intention to support social interactions between the student with disabilities and his/her peers, is equally reinforcing to all participants. Circles may choose to meet during a lunch period, planning period, or after school. The process, once the friendship circle has been established, includes drawing four concentric circles, with the name or picture of the student with a disability in the middle. The members of the group are then asked to include the names of close friends and family members in the first circle, the names of friends or neighbors in the second circle, and the names of acquaintances, team members, and/or friends of a friend in the third circle. In the outer circle, members are asked to identify those individuals that are paid to support the student, such as a teacher, classroom aide, nurse, etc. (see Figure 3). The purpose of this activity is to identify the many people who are a part of the student's life already, to help people see that everyone has value, to help break down barriers, to underscore that people together have a stronger voice, to help people who are excluded get the life they desire, to build a community, to emphasize that relationships are at the center of support, and to develop a plan to add to the names in the first two circles. The following is an example of a circle of friends' lunch meeting involving Matt, a fourth grade student with autism. The teacher began:

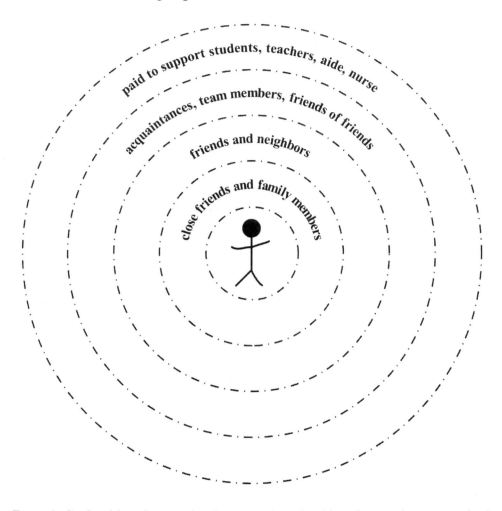

Figure 3. Circle of friends or circle of support. A circle of friends provides a network of support of family and friends.

- Matt, we are going to go around the group to discuss what our favorite sandwich is? I'll go first. . . . I love tuna fish. When I was little I use to love to put potato chips on my sandwich. [students laugh] Can anyone think of a question to ask the group . . . related to what their favorite sandwich is or what they'd like for lunch? [Matt responds]
- [Teacher] Matt, remember . . . when we talk to someone what do we usually do first? [no response] Ask "What kind of food do you like?"
- [Matt responds] What kind of sandwich do you like?
- [Teacher] But who are you talking to?
- [Matt] Nora.

- [Teacher] Ah, so if you say Nora's name first would that get her attention?
- [Matt] Yes.
- [Teacher] Go ahead then.
- [Matt] Nora, what kind of fruit do you like?
- [Nora] Grapes.
- [Matt] I like grapes, too.
- [Teacher] Great! Did you see how Matt addressed Nora by name first? Let's see if you can all remember to do that.

Another section of the discussion went as follows:

- [Teacher] Before we go out to recess, let's share one thing we did this weekend. Anybody want to go first?
- [Matt listens to another student describe a movie he had seen and then asks] What kind of bad guy?
- [Teacher] Good question Matt.
- [Student] A bad guy that was trying to hurt a family. [student continues to share].
- [Student] Matt, did you do something this weekend?
- [Matt] I went to the mountains . . . to go camping . . . I forgot what place it was.
- [Another student] Was it Truckee?
- [Matt] Yes, I went up there to have fun with my parents.
- [Student] Great.
- [Teacher] You all did something very nice. You asked questions and shared your experiences. Many of you have similar experiences. Asking questions and sharing experiences is a very nice way of keeping a conversation going.

In addition to providing support through informal discussions, the teacher was able to model, prompt, and facilitate social interactions that may generalize to other situations and environments.

The Circle of Friends strategy is one of many strategies for promoting friendships between students with and without disabilities. Other strategies include pairing students in a *Think, Pair, Share* activity, cross-age peer buddies, peer advocacy, peer tutoring, cooperative learning opportunities, and the creation of lunch buddies.

COOPERATIVE LEARNING

Successful inclusive communities are ones where teachers prepare the environment and materials in such a way so as to lend themselves more readily to cooperative use. For example, forming flexible heterogeneous groups, in well-defined areas, in proximity to each other, is an excellent inclusive strategy. The use of cooperative grouping supports research (Brown, Fox, & Brady, 1987; Johnson & Johnson, 1989) that indicates interactions are more likely to occur if children are provided with cooperative activity areas near one another. Johnson and Johnson (1989) believe that cooperative learning opportunities fosters differentiated, fundamental, valuable views of group members. Research by Rynders, Johnson, Johnson, & Schmidt (1980) also found that a cooperative group structure, rather than a competitive or individualistic structure, facilitated significantly more positive interactions between those students with severe disabilities and nondisabled students. Consistent with Rynders' et al. study, Slavin (1990) found that students with disabilities made significant gains in a range of educational outcomes when included in cooperative groups within the general education classroom, and without loss to the nondisabled peers in the classroom. Wang et al. (1988) found similar results in a series of studies of the Adaptive Learning Environments Model (ALEM), a general education-based service delivery model. Wang at al. found the ALEM model increased the occurrences of spontaneous sharing, resulting in reciprocal positive social responses by peers. In addition, teachers who briefly involve themselves in a cooperative activity accomplish a number of other goals. Not only are the teachers able to closely monitor and modify the interactions taking place between the disabled student and nondisabled peers, they are also able to demonstrate that, they too, enjoy interacting with the student with disabilities. This "enjoying" behavior may include participating in the cooperative process, playing a game, laughing, joking, and/or sharing. Providing an opportunity for students with severe disabilities to interact with their nondisabled peers is just one piece of the complex structure that must be created if inclusion is to become a reality (Tally & Burnette, 1982).

CURRICULUM ADAPTATION AND SUPPORTIVE
INSTRUCTIONAL PRACTICES

Although each effective inclusive classroom may be unique in itself, most reflect very specific supportive instructional practices and resources. Numerous resources are now available for supplementing, modifying, adapting, and/or expanding, when necessary, the general education curriculum. Additionally, many of the strategies used to promote physical and social inclusion are useful in helping children access the academic environment. Key aspects of curriculum modifications and adaptations for students with special needs are shown in Table II. These practices include opportunities for children to be involved in the same lesson as other students, providing a support person to assist in providing access to materials, equipment and/or instruction, the adaptation of materials, support for students to work at developmentally appropriate curricular areas, multilevel instruction, cooperative learning, mastery learning, and alternative activities that meet primary instructional needs. However, evaluating the effectives of specific adaptations and instructional strategies is often difficult. Specific strategies are rarely implemented in isolation, but nearly always employed in combination. Whether modifying, adapting, or enhancing curriculum, curricular modifications must align the level of achievement of the student and the level of the instructional material, the characteristics of the learner and the level of the instructional material or technique, and the motivational aspects of the learner and of the material (McCoy, 1995; Smith, Polloway, Patton, & Dowdy, 1995). This alignment will, in effect, result in all children benefiting from specialized support and assistance.

UNIVERSAL DESIGN

In an attempt to more effectively meet the unique needs of a diverse learning population many educators are focusing their attention on instructional materials, activities, and strategies that allow learning goals to be attainable by individuals with wide differences in their abilities. They are providing varied approaches for teaching information (*what*), for teaching skills and strategies (*how*), and for teaching students to seek the relevance and enjoyment of learning (*why*). Educators are increasingly applying the principles of Universal Design as a means to address the wide differences in abilities among learners in our schools (Table III). Research supports that merely providing physical access to the regular education classroom does not guarantee that students with

Table II
INCLUSIVE EDUCATION GUIDELINES

As is:	Students are involved in the same lesson as other students with the same objectives and using the same materials.
Providing Physical Assistance:	The teacher or support person assist a student in completing an activity by the actual manipulation of materials, equipment, or his/her body.
Adapting Materials:	Students utilizing materials that allow for participation in age-appropriate activities without having prerequisite basic motor, communicative, or cognitive skills.
Multilevel Curriculum:	Students are working in the same subject area, but working at different levels of curriculum.
Curriculum Overlapping:	Students are involved in the same activity with other students but may have a goal from a different curriculum area.
Substitute Curriculum:	Students are involved in alternative activities that meet primary instructional needs when the general education curriculum at the time does not.

Adapted from Neary, Halvorsen, and Smithey (1992).

disabilities will gain cognitive access to the core general education (Kame'enui & Simmons, 1999). Attention to the architectural requirements of that content must take place in order to support cognitive access.

The recently reauthorized Individuals with Disabilities Education Act (IDEA) defines universal design in conjunction with the Assistive Technology Act. These laws identify universal design as "a concept or philosophy for designing and delivering products and services that are usable by people with the widest possible range of functional capabilities, which include products and services that are directly accessible (without requiring assistive technologies) and products and services that are interoperable with assistive technologies" (IDEA, Section 602, [35]). The principles of Universal Design can be successfully implemented through cooperation and commitment. By changing the focus from the remediation and exclusion of individual disabilities to access and opportunity, we create learning environments where students naturally thrive.

Table III
THE PRINCIPLES OF UNIVERSAL DESIGN

PRINCIPLE 1: Equitable Use

The design is useful and remarkable to people with diverse abilities.

Guidelines:

1a. Provide the same means of use for all users: identical whenever possible; equivalent when not.
1b. Avoid segregating or stigmatizing any users.
1c. Provisions for privacy, security, and safety should be equally available to all users.
1d. Make the design appealing to all users.

PRINCIPLE 2: Flexibility in Use

The design accommodates a wide range of individual preferences and abilities.

Guidelines:

2a. Provide choice in methods of use.
2b. Accommodate right- or left-handed access and use.
2c. Facilitate the user's accuracy and precision.
2d. Provide adaptability to the user's pace.

PRINCIPLE 3: Simple and Intuitive Use

Use of the design is easy to understand, regardless of the user's experience, knowledge, language skills, or current concentration level.

Guidelines:

3a. Eliminate unnecessary complexity.
3b. Be consistent with user expectations and intuition.
3c. Accommodate a wide range of literacy and language skills.
3d. Arrange information consistent with its importance.
3e. Provide effective prompting and feedback during and after task completion.

PRINCIPLE 4: Perceptible Information

The design communicates necessary information effectively to the user, regardless of ambient conditions or the user's sensory abilities.

Guidelines:

4a. Use different modes (pictorial, verbal, tactile) for redundant presentation of essential information.
4b. Provide adequate contrast between essential information and its surroundings.

Table III—*Continued*

4c. Maximize "legibility" of essential information.
4d. Differentiate elements in ways that can be described (i.e., make it easy to give instructions or directions).
4e. Provide compatibility with a variety of techniques or devices used by people with sensory limitations.

PRINCIPLE 5: Tolerance for Error

The design minimizes hazards and the adverse consequences of accidental or unintended actions.

Guidelines:

5a. Arrange elements to minimize hazards and errors: most used elements, most accessible; hazardous elements eliminated, isolated, or shielded.
5b. Provide warnings of hazards and errors.
5c. Provide fail safe features.
5d. Discourage unconscious action in tasks that require vigilance.

PRINCIPLE 6: Low Physical Effort

The design can be used efficiently and comfortably and with a minimum of fatigue.

Guidelines:

6a. Allow user to maintain a neutral body position.
6b. Use reasonable operating forces.
6c. Minimize repetitive actions.
6d. Minimize sustained physical effort.

PRINCIPLE 7: Size and Space for Approach and Use

Appropriate size and space is provided for approach, reach, manipulation, and use regardless of user's body size, posture, or mobility.

Guidelines:

7a. Provide a clear line of sight to important elements for any seated or standing user.
7b. Make reach to all components comfortable for any seated or standing user.
7c. Accommodate variations in hand and grip size.
7d. Provide adequate space for the use of assistive devices or personal assistance.

Source: Connell et al. (1987)

UNIVERSAL DESIGN FOR LEARNING

The approach of applying the universal design ideology to curricular materials and methods usable for as many students as possible regardless of age, ability, and/or placement, has become known as the Universal Design for Learning (UDL). Under IDEA, all students, regardless of their abilities, must be given the opportunity to have access to and progress in the general education curriculum. Hitchcock, Meyer, Rose, and Jackson (2002) note that most classroom curriculum materials rely almost exclusively on printed text. Providing access, however, involves much more than supplying every student with a textbook. Teachers must address the diverse learning needs of each child, and ensure that students are actively engaged in learning, regardless of their developmental level. Universal design for learning benefits students who speak English as a second language, students with disabilities, and teachers whose teaching style is contrary to the student's preferred learning style. Essentially, UDL addresses the needs of *ALL* students. UDL gives learners various ways of acquiring information and knowledge, provides learners alternatives for demonstrating what they know, and places a high priority on the learners' interests (Hitchcock, 2001). Figure 4 illustrates the history, principles, implementation and application of the Universal Design for Learning.

Kame'enui and his colleagues have identified six principles that should form the foundation for effective curriculum design (Kame'enui & Simmons, 1999). They assert that these principles provide teachers with a blueprint for designing and developing cognitive supports to promote universal access to the general education curriculum. Universal Access Principles for Designing Curriculum include:

Big Ideas: Concepts, principles, or heuristics that facilitate the most efficient and broad acquisition of knowledge.
Conspicuous Strategies: Useful steps for accomplishing a goal or task.
Mediated Scaffolding: Instructional guidance provided by teachers, peers, materials, or tasks.
Strategies Integration: Integrating knowledge as a means of promoting higher-level cognition.
Judicious Review: Structured opportunities to recall or apply previously taught information.
Primed Background Knowledge: Preexisting information that affects new learning.

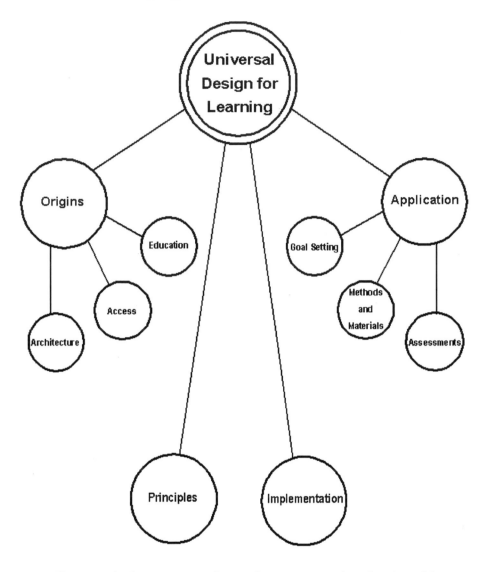

Figure 4. Illustrates the history, principles, implementation and application of the Universal Design for Learning. Adapted from Rose and Meyer (2002).

Kame'enui and Simmons believe that knowledge of these design principles will help teachers evaluate the adequacy of instructional materials and strategies prior to implementation. UDL promotes the development of flexible curricula that can support all learners more effectively thus making learning more accessible. The concept of Universal Design for Learning is committed to improving outcomes for all students, including those with moderate and severe disabilities. It shifts the paradigm from one of focusing on deficits and obstacles to one of focusing on strengths and opportunities.

BENEFITS OF INCLUSIVE CLASSROOMS

There are no quick and easy recipes for building successful inclusive communities. The process of building inclusive communities may be one marked with questions and struggles. However, those who have faced these questions and struggles (Smith et al., 1995) remind us of the benefits of inclusive educational opportunities for students with disabilities. These benefits include:

- Increased interactions between those with and without disabilities.
- Fewer stigmas than being pulled out of the classroom to receive instruction in a separate special education classroom.
- Increased levels of competence/self-esteem.
- Avoidance of the problems often associated with identification and eligibility determination of students for special education.
- Closer interactions among all school personnel in working with all students.
- The dismantling of the artificial dual system of education currently provided in school. (pp. 82-83)

Teachers, staff, and parents often question the benefits of inclusion for typically developing children. It would be an injustice not to conclude the benefits inclusive education provides all children.

- Classmates develop enhanced responsibility, competence and self-esteem.
- Classmates build comfort, confidence, and a better understanding of the range of human diversity.
- Classmates benefit from the knowledge of the special needs student's strengths as well as needs.
- Classmates are enriched by the opportunity to develop new friendships with students with disabilities.

BARRIERS TO BUILDING INCLUSIVE CLASSROOMS

Although there is widespread support for inclusive educational opportunities for children with moderate and severe disabilities, barriers

continue to exist. Smith, Polloway, Patton, and Dowdy (1995) cite a
number of barriers to the successful inclusion of students with disabilities:

- General educators have not been involved sufficiently and are, therefore, not
  likely to support the model.
- General educators as well as special educators do not have the collaboration
  skills necessary to make inclusion successful.
- There is limited empirical data to support the model. Therefore, full implementation should be put on hold until sound research supports the effort.
- The inclusion of students with disabilities into general education classrooms
  may take away from students without disabilities and lessen their quality of
  education.
- Current funding, teacher training, and teacher certification is based on separate educational systems.
- Some students with disabilities do better when served in special education
  classes by special education teachers. (p. 83)

Critics of inclusion continue to assert that inclusive practices are
based on limited empirical evidence and that proponents of inclusion
have traded rhetoric for reason. However, McGregor and
Vogelsberg's (1998) synthesis of research on academic and social outcomes for students with disabilities in general education classes indicate otherwise. The belief that educating children in segregated special
education classrooms would result in more individualized instruction
and improved learning, is not supported by research. In fact, there is
an overwhelming body of evidence that indicates to the contrary
(Freeman & Alkin, 2000). Additionally, no research to date has found
better outcomes when comparing a segregated service delivery model
and an inclusive model. Advocates of inclusive practices remind critics of the extensive amount of research on the negative effects of labeling and separate segregated educational programming.

SUMMARY

Services to children with moderate and severe disabilities have
come a long way since Public Law 94-142 (now IDEA) was enacted.
And although IDEA, related laws and court cases have not eliminated
the discrimination against and segregation of children with disabilities,

they have played a significant role in moving our public schools forward in providing better inclusive educational opportunities for those with disabilities. There is still much to do, however. The idea of an inclusive society potentially forces onto the agenda the broader question of what kind of society we want to live in—and indeed, the question of who "we" are. By working collaboratively, to celebrate the successes, tackle the obstacles, however difficult the experience, schools will discover that a commitment to providing an inclusive education for children and youth with disabilities is good both for the children with disabilities and their nondisabled peers.

DISCUSSION QUESTIONS

1. How have historical events shaped inclusive reform efforts?
2. What specific principles and strategies help to facilitate the building of successful inclusive communities?
3. How can general education teachers provide supports and services to students with moderate and severe disabilities without isolating them from the general population of students?
4. What are the principles of Universal Design and how is it being applied to meet the unique needs of students with diverse learning abilities?
5. How can the general education curriculum be modified in order to meet the diverse learning needs of children with special needs?

REFERENCES

Alper, S., & Ryndak, D. L. (1992). Educating students with severe handicaps in regular classes. *The Elementary School Journal, 92,* 373-384.

Barth, R. S. (1990). *Improving schools from within.* San Francisco: Jossey–Bass.

Biklin, D., & Zollers, N. (1986). The focus of advocacy in the LD field. *Journal of Learning Disabilities, 19*(10), 579–586.

Board of Education, Sacramento City Unified School District, v. Rachel Holland, Civ. S-90-1171-DFL, March, 1992.

Brown, W. H., Fox, J. J., & Brady, M. P. (1987). The effects of spatial density on the socially directed behavior of three and four-year-old children during freeplay: An investigation of a setting factor. *Education and Treatment of Children, 10,* 247–258.

Brown, L., Long, E., Udvari-Solner, A., Schwarz, P., Van-Deventer, P., Ahlgren, S., et al. (1989). Should students with severe disabilities be based in regular or in special education classrooms in home schools? *Journal of the Association for Persons with Severe Handicaps, 14,* 8–12.

Brown v. Board of Education, 347 U.S. 483, (1954).

Bybee, J., Ennis, P., & Zigler, E. (1990). Effects of institutionalization on the self concept and outer directedness of adolescents with mental retardation. *Exceptionality, 1*(4), 215-226.

Byrnes, M. (1990). The regular education initiative debate: A view from the field. *Exceptional Children, 56*(4), 345–349.

Connell, R., Jones, M., Mace, R., Mueller, J., Mullick, A., Ostroff, E., et al. (1997). *The principles of universal design.* Center for Universal Design. Retrieved November 5, 2005 from www.design.ncsu.edu/cud/univ_design/principles/udprinciples.htm.

Davis, W. E. (1989). The regular education initiative debate: Its promises and problems. *Exceptional Children, 55*(5), 440–446.

Deno, E. (1970). Special education as development capital. *Exceptional Children, 37,* 231–237.

Doyle, A., Connolly, J., & Rivest, L. (1989). The effects of playmate familiarity on the social interactions of young children. *Child Development, 51,* 217–223.

Etscheidt, S. K., & Bartlett, L. (1999). The IDEA amendment: A four-step approach for determining supplementary aids and services. *Exceptional Children, 65,* 163–174.

Fisher, D., Sax, C., & Grove, K. (2000). The resilience of changes promoting inclusiveness in an urban elementary school. *The Elementary School Journal, 100*(3).

Forest, M., Pierpoint, J., & Obrien, J. (1996). MAPS, Circle of Friends, and PATH: Powerful tools to help build caring communities. In S. Stainback & W. Stainback (Eds.), *Inclusion: A guide for educators.* Baltimore: Paul H. Brookes.

Freeman, S., & Alkin, M. (2000). Academic and social attainments of children with mental retardation in general and special education settings. *Remedial and Special Education, 21*(1), 3–18.

Friend, M. (2005). *Special education: Contemporary perspectives for school professionals.* Boston: Pearson Education, Inc.

Fuchs, D., & Fuchs, L. S. (1994). Inclusive schools movement and the radicalization of special education reform. *Exceptional Children, 60,* 294–309.

Fuhrman, S. H. (1994). The politics of coherence. In S. H. Fuhrman (Ed.), *Designing coherent policy: Improving the system* (pp. 1–34), San Francisco: Jossey-Bass.

Gardner, P. M. (1994). *A study of exemplary general education teacher behaviors that facilitate positive social interactions between disabled and nondisabled students in a full inclusion classroom.* Unpublished doctoral dissertation, University of San Francisco, California.

Gartner, A., & Lipsky, D. (1987). Beyond special education: Toward a quality system for all students. *Harvard Educational Review, 57,* 367–395.

Gartner, A., & Lipsky, D. (1989). *The yoke of special education: How to break it.* Rochester, NY: National Center on Education & the Economy.

Gerber, M. (1988). Tolerance and technology of instruction: Implications for special education reform. *Exceptional Children, 54,* 309–314.

Gottlieb, J. (1981). Mainstreaming: Fulfilling the promise? *American Journal of Mental Deficiency, 86*, 115–126.

Guralnick, M. J. (1986). The peer relations of young handicapped and nonhandicapped children. In P. S. Strain, M. J. Guralnick, & H. M. Watker (Eds.), *Children's social behavior: Development, assessment, and modification* (pp. 93–140). Orlando, FL: Academic Press.

Hallahan, D., & Kauffman, J. (1994). *Exceptional children: Introduction TO exceptional children* (6th Ed.). Englewood Cliffs, NJ: Prentice-Hall.

Hallahan, D. P., Kauffman, J. M., & Lloyd, J. W. (1988). *Introduction to learning disabilities* (3rd Ed.). Englewood Cliffs, NJ: Prentice-Hall.

Halvorsen, A. T., & Sailor, W. (1990). Integration of students with severe and profound disabilities: A review of the research. In R. Gaylord-Ross (Ed.) *Issues and research in special education: Vol. 1*, 410–472. New York: Teachers College Press.

Hanline, M. F., & Fox, L. (1993). Learning within the context of play: Providing typical early childhood experiences for children with severe disabilities. *Journal of the Association for Parents with Severe Handicaps, 18*(2), 121–129.

Hardman, M., Drew, C., Egan, M., & Wolf, B. (1993). *Human Exceptionality* (4th Ed.). Boston: Allyn & Bacon.

Harris, W. M. (1996). Teaching students with moderate/severe disabilities, including autism. In E. Durán, *Strategies for second language learners in inclusive settings*, (2nd ed., pp. 30–49). Springfield, IL: Charles C Thomas.

Heller, K., Holtzman, W., & Messick, S. (1982). *Placing children in special education: A strategy for equity.* Washington, DC: National Academy of Sciences Press.

Heumann, J. E. (1994). Heumann speaks out on inclusion. *OSERS News Update.* Washington, DC: U.S Office of Special Education & Rehabilitative Services.

Hitchcock, C., Meyer, A., Rose, D., & Jackson, R. (2002). *Technical brief: Access, participation, and progress in the general curricula.* Peabody, MA: National Center on Accessing the General Curricula. Retrieved November 4, 2005, from http://www.cast.org/ncac/index.cfm?i=2830.

Hitchcock, C. G. (2001). Balanced Instructional Support and Challenge in Universally Designed Learning Environments, *Journal of Special Education Technology, 16*(4), 23–30.

Hobbs, N. (1975). *The futures of children: Categories, labels, and their consequences.* San Francisco: Jossey-Bass.

Hobbs, N. (1980). An ecologically oriented service-based system for the classification of handicapped children. In E. Salzinger, J. Antrobus, & J. Glick (Eds.), *The ecosystem of the "risk" child* (pp. 271–290). New York: Academic Press.

Hunt, P., Alwell, M. & Farron-Davis, F. (1996). Creating socially supportive environments for fully included students who experience multiple disabilities. *The Journal of the Association for Persons with Severe Handicaps, 21*, 53–71.

Hunt, P., & Goetz, L. (1997). Research on inclusive educational programs, practices, and outcomes for students with severe disabilities. *Journal of Special Education, 31*, 3–29.

IDEA, 20 U.S.C., section 602. (2005). A users guide to the 2004 IDEA Reauthorization. (P.L. 108-446 & the Conference Report). Retrieved December 2005, from www.thearc.org/ideachanges/usersguide.doc.

IDEA, 20 U.S.C., Section 1400. (2005). Congressional statements and declarations. Retrieved November 8, 2005, from www4.law.cornell.edu/uscode/20/1400.html.

IDEA, 20 U.S.C., Section 1412(5)(B) & 34 C.F.R. Section 300.551. See also Rothstein, L. (1990). *Special education law.* New York: Longman.

Idol, L., & West, F. (1991). Educational collaboration: A catalyst for effective schooling. *Intervention in School and Clinic, 27,* 70–78.

Johnson, D. W., & Johnson, R. T. (1989). *Cooperation and competition: Theory and research.* Edina, MN: Interaction.

Kame'enui, E. J., & Simmons, D. C. (1999). *Toward successful inclusion of students with disabilities: The architecture of instruction.* Reston, VA: Council for Exceptional Children.

Kauffman, J. M. (1989). The regular education initiative as Reagan-Bush education policy: A trickle-down theory of education of the hard to teach. *The Journal of Special Education, 23*(3), 256–278.

Kauffman, J. M., Gerber, M., & Semmell, M. (1988). Arguable assumptions underlying the regular education initiative. *Journal of Learning Disabilities, 21*(1), 6–11.

Kauffman, J. M., & Hallahan, D. P. (1990). What we want for children: A rejoiner to REI proponents. *The Journal of Special Education, 24*(3), 340–345.

Kauffman, J. M., & Hallahan, D. P. (1992). Deinstitutionalization and mainstreaming exceptional children. In M. C. Alkin (Ed.), *Encyclopedia of educational research: Vol.1* (6th ed.) (pp. 229–303). New York: Macmillan Publishing.

Keogh, B. (1988). Improving services for problem learners: Rethinking and restructuring. *Journal of Learning Disabilities, 21*(1), 19–22.

Kode, K. (2002). *Elizabeth Farrell and the history of special education.* Arlington, VA: Council for Exceptional Children.

Kunc, N. (2000). *Do all kids belong in all classes? Equity or excellence in education.* Presentation at the International Summit, Detroit, MI.

Lilly, S. (1988). The regular education initiative: A force for change in general and special education. *Education and Training in Mental Retardation, 23*(4), 253–260.

Lipsky, D. K., & Gartner, A. (1989a). Capable of achievement and worthy of respect: Education for handicapped students as if they were full-fledged human beings. *Exceptional Children, 54*(1), 69–74.

Lipsky, D. K., & Gartner, A. (1989b). *Beyond separate education-quality education for all.* Baltimore: Paul H. Brookes.

Lipton, D. (1994, September). Victory in landmark "full inclusion" case. *Disability rights education and defense fund news.*

Marozas, D., & May, D. (1988). *Issues and practices in special education.* New York: Longman.

McCoy, K. M. (1995). *Teaching special learners in the general education classroom: Methods and techniques.* Denver, CO: Love.

McEvoy, M. A., Shores, R. E., Wehby, J. H., Johnson, S. M., & Fox, J. J. (1990). Special education teachers' implementation of procedures to promote social interaction among children. *Education and training in mental retardation, 25*(3), 267–276.

McGregor, G., & Vogelsberg, T. (1998). *Inclusive school practices: Pedagogical and research foundations: A synthesis of the literature that informs best practices about inclusive schooling.* Baltimore: Paul H. Brookes.

O'Brien, J., Forest, M., Snow, J., & Hasbury, D. (1989). *Action for inclusion.* Toronto, Canada: Frontier College Press.

Peck, C. A., Donaldson, J., & Pezzoli, M. (1990). Some benefits non-handicapped adolescents perceive for themselves from their social relationships with peers who have severe disabilities. *Journal of the Association for Persons with Severe Handicaps, 15*(4), 241–249.

Perske, R., & Perske, M. (1988). *Circle of Friends.* Nashville, TN: Abingdon Press.

Reynolds, M. C., & Wang, M. C. (1981, September). *Restructuring "special" school programs.* Paper presented at National Invitational Conference on Public Policy & the Special Education Task of the 1980s, Racine, WI.

Reynolds, M. C., Wang, M. C. & Walberg, H. J. (1987). The necessary restructuring of special and regular education. *Exceptional Children, 53*(5), 391–398.

Rothstein, L. (1990). *Special education law.* New York: Longman.

Rubin, K. H., Fein, G. G., & Vandenberg, B. (1983). Play. In E. M. Hetherington (Ed.), *Carmichael's manual of child psychology: Socialization, personality, and social development.* New York: John Wiley & Sons.

Rynders, J., Johnson, R., Johnson, D., & Schmidt, B. (1980). Producing positive interaction among Down syndrome and nonhandicapped teenagers through cooperative goal structuring. *American Journal of Mental Deficiency, 85,* 268–283.

Sailor, W. (1991). Special education in the restructured school. *Remedial and Special Education, 12*(6), 8–22.

Santayana, G. (1995). *The birth of reason and other essays by George Santayana.* Edited by D. Cory & with an Introduction by H. J. Saatkamp, Jr. New York: Columbia University Press. Retrieved December 2005, from http://plato.stanford.edu/entries/santayana.

Scheerenberger, R. C. (1983). *A history of mental retardation.* Baltimore: Paul H. Brookes.

Schloss, P. (1992). Mainstreaming revisited. *Elementary School Journal, 92*(3), 233–244.

Scott, B. J., Vitale, M. R., & Masten, W. G. (1998). Implementing instructional adaptations for students with disabilities in inclusive classrooms. *Remedial and Special Education, 19,* 106–119.

Singer, J. (1988). Should special education merge with regular education? *Educational Policy, 2,* 409–424.

Skrtic, T. (1991). *Behind special education.* Denver, CO: Love.

Slavin, R. E. (1990). General education under the regular education initiative: How must it change? *Remedial and Special Education, 11*(3), 40–50.

Smith, A., Hunter, D., & Schrag, J. (1991). *IMPACT: Feature issue on inclusive education, 4*(3), 4–5. Minneapolis, MN: University of Minnesota Institute on Community Integration.

Smith, T. E., Polloway, E. A., Patton, J. R., & Dowdy, C. A. (1995). *Teaching children with special needs in inclusive settings.* Boston: Allyn & Bacon.

Soderhan, A., & Whiren, A. (1985). Mainstreaming the young hearing impaired child: An intensive study. *Journal of Rehabilitation of the Deaf, 18*(3), 7–14.

Soodak, L. C., Podell, D. M., & Lehman, L. R. (1998). Teacher, student and school attributes as predictors of teachers' responses to inclusion. *Journal of Special Education, 31,* 480–497.

Spon-Shevin, M. (1988). Working towards merger together: Seeing beyond distrust and fear. *Teacher Education and Special Education, 11*, 103–110.

Stainback, S., & Stainback, W. (1984). A rationale for the merger of special and regular education. *Exceptional Children, 51*, 102–111.

Stainback, S., & Stainback, W. (1986a). One system, one purpose: The integration of special and general education. *Entourage, 3*(1), 12–16.

Stainback, S., & Stainback, W. (1986b). The merger of special and regular education: Can it be done? *Exceptional Children, 51*, 517–521.

Stainback, S., Stainback, W., & Bunch, G. (1989). A rationale for the merger of regular and special education. In S. Stainback, W. Stainback, & M. Forest, (Eds.), *Educating all students in the mainstream of regular education* (pp. 15–26). Baltimore: Paul H. Brookes.

Stainback, S., Stainback, W., & Forest, M. (Eds.) (1989). *Educating all students in the mainstream of regular education.* Baltimore: Paul H. Brookes.

Stainback, W., & Stainback, S. (Eds.). (1990). *Support networks for inclusive schooling: Interdependent integrated education.* Baltimore: Paul H. Brookes.

Staub , D., Spaulding, M., Peck, C. A., Gallacci, C., & Schwartz, I. (1996). Using nondisabled peers to support the inclusion of students with disabilities in the junior high school level. *Journal of the Association for Persons with Severe Handicaps, 21*(4), 194–205.

Strain, P. S., & Odom, S. L. (1986). Peer social initiations: Effective interventions for social skills development. *Exceptional Children, 52*, 542–551.

Talley, R. C., & Burnette, J. (Eds.) (1982). *Administrators handbook on integrating America's mildly handicapped students. Special education in transition.* Annadale, VA: JWK International Corporation.

Turnbull, H. R. (1993). *Free appropriate public education.* Denver, CO: Love.

Turnbull, H. R., & Turnbull, A. P., Stowe, M., & Wilcox, B. L. (2000). *Free appropriate education: The laws and children with disabilities* (6th ed.). Denver, CO: Love.

Turnbull, P., Pereira, L., & Blue-Banning, M. (2000). Teachers as friendship facilitators. *Teaching Exceptional Children, 32*(5), 66–70.

U.S. Department of Education. (1994). *Goals 2000: Educate America Act.* Washington, DC.

U.S. Department of Education. (2004). *To assure the free appropriate public education of all children with disabilities: Twenty-third annual report to Congress on the implementation of the Individuals with Disabilities Education Act.* Washington, DC: Author.

Wang, M., & Birch, J. (1984). Comparison of a full-time mainstreaming program and a resource room approach. *Exceptional Children, 51*(1), 33–40.

Wang, M., Reynolds, M., & Walberg, H. (1986). Rethinking special education. *Educational Leadership, 44*(1), 26–31.

Wang, M., Reynolds, M., & Waldberg, H. (1987). *Handbook of special education: Research and practice: Vol. I. Learner characteristics and adaptive education.* Oxford, England: Pergamon Press.

Wang, M., Reynolds, M., & Waldberg, H. (1988). Integrating the children of the second system. *Phi Delta Kappan, 70*, 248–251.

Wang, M., Waldberg, H., & Reynolds, M. (1992). A scenario for better-not-separate special education. *Educational Leadership, 50*(2), 35–38.

Will, M. (1986a). Educating children with learning problems: A shared responsibility. *Exceptional Children, 52*(5), 411–416.

Will, M. (1986b). *Educating students with learning problems-A shared responsibility.* A Report to the Secretary, Office of Special Education and Rehabilitative Services, U.S. Department of Education.

Yell, M. (1998). The law and special education. Upper Saddle River, NJ: Merrill/Prentice Hall.

Chapter 2

POWER LANGUAGE

Chris Hagie

The success of students with moderate to severe disabilities who are members of general education classes is, in part, dependent on each student's ability to connect with the peers and teacher in the classroom. Success is not a student working at a desk away from the typical students for long periods of the day, and/or an adult "talking for," or explaining the needs or interests of the separated student. Mastery of classroom participation and lessons occurs when the student with special needs has the skills to communicate his/her needs, access the materials, instruction and curricula, and to join with peers in the educational environment.

THE HUMAN NEED TO BELONG

Abraham Maslow (1970) indicated the requirements for ultimate human satisfaction by describing a hierarchy of needs. At the first level of the hierarchy, all individuals have physiological needs to eat, drink, breathe and so forth. These essentials must be met to move on in the hierarchy to safety needs, or a requirement for security from harm or danger. In a classroom, for example, a student who is hungry might not be able to deal effectively with the fear of threats of aggression from peers.

The need to belong to or feel part of a group and the need for love is the next level of the hierarchy, which can be addressed so long as the earlier physiological and safety needs are met (Maslow, 1970).

Maslow explained that belonging to a group or connecting to other individuals is a necessity for all individuals. This third human need in the Maslow hierarchy must be met in order for the next need of esteem, or the individual experiencing feelings of being competent, is addressed. In school, teachers scaffold instruction and educational activities for success, so that each student's self-esteem improves as they experience success. Maslow suggests that the elevation of esteem can occur only when the student experiences membership of a group.

Finally, at the highest level of the hierarchy of needs, Maslow (1970) identifies "self-actualization" or seeking self-fulfillment and the individual becoming aware of his/her potential so that the work towards living up to that potential is developed and more likely to be mastered. Maslow identified the need for a connection to others and experiencing belongingness as a prerequisite for esteem, which is the prerequisite for self-actualization.

Albert (2003) declares that all students desire to contribute to their class, connect with peers, and to feel capable of participating and working in order to feel part of the class group. Contributing to class can involve, for example, participating in class discussion, completing a "class chore" or taking part in a cooperative group. Connecting with peers could be in the form of making a request, commenting on school activities, or asking to join in a game. Students feel capable in class, for example, when they experience success with assignments and instruction. If any one of these "three Cs" is unsuccessful, the student is at risk for demonstrating challenging behaviors to get his/her needs met.

Language or communication between a student and his/her peers and other adults, allows the individual to be part of the community of the classroom, to share experiences, and to make needs known to others (Garfinkle & Kaiser, 2004). The use of specific types of communication, that will be called Power Language (PL), guarantees that students experience the three Cs, and membership of a class. This section provides the definition and characteristics of Power Language, assessment strategies, the selection of Power Language, and strategies for teaching Power Language with some examples.

DEFINITION OF POWER LANGUAGE (PL)

Power Language is verbal or nonverbal expressive language symbols that facilitate communicative interactions between a student and his/her peers, teachers, key community people (i.e., retail workers, employers, bus drivers, information desk workers, librarians, coworkers, and supervisors), parents, and/or other significant individuals. The forms of Power Language can include, for example, speech, gestures, body posturing, sign language, Picture Exchange Communication Systems (PECS), voice output devices, recorded voice devices, programmable switches, communication books, and/or other picture or drawing communication devices. Power Language helps the student make contributions in his/her daily environments, form connections with other individuals, and feel capable of the work or expectations in school, work, home, and the community. Power Language can be taught and when mastered, the individual experiences the feelings of belonging to the group.

CHARACTERISTICS OF POWER LANGUAGE

The characteristics of Power Language are as follows: (1) the consequence of using Power Language results in an action honoring the intentions of the individual; (2) it is age appropriate, or commensurate with the communicative symbols utilized by typical peers of the same age as the individual; (3) it matches or is appropriate to the cultural characteristics of the setting and the social group of the individual; (4) Power Language can be learned and eventually expressed independently; (5) there are many daily naturally occurring opportunities to use Power Language; (6) other individuals can "read" and understand Power Language; and (7) the use of Power Language contributes to the user becoming more part of a group.

ASSESSMENT OF POWER LANGUAGE

The first step in determining the Power Language to teach a student is to assess the social interactions in the student's environment (Garfinkle & Kaiser, 2004). Direct observation of the interactions between students and teachers in the classroom will provide information about the type of communication that helps typical students in class to connect with others, contribute to the class, and feel capable.

Table IV
POWER LANGUAGE ASSESSMENT

Name of Student: _____ Class: _____ Date: _____ Time: _____

	Power Language observed in Class/ First Name of User	Function or Purpose of the Power Language	Class Activity: indicate type of instruction or activity	Focus Student: Description of Power Language Observed	Discrepancy Analyses	Plan for PL Instruction
Connection Power Language						
Contributing Power Language						
Capable Power Language						

The goal of the assessment of Power Language is to determine specific communicative structures typically used by peers in the class and that would provide a more likely opportunity for the student with a disability to feel connected, capable, and that he/she is contributing to the classroom.

The format that guides the assessment is found in Table IV. The Power Language Assessment form is useful for observation in the classroom of one student (the "focus" student) for whom the goal of increased connection, contributing to the class, and feeling capable has been determined. The first column of the form is divided into the three categories of Power Language that correlate with the ideas suggested by Albert (2004) that are important for a student to experience in order to feel membership in a school. The observer writes in the second column the language used by typical peers in the class in the space next to the type of Power Language that it indicates. The observer hypothesizes or makes a guess based on the observation about the category in which the language sample belongs. It is important to understand the form and type of language that typical peers use that are the same age and familiar with the school culture.

The third column is designed for the observer to indicate the possible function or purpose of the language used by the peer in each of the three categories. The fourth column is provided for the observer to indicate the class activity and/or the type of instruction that is occurring during the observation. For example, the class activity could be a lecture by the teacher who uses a white board on which she writes some important points from the lecture. Power Language used by the focus student is noted in the fifth column and in the row that the observer suspects matches the type of Power Language.

A discrepancy analyses or a note about how the focus student communicates in the respective category without assistance is written in the sixth column. The discrepancy analysis provides a place to indicate the basis for the discrepancy between the focus student's language and the peers' language skills (Downing, 1999). Finally, a brief plan for instruction is provided in the last column. Some strategies that could go into a plan to teach Power Language might be, for example, to increase the pictures in a Picture Exchange Communication (PECS) program, to provide a specific prompt with a plan to fade, or to reinforce the student each specific time for attempts to communicate with peers. Table V is an example of a Power Language Assessment completed for a middle school student, Jamal, in a social studies class.

Table V
POWER LANGUAGE ASSESSMENT

Name of Student: Jamal   Class: Social Studies   Date: Jan. 12th, 2005   Time: 9:05am-9:55

	Power Language observed in Class/ First Name of User	Function or Purpose of the Power Language	Class Activity: indicate type of instruction or activity	Focus Student: Description of Power Language Observed	Discrepancy Analyses	Plan for PL Instruction
Connection Power Language	"Hey, dude, what's up"? with head nod "What page are we on"? "Can I see that?"	greeting; claify teachers' direction; to talk to the peer; to request something from peer	beginning of class; teacher direction about opening text to specific page;	——— slapped text after teacher direction	does not greet peers or techer; does not open book; grabs item from peer	teach a gesture greeting; a hand-shake with a head nod upward; teach requesting using PECs
Contributing Power Language	raised hand to be called on; pointed to the location on a map	to add to the discussion; answer question that was asked by the teacher	teacher asked question about the material	——— ———	does not know how to raise hand to signal for help	teach raising hand; give Jamal a role during the lessons;
Capable Power Language	asked for help from the teacher; answered question about the map	to get assistance; to provide answer to the question posed by the teacher	teacher asked question about the maps on the page of the text	showed the teacher an icon for "help me" ———	——— looks at the photo of the map, but does not answer questions	——— talk to peer in Jamal's group about showing him the page number;

THE SELECTION OF POWER LANGUAGE

Determining the Power Language for intervention depends on (a) the availability of naturally occurring times in the day in which the new language skill can be learned and reinforced, (b) the ease with which, when mastered, the Power Language can be used in several environments such as at school, home, and/or on the bus, (c) the preferences of the student after examining the Power Language Assessment, (d) the preferences of the parents, or significant others in the student's life (Garfinkle & Kaiser, 2004). Successfully learning Power Language is more likely when intervention occurs in the natural environment, rather than in a speech therapy session without peers (Kamps, Kravits, & Ross, 2001), and it most likely happens when the peers and the adults are proficient communicative partners (for example, they are responsive with requests, or comments from others).

Recommended communication functions for intervention include (a) indicating a request, (b) sharing during play, (c) making comments, (d) conversing with peers, (e) responding to initiations from others (Conroy & Brown, 2001), (f) refusing a request, (g) inquiring for information, (h) engaging in greetings and leave-taking, (i) making complaints (Downing, 1999), (j) requesting positive attention, (k) asking for help, (l) indicating a choice, and (m) signaling an interrupted activity (Ford et al., 1989). Power Language is a specific communication function that allows the student to experience increased connections, contributions to a class community, and feelings of being capable in the educational environment.

STRATEGIES FOR TEACHING POWER LANGUAGE

After the assessment has been completed and the selection of Power Language for intervention determined, the intervention strategy is identified. The type of intervention depends on the student's learning style and current language skills baseline, and the situation. The teacher can include any or all of the strategies and intervention methodologies described in the next section.

Antecedent Modifications

When teaching new communication skills, the classroom and social environment can be designed in a manner that is more likely to prompt or encourage the use of the selected Power Language. Garfinkle and Kaiser (2004) stated that the environment can be organized with "Interesting materials . . .", "Out of reach (materials) . . .", "Inadequate portions . . .", "Choice making . . .", "Assistance . . .", and "Unexpected situation . . ." (p. 132) that will facilitate the use of communication. In an example, Chris (a student) is learning to make requests. An item for which she has indicated a preference (an interesting item) is a large ball to play four-square during recess. The balls in the classroom are made available but located in a bin that is out of reach for the students. After working on the form to make a request (in her case this was a picture), the teacher asked, "What do you want?" and she gave the picture to the teacher, who handed her the ball.

In another example, Ben (a student) made a request for paper and glue during a cooperative group activity in social studies class because they were not available to the students. His form of communication was a voice output device. In a third-grade class, the students were given a choice about an item or activity after completing their work. Annika, a student in the class, indicated her choice by pointing to a picture in a communication book. In a high school, Marty used the sign for "help" with a peer during lunch because he had difficulty opening a bag of potato chips. It is noteworthy that in each of these examples, the teachers and paraeducators did not rush in and over-prompt or cue the students.

Least Prompts Strategy

The first steps in the least prompts instructional strategy are (a) to identify 3–5 prompts in a hierarchy, with increasing levels of assistance provided by each prompt, and (b) to task analyze or identify the steps in the activity (Wolery, Ault, & Doyle, 1992). The hierarchy of prompts is designed to match the student's learning style (i.e., visual prompts are used with a more visual learner). A cue (the goal is to use a natural cue, such as the school bell, rather than an artificial cue, such as a teacher direction) indicates the activity. If the student does not independently demonstrate the first step of the activity, then the prompt with the least amount of assistance is provided to the student. If the student does not perform the step, then the next prompt (with just a bit more assistance) is provided to the student. Again, if the student is unsuccessful with that step, another prompt with more assistance is provided to the student and so forth.

An example of using a least prompt strategy with Power Language follows. It was identified that a second grader, Alicia would participate more successfully with her classmates during recess if she indicated a choice about a preferred activity during recess, which was a requirement for all students in the class. She used picture icons on two-inch squares to indicate her preferences, interests and needs. A divider with picture icons of the possible items and/or activities on the playground (i.e., play structures, four-square game, basketball and hoop) attached with Velcro® was placed near the classroom door that led to the playground.

If Alicia did not independently select an icon and hand it to the teacher, she was prompted with a pointing gesture toward the divider. If she chose an icon and handed it to the teacher, she was told, "Great. Have fun on the _____" (the item she chose). If she did not independently select an icon and hand it to the teacher, she was prompted with the pointing prompt accompanied with the comment, "What should you do now, Alicia?" This sequence continued if she was unsuccessful with each step. The prompt hierarchy in this example were, (a) a pointing gesture, (b) an indirect verbal prompt ("What should you do now, Alicia?"), (c) a direct verbal prompt ("Choose an activity, Alicia"), (d) a partial physical guidance prompt, which included the teacher putting her hand over Alicia's hand and guiding toward the divider, and releasing, and finally, (e) a full physical prompt to choose an icon.

Most-to-Least Prompts Strategy

The most-to-least prompts procedure (Wolery et al., 1992) is similar to the least prompts procedure described above, except that the prompt providing the most assistance is delivered first, rather than last. After the student successfully completes the step in the activity with the identified prompt that provides the most assistance (the most prompt), the level of prompt is reduced to one with less assistance. In the example above, the trainer physically guides (using hand-over-hand prompts) Alicia to take an icon from the divider and to hand the icon to the teacher. After a specific number of successful trials with the physical prompt (all trials are successful with a full physical prompt), the trainer provides a partial physical prompt for each trial until the criteria of success is reached, and so forth.

Picture Exchange Communication System (PECS)

Frost and Bondy (1994) developed an instructional procedure for teaching a student Power Language. PECS involves the student initially learning to present a picture of a desired item to another person in exchange for the item (Frost & Bondy, 1994). Power Language that involves initiating a request for items or activities, responding to questions about the students' desires, and commenting about something can be learned using PECS.

The initial PECS training sessions involve two trainers and opportunities throughout the day for the student to request a preferred item in his/her environment (Frost & Bondy, 1994). One trainer, who is the communication partner, sits across from the student and extends his/her open hand. An item that has been determined to be of interest to the student and might be requested is placed on a table between the student and the communication partner (or someplace in easy sight of the student). The second trainer sits behind the student and initially provides physical prompts for him/her to pick up a picture of the item in front of the student and place it in the hand of the second trainer (the communication partner), who acknowledges the request verbally, and gives the student the item. The physical guidance prompt is faded gradually and the open hand of the communication partner is faded as the student masters the skill.

The five training stages that follow the initial training involve expanding the number of pictures so that the student can request additional items, the use of a communication board with many pictures, requesting items using sentences, responding to the question, "What do you want?" and learning to make statements that are comments (Frost & Bondy, 1994). Students learning Power Language through PECS can contribute in class by asking for materials and connecting with peers, which influence the experience of feeling capable.

An example of a student who learned Power Language through PECS instruction is Louise. She was in sixth grade and used a small communication book in which there were about a dozen pages with one-inch square icons attached to each with Velcro. Louise initiated with the book frequently (it seemed she used it about as much as her typical sixth grade peers communicated) to request items, and to make comments. She was learning to talk about her evening or weekends; her mother had a collection of the icon cards and kept her communication book filled with those cards that indicated Louise's activities outside of school. Louise taught her peers to communicate through the book.

REFERENCES

Albert, L. (2003). *Cooperative discipline.* Circle Pines, MN: AGS.

Conroy, M. A., & Brown, W. H. (2001). Preschool children: Putting research into practice. In H. Goldstein, L. A. Kaczmarek, & K. M. English (Eds.), *Promoting social communication: Children with developmental disabilities from birth to adolescence* (pp. 211–237). Baltimore: Paul H. Brookes.

Downing, J. E. (1999). *Teaching communication skills to students with severe disabilities.* Baltimore: Paul H. Brookes.

Ford, A., Schnorr, R., Meyer, L., Davern, L., Black, J., & Dempsey, P. (1989). *The Syracuse community-referenced curriculum guide for students with moderate and severe disabilities.* Baltimore: Paul H. Brookes.

Frost, L. A. & Bondy, A. S. (1994). *PECS: The picture exchange communication system training manual.* Cherry Hill, NJ: Pyramid Educational Consultants.

Garfinkle, A. N., & Kaiser, A. P. (2004). Communication. In C. H. Kennedy & E. M. Horn (Eds.), *Including students with severe disabilities* (pp. 120–140). Boston: Pearson.

Kamps, D. M., Kravits, T., & Ross, M. (2001). Social-communicative strategies for school-age children. In H. Goldstein, L. A. Kaczmarek, & K. M. English (Eds.), *Promoting social communication: Children with developmental disabilities from birth to adolescence* (pp. 239–277). Baltimore: Paul H. Brookes.

Maslow, A. (1970). *Motivation and personality.* New York: Harper & Row.

Wolery, M., Ault, M. J., & Doyle, P. M. (1992). *Teaching students with moderate to severe disabilities: Use of response prompting strategies.* White Plains, NY: Longman.

Chapter 3

FUNCTIONAL LANGUAGE AND OTHER LANGUAGE INTERVENTION STRATEGIES

Elva Durán

Before a teacher can begin to work with a child on any level, some means of communication must be established. With the wide range of problems in teaching handicapped and autistic children, fulfilling this need is no less basic. Some have limited motor abilities, some have undeveloped speech abilities, many have emotional problems, and others have any number of interferences that the teacher must overcome. But of them all, the need for communication—in verbal form or some other means of language—is most fundamental. This chapter will define functional language and will give information on the language intervention strategies which can be used with populations with moderate to severe handicaps.

FUNCTIONAL LANGUAGE

Language, to be functional, must be used in a communicative interaction (Warren & Warren, 1985); that is, it must affect the listener in specific intended ways. For example, a student will communicate with another person by pointing with his/her finger, with or without words. The listener will understand the student and will nod "Yes" to the student after he/she has pointed to a particular object or has noted something to the person. Functional language also means that the words that are to be used are words that the student will need in his/her later life. For instance, some functional words may include vocabulary like "exit," "women," "stop," and "water."

It should also be noted that for language instruction to be useful in everyday life the teacher must use techniques that can be used with students with handicaps in the child's natural environments. In summary, the child's language instruction should include words from his/her environments–home, school, and community. In order to teach these words, the teacher should utilize approaches which would result in language instruction to be taught as the child or student is eating at the cafeteria or is making a sandwich at home.

In the next section of this chapter, natural approaches or techniques which are utilized to teach language to students with handicaps will be discussed.

INCIDENTAL TEACHING

According to Halle (1982), in incidental teaching there is an interaction between an adult and a child that arises naturally in an unstructured situation and is used by the adult to teach information or give the child practice in developing skills. In incidental teaching, the teacher may arrange the environment so that the child will be encouraged to talk or request various items. For example, a series of objects will be placed on a table where the child can see them. These objects should be things the student wants or would like to have. It is important when teaching language to help create in students a desire so that the child will want to speak. Also, in incidental teaching, the teacher, or the parents, will be in various places, in such different environments as the cafeteria, outdoors, at home, at a grocery store, and/or at a fast food restaurant.

Thus, the teacher or parent may ask the child a question about the environment during a particular time. For instance, the teacher may say to the child, "Look at the people standing in line. Let us count the people." The teacher may also say, "Look at Juanita's jacket. What color is it?" According to Halle (1982), incidental teaching produces spontaneous variety in language among students with handicaps who are disadvantaged or come from environments where they are not normally stimulated to speak.

This language model also works well with a student with more moderate handicaps such as one who has Down's syndrome, with a student with severe handicaps, and with a student with autism. Some examples to illustrate this are seen when students with the above handicaps are engaged in vocational and community-based training (learning to shop in grocery stores, or learning to order their food in fast food restaurants) in their own nearby environments and vocational sites.

Teachers or practicum student trainers may ask students questions about their work or purchases they are going to make at stores or restaurants. Students will respond by using short word phrases, will answer teachers or trainers by one-word utterances, or perhaps by pointing.

The writer has noticed as she visits schools where teachers and students are engaged in training that once teachers and trainers are aware of how to ask questions, and further encourage students to talk, these students begin to communicate more in varied locales than they did when language instruction was done just in classrooms or in one environment. It is also important to remember that in incidental teaching the student should be reinforced for initiating a request or should be reinforced for communicating with the adult person. As the child is praised or verbally reinforced for communicating or initiating a request, the child's desire to communicate continues to increase. This reinforcement may be as simple as saying to the student, "Good talking" or "I like the way you said the word" (whatever word or words the student said in the environment).

The effectiveness of using incidental teaching has been widely researched and reported. Hart and Risley (1975) found that using this approach produced spontaneous language in many students who have moderate disabilities. Cavallaro (1983) also found that spontaneous speech increased for several students who have moderate handicaps. Further, Cavallaro and Bambura (1982) discovered that incidental teaching was effective in increasing rates of two-word requests in a language-delayed preschooler. Warren and Kaiser (1986) found that using incidental teaching often generalized to other environments. Hart and Risley also found that incidental teaching resulted in substantial increases both in the frequency of language use and in vocabulary growth. Warren and Kaiser have noted that students tend to use language in a more functional way, or in ways more meaningful to themselves, when they are taught by means of the incidental language approach, rather than in isolated, environmental situations.

MAND MODEL OR MANDING

Another technique which is part of functional language teaching is manding, a method of interaction which *demands* a verbal or other response. Like incidental teaching, manding is used more successfully and efficiently in the child's natural environment. In manding, a response is requested from a child. For instance, the teacher or parent may say to the child, "Tell me what you want" or the teacher may say, "Show me what you want," or "Tell me what you'd like." The teacher during the language instruction session provides the students with interesting materials that will cause the student to request desired objects. Objects are given to the student only if the student explains to the teacher what he/she wants. The teacher will often not give the student the object unless the child points to it or asks for it in a one- or two-word utterance.

According to Halle (1982), the mand model is especially helpful with moderately to severely language-delayed students. This writer has found the mand model especially useful when adolescents (or students of any age) who may have moderate to severe handicaps are supposed to complete a sequence of steps. The teacher may remind them of the step or steps they are forgetting to complete by commanding them to show the teacher what to do next. For example, at the University of Texas at El Paso, this writer directed an adolescent and young adult all-day program. In the program the students or clients were required to wash dishes, bake, cook, and do many other independent types of skills. Since many of the clients in the program had very poor memories due to their extreme mental retardation and/or brain damage, they often forgot the sequence of steps they were to complete for various tasks. In one instance, one of the students was drying dishes and forgot what to do after washing and rinsing the dishes. The writer of this program cued the client by saying, "Show me what to do next." The student then remembered to place the dried dishes in the cabinets.

At the University of Texas at El Paso there is an after-school intervention program where students of all ages and varied handicapped conditions are assisted in language and communication intervention, functional academics, and other areas where teachers and families feel students may need help. In this after-school program, the mand model has also been extremely useful when teaching students language and/or communication. Undergraduate college practicum students may be teaching several language concepts, for instance, learning labels or common noun object names. If the teacher is at a point where he/she wants to see if his/her student remembers a series of words just learned, the teacher may command the child to point to the various objects or vocally to say the names of each object. The teacher can say, "Mary, point to the table" or "Mary, tell me what you want."

In manding, the teacher must remember to show the child interesting materials or objects. If the child responds minimally or not at all, the teacher may model for the child a more satisfactory response. Studies have indicated that the verbalization rates of three children with moderate to severe language delays increased at least twofold from their baseline levels when a manding model was introduced. Vocabulary and complexity of utterance increased, as did the children's display of newly trained words and grammatical forms. McQuarter (1980) found that use of the mand model technique resulted in higher verbalization rates for the children studies, and the student's language complexity increased when the reinforcement pattern changed to include two-word rather than one-word utterances. Manding also showed that generalization–transfer from an initial environment situation to one in another environment–was successful if this procedure was used in a number of environments rather than in a single one (McQuarter, 1980).

DELAY PROCEDURE

Another technique used in functional communication training is the delay procedure. In the delay procedures the teacher or trainer stands at least three feet from the client or student (Halle, 1982; 1987) and waits at least five seconds to see whether the student will give the appropriate response. If the student does not give an appropriate response, then the teacher can model, or give the appropriate response, to the student. It is important to note that the teacher or trainer should not rush to vocalize the response for the student until there has been sufficient time–five seconds at least–for the student to attempt a response. As part of the delay procedure in teaching language, the teacher or adult trainer places a toy or other pertinent object out of reach of the client and delays giving it to him/her until the student properly requests it. Such a procedure has proven very effective in the Special Education Clinic at U.T. El Paso, where college students learn what particular objects to teach first to students, by placing objects on a table away from the student's immediate reach. Students soon realize that the college student trainer is not going to give them the material they want until they ask for items (or point to the item if they are nonvocal students.)

In research conducted by Lovaas (1976) using the delay procedure proved effective with clients who had learned some words or vocabulary prior to using this approach. In each case, "waiting out the child" helped increase the child's vocabulary. The researchers showed the students food trays and waited fifteen seconds before giving what was on the tray. The fifteen-second delay procedure helped the students learn to request their food trays effectively more often than before this procedure was used. Halle (1982) noted that, taken together all of these procedures are capable of making moderately and severely handicapped children, with very low rates of initiation and small expressive vocabularies, into fluent communicators. Thus, it is important to use all of these approaches. When teaching moderately to severely handicapped students language, a combined or integrative model can help increase students' vocabularies, as well as the ease with which they can communicate.

NONVOCAL COMMUNICATION APPROACHES

Nonvocal communication approaches are varied and include several techniques which must be carefully evaluated by the teacher in order to determine which technique is the best approach for teaching communication to a student who is nonverbal or who has some capacity to learn to communicate if given the appropriate stimulus. In the following section, the writer will explain some of these approaches used to teach nonverbal children and will also provide some considerations a teacher can use to determine if a student should be taught by means of a particular technique.

MANUAL OR TOTAL COMMUNICATION

Total or simultaneous communication is referred to as manual communication, a technique which has the teacher or trainer orally saying the word as the sign is modeled for the child. This is signing such as that used by students who are deaf or are partially deaf. The purpose of signing or total communication is to facilitate verbal communication for a student with an intact vocal mechanism. Selection of a total communication approach may be considered, according to Alberto et al. (1983), under a variety of conditions: (1) if the student has poor articulation; (2) if the student has an intelligibility problem; (3) if the student has a minimum vocabulary pool; (4) if the student has more of a receptive ability than an expressive one; (5) if the student has minimal degree of language generalization; or, (6) if the student has some inhibition because of emotional problems.

When teaching a child manual or total communication, it is important to remember to begin with functional words or action words that the child needs in order to communicate in his/her various environments. Brown (1979) noted that using an environmental inventory can help a teacher or trainer discover words to teach a child that are found in the child's home, school, and community. The teacher can develop a table where there are different columns with labels of "Home," "School," and "Community," and the basic words appropriate to each environment listed separately in each column. Functional words are then selected for instruction in each child's environment. The words are prioritized and the most important ones are listed first on each of the columns.

After experimental use of the assumed priorities, the teacher can go through each column and decide which items are in fact more important and therefore should be listed first and should be taught first. Parents can also be encouraged to take part in deciding what their son or daughter should be taught in communication instruction.

Some other considerations which should be noted when teaching students to sign or learn manual communication are to use body movement and facial expression and say the word clearly when the sign is made for the child. The teacher and/or trainer and the student should face each other while the training is being conducted (Dayan et al., 1977). Further, the student should be reinforced for learning correct signs. If the student signs correctly for a particular food item he/she is learning, the student should be rewarded, perhaps by being given some of the food he/she is learning to sign during the lesson.

Additionally, when training the student, it is important to use real objects, concrete objects, and photographs or pictures to help stimulate the student to make the proper sign. The training session should not be confined just to teaching the student in the classroom, but the teacher and parent should stress that the student sign for various objects or other stimuli in the different environments where the student lives, works, and plays. Prizant (1983) found that successful training is more widely seen when the students practice their vocabularies in their various training environments. Again, careful, continuing reexamination of the lists described in Table VI is indicated, stressed particularly those vocabulary words with utility in a variety of situations.

Table VI
ENVIRONMENTAL INVENTORY FUNCTIONAL WORD SELECTION
FOR LANGUAGE COMMUNICATION

Home	School	Community
water	bus	store
glass	pencil	street
bread	paper	car
mild	desk	bus
food	toilet	restaurant

WHAT SIGNED SYSTEM TO USE

There are several educational systems that a teacher can use in teaching signs to students. This particular section will discuss some of these systems and research related to the system.

Signed English

Signed English is an educational signed system. It has the same syntax as spoken English (word order, use of auxiliary verbs, articles, inflections, etc.). The syntactic correspondence among signed and spoken and written English makes possible the close linkage between the two in the teacher's, and, alter, the child's or student's signing (Schaeffer, 1980). Signed English has been reported to be useful in teaching students with autism, those from nonverbal populations, and the severely mentally retarded.

Signing Exact English

Signing Exact English is another educational signed system that was developed to improve other educational systems. This particular signing system consists of nearly 4000 words. Words in Signing Exact English are considered basic, compound, or complex. Basic words are root words with no additions, no plurals or inflected forms such as "girl," "talk," or "sit." Signing Exact English was developed as a manual communication system to represent English for educational purposes (Musselwhite & St. Louis, 1982; Musselwhite, 1986). Signing Exact English parallels the English language and is often used by students who have developed competence in understanding English but who cannot speak it. Alberto et al. (1983) noted that Signing Exact English is not as transparent or ironic–i.e., not as realistic or concrete, so that the concept is less easily grasped with a little imagination–and, therefore, is not as easily remembered by students learning these particular signs. These two educational manual systems are noted here because they are most often used. There are other educational manual systems used with students with autism and those students who have severe handicaps.

OTHER GESTURAL SYSTEMS

One gestural system that has shown great promise is the American Indian Sign or gestures developed by Skelly (1979) from the Iroquois Indians to be used with nonverbal students. It is noted that observers can interpret 50 percent to 80 percent of the signs without previous instruction. The American Indian Sign or gesture system is highly ionic and is used by many students who have been placed in many other systems and have failed to learn to sign (Daniloff, 1981). In the American Indian Sign or gesturing system, the core of signals centers around actions and objects that pertain to the daily needs and desires of students. In a study completed by Daniloff, twenty-one students who were labeled severely and/or profoundly handicapped made progress learning gestures. Some learned one gesture, while others learned thirty gestures. It should be noted that in all manual systems, what is helpful in increasing the number of the gestures the students learn is to have all of the people who come in contact with a particular student (parents, teachers, etc.) practice the gestures with the student. This involvement by others helps to insure maintenance and generalization from one environment to another.

POINTING AND NATURAL GESTURES

In the U.T. El Paso Special Education Clinic, over the past eight years, the practicum students and this writer have found that the use of pointing and other natural gestures are very helpful in teaching some form of communication to students who are severely mentally retarded, since they are less able to learn manual or other types of signed systems. Many are adolescents or young adults when they come to the program, and their parents or guardians have not been able through the years to teach the person any form of communication system. Since time becomes a major factor for these older students, the simpler the communication system is for them the faster they will be able to use these systems in the various environments where they live, work, and play. Many are taught to use natural gestures and to point to various things they want or desire. In our experience, if the students are training in the Student Union cafeteria, for example, and need to communicate that they are tired and need a break, we have taught them to gesture naturally by placing their hand over their forehead and wipe their forehead clean of sweat. This immediately cues the workers or supervisor of the student that the clients should be allowed to take a five-minute break in the lunchroom.

Pointing is also widely used by students and their trainers as the students are crossing streets or are grocery shopping. The clients or students point to the light when it is green and they know they can cross the street. If the light is red the trainer points to the student so that he/she may look up and the student stops the moment the trainer points to the red light. Many older students are not able to learn signs as readily as younger students, and pointing and gesturing naturally is the only way they are able to communicate or understand how to get around in their different environments. As part of the programming, parents and/or guardians are taught how to point or gesture naturally so they can do the same once their sons and/or daughters are at home or are with them in community environments. Some of the students who are enrolled in the All Day Program for Adults with Autism and Other Severe Handicaps come to the program not knowing basic gestures or pointing, and can now after several months move about the community and can let others know what they would like or can request various objects or food from their environments.

Nietupski (1977) noted that natural gestures are easily understood by others, and no additional equipment is needed to have the students participate in communicating with other people around these particular populations. Natural gestures and pointing can easily supplement other communication systems.

OTHER COMMUNICATION SYSTEMS

Communication boards can be effectively used with nonverbal students in order to teach them to communicate. The communication board can be made of cardboard or other firm material and is usually divided into small squares that are neatly divided by lines running vertically and horizontally to separate each square from the other square. The square and line pattern is much like a Chinese checkerboard or a tic-tac-toe board. Each square on the communication board is big enough to hold a picture or photograph so that the student can point to the picture or photograph in order to tell others what he/she wants or needs.

The board is organized in the Fitzgerald key and the organization is usually one row for the subjects or agents such as "I" or "me." There is an additional column for the verbs such as "want" and there is a column for prepositions such as "in." Finally, there are columns for objects such as "big" and an additional column for nouns which represent objects; for instance, one of the object names placed on this particular column may be a commonly used food item such as "milk."

Also, at the top of the communication board, there is a place for a "Yes" on the upper left-hand corner of the board. There will also be a "No" placed at the upper right-hand corner. The "Yes" and "No" are used by the student to communicate wanting or not wanting certain items. Numbers one through ten are also placed at the upper right-hand corner for the student so that he/she may communicate how much or how little of each he/she would like of various things. The alphabet (in upper-case letters) is placed towards the bottom of the communication board. As the student learns the alphabet, he/she will also learn that he/she can spell different words with the letters of the alphabet. Again, the words (nouns) placed on the communication board should be words that are used very often by students.

The environmental inventory that was discussed earlier as being useful for helping the teacher discover words for the students to learn is practical here as well. The same procedure should be used to help students learn words from the communication board. Verbs "want" and "go" should be taught to the student immediately, since they are action words that are commonly used to express various activities. On the communication board, the printed word should appear above each picture or symbol, for fullest utility. Thus, if there is a drawing or a photograph of milk or bread, the printed word "MILK" or "BREAD" should appear above it. Some instruction or cueing should be given to the student so he/she can learn to respond to the object pictured or photographed on the communication board. For example, the teacher or adult teaching the student to communicate using the board can say, "What do you want?" (Dayan et al., 1977; Firling, 1975; Snyder et al., 1975). If the student does not respond to the teacher's inquiring after the teacher has waited approximately five seconds, then the teacher can ask the question once again and at this time place the student's hand over the photograph or picture being requested. This type of practice is important to do with a student learning to use the communication board because such practice will help train the student so that if he/she is asked such a question, then the student can learn to use the communication board to request items from the environments he/she participates in.

Obviously, in order for the board to be useful to the student in different environments it must be portable. Placing a small handle on the board will help the student carry the board from one place to another.

COMMUNICATION BOOKLETS

Communication booklets are becoming widely used by special education teachers who teach students with severe handicaps (Brown, 1987; Sailor, 1985; Wilcox, 1984). Communication booklets are often made quite easily by placing colored photographs in a 5 x 7 spiral notebook. Pictures or photographs can also be placed on cards and then laminated so they will not become destroyed and can be used over and over by the student. As with the booklets, the printed words are usually written above each photograph to allow the student the opportunity to read or learn to recognize the words. Vocabulary selected for the booklets, of course, should be chosen by using the environmental approach that was noted earlier in this chapter.

In the U.T. El Paso Special Education Clinic, the communication has been widely and successfully used with several students who attend the program for remediation and/or additional help. For example, a boy I will call Rene was one student who made excellent progress learning languages by using the communication booklet. He was a Spanish-dominant, severely language-delayed student. He was five years old when enrolled in the Clinic. He was nonverbal and quite aggressive. Rene would cry most of the time he was being taught language or any other skill area; he was extremely stubborn and inflexible. His mother naturally wanted desperately for Rene to be able to communicate some of his desires. We first completed an inventory to see which words the student would learn from home, school, and community. A total communication system approach was used with the student. Along with a signed speech approach and/or total communication, an alternative system consisting of a communication booklet was used with the student. Rene's mother was instructed to teach him utilizing this approach. After six months he had learned several signs. His aggressive behavior diminished almost completely. During the hour and a half instruction (for the first six months) at the Clinic, the student was also given help learning to use the communication booklet. He was also taught signs and the use of the booklet at home and in other environments. Rene learned to also request various items using his communication booklet. His communication booklet was organized into several sections, involving each of his environments, including one for restaurants. Photographs useful in each of the different areas were included in the appropriate section.

As the student needed to learn additional vocabulary items, more photographs were placed in each section. He used his booklet daily, and by the end of the year had increased considerably the number of symbols he comprehended, as well as developing more and more facility in using his communication booklet. Both his mother and his teacher continued to observe that his aggressive actions decreased markedly in addition, probably because he had become less frustrated with matters of communication.

In using an alternative mode of communication such as a picture or a photography booklet, it is obviously important to involve the parents. They must be taught how to use such a system or any system of communication used with the child. If they learn to use the system being employed, their son or daughter will increase in functional vocabulary, and parents themselves will add more items to the booklet as they become increasingly aware of the usefulness of this communication device and of the importance of enriching it. In the eight years this writer has been working with parents of language-delayed students, both at the university clinic and as a consultant in public schools, she has noted repeatedly that when parents are not fully behind a procedure or technique, the son or daughter will make considerably less progress, whatever system is used.

It should be pointed out that little information has been written on the effectiveness on using communication booklets because this technique has only recently come into use as an alternative system of communication for students who have been successful learning by other systems. The versatility of the booklet and the ease with which it can be carried about by students gives this means of communication great promise for wider use with language-delayed populations. And, in this case, the gratification the student receives from achieving success where little or none was felt before has infinite possibilities.

PICTURE EXCHANGE COMMUNICATION SYSTEM

The Picture Exchange Communication System (PECS) (Bondy & Frost, 1985) was developed to provide a means of functional communication for children with autism. This system uses pictures and the exchange of these pictures to effectively teach children how to initiate a social request for a desired item. This system incorporates behavior analysis techniques and a functional communication approach to teaching children to use meaningful communication (Germany & Williams, 2004).

PECS originally was developed for use with preschool-aged children with Autism Spectrum Disorders (ASD), and other social communicative disorders who display no functional or socially acceptable speech. By this it is meant that these children do not speak at all, speak only in "self-stimulatory" manner, and/or speak only when promoted to do so (Germany & Williams, 2004). These children's communicative difficulties are socially related in that the children do not routinely approach others to communicate, actively avoid interaction with others or only communicate in response to a direct cue to do so.

Over the years, Bondy and Frost (1985) have recognized that many children, in addition to children with ASD, have difficulty learning speech. PECS is taught to a variety of children and adults with a variety of diagnoses or educational classifications. PECS have been taught to thousands of children from around the world, in family and educational settings. Children using PECS first learn to approach and give a picture of a desired item to a communicative partner in exchange for that item. By doing this, the child initiates a communicative act for a concrete outcome with a social context (Germany & Williams, 2004).

There are no prerequisites for children utilizing the Picture Exchange Communication system. Students do not have to possess fine motor skills. A child having difficulty grasping small items may benefit from pictures glued to a wood or foam blocks or dowels, which would aid the child in picking up the picture. The size of the picture can be modified as well to help in manipulation (Germany & Williams, 2004). Also, children do not need to know the meaning of the picture before starting PECS and there are no cognitive prerequisites indicated by scores on a standardized development test. Also, children do not have to have minimum developmental age before they can successfully learn PECS. Further, such eye-to-eye contact, sitting quietly in a chair, responding to a series of simple instructions, or being able to match pictures to objects or other pictures are not prerequisites for PECS (Germany & Williams, 2004).

The PECS training protocol is based on research and practices of applied behavior analysis. In PECS the teacher or trainer will use reinforcement, error correction strategies and generalization strategies to teach each skill. PECS training protocol also closely parallels typical language developments in that it first teaches the child how to communicate or teaches the child what the basic rules of communication are (Germany & Williams, 2004). Children using PECS learn to communicate first with single pictures, but later learn to combine pictures to learn a variety of grammatical structures, semantic relationships and communicative functions.

In order to begin using the program successfully the trainer must observe the student to see what the student wants. By observing the student the trainer or teacher will be more successful in making sure the program begins to work immediately for the student. This will occur because the student will be highly motivated to want to request the item that is being presented to him/her.

Bondy and Frost (1985) believe that it is important to teach children to be spontaneous communicators. Thus, the first step in PECS is to teach the child to initiate a request. Once the teacher or trainer has discovered a powerful incentive for the child, the teacher can start introducing PECS by teaching the child to pick up and exchange a picture that corresponds to the item the child wants. It is important to make sure the child is interested in the item when beginning the instruction with PECS. To increase the likelihood that the child will be interested in the item, it is important to withhold the item for a short period of time so that the child comes to want the item. Then, the teacher will show the child the item and the child will be motivated to obtain the item.

During the initial phase it is best to have two people involved with directing the child. One person is placed directly in front of the child (may be seated at the table or standing in front of the partner), uses no verbal prompts (Germany & Williams, 2004). When the child reaches for the enticing item, the second adult, called the physical prompter, sitting or standing behind the child guides the child to pick up the picture (with or without assistance), reach toward the first person, and place the picture in the open hand of the first person. The communicative partner immediately gives the child the item while saying the name of the item.

During Phase II where the child's pictures are expanded the child is introduced to the more realistic aspect of communication. During this phase the picture is placed further from the child but still so that the child can see the picture and bring the picture to the teacher.

It is during Phase II that a communication binder for the child is introduced. This may be a three-ring binder that has a square of Velcro® affixed to the middle of the front cover. A single picture to communicate is displayed on the outside of this binder (placed there by the teacher) while other pictures can be stored within the binder. The binder will help the child identify his/her own set of pictures, as well as provide a location to place all pictures the child will eventually be using.

During this phase of PECS instruction, the number of motivational items is expanded. For instance, if candy was used as the reward in PECS previously then other items are introduced. Also, it is important to add items that are not similar to the first item, that is, something that is not food. The use of a favorite toy or access to music or television may be used (Germany & Williams, 2004). It must be kept in mind that the goal is to teach the child how to initiate functional communication in all situations in which the child desires something, rather than as the system used only during snack or mealtime.

In Phase III the child learns to discriminate between pictures. When discrimination training begins, a second picture will be associated with something that the child greatly prefers (Germany & Williams, 2004). The distracter picture can either be a picture of something neutral or the picture can be something the child dislikes and or the picture that looks distinctly different from the picture of the preferred item.

With the use of the neutral distracter, there would be a picture of the preferred item, for example, a piece of candy and a picture of something neutral or disliked by the student, for instance, a Kleenex®. When using this strategy, the child is given the corresponding item when he/she gives the picture to the communicator. For example, the child hands the teacher the card with the candy, the teacher gives the student the candy. If the child hands the teacher the card displaying the Kleenex, the Kleenex is given to the child. This strategy generally is successful if the child appears to be somewhat upset if handed the Kleenex.

In discrimination training, the focus is now on teaching the child to select the correct picture, since the child has previously learned to hand a single picture to the communicator. Also, at this stage only one trainer is needed.

It has been found that providing some vocal (as in verbally voicing "Oh!") or visual (as in showing the desired item) feedback at the point of the picture selection can hasten the acquisition of this skill. These cues signal the child that he/she will soon receive what he/she has asked for. While the communicator may respond vocally as the child selects a picture, the communicator only provides the item when the child puts the picture into the hand.

Once a child has learned to successfully select from two pictures, more pictures are added. As more pictures are included, the child is offered a choice between items that are more and more similar in preference. In time, the choice may be between two types of cookies or two types of chips.

When two equally preferred items are offered, the trainer will seek to determine whether there is correspondence between what the child requests and what item the child wants. Therefore, in situations where both (or many) items are enjoyed, when the child gives the card to the communicator, the communicator will say, "Ok, take it." The communicator watches the child carefully to see if the child takes the item requested. If the child takes the wrong item, an error is made and corrections must be made to teach the child to take the correct item.

When a child can discriminate between two pictures, the child is presented with three, four, and then five pictures presenting preferred items. Periodically, checks are made for accuracy by being told to "Go get" what the child is asking for. Eventually, the child learns the pictures in his/her PECS book.

In Phase IV, the child learns to use the sentence strip. In this phase the child is introduced to the pictures "I want" and "I see." With long-term goal in mind, we must also introduce a new structure to help children learn to express different communication purposes.

The new structure (sentence) is taught using the function the child already knows. First, a sentence strip that can be easily removed from the communication book is designed. This communication book will hold different pictures upon which the child will be able to use when constructing his/her sentence. The first picture that the teacher constructs is one that states, "I want." (The words are on one card, not separated.) At this time, it is not possible to teach the child what the word "I" means because the child has not had any other pronouns in his/her picture dictionary yet to contrast "I."

The lesson is presented to the child with the "I want" picture already on the sentence strip. The child is then guided to exchange the whole sentence strip. Next, the child is taught to place both the "I want" icon and the picture of what is desired onto the strip before giving the strip to another person.

When the communicator is handed the strip, he/she encourages the child to touch each picture while the communicator reads the sentence to the child, for example, "I want cookie." While the child is learning where to place each picture and what to do with the entire sentence strip, the communicator reads the sentence strip quickly so as not to delay giving the requested item. Once the sequence has been learned fluently, then a pause is introduced between the words; for instance, the teacher will note, "I want" and then the item is requested. This pause tends to encourage the child to initially imitate and often say the final spoken word before the communicator does. The communicator does not want to force the child to speak if the child is not willing or able to do so, so that the child does not avoid the use of PECS.

Once the child has learned how to use the sentence strip to make direct requests, the communicator can now teach the child to clarify what is being requested. An example would be to place a preferred object into the red box and place that box next to a blue box. To gain access to the box, the child must request, "I want RED box." Additional games can be created with different preferred objects and different colored objects. This type of instruction can occur with other objects that the child may wish to request. If the child wants cookies, for example, the teacher can show the child a large and small cookie and the child will have to let the teacher know which cookie he/she may want. Such advanced training helps the child expand requests using different attributes of things the child may want or need.

ALTERNATIVE AND AUGMENTATIVE COMMUNICATION

Communication devices, referred to as Alternative and Augmentative Communication devices (AAC), enable students who cannot speak to communicate using another means. The device may be as simple as pictures or symbols pasted onto cardboard (an example of a low-tech assistive device) or as complicated as a computerized device that both speaks and writes (an example of a high-tech device) (Snell & Brown, 2006). Accommodations, adaptations, and assistive technology all enable children with disabilities to fully participate in typical home, school, and community activities. For example, a child who is unable to write the letters may still be able to participate in a general education class because he/she may have another child in general education help the child with disabilities by pointing to a keyboard that indicates the letters and the child in general education may help the child write some of the letters that the child with disabilities may be unable to write even with his assistive technology. Assistive technology includes a variety of items, ranging from items that are readily available and used by people with or without disabilities to those that have been developed specifically for use by individuals with disabilities. Simple adaptations of readily available items are often classified as "low tech," while those that are specific to individuals with disabilities are defined as "high tech" (Snell & Brown, 2006). Assistive technology can help individuals perform specific skills in a different way than is typically done.

There are some considerations for using Alternative and Augmentative Communication (Snell & Brown, 2006). Multimodal teaching approaches are needed to teach communication through an Alternative and Augmentative Communication (Snell & Brown, 2006). Thus, a teacher may model and respond with spoken language and will also use the student's Alternative and Augmentative Communication by pointing to a picture in the PECS book and/or communication booklet.

Some considerations for using Alternative and Augmentative Communication are as follows: the selection of the communication mode should be based on current and student and environmental assessments (Snell & Brown, 2006) and requires knowledge of the student's physical, cognitive, and intentional communication abilities as well as the barriers that may interfere in the student's communication. Some students, for example, can wave and identify pictures. Therefore, the two modes of communication should be taught to the student so the student can communicate in different environments.

Whichever system or systems are used to help students with severe disabilities to communicate, the teacher and parent should seek expert advice on whether the student may need Alternative and Augmentative Communication devices. The student may need to begin with a very low technical option such as pictures and gradually move into a more complex computer-based system. A student may begin with a simple system and later be moved to a more complex system like a computer-based system like Freestyle/Speaking Dynamically Pro™ (Snell & Brown, 2006).

Another consideration for using Alternative and Augmentative Communication with students is that students may need practice using a new mode of communication in addition to naturalistic teaching. For example, students may need to be given practice initially in operating a computer-based system or in learning enough motor imitation skills to be able to imitate a sign. All of this practice should occur in natural settings rather than wait until the student is "ready" to begin using this information in functional contexts. A teacher, for instance, may need to make certain that the student he/she is working with on PECS can match pictures to items. This first practice can occur in a classroom then instruction can occur naturally while the student is in the cafeteria.

Additionally, another consideration when using Alternative and Augmentative Communication with students with severe disabilities is to make sure that the student's communication partners know enough about the communication system so that the communication system can be functional. Communication partners who are teaching new forms (signs, pictures) need a variety of those forms so that they can model and expand in natural environments (Snell & Brown, 2006). Peers who have been taught to use pictures to communicate with a student who has been fully-included in a general education classroom for example, will use pictures to communicate with the student who has severe disabilities in a variety of natural environments. Thus, the important thing to do here to facilitate this use between students with and without disabilities is to teach peers how to use these pictures with the fully-included student in their class.

Further, another consideration to keep in mind when using Alternative and Augmentative Communication is that it is not going to reduce the amount of communication a child will perform by using the alternative and augmentative devices. Research shows that utilizing different systems of communication with the child will actually enhance the child to communicate more in different environments. For example, this writer has often used total communication signed systems with students with autism because they were nonverbal. As the student learned several systems with the total communication system or approach, the student was also introduced to using pictures or pointing and requesting with pictures. The student with autism started communicating more because the total communication or signed system was used along with pictures and spoken language from the communicator partners. Parents indicated to the writer that their child's communication actually expanded because signs, spoken language and pictures were used with their child.

VOCAL SYSTEMS

There are few programs that have the special features that are needed to teach students who have some ability to say one-word or two-word phrases. The Functional Speech and Language Program has appeared in the literature several times as being a very worthwhile program to teach verbal students with language delays (Booth, 1978; Guess et al., 1976; Gullo & Gullo, 1984; Haring & Brown, 1976; Musselwhite, 1982; Wilcox, 1984). This program is a behavioral approach designed to increase the student's expressive language. Unlike the few other programs that have been developed for nonvocal students, it is a program that is designed to increase the student's vocalization because the structured program stresses generalization training. The program is divided into four parts. The program emphasizes Persons, Things, Action with Persons, and Action with Things. Other content areas include Possession, Color, Size, Relation, and Morphological Grammar (plurals, suffixes, tenses, inflections). The program has easy-to-follow lessons where the teacher or trainer is told the exact dialogue to say to the child. For example, in the first lesson, the student is asked by the teacher, "What want?" At this point, the teacher holds up one object at a time as she asks the child the above question. As the child responds to the object name, the teacher records a "+" in the space next to the object. This indicates that the student responded correctly. This continues until all of the objects are shown to the student for the lesson's objective. The teacher or trainer is given suggestions as to which object to use in each lesson.

It is important to remember that when teaching students with severe language delays, there have to be very motivating objects shown to the student at first to help create a desire to want to communicate. Few students with severe language delays learn language unless a strong desire is created to communicate (Warren & Warren, 1985). This writer has used the Functional Speech and Language Training Program in the U.T. El Paso Special Education Clinic for approximately four years and has found it to be very helpful for various students who have come to the program with some expressive language abilities.

Roberta was a four-year-old with extreme mental retardation and language delay. She could vocalize only a few words, and the words she vocalized were not easily understood. In conferencing with Roberta's parents, we learned that Roberta cried and became extremely aggressive with others when she was not given what she demanded. The student acting as her tutor interviewed one of the parents and did an environmental inventory on Roberta in order to determine what words in home and community she needed to know. The public school teacher provided the practicum students with words that were important for Roberta to know in school.

After completing the child's environmental inventory, the practicum student started with the first lesson in the program. The parent and teacher also reinforced the same lessons with Roberta at home and school. She was taught twice weekly in the clinic for one hour each session. At first, all words selected for Roberta were functional. Later some functional words were interspersed with words that would be also highly motivational to her. Roberta, for example, found music and toys highly motivational, and these were often added to each of her language lessons. In one year, Roberta began speaking one-word and two-word utterances. By the end of two years, she started to request more items and also asked more questions as she went around her different environments. Roberta continues to be in the Functional Speech and Language Training Program and continues to make more progress daily. Her vocabulary has increased to the point that she is requesting and naming approximately ten more items in the immediate environment on a weekly basis.

DEVELOPING ATTENDING SKILLS AND ELIMINATING INAPPROPRIATE BEHAVIORS WHICH INTERFERE WITH COMMUNICATION TRAINING

As with many nonvocal programs, the few vocal programs that have been developed, including the Functional Speech and Language Training Program, do not have guide manuals explaining the areas in which a teacher can develop attending skills. Attending skills are seen when a student looks at the item or training object or person or teacher who is attempting to get a response from the student (Campbell & Campbell, 1982; Snell, 1987; Warren & Warren, 1985). Attending skills, simply stated, involve the ability to pay attention, to respond appropriately to the teacher, parent, or as the situation demands.

When beginning any language or communication program, the first thing a teacher or trainer must do is to teach the student to look at the stimulus or object that the teacher is using to teach the student (Snell, 1987). The teacher begins by teaching the student to look at the teacher when the teacher says, "Look at me." The teacher should give the student reinforcement, or praise the student for looking at the object or stimulus the teacher is holding in his/her hands. If the student is aggressive or swings at the teacher or trainer, the teacher can hold the student's hands for about three seconds and say, "No hitting" (Lovaas, 1981; Prizant, 1983). If the student kicks, the teacher can also hold down the student's legs for three seconds and say, "No kicking."

As the teacher or trainer holds the stimulus, and the student responds by not kicking and looks at the trainer, then the trainer should continue praising the student. For example, the trainer should say, "Good not kicking" or "Good looking." With constant reinforcement (Wehman, 1979) and work, the delayed-language student will gradually begin to focus on the training object or stimulus and will further learn to replace kicking with other less aggressive behaviors.

It has been the experience of this writer that many students who have not had training in language make more progress when they are taught how to attend and to be less aggressive. It usually takes several lessons, plus consistent training time at home, before attending becomes a major part of the student's repertoire. As the instruction continues, the student needs a continuation of this type of instruction in attending and in eliminating his/her interfering behaviors. Students with autism and those with autism plus severe mental retardation have the most difficulty learning to attend. Also, students with autism have extreme difficulty learning new behaviors such as kicking and hitting.

In the U.T. El Paso Clinic, approximately eight students with autism have been assisted in language training. With all of the students some time was spent initially teaching them to sit up and look at the trainer or teacher. With some it took approximately one week and with others it took two or three weeks to accomplish these goals. Unless these particular skills are taught, the students make little progress in their language instruction.

SOME OTHER CONSIDERATIONS IN TEACHING LANGUAGE AND COMMUNICATION TO STUDENTS WITH SEVERE HANDICAPS

In the past five years, much has been written about teaching functional and chronological age-appropriate materials to students with severe handicaps (Brown, 1979, 1980; Wilcox & Bellamy, 1984). It is important to remember that students who are severely and/or developmentally delayed need to be shown materials that are age-appropriate. For instance, a seventeen-year-old nonverbal student with handicaps should not be instructed in a separate speech room and taught the colors and the letters of the alphabet, as one would teach developmental skills to young children who are beginning to learn language. It would be far more appropriate to teach a nonverbal seventeen-year-old how to order food in a restaurant, or buy groceries, by using picture or photograph cards as he/she goes out into the community.

In short, rather than using an artificial approach, one should use a natural one, reaching the student language in context, not in meaningless isolation. By following this method, the student is taught to generalize, applying what is learned in one environment to another environment; once again, this generalization is necessary in making certain that students learn language or how to communicate with others.

It should be obvious that basic to successful language instruction is teaching elementary age student material which is functional and appropriate to the environments in which they live. But all too often there are language programs which devote themselves to nonfunctional, illogical vocabulary almost entirely related to the student's real life. The majority of words used are school-related, and the program had few if any words from other environments.

Another important consideration in teaching students with severe handicaps language is allowing time to train or teach parents to use or learn the different manual or vocal systems. It has been the experience of this writer that if parents are not given instruction on how to teach their son or daughter the different language or manual systems, generalization will not carry over to other environments.

Too often teachers have indicated that many parents do not work with their son or daughter on language or communication training at home. If more time is taken to teach parents how to use various programs or techniques, then they will try harder to use these particular materials with their child at home. Language and/or communication systems are considerably less effective unless parents teach these systems at home and in the other environments where their son or daughter may live, work and/or play (Brown, 1987; Firling, 1975; Warren & Warren, 1985). Parents work with their child at least two or three times weekly for twenty-minute sessions. Natural use of these techniques on a daily basis is an easy addition to the training.

Another important aspect of language training is to consider the sequence of instruction for the students. Schaeffer (1980) believes that students should be taught to express their desires first, because students with developmental delays, or those who are severely handicapped, express desires more easily and naturally than they address people or ask questions. Earlier in this chapter when speaking about signing communication, some of the actions that could be taught were indicated.

When deciding what noun labels to teach, it is important once again to do an environmental inventory and select words from the child's home, school, and community. Evaluating daily where the student is successful in learning words is important, because that gives the teacher information on what words should be taught once again, reviewed, or presented by using different objects or materials to teach the concepts. The student's progress on the various language concepts being presented can be noted as follows: a plus (+) is used for correct words and a minus (-) is used for incorrect words. If a student does not respond, an "N" is placed beside the word. This progress can be noted each time the trainer or teacher teaches the child in his/her particular language lesson. Additionally, when teaching language and/or communication strategies to students with disabilities, it is necessary to consider the student's primary language as part of his/her instruction. The teacher should determine if the student, who may be from another country, speaks English or another language as the primary language. If the student is nonverbal, the teacher should also determine the student's primary language at home. Receptively, the student whose first language is not English still needs support and instruction in his/her primary language no matter what system(s) of communication is/are employed by the teacher. Parents, by law, can request that some primary language support be allowed for their son and/or daughter at school. Parents should request primary language support for their son and/or daughter in their child's individualized education program.

In conclusion, when teaching language instruction to students with severe handicaps, it is necessary to realize that there are many different approaches and systems that are available to teach these populations. Furthermore, it is important to consider many systems in order to decide on the best one for a particular student. Finally, the vocabulary taught to the students should be age-appropriate and should more importantly include words from the different environments where the student lives, works, and plays.

DISCUSSION QUESTIONS

1. What is functional language?
2. Define incidental teaching. Explain how it is used with persons with moderate handicaps.
3. What is manding and how is it used with moderately handicapped students?
4. What is the delay procedure?
5. List and explain two nonverbal approaches.
6. What is signed English and when should you use this manual communication?
7. What other communication systems can you use with nonvocal students?
8. What is Picture Exchange Communication System or PECS? When is it used to help students communicate?
9. What is Alternative and Augmentative Communication? When do we use this type of communication?

REFERENCES

Alberto, P., et al. (1983). Selection and initiation of a non-vocal communication program for severely handicapped students. *Focus on Exceptional Children, 15*(7), 1–16.

Biklen, D. (1990). Communication unbound: Autism and praxis. *Harvard Educational Review, 60*(3), 291–314.

Biklen, D. (1992). Typing to talk: Facilitated communication. *American Journal of Speech and Language Pathology, 1*(2), 15–17.

Biklen, D. (1993). *Communication unbound: How facilitated communication is challenging traditional views of autism and ability.* New York: Teacher's College Press.

Biklen, D., & Schubert, A. (1991). New words: The communication of students with autism. *Remedial and Special Education, 12*(6), 46–57.

Biklen, D. & Schubert, A. (1992). *Communication unbound: The story of facilitated communication.* Paper presented at 1992 National Symposium, Current Issues in the Nature and Treatment of Autism. St. Louis: Missouri Department of Mental Health Conference.

Bondy, A., & Frost, L. (1985). *Picture exchange communication system.* Newark, DE: Pyramid Educational Products.

Booth, T. (1978). Early receptive language training for the severely and profoundly retarded. *Language, Speech and Hearing Services in School, 9*, 142–150.

Brown, L. (1979). A strategy for developing chronological age appropriate and functional curricular content for severely handicapped adolescents and young adults. *Journal of Special Education, 13*(1), 81–90.

Brown, L. (1987). *Transition and educating the person with moderate to severe handicaps.* Paper presented at workshop, El Paso Independent School District, El Paso, TX.

Calculator, S. N. (1992). Perhaps the emperor has clothes after all: A response to Biklen. *American Journal of Speech and Language Pathology, 1*(2), 18–20.

Calculator, S., & Slinger, K. (1992). Letter to the editor: Preliminary validation of facilitated communication. *Topics in Language Disorders, 13*, 9–16.

Campbell, R. C., & Campbell, K. (1982). Programming loose training as a strategy to facilitate language generalization. *Journal of Applied Behavior Analysis, 15*(2), 295–301.

Cavallero, C. (1983). Language interventions in natural settings. *Teaching Exceptional Children, 16*(1), 65–70.

Cavallero, C. C., & Bambura, L. M. (1982). Two strategies for teaching language during free play. *Journal of the Association for the Severely Handicapped, 7*(21), 80–92.

Crossley, R. (1988, October). *Unexpected communication attainments by persons diagnosed as autistic and intellectually impaired.* Unpublished paper presented at International Society for Augmentative and Alternative Communication, Los Angeles, CA.

Crossley, R. (1992a). Communication training involving facilitated communication. In DEAL Communication Centre (Eds.), *Facilitated communication training,* (pp. 1–9). Melbourne, Australia: DEAL Communication Centre.

Crossley, R. (1992b). Who said that? In DEAL Communication Centre (Eds.), *Facilitated communication training,* (pp. 42–54). Melbourne, Australia: DEAL Communication Centre.

Dandiloff, J. (1981). A gestural communication program for severely and profoundly handicapped children. *Language, Speech and Hearing Services in School, 12,* 258–268.

Dayan, M., et al. (1977). *Communication for the severely and profoundly handicapped.* Denver, CO: Love.

Firling, J. D. (1975). Functional language for a severely handicapped child: A case study. *AAESPH Review, 1*(7), 54–71.

Germany, D., & Williams, J. (2004, April). *Picture exchange communication system.* Paper presented in Language and Literacy II class. California State University, Sacramento.

Gullo, D. F., & Gullo, J. C. (1984). An ecological language intervention approach with mentally retarded adolescents. *Language, Speech and Hearing Services in Schools, 15,* 182–191.

Halle, J. W. (1982). Teaching functional language to the handicapped: An integrative model of natural environment teaching techniques. *TASH Journal, 7,* 29–37.

Halle, J. W. (1987). Teaching language in the natural environment: An analysis of spontaneity. *Journal for the Association for Persons with Severe Handicaps, 12*(1), 28–37.

Halle, J. B., & Spradlin, D. (1981). Teacher's generalized use of delay as a stimulus control procedure to increase language use in handicapped children. *Journal of Applied Behavior Analysis, 14,* 389–409.

Haring, N. G., & Brown, L. (1976). *Teaching the severely handicapped.* New York: Grune & Stratton.

Hart, B., & Risely, T. R. (1975). Incidental teaching of language in the preschool. *Journal of Applied Behavior Analysis, 8,* 411–420.

Lovaas, I. O. (1976). A program for the establishment of speech in psychotic children. In J. K. Wing (Ed.), *Childhood autism.* Oxford: Pergamon Press.

Lovaas, I. O. (1981). *Teaching developmentally disabled children the me book.* Baltimore: University Park Press.

McQuarter, R. (1980). *Milieu language training: A functional alternative to traditional remediation strategies.* Unpublished master's thesis, University of Kansas.

Musselwhite, C. R. (1986). Using signs as gestural cues for children with communicative impairments. *Teaching Exceptional Children, 19*(6), 32–35.

Musselwhite, C. R., & St. Louis, K. (1982). *Communication programming for the severely handicapped vocal and nonvocal strategies.* San Diego, CA: College Hill Press.

Myles, B. S., & Simpson, R. L. (1994). Facilitated communication with children diagnosed as autistic in public school settings. *Psychology in the Schools, 31,* 208–220.

Nietupski, H. (1977). Curricular strategies for teaching selected nonverbal communication skills to severely handicapped students. In L. Brown, et al., *Curricular strategies for teaching nonverbal communication, functional object use, problem solving and mealtime skills to severely handicapped students, 7,* (Part 1). Madison, WI: University of Wisconsin-Madison & Madison Metropolitan School District.

Prizant, B. M. (1983). Language acquisition and communication behavior in autism toward an understanding of the whole of it. *Journal of Speech and Hearing Disorders, 48*(3), 286–296.

Rimland, B. (1992a). A facilitated communication "horror story." *Autism Research Review, 6*(1), 1, 7.

Rimland, B. (1992b). Facilitated communication: Problems, puzzles, and paradoxes: Six challenges for researches. *Autism Research Review, 5*(4), 3.

Rimland, B. (1993). Facilitated communication under siege. *Autism Research Review International, 7*(1), 2, 7.

Sailor, W. (1985). *Strategies for teaching persons with severe handicaps.* Paper presented at a workshop held at the University of Texas at El Paso.

Sailor, W., et al. (1976). Functional language for verbally deficient children: An experimental design. *Mental Retardation,* 27–29.

Sailor, W., & Guess, C. (1982). *Severely handicapped students: An instrumental design.* Boston: Houghton Mifflin.

Schaeffer, B. (1980). Teaching signed speech to nonverbal children theory and method. *Sign Language Studies, 26,* 29–63.

Simpson, R. L., & Myles, B. S. (1995). Effectiveness of facilitated communication with children and youth with autism. *Journal of Special Education, 28*(4), 424–439.

Simpson, R. L., & Myles, B. S. (1995). Facilitated communication and children with disabilities: An enigma in search of a perspective. *Focus on Exceptional Children, 27*(9), 1–16.

Skelly, M. (Ed.). (1979). *American-Indian gestural code based on universal American Indian hand talk.* New York: Elsevier North Holland.

Snell, M. (1987). *Systematic instruction of persons with severe handicaps* (3rd Ed.). Columbus, OH: Merrill.

Snell, M. E., & Brown, F. (2006). *Instruction of students with severe disabilities* (6th Ed.). Upper Saddle River, NJ: Pearson Merrill Prentice Hall.

Snyder, L. K., et al. (1975). Language training for the severely retarded: Five years of behavior analysis research. *Exceptional Children,* 7–15.

Warren, S. F., & Kaiser, A. P. (1986). Incidental language teaching: A critical review. *Journal of Speech and Hearing Disorders, 15,* 291–299.

Warren, S. F., & Warren, A. K. (1985). *Teaching functional language, language intervention series.* Austin, TX: Pro-ed.

Wehman, P. (1979). *Curriculum design for the severely and profoundly handicapped.* New York: Human Services.

Wilcox, B. (1984). *Teaching language to persons with moderate to severe handicaps.* Lecture series from workshop taken at the University of Oregon, Eugene.

Wilcox, B., & Bellamy, T. G. (1984). *Programming for secondary students with severe handicaps.* Lecture series given at the University of Oregon, Eugene.

Chapter 4

TRANSITION PLANNING FOR STUDENTS WITH DISABILITIES FROM CULTURALLY AND LINGUISTICALLY DIVERSE BACKGROUNDS

HYUN-SOOK PARK

Transition planning from school to adult life has been an important element in educational programs for students with disabilities for more than two decades. This emphasis on transition planning and particularly on vocational training that can result in independent employment or "supported employment," stemmed from the fact that the employment rate for secondary school graduates with disabilities lagged behind their peers without disabilities (Blackorby & Wagner, 1996). Here the term "supported employment" refers to paid employment in a nonsheltered, competitive work environment with ongoing support provided by employment specialists (Rusch, 1990). In an effort to improve the discouraging post-secondary employment outcome, in 1984 the Office of Special Education and Rehabilitation Services (OSERS) institutionalized the policy on transition planning for students with disabilities that can lead to a successful employment after graduating from high school (Will, 1984). The OSERS priority on transition planning has continuously encouraged professionals and service providers to demonstrate ways to deliver vocational training effectively and to document best practices in transition planning, which resulted in numerous successful demonstration programs supported by federal grants over the past two decades. The development and refinement of best practices for transition still continues, however, as professionals, service providers, and consumers expand the ways to help persons with disabilities attain the highest possible quality of life in their post-secondary years and adult lives. This chapter provides an overview of legislation related to transition/school-to-work programs and best practice transition model components. In particular, the chapter highlights best practice strategies for working with students and families from culturally and linguistically diverse backgrounds.

OVERVIEW OF TRANSITION/SCHOOL-TO-WORK LEGISLATION

A focus on transition planning for students with disabilities initially began with vocational training that would lead to successful post-secondary employment, as supported by the 1984 OSERS transition initiative. Since then, the term "transition" often has been used interchangeably with "work experience or employment training programs." However, the current best practice transition planning addresses broader quality of life issues not only in employment but also in other areas such as social relationships, self-determination, and independent/supportive living. Because vocational training, rehabilitation, and the broader quality of life issues for people with disabilities have been addressed through legislation, government policies, and government-supported programs, it will be helpful to overview the major legislation that has influenced transition/school-to-work programs for persons with disabilities.

It was not until after the World War I that vocational rehabilitation and employment programs for persons with disabilities were guaranteed by law (Smith-Hughes Act, P.L. 64-347) because of the need to provide rehabilitation training to disabled veterans of World War I. This legislation provided for the first federally-funded vocational education programs in secondary schools in the areas of agriculture, home economics, trade, and industrial education (Stodden, 1998). Similarly, the need to train industrial workers during World War II prompted the legislation to offer vocational training to persons who did not qualify for military service and for the first time included persons with developmental disabilities in rehabilitation and vocational training programs, resulting in the birth of "sheltered workshops" and work study programs.

The Rehabilitation Act of 1973, in particular, Sections 503 and 504 (P.L. 93-112) introduced significant changes to vocational training and employment for persons with disabilities by mandating business sectors with federal contracts to initiate a plan for hiring and training persons with disabilities and by ensuring nondiscriminatory treatment for persons with disabilities. Another important law passed in 1973, the Comprehensive Employment and Training Act (CETA, P.L. 93-203), purported to provide manpower training for persons who did not possess any employment skills, in order to decrease the high unemployment rate. Although this Act did not specify the population of persons with disability, it benefited this population. The CETA programs were reshaped and reinforced through 1982 legislation, the Job Training Partnership Act (JTPA, P.L. 97-300) that included job training and placement services for youth with disabilities. The landmark 1975 legislation, the Individuals with Disabilities Education Act (IDEA, P.L. 94-142) required the development of the Individualized Educational Program (IEP) to guarantee free, appropriate public education (FAPE) for all children and young adults with disabilities. Although it did not mandate the transition/vocational goals in the IEPs, this law implied that the IEP could include career and vocational goals if deemed appropriate by the IEP teams. In 1984, the Carl Perkins Vocational and Technical Education Act mandated vocational assessment, counseling, support, and transition services for youth with disabilities and disadvantages. This legislation required that vocational goals and objectives be included in the IEPs of students with disabilities.

Among all the legislation reviewed, the policy developed by Madeline Will, Assistant Secretary for the OSERS in 1984, played a key role in shaping the current transition program requirement for persons with disabilities. This OSERS Transition policy emphasized the need to provide work experience programs for students with disabilities in secondary schools in order to help them transition from school to work successfully. Will (1984) regarded employment as the desired outcome of transition services and proposed three levels of interventions: (1) transition without special services; (2) transition with time-limited services, and (3) transition with ongoing services. Among these three distinct interventions, the third category, "transition with ongoing services," became the basis for the concept of "supported employment" that provided ongoing services for persons with moderate/severe disabilities who otherwise could not secure and maintain employment on their own. Under this most influential OSERS Priority on Transition, numerous federal demonstration grants reshaped the way that service providers prepare persons with disabilities for employment.

The IDEA Reauthorization in 1990 mandated a "statement of transition services to be written in the IEPs for each student by age of 16 and older." Specifically the statement should include "the needed transition services and a statement of each participating agency's responsibilities and linkages." It also required a rationale for not providing transition services if the IEP team determined that no such services were necessary. This requirement of transition services in the IEPs ensured that it was the school's responsibility to provide transition planning activities for assisting students with disabilities to transition from school to adult life successfully, accompanied by positive post-school quality of life outcomes. It also ensured that transition planning should involve long-term planning with goals spanning several years in the students' educational planning. This established a solid foundation for including transition components in the IEPs for students with disabilities.

Following the IDEA's 1990 mandate to include transition components in the IEPs, several other laws contributed to reinforcing the importance of vocational training and placements for persons with disabilities. For example, the Americans with Disabilities Act of 1990 (ADA, P.L. 101-336) ensured the rights of individuals with disabilities in private sector employment, public accommodations and services, transportation, and telecommunications. Also the Rehabilitation Act Amendment of 1992 sought to end the fragmentation among services that assist persons with disabilities transition from school to adult life. It emphasized the integration of services offered by vocational rehabilitation and education programs. The amendment also promoted quality of life outcomes and the provision of consumer-oriented services that required service providers to consider individual preferences and desires in transition planning. This legislation laid the groundwork for the later focus on self-determination of persons with disabilities in transition planning–still considered an essential component of the best practice transition model. In the mid-1900s, Congress sought strategies to reform and consolidate federal employment and training programs such as JTPA, Carl Perkins Vocational and Applied Technology Education Act, the School-to-Work Transition Act, and other employment legislation in an effort to eliminate the duplication and overlap of services and to give fiscal flexibility to states within the consolidated structure (Stodden, 1998).

The 1997 IDEA Reauthorization improved requirements for transition programs. It required that transition planning begin at the age of 14 years for youth with disabilities and emphasized self-determination for students and the involvement of their families in the planning process. In addition, it focused on integrated interagency services requiring the participation of post-school agencies in transition planning for students who are 16 years and older. It also required that educational programs be based on post-school outcomes that could lead to quality of life for individuals with disabilities. The 2004 IDEA Reauthorization reaffirmed that schools should develop clear post-secondary goals for life after school and should provide transition services to students beginning at age of 16. Also it emphasized the involvement of the vocational rehabilitation system in transition planning in secondary schools. Furthermore, it required that all students with disabilities leaving secondary schools receive a summary of their accomplishments and transition needs along with their report cards. Table VII summarizes changes in the transition requirements as stated in the IDEA Amendments over the past two decades.

As reviewed above, several pieces of legislation ensured transition services for individuals with disabilities in their education planning and expanded them from focusing solely on vocational training to encompassing other areas that are critical to successful post-school outcomes. These areas include integrated services among responsible agencies, consumer-centered planning, and services that honor individual preferences and interests. The success of a transition program depends on careful transition planning based on the post-school outcomes desired by the students. Success also requires collaboration among agencies providing different services to students with disabilities who transition from school to adult life. To achieve these ends, educators and other professionals working with students with disabilities need to be knowledgeable about current developments in the best practice transition model. They also need to learn skills to implement the model in the educational programs for these students. The following section discusses the components of the best practice transition model.

Table VII
CHANGES IN TRANSITION REQUIREMENTS STATED WITHIN IDEA

1975 IDEA (P.L. 94-142)	1983 IDEA (P.L. 98-199)	1990 IDEA (P.L. 101-476)	1997 IDEA (P.L. 105-17)	2004 IDEA (P.L. 108-446)
• Ensured FAPE for children with disabilities. • Required IEP for each child with disability. • Did not specify but implied that IEP could include career/vocational goals, if deemed appropriate by the IEP teams.	• Provided federal funds for transition demonstration models. • OSERS transition model developed. • Transition outcomes were specified in legislative language.	• Transition services are defined in legislation. • Required transition services to be written in the IEP for each student by age of 16 or older. • Emphasized that educational planning focus on post school outcomes.	• Emphasized self-determination for students and families. • Required that transition planning begin at the age of 14. • Focused on integrated interagency services. • Focused on student participation in general education curriculum.	• Required that transition services in IEP begin at the age of 16. • Change in the definition of "transition services": • Deleted "student" and inserted "child." • Deleted "outcome-oriented" and inserted "results-oriented." • Clarified that the results-oriented process is "focused on improving the academic and functional achievement of the child with a disability to facilitate the child's movement from school to post-school activities, including postsecondary education; vocational education (instead of training); integrated employment (including supported employment); continuing and adult education; adult services; independent living or community participation.

Adapted from Stodden (1998).

BEST PRACTICE COMPONENTS IN TRANSITION MODEL

As discussed earlier, the OSERS Transition Model (Will 1984) focused mainly on employment as a post-secondary education outcome. Halpern (1985) added two further components to the OSERS transition model: independent living and social support network domains. Halpern considered that in addition to the importance of employment, independent living and social/interpersonal network also needed to be addressed when planning for successful community adjustment after schooling. Ongoing research in transition has refined transitional planning and added more elements to the Halpern model, including self-determination, person-centered planning, post-secondary college education, interagency collaboration, and involvement of families (Baer, Flexer, & McMahan, 2005). Therefore, the current best practice transition model includes eight components: (1) person-centered planning, (2) self-determination, (3) work experience/employment training, (4) social support network intervention, (5) daily living skills training, (6) post-secondary college education, (7) interagency collaboration, and (8) involvement of families. The remainder of the chapter discusses each of these best practice components, illustrating them with a case study.

PERSON-CENTERED PLANNING

Person-centered planning refers to a process in which the interests, strengths, and preferences of a focus person with disabilities are considered when developing a plan for his or her future. The person-centered planning process utilizes resources and support from a circle of support of those at school, home, and in the community who are important to the person (cf., Mount, 1994). In transition planning, person-centered planning encourages active participation from the student and family. In this process, students can take the leading role in their transition planning by setting the goals for their future and making decisions about what to include in their Individualized Transition Plan (ITP), which will be drafted to help achieve these goals. Family participation and input are actively sought in person-centered planning. A teacher of students with disabilities should utilize this person-centered planning as the initial step in transition planning and conduct this informal meeting prior to the formal IEP/ITP meeting.

Common Principles of a Person-Centered Planning

Many different person-centered formats have been proposed, including Life Style Planning (O'Brien, 1987; O'Brien & Lyle, 1987), Personal Profile and Future Planning (Kincaid, 1996), Planning Alternative Tomorrow with Hope (PATH) (Pearpoint, O'Brien, & Forest, 1995), and Personal Future Planning (Mount & Zwernick, 1988). Despite the different names, these person-centered planning formats share the following common principles. First, an individual with disabilities (focus person) is encouraged to express preferences and makes choices about everyday life. The person-centered planning process is "driven by the individual's needs and goals rather than the goals of an agency or a professional" (Anderson, Bahl, & Kincaid, 1999, p. 387). For example, the individual's preference regarding job placement is honored—not someone else's preference. Second, the person-centered planning approach utilizes the resources provided by the individual's circle of support for helping achieve his or her own future goals. This approach acknowledges the need for support from the community and the team members in order for the individual to engage in activities that enhance the quality of life. It also allows the team members to be creative in overcoming barriers. For example, the planning team can brainstorm about employment opportunities that suit the individual's interest such as a job at a zoo for someone with an interest in animals. Third, support is provided to help the individual increase and maintain satisfying relationships. Because of the importance of satisfying relationships for peer modeling of appropriate behaviors as well as for social support, the individual with disabilities should be assisted in developing and maintaining satisfying relationships. Fourth, support is provided to help the individual fulfill respected social roles and live with dignity. A key principle of the person-centered approach is that each person, regardless of the severity of the disability, can contribute to the community and should be allowed to do so with dignity. For instance, an individual with disabilities should not be placed in a demeaning job that nobody else wants solely based on the disability. Fifth, this approach assumes that an individual with disabilities should be present and participating in community life. In other words, the individual should engage in community activities similar to those performed by same age peers, for example, grocery shopping, going to a movie theater, and going out to eat. Sixth, the person-centered approach believes that the individual should have opportunities to develop personal competencies, including new skills and expertise. Finally, this approach respects the individual's culture and heritage.

Steps for a Person-Centered Planning Meeting

"Mapping" is a user-friendly format used for person-centered planning for transition (Mount & Zwernik, 1988). Mapping starts with creating a personal profile of the student highlighting achievements, strengths and talents. The facilitator, who may be a teacher or transition specialist, draws diagrams showing life history, current and past relationships, choice-making opportunities, community presence, and preferences. In addition, the team develops a future map including the student's desires regarding residence, employment, socialization, and leisure. Areas for improvement such as behavior problems are also noted, exploring possible explanations for the problems. By understanding the reason and function that may underlie the problem behaviors, the team can discuss strategies to help the student alter the problem behaviors. Based on this activity, the facilitator summarizes the student's preferences and desires. This information is utilized later at an ITP meeting to develop an action plan for supporting the individual to achieve the desired lifestyle. The following case study illustrates the application of this person-centered approach in transition planning. Pseudonyms are used in the case studies to protect the privacy of the individuals under discussion.

Sam, a 17 year-old Chinese American boy, lived with his parents, sister, brother, and his aunt (his father's younger sister). Sam was the youngest in the family. Sam was enrolled in a special education program in a local high school. He took P.E., Art, and Health classes with general education peers while spending a major portion of the day in a self-contained class participating in an independent living skills program. He could read simple sentences and use a calculator for simple addition and subtraction. Sam had participated in a community-based work experience program and gained experience washing dishes in restaurants and doing maintenance work at a local zoo park. Unfortunately, he lost his jobs soon after he started working because he was not focusing on the tasks and often did not complete them. His speech was not clear due to his tongue thrust problem. He mumbled most of the time. He had been receiving speech therapy once a week at school.

For Sam's person-centered planning, his teacher Ms. Smith met with his mother, sister, brother, and his aunt at his home. His father did not want to participate in the meeting. Ms. Smith decided to hold the meeting at his home because Sam wanted to include his family members; they felt comfortable having his teacher visit the home and it was easier for them to meet there. Since his parents did not speak English, his 23-year-old sister, Melanie was the designated family spokesperson for Sam and translated for his mother and aunt at the meeting.

Ms. Smith began the meeting by complimenting Sam's recent accomplishments in improving his speech and his hard work on the class horticulture fundraising project during which he prepared flowering plants (the class previously had potted them) for sale at a school fundraising carnival. This compliment about Sam made everyone at the meeting feel happy to be there and comfortable about talking about Sam further. It also helped in gaining the family's trust and respect. Later his sister told Ms. Smith that his family was relieved to hear positive things about Sam because they expected to hear—as they had in previous meetings—negative comments about what Sam could not do, which turned out to be false. The compliments about Sam made them feel positive about both the meeting and Ms. Smith; they felt they could count on her to help Sam learn better at school. Next, Ms. Smith briefly introduced the person-centered planning meeting, saying "The purpose of today's meeting is to get to know Sam better, about his family and friends, what he is good at, things he likes to do now and in the future after graduating from high school." She also asked the family members to refer to the questions that she had sent home prior to the meeting, questions intended to familiarize family members with the topics to be discussed at the meeting. Ms. Smith took out a marker and a large piece of paper and drew diagrams, indicating Sam's life history, circle of support, his likes and dislikes, community presence, his talents, and his desired future lifestyle (see Figure 5).

WHO IS SAM?

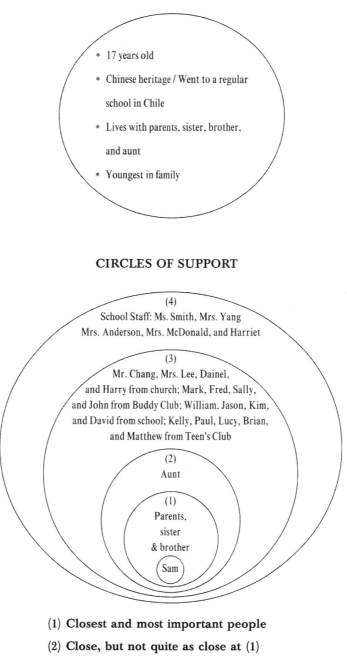

* 17 years old

* Chinese heritage / Went to a regular school in Chile

* Lives with parents, sister, brother, and aunt

* Youngest in family

CIRCLES OF SUPPORT

(4)
School Staff: Ms. Smith, Mrs. Yang
Mrs. Anderson, Mrs. McDonald, and Harriet

(3)
Mr. Chang, Mrs. Lee, Dainel,
and Harry from church; Mark, Fred, Sally,
and John from Buddy Club; William, Jason, Kim,
and David from school; Kelly, Paul, Lucy, Brian,
and Matthew from Teen's Club

(2)
Aunt

(1)
Parents,
sister
& brother

Sam

(1) **Closest and most important people**

(2) **Close, but not quite as close at (1)**

(3) **People from the community**

(4) **Paid staff/professional**

Figure 5. Diagrams used in Sam's person-centered planning meeting. Sam is a fictitous student. Adapted from Mount and Zwernik (1988).

Figure 5–*Continued*

COMMUNITY PRESENCE

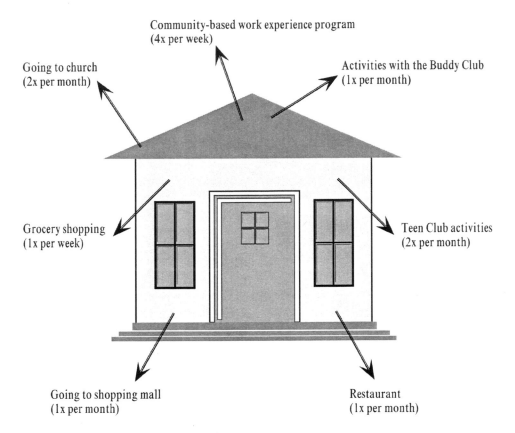

Community-based work experience program
(4x per week)

Going to church
(2x per month)

Activities with the Buddy Club
(1x per month)

Grocery shopping
(1x per week)

Teen Club activities
(2x per month)

Going to shopping mall
(1x per month)

Restaurant
(1x per month)

LIKES/DISLIKES, STRENGTHS/TALENTS, AND FUTURE LIFE STYLE

Likes:	Dislikes:
Speaking Spanish	Working alone
Watching Spanish TV programs	Doing maintenance work
Meeting people	Brushing teeth
Looking at travel/ food magazine	Cleaning house or room
Buddy Club	
Play/ watch basketball	
Going to shopping mall	
Eating different kinds of foods	

Figure 5–*Continued*

Strengths/Talents:

Speaking Spanish

Being honest

Being punctual

Being consistent

Being helpful

Future Life Style:

Living with parents

Going to college

Working in a Mexican restaurant

 or travel office

Continue with the Buddy Club

Going to basketball games

Ms. Smith then asked the participants to freely provide information on a specific area in each diagram. His sister began sharing his life history, verifying the facts with her mother in Chinese. Before immigrating to the U.S. eight years ago, his parents emigrated from China to Chile, where they lived for five years until Sam was nine years old. Sam attended school in Chile and learned Spanish. His siblings often spoke Spanish to each other at home. She also learned that Sam had attended a general education class in Chile. This information was new and interesting to Ms. Smith. As for his circle of support, his sister, brother, and aunt named people Sam usually spent time with, for example, people from his church, members of the Teen Club (leisure activity club for youth with disabilities), and relatives. Ms. Smith added the names of people with whom Sam had social contact with in school and asked Sam for additional names.

When Sam named Fred from the Buddy Club at his high school, his face brightened with a big smile. Fred was a senior and president of the school's Buddy Club. Along with other general education peers who signed up for the leadership building elective, Fred organized a variety of monthly social activities for students with disabilities such as going out for pizza and bowling. Although Sam only saw Fred and the other buddies once a month, these were the activities he most enjoyed. His sister commented that Sam often mentioned the Buddy Club activities. Sam thought Fred was cool and tried to emulate him, for example, styling his hair like Fred's. As for community presence, once a month Sam's sister or aunt took Sam to the mall or to the Teen Club, which arranged sports and games for students with disabilities. However, Sam expressed that he wanted to go out more often. At the Teen Club, he often preferred watching others play rather than participating in the games himself. In terms of his likes and dislikes, Sam mentioned he liked watching Spanish programs on television at home and eating foods from different cultures. He did not like working outside doing maintenance work at the zoo or park. His family agreed that his talents included his ability to speak and understand Spanish, his honesty, punctuality, consistency, and helpfulness.

At first Sam did not have much to say about the lifestyle he would like in the future, but when Ms. Smith asked specific questions, including yes/no questions, about living arrangements, post-secondary education, employment, and leisure activities, Sam was able to express his preferences. His family had a definite plan about Sam's living arrangements. His parents wanted him to continue to live with them; when they were no longer able to take care of him, he would live with his sister. Sam agreed that he would like to live with his family for a while after graduation. Maybe later he would like to live in a house with roommates rather than in an apartment. He liked being part of a big family because he enjoyed being around people. He would like to go to college like his brother. He would like to work as a busboy in a restaurant, preferably one with Spanish speaking employees, or as an office assistant in a travel agency where he could look at maps and travel brochures. For his leisure activities, he would like to continue to participate in social activities with his peers from the Buddy Club and go to basketball games, particularly his brother's college basketball games. The participants discussed why he did not complete the job tasks at his previous job. He might have not liked his previous jobs because he worked alone; he expressed an interest in a more social work environment.

Ms. Smith summarized the information discussed at the meeting and stated that she would share the information at his upcoming ITP meeting. She also would prepare Sam to share his preferences and desired future lifestyle at the meeting. Based on the valuable information obtained from the person-centered planning meeting, she and the ITP team members would develop a transition plan that would help

Sam achieve his desired lifestyle after graduation. Ms. Smith invited his family to attend the ITP meeting and it was agreed that his sister and aunt would be there.

SELF-DETERMINATION

Self-determination is defined as "a broader array of conducts that enable one to act as the primary causal agent in one's life and making choices and decisions regarding one's quality of life, free from undue external influence or interference, as an impetus for achieving dignity and respect, perception of self-value and worth, and contribution" (Nirje, 1972; Wehmeyer, 1998). Self-determination is the unique component of current best practice in transition planning. The focus student is encouraged to actively participate in the person-planning and transition meetings by leading the meetings and expressing interests and preferences regarding work, residence, social, leisure and recreational activities, community living, and other areas that affect quality of life after graduation from high school. Even when the student is not able to lead or actively participate in the meeting due to limitations such as difficulty communicating, the student should attend the meeting. The student's presence reminds participants that the meeting concerns the student's future and encourages them to consider the student's interests and preferences as obtained from alternative methods such as family input, preference assessment, and observation. Honoring the student's preferences, interests, and strengths is a requirement in person-centered transition planning.

Most students with disabilities lack the skills to actively lead and participate in their own transition meeting, and therefore, teachers need to teach these skills (Lehmann, Bassett, & Sands, 1999; Lovitt, Cushing, & Stump, 1994; Powers 1997). In Sam's case, prior to his ITP meeting, the teacher taught him how to recognize the page number of the report and key words in the report such as his name, to make a list of questions, and to present his interests and preferences (Browder & Grasso, 2001). As an adaptation, the teacher utilized photos and symbols for prompting the student to talk about his interests and preferences. For example, a "picture of a $100 bill" would remind him to talk about his desire to earn money; a "picture of a restaurant with a

Spanish name" would prompt him to talk about his interest in working at a restaurant where Spanish-speaking employees work; and a "university banner" would remind him to express his interest in attending college like his brother (Browder & Grasso, 2001). To further facilitate Sam's presentation, the teacher helped Sam place these symbols in order in a binder and write out the verbal scripts of what he wanted to say about each symbol as shown in Figure 6.

Materials Used to Facilitate Sam's Participation in Transition Meeting

Material	Topic	Script
 $100 ⑤ 001$	Working for money	"I would like to work and earn money."
 AMIGOS MEXICAN RESTAURANT	Work place	"I would like to work in a restaurant and speak Spanish."
 Luke College	College	"I would like to go to college like my brother."

Figure 6. Materials used to facilitate Sam's participation in transition meeting. Adapted from Browder and Grasso (2001).

Additionally, teachers need to teach appropriate social skills required at a meeting such as taking turns, speaking clearly, and shaking hands to greet the participants. In order to teach these skills, teachers can use direct instruction strategies including verbal cues, modeling, role-play, feedback, physical prompts, and reinforcements. When necessary, teachers may need to facilitate the student's participation during the meeting by providing cues and prompts such as showing a picture of a person talking to signal the student's turn to speak, or asking the student to point to a "yes" or "no" card when answering questions. In Sam's case, the teacher engaged in role-playing with him to practice greetings, thanking others for compliments, saying goodbye at the end of meeting, paying attention to the teacher's verbal or visual cues, and presenting his preference list in his picture binder slowly and clearly.

The 1997 Reauthorization of the IDEA ensures that students lead and actively participate in their own transition meeting as well as learn goal setting and problem-solving skills. These skills need to be taught not only in transition programs but also throughout the students' schooling. Teaching students skills in making choices and self-management, including self-instruction, self-monitoring, and self-evaluation will be critical in helping them take charge of their own learning and decision-making regarding their adult lives after graduation. Wehmeyer, Agran, and Hughes (1998) discuss specific strategies to teach self-determination skills. Teachers may consider adopting a commercially available self-determination curriculum from the list provided in Table VIII.

COMMUNITY-BASED WORK EXPERIENCE/ EMPLOYMENT TRAINING

For a person with disability entering adult life, working in a nonsheltered or competitive work environment helps the individual to become a productive member of the community, interact with other typical adults, and earn employment income. Employment in competitive settings can contribute to the overall quality of lives of adults with disabilities. Therefore, work experience is considered a major component of any transition program, and it should be provided in real work environments, preferably at job sites in the community. When utilizing community-based work sites, teachers must comply with the Fair Labor Standards Act. In general, nonpaid community-based work experience programs for an individual student should be limited to: fiv hours per job for vocational exploration, 90 hours per job for vocational assessment, and 120 hours per job in a single school

Table VIII
SELECTED EXAMPLES OF COMMERCIAL SELF-DETERMINATION CURRICULA

Curriculum	Authors	Publisher	Major Content Area
Choicemaker Self-determination Transition Curriculum	L. Huber-Marshall, J. Martin, L. Maxson, & P. Jerman	Sopris West, Inc. 4093 Specialty Place Longmont, CO 80504 1-800-547-6747	Choosing goals. Expressing goal. Taking action. Self-directed IEP.
Take Charge and Take Charge for the Future	L. Powers	Oregon Health Science University Child Development & Rehabilitation Center P. O. Box 574 Portland, OR 97202-0574 1-503-232-9154	Achievement skills. Partnership skills. Coping skills.
Next S.T.E.P. (Student Transition and Educational Planning)	A. Halpern, C. Herr, N. Wolf, J. Lawson, B. Doren, & M. Johnson	Pro-Ed Publishing Co. 8700 Shoal Creek Blvd. Austin, TX 78757-6897	Understanding transition planning. Self-evaluate transition needs. Identify and select goals and activities. Implementing and monitoring own plans.
Whose Future Is It Anyway?	M. Wehmeyer & K. Kelchner	The ARC National Headquarters 500 East Border Street, Suite # 300 Arlington, TX 76010 1-888-368-8009	Self-awareness and disability awareness. Making decisions about transition related-outcomes. Identifying and securing community resources to support transition services. Writing and evaluating transition goals and objectives. Communicating effectively in small groups. Developing skills to become an effective team member, leader, or self-advocate.

Source: Browder and Lohrmann-O'Rourke (2001); Wehmeyer, Agran, and Hughes (1998).

year for vocational training purposes (Browder & Grasso, 2001). Moon and Inge (1993) and Browder and Grasso list the following criteria that a community-based work program should meet in order for a student to be placed in a non-paid job:

1. A student must be a person with disability for whom competitive employment is not immediately available and who needs intensive ongoing support to perform on the job.
2. The student's participation in the nonpaid community-based work program is for vocational exploration, assessment, or training, and the student is under general supervision of public school personnel.
3. The community-based work program is clearly stated in the student's IEP/ITP and it is designed for the student's benefit.
4. The student and family must be fully informed of the job placement and must have agreed that the student's participation is voluntary and that the student is not entitled to wages.
5. Student's participation must not result in an immediate advantage to the business. Student must not displace any regular employee of the business or relieve regular employees of their duties. Student's work must be related to his/her IEP/ITP and the student must receive direct supervision from the school or workplace staff.
6. The student is not necessarily entitled to employment at the end of the IEP/ITPs.

It is important that teachers should not interpret these regulations as a ban on paid employment for students during their training placements (Browder & Grasso, 2001). Once teachers confirm that their community-based work experience programs meet these regulations, then they can begin exploring job sites in the community and develop training programs for their students. In order to establish successful community-based work programs, teachers and job coaches need to implement carefully planned, research-based strategies in each phase of the program: identifying job sites, job analysis, job training, and job evaluation.

Identifying Job Sites

Surveying and identifying potential job sites is the first step in developing a community-based work experience program. However, before surveying and identifying job sites, a teacher needs to identify the types of jobs the student likes or needs to explore as indicated by the goal of the student's transition program. Job preference can be identified through the person-centered planning process, i.e., as expressed by the student, the family, or both; by teacher observation; or by conducting a career preference assessment. For example, career interest assessment tools offered by Career Kids (2005) use picture cues to help students identify specific features of a particular job.

When identifying the student's job preference through person-centered planning, sometimes a teacher may find that the student's desire for certain types of jobs appears unrealistic. In these instances, it is important to actively listen to the student and identify the student's underlying interest. For instance, a student with moderate/severe cognitive disabilities wanted to be a medical doctor like his father. The teacher asked additional questions to discover why he wanted to be a doctor. He said that he liked wearing a doctor's gown and working with other doctors like his father. The teacher explained that different people in a doctors' office engage in different tasks wearing different uniform gowns, and explored other tasks that might interest the student. Through this process the student identified the position of internal mail delivery person in a hospital setting as a job that he would like.

It is also important to identify the student's strengths and find a job that utilizes them. In Sam's case, discovering that he liked speaking and listening to Spanish was a turning point for the successful planning of his transition. Other key items for understanding Sam's employment preferences included: learning that he liked working in a setting alongside coworkers, and his preferences to work as a busboy in a restaurant where employees speak Spanish or as an office assistant in a travel agency. Utilizing this new information about his interests and ability in Spanish, his transition team developed a plan to identify potential job sites including a Mexican restaurant and travel agency. One ITP team member knew someone who owned a Mexican restaurant near Sam's high school and volunteered to talk to the owner. His teacher offered to explore travel agencies.

It is equally important that the transition program provides work experience at a range of sites that involve a variety of tasks as it is to use and develop the student's strengths. A range of work experience can help the student later when seeking employment; it also helps the student discover abilities and preferences regarding work.

After determining the type of work site, a teacher can identify potential work sites located close to school. Sometimes a job site may require taking public transportation, which presents an excellent opportunity for the student to learn about using public transportation. The teacher can help students send out their resumes and/or introduction letters explaining the goal of the transition program and the strengths of the student. (See a sample letter of introduction in Table IX.) Including photos of the student performing different job tasks sometimes helps potential employers understand the tasks that the student can perform. Seeing can be believing! In addition, teachers and job coaches can solicit assistance from parents and school personnel, and, as in Sam's case, from larger personal networks. They can also make presentations about the transition program at meetings of local business associations, asking for assistance in providing worksites. Teachers and job coaches need to inform potential employers that support for these students is available through the transition program and includes initial training and supervision. Potential employers should also be informed of the tax benefits associated with hiring people with disabilities. Furthermore, teachers and job coaches need to understand the school district's liability policy and discuss it when meeting with potential employers. If no work site is available in the community, employment at the school can be a good starting point for learning positive work habits, social skills, and other important work-related skills.

Job Analysis

After identifying potential job sites, the next step is to identify not only the skills required to perform the given tasks but also the natural supports available for workers with disabilities. In this context "natural supports" refers to supports in the work environment that are available to typical workers such as consultation and feedback from coworkers and supervisors and the use of vocational jig (adaptive

Table IX
SAMPLE LETTER OF INTRODUCTION

October 12, 2003
To Whom It May Concern:

My name is Fred Fillmore. I am 17 years old. I live with my mom, my brother and sister. I attend Sierra High School.

I am going to graduate soon and so I am looking for a job. I have worked at several job sites while attending school. I worked in a school cafeteria and restaurants bussing tables and washing dishes, in a hospital delivering mails, and in an office helping clerical work. I especially like office work because I love working with papers and making copies.

I like helping people. I am honest and dependable. I work hard.
My hobbies are collecting mini-cars and stamps. I also love to watch football and basketball games.

I have a cognitive disability. Some people think I can't do things because I have a disability. That is not true. If they give me a chance to try, I can learn to do a good job. I can ride the public bus and have friends. I like to show people that I work hard and I can do the same things as other young people my age.

Thank you very much for considering me.

Sincerely,

Adapted from Whaley and Hoffman (1997).

devices). In conducting a job analysis, teachers and job coaches need to identify the gross and fine motor skills as well as social skills required for performing each job task, utilizing a job analysis form (see Table X). By shadowing potential coworkers at a job site for a day or two, the teacher or job coach can generate a list of specific work tasks and the expectations for performance, for example, speed, rate, and quality of production. Job-related social skills such as asking for help when materials run out or taking a break and returning on time also need to be identified.

Table X
JOB ANALYSIS FORM

Job Site: *Mace's Restaurant*   **Date:** *October 15*
Address: *2345 Addison Street*
Contact Person and Phone Number: *Ellen, 269-8456*
Access to Public Transportation: *Yes. The restaurant is located on the third floor in the Valley Shopping Mall. Public transportation available right in front of the mall. Jeff can ride a bus from both school and home.*

Job Requirements

1. **Job Tasks Required:** *Bussing, washing dishes, and restocking condiments. Sometimes needs to respond to customer's request (e.g., water, napkins etc.).*
2. **General Mobility Requirement:** *Moving a cart up and down aisles, walking around tables.*
3. **Gross Motor Skills Required:** *Bending down, reaching, and pushing cart.*
4. **Fine Motor Skills Required:** *Turning on and off water facet, rinsing dishes, placing dishes in dishwasher, turning on dishwasher, taking dishes out from dishwasher, placing clean dishes in cupboard, wiping table with one hand, restocking salt/pepper shakers.*
5. **Length of Job Task:** *Bussing tables, rinsing dishes and placing them in dishwasher are continuous. The length of tasks varies depending on the time and number of customers.*
6. **Production Rate Expected:** *Must be able to work continuously during shift. Must have clean dishes on stock. Average production rate for other employees who had done the same task is rinsing and placing ten dishes per minute in dishwasher.*
7. **Quality of Product Required:** *Clean dishes.*
8. **Variability of Daily Job Task:** *The number of dishes needs to be washed varies each day and depending on the time of the day. When done with dish wash, check with the manager, Ellen for next task.*
9. **Problem-Solving Requirement:** *Must have ability to recognize whether there are not enough clean dishes on stock and ask for help from the manager. When it is not busy and dishwashing is done, a worker needs to find a next task to do such as restocking salt and pepper shakers, or ask manager for next task.*
10. **Break Time:** *20 minute break usually between 3:00 and 4:00.*

Table X—*Continued*

Natural Supports

11. **Job-Related Contact/Supervisor:** *Manager, Ellen.*
12. **Co-Worker Presence:** *Yes, many co-workers are present.*
13. **Supervisor/Co-Worker Support:** *Even though many co-workers are present during shift, they are usually busy with their own tasks. Best to check with Ellen when needing help.*
14. **Adaptive Material Support:** *Masking tape with number placed on a dish washer to prompt the worker to press the correct buttons in sequence.*
15. **Non-Job Related Social Contact During Task:** *Can engage in casual social conversation during non-busy hours. Sometimes regular customers initiate conversations.*
16. **General Social Atmosphere:** *Friendly and supportive. The manger, Ellen is very flexible and helping workers when needed.*

Environmental Factors

17. **Noise/Visual:** *Can be very noisy during busy hours. Kitchen is generally noisy.*
18. **Comfort Factors (temperature, space, lighting, odor, sensory, etc.):** *Temperature in the dining hall is comfortable, but the kitchen can get very warm and doesn't have much space. Space between tables is not large either. Need to walk around the tables carefully. Lighting is adequate and there is food odor.*
19. **Tools/Equipment Used:** *Operating a commercial dish washer.*

Adapted from Hughes and Carter (2000).

Worksites with more potential natural supports, for instance, where coworkers are willing to help out, are obviously preferable to those with fewer natural supports. However, due to the challenge of obtaining a work site, in some cases the teacher or job coach may need to take one that is available albeit lacking in natural supports. In these instances, intervention by the teacher or job coach may be necessary to facilitate social acceptance of the worker with disabilities and gradual provision of support by coworkers. Strategies for promoting social acceptance are discussed later in the section on Social Support Network Intervention.

Job Training

After specific job tasks are identified, the next step involves assessing the baseline performance of the worker with disabilities—how well the worker performs on the task without training—and comparing it with the performance of coworkers. Known as a Discrepancy Analysis, this assessment strategy utilizes a task or routine analysis (Browder, 2001). By conducting the Discrepancy Analysis, the teacher identifies the steps in a task or routine that the worker needs to learn. The teacher then can confer with a supervisor or coworker to see if any adaptations or accommodations can be made so that the worker can perform the task as independently as possible. For example, when Sam was learning skills as an office assistant in a travel office, he was not able to staple a stack of collated papers in the proper place (see Discrepancy Analysis in Table XI). The teacher made a vocational jig with a wooden panel and stapler so that Sam could place the collated papers easily within the jig and staple them without making errors. This simple adaptation facilitated Sam's independent job performance and increased his productivity and accuracy.

When simple adaptation is not available, a teacher or job coach then needs to teach specific job tasks to the worker using a variety of direct instructional strategies such as verbal prompt, modeling, physical prompt, and reinforcement. Once the student learns the specific job task, the teacher needs to fade out instructional prompts so that the student can perform the task independently as much as possible. Teachers can also check on the availability of natural supports. For example, pairing up with a coworker can help the worker perform tasks successfully. Coworkers can be asked to check on the student's performance and the products in order to ensure meeting targets for productivity and quality. In addition, self-instruction, self-monitoring, and self-evaluation skills can be also taught to help the student maintain independent performance and enhance self-determination.

Wehmeyer, Agran, and Hughes (1998) explain the successful use of self-instructional strategies using the "Did-Next-Now" and the "What/Where" models. In the Did-Next-Now model, students with cognitive disabilities were taught to perform a series of tasks in a sequence. In the Did-Next-Now model, a student states the step that he/she just completed ("Did") and the next step to be performed ("Next") and then direct himself/herself to perform that step ("Now"). For example, in operating a dishwasher, a student can state a verbal script such as "I poured dishwasher soap," "Next, I need to press the button," and "I need to do it now." The student needs to perform the target step immediately following the verbal script and self-reinforce ("Good job! I did it!") or self-correct ("Oops, I was supposed to press

Table XI
DISCREPANCY ANALYSIS

Name: Sam   Date: November 13   Activity: Collating and Stapling Papers

Routine/Steps of the Task	Student Performance +/- Comments	Specific Adaptation/ Accommodation	Skills in need of instruction
1. Get/check paper	-		Ask manager/co-worker if all materials are not found.
2. Get/check stapler	+		
3. Get/check trays	-		
4. Pick up first page	+	Place copies of each page in separate tray, starting from left to right	
5. Pick up next page	+	Use a picture sequence with an arrow indicating "behind the previous page."	
6. Place it behind the previous page	-		
7. Get all pages	+	Use a jig made of wooden panel	
8. Straighten out all pages	-		
9. Staple the packet in the upper left corner	-	Use a jig made of wooden panel with a stapler attached	If materials run out, ask for help.
10. Place finished packet in tray	+		

the button next. I will do it now."). In the What/Where model, a student is taught to guide himself/herself to perform in response to an instruction. The student is taught to select a key word (s) from a verbal/written instruction and determine *what* he/she is to do and *where* he/she is to do it. For example, a student working in a hospital as a mail deliverer receives an instruction from his supervisor, "These envelopes with red stamps on them are to be delivered to all the doctors in Building Two." The student repeats the key words, using the What/Where model, "Red Stamps, Building Two," and delivers the mail to Building Two.

Job Evaluation

As stated earlier, when a worker learns the task, then the teacher/job coach needs to step back and encourage the worker to perform it as independently as possible. The teacher or job coach may need to evaluate job performance regularly checking to see that the worker continues to complete tasks correctly and the products meet the quality criteria. The job coach may need to retrain the worker on specific steps of the task. Here again, it is best if the job coach utilizes natural support, such as help from coworkers and supervisors whenever possible. For example, if the supervisor at the work site evaluates the products/tasks done by other coworkers, the job coach may check to see if the supervisor also can evaluate the products made by the worker with disabilities. Or a coworker next to the worker with disabilities can check intermittently on the products and can give feedback to the worker with disabilities.

This use of natural support cannot be assumed without promoting the social acceptance among coworkers and supervisors. The availability, type, and extent of natural support may vary from work site to worksite. Therefore, it is best to involve employers, coworkers, and supervisors in the decision making process from the beginning of the work experience program. In Sam's case, the teacher attended a meeting of supervisor and coworkers and shared the philosophy and goals of the work experience program. She also shared Sam's strengths, such as working hard, communicating in Spanish, and being sociable, as well as his needs to be reminded to ask for help and to be checked on his task performance when the teacher faded out after the initial training. Finally, the teacher requested supervisors and coworkers to contribute their support for helping Sam succeed on the job. One supervisor who was taking a Spanish class in a city college volunteered to serve as his immediate supervisor, and as natural support later, checking on his performance and giving him feedback.

SOCIAL SUPPORT NETWORK INTERVENTION

Since social support has been consistently shown in the literature to be positively related to the psychological adjustment and well-being of all adults (Broadhead et al., 1983; Dean & Lin, 1977; Mitchell, Billings, & Moos, 1982; Wallston, Alagna, DeVellis, & DeVellis, 1983), it is reasonable to assume that this holds for students with disabilities who are entering adult lives in the community. Therefore, as proposed in the Halpern's transition model (1985), transition programs should include components that help individuals with disabilities increase and maintain a social support network/relationships with others in the community. Interventions aimed at supporting the development of such network/relationships should be implemented throughout schooling. This section, however, focuses on interventions at work sites.

In the past, as an intervention for increasing social interaction and developing social support networks with others at work sites, teachers and job coaches typically concentrated on the social skills of persons with disabilities. It was assumed that the persons' social skill deficits alone were responsible for the lack of social interaction and social networks. However, in addition to the lack of social skills, a number of ecological factors affect the availability of social opportunities and the development of a social support network. Therefore, intervention efforts to support the social network and social relationships must address both the person and other ecological factors. The Consortium for Collaborative Research on Social Relationships of Children and Youth with Disabilities (hereafter the Consortium) (Meyer, Park, Grenot-Scheyer, Schwartz, & Harry, 1997) identified four critical variables (three ecological variables and one person variable), through its in-depth qualitative study that can affect the formation of social relationships/social network between persons with disabilities and their peers without disabilities: (1) social ecology; (2) person's repertoire; (3) peer skills, support, and expectations; and (4) adult mediation. Of these four variables, the second variable, "person's repertoire" focuses on the individual with disability while the other three variables focus on environmental factors other than the person.

The first ecological variable, "Social Ecology" refers to environmental variables that may affect social opportunities and interactions, such as a student worker's placement. The second variable, "Person's Repertoire" refers to skills of the student that may facilitate or hinder social interactions and involvement in activities with other peers such as communication skills and behavior problems. The third variable, "Peer Skills, Support, and Expectations" refers to the knowledge, skills, attitudes and expectations of nondisabled peers that can assist or impede the emergence of social interactions and social relationships with a person with disabilities. For example, if peers without disabilities have low expectations toward individuals with disabilities, social interactions may be less likely to occur between them. The last ecological variable, "Adult Mediation" refers to the roles that caregivers, teachers, instructional assistants, job coaches, and other service providers play in assisting students with disabilities in learning academic, work, and daily living skills and in developing social relationships. Depending on the type and level, this adult support can have a positive or negative impact on the emergence of social interactions between students with disabilities and their peers without disabilities.

To promote long-lasting social networks for persons with disabilities, interventions for supporting social networks and social relationships between persons with disabilities and those without disabilities should focus on all four variables. These four variables form the base that supports a pyramid. The quality of social relationships and social networks is affected when any one of the variables is ignored. The following section discusses different strategies that focus on each of the four variables at work sites.

Social Ecology

Social interactions do not occur without social opportunities. It is important for a teacher/job coach to note that some job sites provide more social opportunities than others, and to identify environmental variables that might affect the availability and quality of social opportunities at work sites. By their very nature, certain jobs offer more social opportunities than others. For example, a small, family-run store presents more social opportunities than a large warehouse where a worker seldom sees other employees. Also social interactions are more likely to occur at a work site where the manager allows nonjob-related interactions and conversations than at a site where such interactions are not permitted. If a worker shares a common space or equipment like a breakroom or copy machine or engages in the same job task with another employee, the worker may have more social opportunities than working alone in a corner room unused by other employees.

The Job Site Social Ecology Checklist developed by the Consortium (Park, Meyer, Grenot-Scheyer, & Henry, 1994) presents the list of environment variables that may affect social interactions at work sites (see Table XII). A teacher or job coach can use this checklist for evaluating potential job sites and selecting sites with higher scores on this social ecology measure. If the work site has a management style that does not allow nonjob-related social interaction or the job itself has no social opportunities–such as setting up tables alone in a restaurant in the morning before customers come–the job site may be inappropriate for supporting social relationship building of workers with disabilities. However, teachers sometimes may have to take job sites that do not offer many social opportunities. In this case, the job coach or teacher can evaluate each variable in the checklist that scored "no" to see if it can be modified to offer more scope for social interaction. For example, the job coach can explain to the manager of the work site that one of the goals for the student is to learn to interact appropriately with others on the job, and that by working during lunchtime at a restaurant the student benefits by having opportunities to interact with coworkers and customers. An understanding of the purpose of the work experience program frequently helps employers and supervisors to become supportive of the program. Thus, the Job Site Social Ecology Checklist can be used in a broad range of circumstances to increase awareness of environmental variables; it can help the teacher or job coach in screening, evaluating, and intervening in a potential job site in terms of the availability of social opportunities.

Person's Repertoire

Certain functional skills such as those related to mobility/transportation, making purchases, using the telephone, grooming and hygiene, leisure and recreation, socialization, communication, friendship, and self-determination also can facilitate social interaction and develop social relationships. For example, when students are able to use public transportation services like buses and paratransit, they may have more access to social activities outside of work or school, such as visiting each other's homes or work sites and going to the mall with friends. Even when they can depend on others for transportation, developing their own transportation skills can help make these social outings easier to arrange and more spontaneous because they do not require waiting for rides, which can be difficult to arrange sometimes.

Table XII
JOB SITE SOCIAL ECOLOGY CHECKLIST

Instruction: Please evaluate the potential worksite in the following areas.
Check "yes" or "no"

VARIABLE	YES	NO
1. *Location of Business*–Does the town or community provide social opportunities and public transportation?	___	___
2. *Physical Location*–Is a worker(s) with disabilities located in the same room/work area shared with the supervisor and co-workers without disabilities and/or customers?	___	___
3. *Physical Presence*–Are co-workers without disabilities, supervisors without disabilities, and/or customers present at same time period?	___	___
4. *Common Space*–Is there overlap of use of areas such as supply sources, travel to and from work area, and so forth?	___	___
5. *Size of Jobsite*–Is this a large job site or a small business/office?	___	___
6. *Schedule*–Do typical co-workers' schedules overlap with those of worker(s) with disabilities?	___	___
7. *Break or Lunch*–Is there overlap for break times, between co-workers with and without disabilities?	___	___
8. *Management Style*–Is the management style flexible so that employees have positive attitudes toward variation in schedule, rate, and so forth?	___	___
9. *Supervisor Responsibilities*–Is supervision shared between job coach and regular supervisor?	___	___
10. *Job Status*–Is the job performed by a worker(s) with disabilities of "lower" status?	___	___
11. *Non Job*–Related Social Interaction-Do supervisors/co-workers without disabilities interact with a worker(s) with disabilities for non-job-related matters?	___	___
12. *Attitude*–Do supervisors and co-workers have positive attitudes about people with disabilities and the supported employment model?	___	___
13. *Social Activities*–Does the jobsite include planned social events by the "group," such as an office party, a picnic, a gathering after work, and so on?	___	___

Table XII–*Continued*

VARIABLE	YES	NO
14. *Co-worker Age, Gender, Ethnicity*–Is there a "match" between these variables and the characteristics of the worker(s) with disabilities?	____	____
15. *Social Class and Status of Co-workers*–Are co-workers "typical" or much more educated, performing higher-status job, and so forth, in comparison to the worker(s) with disabilities?	____	____
16. *Past Experience*–How much previous contact have the jobsite/people at the jobsite had with people with disabilities?	____	____
17. *Specific Information*–How much information do supervisors/co-workers have about the worker(s) with disabilities?	____	____
18. *Joint Activity*–Does a worker(s) with disabilities perform shared job tasks rather than discrete jobs?	____	____
19. *Wait Time*–Does the job itself require "standing around" during performance of tasks that provides social interaction opportunities (e.g., photocopying, drying clothes, picking up mail)?	____	____
20. *Expectations*–Do expectations for social behavior and job performance differ or are they the same for worker(s) with and without disabilities?	____	____
21. *Contact with the Public*–Does the job involve opportunities to interact with customers and other members of the public who have contact with the place of employment?	____	____
22. *Job Overlap*–Do co-workers without disabilities perform job tasks that overlap with those performed by a worker(s) with disabilities?	____	____
23. *Job-Related Contact*–Does the job involve contact with supervisors/co-workers without disabilities as part of the job assignment?	____	____

Total # of YES: ____
Total # of NO: ____
Number of variables that
have potential for change: ____

Developed by the Consortium (Park, Meyer, Grenot-Scheyer, & Harry, 1994).

Therefore, a range of functional skills should be taught in natural contexts with adaptations if necessary. For example, Mark, a student with a visual impairment with minimal fine motor skills, was taught how to use a telephone with enlarged number buttons programmed to call friends and transportation services such as the paratransit service. Enhancing his ability to use the telephone helped him to arrange social outings which otherwise would not have been possible because his caregivers were not able to help him in this way. Some professionals argue that students with disabilities should only be taught the general education academic curriculum, with instruction in functional skills reserved for the time when these students enter transition programs. However, this writer contends that some functional skills should be taught in a natural context in school prior to enrollment in a transition program, particularly because such skills can facilitate the student's social relationships. The development of social networks/ social relationships needs to be supported throughout the students' schooling as well as later in their adult community lives.

Leisure/Recreational Skills

Developing hobbies and leisure skills should be an important part of transition program objectives for students with disabilities. Such activities not only would increase the student's range of topics for conversation, but also would increase the probability and opportunities for developing social relationships. Park (1998) found that coworkers without disabilities found it easier to initiate social interactions with workers with disabilities if they shared a range of conversational topics based on hobbies or sports, for example, collecting minicars or stamps and watching basketball or football games. Other leisure and recreational skills that may facilitate social interactions include bowling, playing pinball or computer games, drawing, renting a video at a video store, and ordering takeout pizza (cf. Schleien, Mustonen, & Rynders, 1995; Taylor, McKelvey, & Sisson, 1993). When identifying potential leisure skills, teachers should consider the following four points: (1) Select activities that are age appropriate and appealing to nondisabled peers; (2) Select leisure activities enjoyed by the student's family so that the student can be taught skills that may increase the student's participation in family activities; (3) Select leisure skills used both for spending time alone and for interacting with others; and (4) Explore adaptations that could enhance the student's participation in leisure activities (e.g., adaptive switches for computer games). The best resources for supporting leisure and recreational skills for persons with disabilities are programs offered by local parks and recreation departments such as youth theatre, arts, sports, and fitness classes (for more examples, see Schleien, Ray, & Green, 1997). Using these resources eliminates the need to create a new program that serves both persons with disabilities and those without disabilities. In Sam's case, his transition team developed a leisure plan that honored his interest in attending basketball games, playing basketball, and learning about different places, people, and foods. It included signing him up for a basketball class in a community recreational program, asking Sam's brother to take him to college basketball games, and having a peer from the Buddy Club help him check out travel books and magazines from his high school library.

Social/Communication/Friendship Skills

In addition to effort and commitment, other skills are necessary for developing and maintaining social relationships. Social relationships and friendships require a variety of embodiments–the "physical enactment of interrelationship" (Hunt, 1991)–that encompass different skills: initiating conversations; sharing information about self, including hobbies and leisure activities; planning and initiating social activities; following through with activities; engaging in reciprocity to reinforce relationships; and working through conflicts. An effective way to teach social activity planning is through the use of pictures. Teachers can arrange relevant cue cards so that the student can scan each picture and answer corresponding planning questions: What do you like to do socially? With whom do you like to do it? How would you want to invite the person (e.g., by telephone)? How will you get together with the person (e.g., what form of transportation do you need?)? What things do you need (e.g., money, emergency phone numbers)? How did the activity go? Did it make you happy or sad? In the future, would you do the same or a different activity with that person again? (Hoffman & Whaley, 2004).

When teaching specific social skills such as initiating, expanding, and terminating a conversation, the teacher can use typical social skills training package strategies including rationale, modeling, role playing, providing feedback, and homework. For example, a teacher can explain why it is important for the student to initiate social interactions such as greetings. Then the teacher can model a daily greeting for coworkers, e.g., saying, "Good Morning," or "Hi" in a pleasant tone of voice. Next, the teacher can ask the worker to try it out in role playing and give feedback on the student's performance. The student is given homework to practice the skills, and the teacher and student evaluate the outcome of the homework together.

Table XIII

EXAMPLES OF THE SEVEN RULES FOR PROBLEM SOLVING
PREPARED BY SAM AND HIS TEACHER

Student: Sam	
Target Behavior: Speaking Clearly	
1. What's Happening?	I speak to some one.
2. What Choices?	1. I speak clearly. *OR* 2. I mumble.
3. What Might Happen?	1. If I speak clearly, then the person will understand what I say. 2. If I mumble, then the person will not understand what I say.
4. Which is Better?	Speak clearly.
5. How Could I do It?	Slow down. Open mouth. Wait for a second before I start another sentence.
6. Do It.	
7. How Did I Do It?	Check if the person understands me. If he or she does, I feel good. If he or she does not, I repeat what I have said before and slow down more.

Table XIII–*Continued*

Student: Sam	
Target Behavior: Asking for Help	
1. What's Happening?	I ran out of paper (staples, etc.).
2. What Choices?	1. I ask for help. *OR* 2. I sit and wait.
3. What Might Happen If...	1. If I ask for help, I will not be behind. 2. If I sit and wait, it might take awhile for anyone to come and help. Then I will be behind.
4. Which is Better?	Ask for Help.
5. How Could I Do It?	Ask Marie or someone to help. When I speak clearly and politely and look at her.
6. Do It.	Do It.
7. How Did I Do It?	Did anyone help me? If yes, I feel good. If no, check if I spoke clearly and politely. If I did not speak clearly and politely, speak clearly and politely.

When workers already possess these social skills but do not use them appropriately, they can be taught a problem-solving approach such as the "Seven Rules" (Park & Gaylord, 1989). For instance, if a worker with disabilities does not respond to a co-worker's greeting, the job coach can teach the worker to follow the Seven Rules by asking the following questions: (1) What is happening? (2) What are the choices? (3) What are the consequences of each choice? (4) Which choice is better? (5) How to do it? (6) Do it. (7) How did I do it? In Sam's case, the teacher taught him how to use these Seven Rules for speaking clearly and for asking for help at work, as shown in Table XIII. The Seven Rules can be also applied for teaching other social skills such as expanding and terminating conversations.

Self-Determination Skills

The friendships of youth with disabilities may depend on some adult support and assistance. However, Park (1998) found a strong association between developed self-determination skills—for example, being self-confident, making choices, and playing a major role in initiating, planning, and implementing social activities—and the level of success in forming stable and fulfilling social relationships. Students with disabilities who initiated and facilitated social activities with minimal family support had more social events and more active social contacts than those who were completely dependent on family members or other adults. In addition, as they gained self-confidence through a range of successful work and social experiences, these more active young adults developed friendships more frequently and were more willing to plan and carry out social activities. For example, one active young adult, Jason, belonged to a church choir, attended ball games, and frequently met with friends at the restaurant where one of his friends worked. He had definite goals for his life and had specific action plans to fulfill them, keeping busy with two jobs, enjoying living independently, and making arrangements to see his friends.

In Sam's case, on the other hand, his family and his teacher arranged most of his social activities either in school or at home. As a result, Sam lacked the skills to make his own arrangements and had a less active social life than Jason. This corresponds to Walker's findings (1999) that people who actively initiated social interactions on their own were known in their community and those who primarily relied on family members for their outings were not known in their community. Therefore, transition programs should foster self-determination skills among students so that they can build the confidence and skills necessary to make choices for developing positive social relationships and friendships. Such skills include initiating activities oneself, using critical thinking skills to make informed choices and decisions, and assuming responsibility. In Sam's case, his teacher began to assign Sam more responsibilities in the classroom and at work, e.g., encouraging him to advocate for himself. The teacher also began teaching Sam how to plan his social activities utilizing picture cues as explained earlier.

Peer Skills, Support, and Expectations

The ways that persons without disabilities perceive peers with disabilities can affect the quality and level of social interaction. When a person without disability(ies) sees a person with disability(ies) as equal, capable, interesting, having something to offer, and having the same need for social contact and friendship, the person with disability(ies) is more likely to have opportunities for social interaction and for developing a satisfying social relationships with the person without disabilities. Changing the negative perception and attitude toward people with disabilities is a challenging task requiring continued study. Fortunately, we have several studies that document close social relationships between persons with disabilities and those without disabilities (Bogdan & Taylor, 1987; Green, Schleien, MacTavish, & Benepe, 1995; Park, Chadsey-Rusch, & Storey, 1998). For example, in their explanation of the sociology of acceptance, Bogdan and Taylor (1987) refer to this as "accepting relationships." Such a relationship is formed when a person with disabilities receives unconditional acceptance that neither denies the disability nor stigmatizes the person on the basis of that disability.

Several strategies can help build positive peer expectations and social acceptance. First, sharing accurate information about workers with disabilities can help reduce fear and discomfort about interacting with them. The lack of information and misperceptions about workers with disabilities often contributes to coworkers' low expectations and negative stereotypes and attitudes about workers with disabilities. Sharing personal information such as hobbies and interests, related either by a job coach or the student, can allow the coworkers to perceive workers with disabilities as individuals and fellow human beings, and not stigmatize them because of their disabilities. In particular, sharing information about the strengths of workers with disabilities is critical to building social acceptance among coworkers. For instance, Sam wrote a short biographical note with the help of his teacher describing his work experiences, his interest and hobbies, and his goals at the work site, and shared the note with his coworkers at the employees' meeting. This helped familiarize Sam's coworkers with him and prompted them to initiate conversations. In addition to the worker's hobbies and talents, good work habits, such as punctuality and dependability can be emphasized to supervisors and managers so that they can value those strengths, particularly in situations where a worker with disability is less productive than coworkers without disabilities (Hughes & Carter, 2000).

Second, sharing the goal of the transition work program for individual workers can help coworkers understand why the workers with disabilities are employed at the work site and support them in achieving their own goals, such as developing good work habits, working on tasks independently, and socializing appropriately (Hughes & Carter, 2000). When coworkers and managers know the goals of the transition work program, they are more likely to participate in brainstorming to help student workers succeed on the job. Maintaining open communication with coworkers and supervisors can help the job coach monitor the worker's performance and be proactive when problems arise.

Third, it is important to express appreciation to supportive coworkers and supervisors at the end of the academic year by presenting certificates of appreciation or awards from the school's principal or director. Working with local newspapers and other media to publicize stories about students and supportive coworkers can bring recognition to the work site and increase awareness about the transition program in the local community.

In addition to facilitating positive perceptions about people with disabilities and their social acceptance, transition programs may need to teach workers without disabilities how to interact appropriately with workers with disabilities. For example, if the worker with a disability uses an augmentative communication device, then his coworkers need to be taught how to ask or respond to questions using the communication device. Also the coworkers can be taught skills for improving communication with the workers with disabilities, for example, basic and specific sign language relevant to the person and how to interpret certain communication and behavior modes. It can be explained to coworkers that when a nonverbal worker with disability stands near you, it may mean that he or she wants to ask a question. Any other skills that may facilitate social interaction should be taught to coworkers without disabilities. In addition, coworkers should be instructed about appropriate responses to behavioral problems of workers with disabilities. Knowing how to handle problems helps reduce the anxiety and discomfort coworkers may feel regarding a worker with disabilities.

Adult Mediation

Self-determination skills are necessary for maximizing social opportunities and developing satisfying social relationships and friendships. However, these skills do not diminish the importance of support by family members and other adults in the community (Strully & Strully, 1985). These external support individuals must facilitate and not impede or undermine the efforts and intentions of workers with disabilities to socially interact with coworkers. Many studies found that job coaches often acted as barriers to social opportunities for workers with disabilities because coworkers tended to communicate with job coaches regarding job and nonjob-related matters rather than directly with workers with disabilities (Park, Chadsey-Rusch, & Storey, 1998). Job coaches and teachers need to be "social coaches" who facilitate social interaction as discreetly as possible. For example, a job coach can identify a coworker who has the same hobby as the student worker and can facilitate interaction between them by introducing the student to the coworker. The job coach may stand behind the worker and provide a prompt such as a verbal script. The job coach can also help the worker plan and carry out social activities that facilitate social interaction among coworkers such as bringing baked goods for coworkers' birthday celebrations.

Despite the good intentions of family members, their efforts often serve as barriers. Parents may have lower expectations for their children in terms of their need and ability to develop and maintain friendships. In addition, due to fears about their children's safety, parents often neither allow their involvement in social activities outside of the home nor allow them to learn transportation skills. Their fear of letting go can make it difficult for parents to allow their children to take reasonable risks—sometimes compounded by not understanding the need for the person with disabilities to have social relationships—further reducing access to social opportunities and impede their learning experiences in social situations. These concerns also become barriers to parents' support of their children's social relationships and friendships. For parents, sometimes seeing a photo or video that shows their child in a competitive work setting provides a fresh perspective, often helping them understand that their child is capable of functioning in an environment with higher expectations. Another way to help parents develop reasonable expectations for their children is to introduce them to parent advocacy and support groups. Such groups offer accurate and relevant information about particular disabilities, which can foster a better understanding of each child's potential and the supports needed to realize it.

In Sam's case, his family members had low expectations for him, and therefore, most things at home were done for him. Unlike his brother, he was not given any responsibility to help out with household chores. He was treated like a young child and he seemed to enjoy it. When the Buddy Club planned a camping trip in collaboration with the local parks and recreation department, Sam was invited. He was enthusiastic about the trip, but his parents did not want to sign the permission slip, indicating that he would not be able to take care of himself. Although his teacher discussed Sam's ability to do a variety of tasks at school and work, the family remained hesitant. The teacher sent home a videotape of Sam working as an office helper at the travel agency and participating in the class's horticulture fundraising project. They were pleasantly surprised to find out how well he engaged in these tasks without constant prompting. After being assured that Sam was more independent than they thought and that staff from the city recreational program would supervise the trip, Sam's parents signed the permission slip. Thus, Sam was able to go camping with his favorite group of peers from the Bubby Club. As a result of these discussions, his family began to have Sam assume more responsibility for household chores and encouraged him to make choices about food and social outings, which in turn helped build his self-confidence.

DAILY LIVING SKILLS TRAINING

Teaching daily living skills in transition programs is important for both students with mild/moderate disabilities and those with moderate/severe disabilities. Acquisition of these skills can increase the individual's autonomy, self-confidence, and dignity, especially for those with moderate/severe disabilities. Daily living skills include budgeting and money management; time management, including making and keeping medical appointments and social engagements; domestic skills, including food preparation, housekeeping, and doing laundry; mobility skills; personal safety skills, including sex education; and self-care skills, including dressing, grooming, and personal hygiene. Teachers can select target skills according to the needs of the student, which are often identified at person-centered planning meetings. For example, some students may focus more on budgeting and money management while others, and particularly those with moderate/severe disabilities, may focus on self-care and mobility skills. For lists of daily living skills, teachers can refer to published resources, such as Syracuse Community-Referenced Curriculum Guide for Students with Moderate/Severe Disabilities (Ford et al., 1989), Life Centered Career Education: Modified Curriculum for Individuals with Moderate Disabilities (Loyd & Brolin, 1997), and Choosing Outcomes and Accommodations for Children (Giangreco, Cloninger, & Iverson, 1998).

When selecting target skills, it is important to remember that not all students can learn to be fully independent in their daily living. Therefore, there are students who will require lifelong support and assistance from caregivers (Browder, 2001). Given the importance that transition planning places on self-determination and quality of life, students who require lifelong support from caregivers must nevertheless maintain their autonomy and personal dignity. Teachers can teach choice-making and "take charge" skills. These skills enable the students to direct the actions of their caregivers, thereby ensuring that these actions reflect the student's choices and preferences (Browder, 2001). For example, although the student has to rely on lifelong support, the student can learn how to communicate and make choices about clothing or when to go to the bathroom or how to ask for help. By directing the caregiver's action, the student can still "take charge" of his or her own life. Unfortunately, many curriculum materials teaching self-care skills to individuals with moderate/severe disabilities lack this perspective on self-determination. Therefore, teachers must be aware and vigilant about the need for instructional programs that address the importance of self-determination.

When selecting target skills, the cultural background, customs, and family traditions of students, such as those related to diet and use of utensils, also require careful consideration. For example, if a student and family members eat rice and noodle dishes at home, the teacher might want to include preparing rice or noodle dishes using a microwave oven as a target skill for food preparation. Often parents from nonmainstream cultural backgrounds express concern that the foods used at school for teaching domestic skills are inconsistent with the family's diet (Park, 1998).

After having selected the target skills, teachers can apply the Discrepancy Analysis to identify the steps for teaching the skills (Browder, 2001). Teachers may need to develop a task analysis for a specific target activity such as reheating food, and evaluate the individual's ability to perform the target activity. For the steps that the student misses, the teacher can evaluate potential adaptations for enabling the student to perform the task as independently as possible. For example, when using a microwave oven, the student presses one preprogrammed button identified by a numerical sequence and picture without needing to remember a sequence of buttons. For steps that are not feasible to adapt, the teacher can utilize instructional strategies such as prompts, modeling, and feedback. Teachers may refer to studies that demonstrate the effectiveness of teaching students with moderate/severe disabilities self-care skills including: eating, dressing, using the toilet, oral hygiene, housekeeping, preparing food, and doing laundry (Konarski & Diorio, 1985; Westling & Fox, 1995). Also, various commercial life skills curriculum materials such as those published by Attainment Company (2002) can be good resources for teaching daily living skills. Picture sequences that prompt the student to follow a series of steps to self-monitor performance is a powerful strategy for teaching these skills.

Students with disabilities often fail to generalize skills learned in a simulated environment to real situations. Furthermore, the real environment is usually more stimulating and motivating than a simulated one. Therefore, daily living skills should be taught in the real environment including the community. For example, money management and banking skills initially can be taught in the classroom but they should be practiced in the bank, particularly after students began earning an income. Also, the transition program can use a home or apartment as a classroom for teaching domestic and housekeeping skills.

Skills related to personal safety are crucial areas to be taught in the transition program. As students actively participate in the community, caregivers and parents are concerned about safety; students with disabilities require instruction in protecting themselves from predators. People with disabilities are victimized and revictimized five to ten times more often than people without disabilities (Petersilia, 1998; Watson, Bain, & Houghton, 1992; Wilson, Seaman, & Nettelbeck,

1996). Therefore, students need to be taught personal safety skills, which include self-determination/self-advocacy skills to resist potential victimization by saying "no" to unwanted propositions; general safety skills in the community, including dealing with solicitations by strangers; protecting personal information; and sex education. Although the provision of sex education to students with or without disabilities is controversial, parents of children with disabilities increasingly are accepting the need for it (Hoffman, Whaley, & Park, 2005). While students with disabilities lack knowledge about sexuality and sexually transmitted diseases, they were found to have high rates of pregnancy and sexually transmitted disease (McCabe & Cummins, 1996). Sex education for students with disabilities is necessary for helping them to understand and manage their own sexuality and for teaching them to protect themselves from sexual predators and sexual abuse (Wolfe & Blanchett, 1997). Therefore, sex education is included in the personal safety curriculum. A research-based curriculum developed by Hoffman, Whaley, and Park covers a comprehensive list of personal safety knowledge and skills: identifying feelings; knowing body parts and the right to privacy; knowing the dynamics of abuse (who are potential perpetrators, where and when abuse can occur); being skilled in saying "no," walking away and reporting the incident to a safe person; making good choices and developing healthy social relationships; knowing what constitutes illegal behavior; and preparing for emergencies. Students can learn these skills through discussion, role-playing, and visual media. The use of set-up situations in which students practice learned personal safety skills during the school day is a unique feature of this curriculum. For example, an actor unknown to the student tries to lure the student to provide personal information or to get into a car. The student has been taught to say "no," walk away, and report the incident to a safe person (cf., Lumley, Miltenberger, Long, Rapp, & Roberts, 1998). In this context, a safe person is an adult whom the student trusts; the student is advised to designate two or three safe persons in the circle of support. If the student does not respond appropriately in the set-up situation (e.g., going to a car with the actor), the teacher provides immediate feedback by pointing out the possible unsafe consequences. If the student acts correctly in the situation, then the teacher delays feedback until all the students complete the exercise and have had enough time to report to the teacher or teacher aides. Feedback is provided on both their actions in the simulated situations and their reporting skills. This type of teaching in simulated situations is called an "in-situ probe." Although previous studies utilized in-situ probes only as an assessment tool, this method has been found to be effective and essential with many students with disabilities, especially students with autism who have difficulty understanding concepts such as abuse and safety (Hoffman, Whaley, & Park, 2005).

POST-SECONDARY COLLEGE EDUCATION

Post-secondary education not only enhances the employability of students with learning, cognitive, and intellectual disabilities, but also offers opportunities for continued learning in the students' areas of interest. However, information about how to establish effective post-secondary education programs for students with disabilities is limited (Hart, Mele-McCarthy, Pasternack, Zimbrich, & Parker, 2004). Only thirty-seven percent of students with learning disabilities were found to enter some type of post-secondary education compared to seventy-eight percent of all high school graduates (Blackorby & Wagner, 1996). Students with disabilities typically drop out of high school or remain in special education programs beyond 18 years of age. The lack of a high school diploma restricts opportunities to pursue post-secondary education and makes it difficult to enroll in college classes. The new concept of "dual enrollment" allows students with disabilities to simultaneously complete high school and attend community college with age peers without disabilities, pursuing academic or vocational classes in an inclusive setting. According to Hart et al., dual enrollment permits students with disabilities to remain eligible for services under the IDEA up to age 21, if deemed appropriate by their IEP team. Under IDEA, students with disabilities are no longer eligible for special education services when they graduate from high school or if the state allows, when they reach the age of 21, whichever comes first.

Dual enrollment facilitates high school graduation as well as post-secondary education. Transition teachers should utilize this dual enrollment model in transition planning especially for those who might not be able to graduate from high school. Once a potential college(s) is identified, teachers and transition specialists can ask the director of the college's disability program about the range of services available for students with disabilities: Are there services that fit the specific needs of the student? What procedures do students with disabilities need to follow to receive services? What types of accommodations are available to students with disabilities? How many students are receiving services from the disabilities program? Furthermore, Skinner and Lindstrom (2003) advocate that students with learning disabilities should begin preparing for post-secondary education during their freshman year in high school. They suggest a number of post-secondary preparation activities to be taught in high school: encouraging students to self-identify their disability and areas for which they need assistance and then to seek the appropriate assistance; teaching students organizational skills for learning and living; encouraging students to develop their own strategies for improving long- and short-term memory (e.g., mnemonic techniques); facilitating and expanding social support networks of students; assisting students to obtain a comprehensive psychoeducational evaluation in high school; and encouraging students to participate in post-secondary education programs. Teachers may utilize commercial post-secondary education preparation programs such as *I Can Do This!* (Bresette et al., 1994) or *Transition to Postsecondary Learning* (Coull & Eaton, 1998).

There is no commercial post-secondary curriculum available for students with moderate/severe disabilities, more transition programs are now enrolling these students in community college classes. These programs utilize resources from the college's disability program and individually approach prospective instructors to survey classroom ecology for its effects on the student's ability to learn, considering factors such as class size, teaching style, and the grading system. For example, if the class is relatively small and the instructor is willing to allow accommodations in terms of assignments and grading, and there is external/internal peer support, then students with disabilities can engage in meaningful learning and activities. Peers without disabilities can serve as note-takers, tutors, and facilitators in the class, and they can be compensated through an interagency agreement to support post-secondary education for the students as stated in their Individualized Transition Plans. When developing post-secondary education programs for students with disabilities, it is important to select classes that match the student's needs and preferences as expressed in the person-centered planning meetings. In Sam's case, the transition team enrolled him in

Spanish class to give him more opportunity to speak Spanish and meet peers who enjoy speaking Spanish. This, in turn, would have the potential to increase his social support network in the college and the community. Enrolling in Spanish class resulted in many positive outcomes for Sam. It fulfilled his wish to go to college like his brother; it increased his social network, giving him more peers interested in interacting with him in Spanish or in English; and it enhanced his overall self-confidence.

INTERAGENCY COLLABORATION

The 1990 IDEA requires that by age 16, the Individualized Transition Plan (ITP) must include a statement that outlines the projected services that will lead to successful transition into adult life, and a corresponding statement of interagency collaboration, e.g., among the educational agency, Department of Rehabilitation, and Department of Developmental Disabilities. The Amendments of 1997 and 2004 further specify that "if an adult partner agency such as the Department of Rehabilitation does not fulfill the agreed-upon services, the educational agency must reconvene the Individualized Educational Plan (IEP) team and develop alternative methods to meet the transition objectives" [IDEA, 602(a) (20)]. In addition, many studies clearly have demonstrated the importance of interagency collaboration for the successful transition of students with disabilities into their adult lives.

Department of Rehabilitation and Regional Center

Early intervention, shared funding, and regular interagency committee meetings were found to be effective in providing seamless services to students during their transition into adult life (Noyes & Sax, 2004; Certo et al., 2003). For example, both the Department of Rehabilitation (DR) and the regional center can provide students with funding "at the same time for different services eliminating the 'either/or' dilemma for choosing the programs" (Noyes & Sax, 2004). In other words, DR can pay wages to students for their work in supported employment settings while the regional center can pay for the supports that students need to engage in nonwork activities in the community such as community access, recreation, and education. In particular, DR can provide students with early funding during their final years in school, which allows the students to receive the services in work and nonwork activities without interruption after graduation. When collaborating with different agencies, the involved parties need to meet regularly to facilitate communication and address potential barriers that may prevent a synergy of services. For example, Noyes and Sax held meetings of the transition teacher, rehabilitation personnel, and regional center staff every three months.

Further, Certo et al. (2003) housed a transition teacher in the hybrid agency to provide students with services for community activities during nonwork hours and paid wages for work in supported employment. Sharing an office allowed the transition teacher to plan and schedule activities jointly with the agency staff and director. This hybrid and nonprofit agency served adults with significant support needs and agreed to work with students prior to and after graduation from school. The funding for this hybrid agency was vendorized as a provider by both the DR and the regional center. The school dedicated a teacher to the students but subcontracted with the hybrid agency to provide the equivalent of instructional aides, thus, redirecting existing staffing funds generated by the instructional student load. This model minimized the disruption that students typically experience when transitioning from school to adult life, produced a higher employment rate, and supported students engaged in nonwork activities in the community. The school transition team may want to explore adopting this model as its transition framework.

Social Security Administration

Policy in Social Security Administration significantly impacts the paid community-based work experience program and the employment of students with disabilities over eighteen years old who are in transition programs. Therefore, teachers of transition programs must be familiar with Social Security Administration programs and rules related to the employment of students with disabilities. Social Security Administration provides the Supplemental Security Income (SSI) to individuals whose disability prevents them from working currently and is likely to continue in the future, at least for twelve months. SSI may be critical to some individuals with disabilities for their daily living and for their ability to participate in educational and employment programs. The eligibility rules for SSI change when a student becomes eighteen years old (Mellard & Lancaster, 2003). Therefore, teachers should communicate with the families so that they can assist their child with disability in filing for eligibility determination prior to their eighteenth birthday. SSI is for people with disabilities whose disability prevents their employment and it seems contradictory to one of the goals of transition programs, supported or independent employment. However, several programs within Social Security Administration encourage people with disabilities to obtain support for vocational training and employment such as the Student Earned Income Exclusion, Ticket to Work Program, and Plan to Achieve Self-Support (PASS). Transition program specialists/teachers should be familiar with these programs so that they can best assist their students in obtaining support for their work experience/employment programs during the transition years.

The Student Earned Income Exclusion (SEIE) is "a work incentive that allows certain SSI recipients who are under age twenty-two and regularly attending school to exclude a specified amount of gross earned income per month up to a maximum annual exclusion. The student earned income exclusion (SEIE) decreases the amount of countable earned income, thus permitting SSI recipients to keep more of the SSI check when they work" (Benefits Assistance Resources Center, 2005). Therefore, the SEIE allows students in transition programs to participate in work experience/supported employment programs without any reduction in their SSI payments. Each year the Social Security Administration adjusts the monthly amount and the annual limit based on changes in the cost-of-living index. For example, in the calendar year 2005, approximately $1,410 per month of a student's income could be excluded from their gross earnings (Benefits Assistance Resources Center, 2005). This feature provides an incentive for individuals with disabilities to participate in work-related training programs as part of their transition plans without a reduction in their SSI benefit.

In addition, the Ticket to Work Program serves as another work incentive for individuals with disabilities. Enacted by the Ticket to Work and Work Incentives Improvement Act of 1999 (P.L. 106-170), this legislation removed or reduced several disincentives for people with disabilities to work (Mellard & Lancaster, 2003). Under this law, individuals over eighteen years old who receive SSI receive a "ticket" in the mail. They can use this ticket or voucher to obtain employment/vocational rehabilitation services from an approved provider of their choice (Social Security Administration, 2006). The ticket is given to an employment or rehabilitation provider, who provides individuals with disabilities with supports for developing work/employment skills without giving up the full amount of the SSI benefit until they no longer need SSI (Mellard & Lancaster, 2003). The employment training provider may include transition program services, supported employment services, vocational rehabilitation services, and other private and public services such as centers for independent living (Mellard & Lancaster, 2003). Further, the PASS program provides an incentive for individuals with disabilities to enroll in work experience/vocational rehabilitation training programs by encouraging them to develop a plan for self-support. The PASS plan includes goal statements, disability information, income and resource levels, and anticipated expenses for services or items needed for achieving self-support (Millar & Lancaster, 2003). The list of expenses may include educational items such as books, transportation, tuition, fees, and clothing. Therefore, students who are enrolled in transition programs and other post-secondary education programs during their nonwork hours can receive these educational expenses through their PASS plans and still be eligible for SSI or receive SSI without any reduction; the income and/or resources set aside in a PASS plan are not counted in determining eligibility for SSI or in calculating the amount of the SSI benefit (Rehabilitation Research and Training Center on Workplace Supports, 2006). More information about SSI in relation to work experience/supported employment program can be found in several websites such as http://www.disabilitybenefits101.org; http://worksupport.com; or http://www.ssa.gov.

INVOLVEMENT OF FAMILIES

The 1997 IDEA and the recent 2004 IDEA amendments mandate family involvement and collaboration in transition planning. Families play a major role in the adult life of children with disabilities, making it vital that transition teams consider the family's input in transition planning. This family involvement in planning ensures that students can achieve outcomes that are socially and ecologically valid within their intimate circle of support. In addition, students with disabilities want their families to participate in planning the transition program (Morningstar, Turnbull, & Turnbull, 1995). However, the literature indicates that family involvement in transition planning continues to be limited, especially in families from culturally and linguistically diverse (CLD) backgrounds (Baer, Flexer, & McMahan, 2005; McDowell, Wilcox, Boles, & Bellamy, 1985; McNair & Rusch, 1991). This lack of involvement may be due to several factors: the common practice of holding transition planning meetings at school sites where culturally and linguistically diverse families often feel intimidated; the overly formal format of the meeting that makes CLD families feel uncomfortable and vulnerable. Furthermore, the values and beliefs underpinning the current best practices in transition may not corre-spond to those of CLD families (Greenen, Powers, & Lopez-Vasquez, 2001; deFur & Williams, 2002; Kalyanpur & Harry, 1999).

Some of the values emphasized in the current best practice in tran-sition planning may not correspond to the values of particular cultur-al groups. For example, independent living arrangements and employ-ment may be valued differently in different cultures. While one culture may value highly independent living and self-reliance, other cultures may value interdependence as more important. Also the value of hon-oring the student's preferences may conflict with the cultural value of deferring to group consensus or to the authority of the parents' judg-ment in the face of the student's differing preferences. Therefore, situ-ations may require honoring the preferences of the families or students even when they do not correspond to those shared in the best practice in transition planning. However, students and their families must be provided with all available information so that they can make informed choices. In Sam's case, he preferred to live with his parents in his adult life—at least for the time being—because this practice was familiar from his adult relatives who lived with their parents until after marriage. The transition planning team honored Sam's preference based on his and his family's cultural values and developed a transi-tion plan that incorporated this residential choice.

Discrepancies may occasionally arise between preferences of the student and those of the family. Person-centered planning respects the culture and heritage of the student and family; however, it also honors self-determination by the student. This approach can result in disagreement between the family's and the student's preferences. For example, a student may prefer to live with a roommate in a supported living facility, but the family prefers that the student follows the family's cultural practice and continue to live with the parents. In such cases, the facilitator needs to allow time for the student and the family to communicate and discuss each other's perspectives. Sometimes this means delaying the decision about residence in the transition plan. However, the team can still focus on skills that are required in different residential settings. The transition planning process needs to facilitate the involvement of CLD families in decision making so that they have opportunities to voice their perspective and hear perspectives that may be different from their own. The literature has identified many strategies that can help facilitate family involvement and collaboration in transition planning (see Table XIV). This range of strategies gives teachers scope for selecting those that best fit the needs of particular students and their families.

Table XIV

TIPS ON COLLABORATING WITH FAMILIES FROM CULTURALLY AND LINGUISTICALLY DIVERSE BACKGROUNDS

Be Aware that:

- Barriers to parental participation are more commonly related to differences, in languages, dialects, value, and belief systems or insensitivity to religious beliefs, family traditions, family pride, or patterns of interactions with non-family members.
- Participation on the part of these families may be more adversely affected by logistic barriers related to income, material resources, transportation, time, educational competence, and knowledge about the school system.

Things to Consider Before Meeting with Family:

- Seek help from "cultural interpreters."
- Carefully ascertain literacy and language status of family members.
- Involve family members in planning a meeting.
- Preview questions or topics, if available, with family members.
- Be flexible and responsive to the family's interaction style.
- Adapt the time frame to meet the needs of the family.
- Carefully examine the nature of the questions to ask.
- Appreciate the uniqueness in each family.
- Be aware of the influence of your role as professional.
- Acknowledge cultures.
- Develop an awareness of cultural norms.
- Learn with families.

Skills that Help Develop Cultural Sensitivity:

- Approach from a view of "Cultural reciprocity."
- Be flexible
- Accept different views of time and punctuality.
- Be accessible.
- Speak the language.
- Be aware of the family's view of authority.
- Understand why families may not follow up on recommendations.
- Be aware of the heterogeneity within the diverse groups you serve.

Sources: Dennis & Giangreco (1996), Harry, Kalyanpur, & Day (1999), and Rodriguez-Diaz & Rohena (2000).

REFERENCES

Anderson, C. M., Bahl, A. B., & Kincaid, D. W. (1999). A person-centered approach to providing support to an adolescent with a history of parental abuse. In J. Scotti & L. Meyer (Eds.), *Behavioral interventions, principles, models, and practices.* Baltimore: Paul H. Brookes.

Attainment Company. (2002). *Life skill curricula series.* Verona, WI. Retrieved February 6, 2006. from http://www.attainmentcompany.com/index.html or 1-800-327-4269.

Baer, R., Flexer, R. W., & McMahan, R. K. (2005). Transition models and promising practices. In R. W. Flexer, T. J. Simmons, P. Luft, & R. M. Baer (Eds.), *Transition planning for secondary students with disabilities* (2nd ed., pp. 53–82). Upper Saddle River, NJ: Pearson Education, Inc.

Benefits Assistance Resource Center. (2005, March). *2005 Student earned income exclusion. Key Facts, Vol. I,* No.3. Virginia Commonwealth University, Rehabilitation Research and Training Center on Workplace Supports. Retrieved February 4, 2006, from http://www.worksupport.com/ documents/ seie2005.txt.

Blackorby, J., & Wagner, M. (1996). Longitudinal post-school outcomes of youth with disabilities: Findings from the National Longitudinal Transition Study. *Exceptional Children, 62,* 399–413.

Bogdan, R., & Taylor, S. (1987). Toward a sociology of acceptance: The other side of the study of deviance. *Social Policy, 18,* 34–39.

Bresette, K., Greene, C., Moore, A., Palmer, M. A., Prysock, P., Walker, K., & Whitaker, S. (1994). *I can do this! An instructional unit in self-advocacy for students with disabilities.* Spartanburg, SC: Spartanburg County School District #7.

Broadhead, W. E., Kaplan, B. H., James, S. A. Wagner, E. H., Schoenbach, V. J., Grimson, R., et al. (1983). The epidemiologic evidence for a relationship between social support and health. *American Journal of Epidemiology, 117,* 521–537.

Browder, D. M. (2001). Ecological assessment and person-centered planning. In D. M. Browder (Ed.), *Curriculum and assessment for students with moderate and severe disabilities* (pp. 23–67). New York: Guilford Press.

Browder, D. M., & Grasso, E. (2001). Using ecological assessment in planning transition and employment. In D. M. Browder (Ed.), *Curriculum and assessment for students with moderate and severe disabilities* (pp. 361–390). New York: Guilford Press.

Browder, D. M., & Lohrmann-O'Rourke, S. (2001). Promoting self-determination in planning and instruction. In D.M. Browder (Ed.), *Curriculum and assessment for students with moderate and severe disabilities* (pp. 148–178). New York: Guilford Press.

Career Kids. (2005). Retrieved on February 4, 2006, from http://www.careerkids.com or 1-800-537-0909.

Certo, N. J., Mautz, D., Pumpian, I., Sax, C., Smalley, K., Wade, H., et al. (2003). Review and discussion of a model for seamless transition to adulthood. *Education and Training in Developmental Disabilities, 38*(1), 3–17.

Coull, L., & Eaton, H. (1998). *Transition to post-secondary learning for students with learning disabilities and/or Attention Deficit Disorder.* Vancouver, BC, Canada: Eaton Coull Learning Group.

Dean, A., & Lin, N. (1977). The stress buffering role of social support. *Journal of Nervous and Mental Disease, 165,* 403–413.

deFur, S., & Williams, B. T. (2002). Cultural considerations in transition process and standards-based education, In C. A. Kochhar-Bryant & D. S. Bassett (Eds.), *Aligning transition and standards-based education: Issues and strategies* (pp. 105–123). Arlington, VA: Council for Educational Children.

Dennis, R. E., & Giangreco, M. F. (1996). Creating conversation: Reflections on cultural sensitivity in family interviewing. *Exceptional Children, 61*(1), 103–116.

Ford, A., Schnorr, R., Meyer, L., Davern, L., Black, J., Dempsey, P. (1989). *The Syracuse Community-Referenced Curriculum Guide for students with moderate and severe disabilities.* Baltimore: Paul H. Brookes.

Giangreco, M. F., Cloninger, C. J., & Iverson, V. S. (1998). *Choosing outcomes and accommodations for children* (2nd Ed.) Baltimore: Paul H. Brookes.

Green, F. P., Schleien, S. J., MacTavish, J., & Benepe, S. (1995). Non-disabled adults' perceptions of relationships in early stages of arranged partnerships with peers with mental retardation. *Education and Training in Mental Retardation and Developmental Disabilities, 30*(2), 91–108.

Greenen, S., Powers, L. E., & Lopez-Vasquez, A. (2001). Multicultural aspects of parent involvement in transition planning. *Exceptional Children, 67,* 265–282.

Halpern, A. S. (1985). Transition: A look at the foundations. *Exceptional Children, 51,* 479–486.

Harry, B., Kalyanpur, M., & Day, M. (1999). *Building cultural reciprocity with families.* Baltimore: Paul H. Brookes.

Hart, D., Mele-McCarthy, J., Pasternack, R. H., Zimbrich, K., & Parker, D. R. (2004). Community college: A pathway to success for youth with learning, cognitive, and intellectual disabilities in secondary settings. *Education and Training in Developmental Disabilities, 39*(1), 54–66.

Hoffman, S., & Whaley, S. (2004). *Social activity planning guide.* Unpublished materials used in Sacramento Unified School District Transition Program. Sacramento, California.

Hoffman, S., Whaley, S., & Park, H. S. (2005). *Personal safety curriculum for students with disabilities.* Sacramento, CA: Sacramento Unified School District.

Hughes, C., & Carter, E. W. (2000). *The transition handbook: Strategies high school teachers use that work!* Baltimore,: Paul H. Brookes.

Hunt, M. E. (1991). Fierce tenderness: A feminist theology of friendship. New York: Crossroad.

Kalyanpur, M., & Harry, B. (1999). *Culture in special education: Building reciprocal family-professional relationships.* Baltimore: Paul H. Brookes.

Kincaid, D. (1996). Person-centered planning. In L. K. Koegel, R. L. Koegel, & G. Dunlap (Eds.), *Positive behavioral support: Including people with difficult behavior in the community* (pp. 439–465). Baltimore: Paul H. Brookes.

Konarski, E. A., & Diorio, M. S. (1985). A quantitative review of self-help research with the severely and profoundly mentally retarded. *Applied Research in Mental Retardation, 6,* 229–245

Lehmann, J. P., Bassett, D. S., & Sands, D. J. (1999). Students' participation in transition-related actions: A qualitative study. *Remedial and Special Education, 20,* 160–169.

Lovitt, T. C., Cushing, S. S., & Stump, C. S. (1994). High school students rate their IEPs: Low opinions and lack of ownership. *Intervention in School and Clinic. 30,* 34–37.

Loyd, R. J., & Brolin, D. E. (1997). *Life centered career education: Modified curriculum for individuals with moderate disabilities.* Reston, VA: Council for Exceptional Children.

Lumley, V. A., Miltenberger, R. G., Long, E. S., Rapp, J. T., & Roberts, J. A. (1998). Evaluation of sexual abuse prevention program for adults with mental retardation. *Journal of Applied Behavior Analysis, 31,* 91–101.

Martin, J. E., & Huber-Marshall, L. H. (1996). *Choicemaker self-determination transition assessment.* Longmont, CO: Sopris West.

McCabe, M. P., & Cummins, R. A. (1996). The sexual knowledge, experience, feelings, and needs of people with mild intellectual disability. *Education and Training in Mental Retardation and Developmental Disabilities, 31,* 13–21.

McDonnell, J., Wilcox, B., Boles, S. M., & Bellamy, G. T. (1985). Issues in transition from school to adult services: A survey of parents of secondary students with severe handicaps. *The Journal of Association for Persons with Severe Handicaps, 10*(1), 61–65.

McNair, J., & Rusch, F. R. (1991). Parent survey: Identification and validation of transition issues. *Interchange, 7*(4), Urbana-Champaign, IL: University of Illinois, Transition Institute.

Mellard, D. F., & Lancaster, P. E. (2003). Incorporating adult community services in students' transition planning. *Remedial and Special Education, 24*(6), 359–368.

Meyer, L. H., Park, H. S., Grenot-Sheyer, M., Schwartz, I., & Harry, B (1997). *Social relationships model.* Presented at the working conference on naturalistic interventions to facilitate social relationships for children and youth with diverse abilities. Consortium for Collaborative Research on Social Relationships of Children and Youth with Diverse Abilities. Syracuse, NY: Syracuse University.

Mitchell, R. E., Billings, A. G., & Moos, R. H. (1982). Social support and well-being: Implications for prevention programs. *Journal of Primary Prevention, 3,* 77–98.

Moon, M. S., & Inge, K. (1993). Vocational preparation and transition. In M. E. Snell (Ed.), *Instruction of students with severe disabilities* (pp. 556–587). New York: Macmillan/Merrill.

Morningstar, M. E., Turnbull, A. P., & Turnbull, H. R. (1995). What do students with disabilities tell us about the importance of family involvement in the transition from school to adult life? *Exceptional Children, 62,* 249–260.

Mount, B. (1994). Benefits and limitations of personal futures planning. In V. J. Bradley, J. W. Ashbaugh, & B. C. Blaney (Eds.), *Creating individual supports for people with developmental disabilities* (pp. 97–108). Baltimore: Paul H. Brookes.

Mount, B., & Zwernik, K. (1988). *It's never too early, it's never too late: A booklet about personal-futures planning for persons with developmental disabilities, their families, and friends, case mangers, service providers, and advocates.* St. Paul, MN: St. Paul Metropolitan Council.

Nirje, B. (1972). The right to self-determination. In W. Wolfensberger (Ed.), *The principle of normalization in human services* (pp. 176–193). Toronto, Ontario, Canada: Leonard Crainford.

Noyes, D. A., & Sax, C. L. (2004). Changing systems for transition: Students, families and professionals working together. *Education and Training in Developmental Disabilities, 39*(1), 35–44.

O'Brien, J. (1987). A guide to life-style planning. In B. Wilcox & G. T. Bellamy (Eds.), *A comprehensive guide to the activities catalog: An alternative curriculum for youth and adults with severe disabilities* (pp. 175–189). Baltimore: Paul H. Brookes.

O'Brien, J., & Lyle, C. (1987). *Framework for accomplishment.* Decatur, GA: Responsive Systems Associates.

Park, H. S. (1998). Qualitative study on family support and social relationship of children with disabilities. Unpublished document from the Consortium for Collaborative Research on Social Relationships of Children and Youth with Diverse Abilities. Syracuse, NY: Syracuse University.

Park, H. S., Chadsey-Rusch, J. G., & Storey, K. (1998). Social relationships or no social relationships: Social experiences at worksites. In L. Meyer, H. S. Park, M. Grenot-Scheyer, I. S. Schwartz, & B. Harry (Eds.), *Making Friends: The influences of culture and development.* Baltimore: Paul H. Brookes.

Park, H. S., & Gaylord-Ross, R. (1989). Problem-solving social skills training in employment settings with mentally retarded youth. Special Issue on Supported Employment, *Journal of Applied Behavior Analysis, 22,* 373–380.

Park, H. S., Meyer, L., Grenot-Scheyer, M., & Henry, L. (1994). *Ecological dimensions of sociality of job sites.* Unpublished document from the Consortium for Collaborative Research on Social Relationships of Children and Youth with Diverse Abilities. Syracuse, NY: Syracuse University.

Pearpoint, J., O'Brien, J., & Forest, M. (1995). *PATH: A workbook for planning positive possible futures and planning alternative tomorrows with hope for schools, organizations, businesses, families.* Toronto, Ontario, Canada: Inclusion Press.

Petersilia, J. (1998). *Persons with developmental disabilities in the criminal justice system: Victims, defendants, and inmates.* Statement prepared for the California Senate Public Safety Committee hearings on "Persons with Developmental Disabilities in the Criminal Justice Systems." Sacramento, CA.

Powers, L. E. (1997). *Self-determination research results.* Unpublished paper presented at University of Colorado Self-Determination Meeting, Colorado Springs.

Rehabilitation Research and Training Center on Workplace Supports. (2006). *Effects of PASS on SSI benefits.* Virginia Commonwealth University. Retrieved February 4, 2006, from http://www.worksupport.com/ resources/viewContent.cfm/381.

Rodriguez-Diaz, V., & Rohena, E. (2000). *CLD learners with moderate/severe mental retardation; language of instruction and family participation.* Unpublished paper presented at the 2000 Symposium on Culturally and Linguistically Diverse Exceptional Children, Albuquerque, New Mexico.

Rusch, F. R. (1990). *Supported employment: Models, methods, and issues.* Sycamore, IL: Sycamore.

Schleien, S., Mustonen, T., & Rynders, J. (1995). Participation of children with autism and nondisabled peers in a cooperative structured community art program. *Journal of Autism and Developmental Disorders, 25,* 397–413.

Schleien, S. J., Ray, M. T., & Green, F. P. (1997). *Community recreation and people with disabilities: Strategies for inclusion.* Baltimore: Paul H. Brookes.

Skinner, M. E., & Lindstrom, B. D. (2003). Bridging the gap between high school and college: Strategies for the successful transition of students with learning disabilities. *Preventing Social Failure, 47*(3), 132–137.

Social Security Administration. (2006). *Fact sheet: Ticket to Work and Work Incentive Improvement Act of 1999.* Retrieved February 4, 2006, from http://www.ssa.gov/work/ResourcesToolkit/legisregfact.html.

Stodden, R. (1998). School-to-work transition. In F. R. Rusch & J. G. Chadesy, *Beyond high school, transition from school to work* (pp. 60–76). Belmont, CA: Wadsworth Publishing Company.

Strully, J. L., & Strully, C. (1985). Friendship and our children. *Journal of the Association for Persons with Severe Handicaps, 10*(4), 224–227.

Taylor, J., McKelvey, J., & Sisson, L. (1993). Community-referenced leisure skills clusters for adolescents with multiple disabilities. *Journal of Behavioral Education, 3,* 363–386.

Walker, P. (1999). From community presence to sense of place: community experiences of adults with developmental disabilities. *Journal of the Association for Persons with Severe Handicaps, 24*(1), 23–32.

Wallston, B. S., Alagna, S. W., DeVellis, B. M., & DeVellis, R. F. (1983). Social support and physical health. *Health Psychology, 2,* 367–391.

Watson, M., Bain, A., & Houghton, S. (1992). A preliminary study in teaching self-protective skills to children with moderate and severe mental retardation. *The Journal of Special Education, 26*(2). 181–194.

Wehmeyer, M. L. (1998). Self-determination and individuals with significant disabilities: Examining the meaning and misinterpretations. *Journal of the Association for Persons with Severe Handicaps, 23,* 5–6.

Wehmeyer, M., Agran, M., & Hughes, C. (1998). Transition services and self-determination. In M. Wehmeyer, M. Agran, & C. Hughes (Eds.), *Teaching Self-Determination to Students with Disabilities.* Baltimore: Paul H. Brookes.

Westling, D. L., & Fox, L. (1995). *Teaching student with severe disabilities* (pp. 384–415). Upper Saddle River, NJ: Prentice Hall.

Whaley, S., & Hoffman, S. (1997). *Letter of introduction.* Unpublished materials used in Sacramento Unified School District Transition Program. Sacramento, California.

Will, M. (1984). *OSERS programming for the transition of youth with disabilities: Bridges from school to working life.* Washington, DC: U.S. Department of Education, Office of Special Education and Rehabilitative Services.

Wilson, C., Seaman, L., & Nettelbeck, T. (1996). Vulnerability to criminal exploitation: Influence of interpersonal competence differences among people with mental retardation. *Journal of Intellectual Disability and Research, 40*(1), 8–16.

Wolfe, P. S., & Blanchett, W. J. (1997). Infusion of sex education curricula into transition planning: Obstacles and solutions. *Journal of Vocational Rehabilitation, 8,* 143–154.

Chapter 5

TEACHING ADOLESCENTS STUDENTS WITH AUTISM AND OTHER SPECTRUM DISORDERS

ELVA DURÁN

INTRODUCTION

This chapter will define and give characteristics of autism. Also, some of the training and employment information of the adolescent student with autism will be given. Additionally, information will be noted on some particular programming techniques that can be used with students with autism in the public schools.

DEFINITION AND CHARACTERISTICS OF AUTISM

Since the late 1970s the description and definition of autism has been refined and extended to include the term, spectrum disorder (Gillberg et al., 1990; Wing & Gould, 1979). The term spectrum is appropriately indicated when defining autism because the students have many learning difficulties which are varied in degree and amount of disability. Many of the students have difficulties in the area of social interactions, communication, and exhibit repetitive behaviors or interests in the areas that often occur in students with autism. Students with autism who have these difficulties vary significantly in the degree to which they are affected by these behaviors which are associated with the condition of autism (Wetherby & Prizant, 2000).

Also, some students with autism may not exhibit all three characteristics noted above, but they may exhibit one or two of the characteristics. For example, a student may have difficulties communicating
and interacting socially but will not show any problems with repetitive
behaviors. The student may still have lifelong delays but will not meet
the three-domain definition of autism.

Years ago, the term pervasive developmental disorders (PDDs) was
first adopted to provide a formal diagnosis for students who shared
similar deficits in the area of autism but who did not have all three
characteristics for diagnosing the condition of autism (Wetherby &
Prizant, 2000).

According to Wetherby and Prizant (2000), it is not clear from the
many researchers who are writing in this area which disorders should
be included in the spectrum but all agree that there is a spectrum of
disorders. More and more researchers who work closely with autism
are also recommending that the term autism spectrum disorders
(ASDs) be used instead of the term pervasive development disorder.
The reason there is a shift in defining autism as a spectrum disorder is
because the term autism spectrum disorders is a broader term that
includes all of the different categories of autism instead of just highlighting one or two of the categories within the definition.

Even though there is some difference in the terms (atypical autism
versus pervasive developmental disorder) among investigators and
those persons who do diagnostic evaluations of atypical autism and
pervasive developmental disorder, there is overall agreement that students with lesser degrees of deficit should be considered as part of the
autism spectrum.

LANGUAGE AND/OR COMMUNICATION

In the chapter on Functional Language and Other Language Intervention Strategies, much information has already been discussed on
how to teach students with moderate to severe disabilities language. In
this chapter we will continue our discussion on the strategies which
will be helpful with students who have autism. In this section some
intervention strategies will be noted when teaching communication
skills to students with autism. The last time this textbook was pub-

lished (1996) there were not that many intervention strategies given to help the students with autism communicate. It was mentioned that the students should learn functional information as they are learning to speak and/or communicate. The literature reports that whatever is presented to the students should be functional (Brown, 1978; Carr, 1980; Kluth, 2003; Schuler, 1980). Functional means that the student will be able to use the vocabulary or language material because it is found in his/her various environments. Functional also means that the student is taught in the context of his/her particular environments. For example, a younger student with autism may need to request some food item because he/she is hungry and the child would select this photograph or picture icon from other photos or icons and would let the teacher, parent or care provider know what he/she wanted. An older student with autism may point to a photo or picture icon of a bus indicating to his/her teacher that he/she was ready to go home.

An environmental inventory should be completed by the teacher and the parents in order to determine what vocabulary should be emphasized to the student. If, for example, the student is learning to do a job, he/she should learn words related to what the student is performing in his/her work. For example, the adolescent student with autism may learn that "on" is the red button on the machine which will turn the equipment on. Here, the student is learning language in the context of his/her particular job training (Durán, 1986, 1987, 2005). Also, if the student is unable to communicate verbally, he/she can learn to point or gesture to whatever he/she would like to obtain. Communication booklets containing photographs of foods and/or other materials he/she may need to request or purchase at a grocery or department store can also be used by these students. The communication booklets are small enough so that students can carry them easily in the community. Color photographs are taken frequently in order that they may be inserted; new photographs will expand the materials that the student can learn by means of the booklet. With repeated practice in all environments, and by instructing all the people who work with the adolescent, the student can learn to use his/her booklet in whatever environment(s) he/she may be associated with.

Additionally, PECS or the Picture Exchange Communication System (Bondy & Frost, 1985) can also be used successfully with students with autism (mild, moderate to more severe in terms of their abilities to communicate). PECS is an alternative communication system that was developed to provide a means of functional communication for children with autism. The system uses pictures and/or picture icons and the exchange of these pictures effectively teach children how to initiate a social request for a desired item. This system utilizes behavior analysis techniques and a functional communication approach to teach children to use meaningful communication. Children are taught to request items through the use of picture icons, discrimination, and are taught to request items utilizing, "I want _____" sequence when requesting an item, and thus are taught to comment about the environment. There are correction procedures in place if a student selects the incorrect picture icon. For example, if the teacher or parent ask the child or young adult, "What day is it?" and the child or young adult says, "Friday" when the child should have said, "Thursday" the teacher or parent can correct by saying, "No, it is Thursday." Then the child will repeat, "It is Thursday" and the teacher will ask the student once again, "What day is it?" The child will say, "Thursday." The teacher/parent will then say, "That is right! What is your name?" The child/young adult will respond "Mary" and the teacher/parent will repeat once again the question to the child, "What day is it?" and the child/young adult will say, "Thursday." The strategy here is to ask Mary something totally unrelated to the day of the week such as her name and this will help Mary give the correct response because the correct day of the week was given to her just moments earlier and Mary will respond correctly to this question.

This writer knows of several of her teacher candidates who have had excellent results with their students learning vocabulary and students have also learned how to discriminate words by using the PECS.

Another form of communication students may learn is total or simultaneous communication. Students who learn to communicate utilizing signs or simultaneous communication during the early years of training continue to do very nicely, learning a few more functional signs during adolescence. According to Carr (1980) and Koegel and Koegel (2000), if students are nonverbal and learn to communicate before the age of five, they can learn some expressive language. At least 50 percent of the children with autism who are completely nonverbal learn some expressive language if they are taught before the age of five. According to Koegel and Koegel, nonverbal communication includes use of gestures, simple signs or pictures. Those students with autism who do not have speech have marked delays in phonology, syntax, and semantics. Thus, teaching students with autism some form of communication through signs, gestures or pictures is important.

As with the PECS (Picture Exchange Communication System) it is important to use functional signs and or gestures so that the students can utilize these functional signs in a variety of environments. Additionally, some students learn some signs and are able to also communicate with others in different environments utilizing different forms of communication such as gestures and pictures. According to various teachers of students with autism, it is helpful to teach their students more than one form of communication so that if someone, for example, does not know how to sign he/she will be able to communicate with the student. Koegel and Koegel (2000) suggest that teaching students more than one form of communication will allow them to be able to communicate with different people in different environments. Whatever means of communication is used with the students, it is important that parents be part of the education of these students. If parents are not taught how to use the different forms of communication, then they will not use the various forms to communicate with their children and or youth. This writer has seen many parents who are told, for example, at IEP meetings that various forms of communication are to be used at home but parents are not given direct instruction on how to utilize each of these forms of communication. Showing parents one time how to teach their children is not often enough practice time for many parents who have several things to keep in mind when teaching their children and/or youth. When parents can do the various steps in the communication process, they will more than likely continue doing this much needed instruction in a variety of environments.

The success of having parents accomplish any teaching strategy that the parents or guardians are shown to do with their sons/daughters will depend in great part on how much time the teachers assist the parents to learn the strategies, record results of using the strategies, and following up with the parents as the children/youth learn the various alternative forms of communication. Parents of various cultural and linguistic backgrounds will need additional support and follow up because they often have language and cultural barriers when trying to learn various alternative forms of communication. Starting to work with them to learn one form of communication at a time may be the best way to help them achieve success with their sons and daughters as they learn to request and select different words in their environment.

SOCIAL SKILLS

The area of social skill training, like language training, is also very important for the student with autism. This area is also especially important if the student is an adolescent and/or adult with autism. Many adolescents and adults with autism do not get jobs or have extreme difficulties living in their communities because they act inappropriately. Schopler and Mesibov, (1983) indicates that this is one of the main reasons the adolescent fails to get a permanent job in some instances. More recent literature and research (Smith, Belcher, & Juhrs, 1995) indicates that if persons with autism are offered support on the job then they will more likely be able to continue the job where they have been placed. Because the adolescents are going through many bodily changes, many of their behaviors will be even more pronounced and severe than at other stages of their lives.

According to Mesibov (1984), the adolescent student with autism can be taught social skills by teaching the student to role play. During the role-playing process, the student is taught to smile and shake hands and is taught directly how to respond to another person when the person says, "Hi, how are you?" Mesibov suggested that role playing should be done in different environments with the individuals with autism so that the persons with autism will learn appropriate social behaviors in each environment where he/she may be active.

At a program for children and adolescents with autism that this writer was directing at the University of Texas at El Paso, parents were asked to come into the program area practice with their son and/or daughter and observe the college interns as they have the individual with autism respond if someone says, "Hi, how are you?" If the persons with autism are bilingual and the parents want the individuals to know both languages as was the case in the university program then the students were asked in Spanish, "¿Cómo esta usted?" (How are you?) The parents are taken to other locations where their son and/or daughter may be participating in a variety of activities. As this is done, parents learn how they are to prompt their son and/or daughter so he/she can respond to questions directed to them. Another skill that is important to teach students is to make sure they do not go with strangers to different places. This writer is aware that in a transition program through Sacramento City Unified the student with disabilities are taught that if other college students ask them to go with them or do an activity with them, the students with disabilities are not to go with them. Different students are brought to the transition program so that the students with disabilities can learn to generalize across different people and different locations on the junior college campus. After different people are presented to the students and they continue not to go with the different people, the staff then knows it is time to move on to a different social skill. Such training has proven to be a safety program for the different students with disabilities in the transition program.

It is important for the people working with these populations to realize that special time must be set aside in order to have social skills be an important part of the curriculum. It is further important for teachers to be aware that parents are an important part of this information and social skill instruction.

MANAGING THE ADOLESCENT WITH AUTISM

Because the adolescent with autism gets larger as he/she grows older, the adolescent with autism often becomes more difficult to manage especially if he/she has not learned appropriate behaviors when the teenager is younger. During this period the adolescent will be undergoing some major bodily changes, may be aggressive, and once again difficult to manage. This is one group of students who are a challenge for anyone working with them. It is recommended that when working with an adolescent in the community, or whatever environment, that some of the following guidelines be followed:

1. Use positive reinforcement with the adolescent student with autism. Find out what he/she likes and tell him/her that if he/she completes the task or does not engage in self-abusive or self-stimulatory behaviors, he/she can choose what he/she would like to

do (preferred activity) or eat, or have (some particular object he/she would like to have, whatever object is reinforcing to the adolescent).

2. Utilize positive behavior supports (K. Gee, personal communication, February 2005) to assist students with various inappropriate behaviors that they may exhibit. For example, if a student is being noncompliant or will not complete an activity, then the team (consisting of the teacher and parent and/or guardian) can set up a behavioral contract with the student to discover how the target behavior can be better managed. If the student will not set the table for the group home dinner, the team can talk about what are the antecedents which may be triggering the behavior. Also, the student should explain what he/she is doing that is causing him/her not to set the table. Pictures of activities he/she can engage in will be displayed in front of the student. He/she is to select what he/she would like to complete once finished the task or as indicated in this example, setting the table. The choices the student is selecting are written in the positive behavior plan and will be part of the student's reinforcer as he/she works on the various tasks at hand. Having the pictures in front of the student's visual field will help the teacher remind the student each time he/she is doing the task that he/she will be able to select from a desired activity once he/she completes the task that he/she may be engaged in doing.

3. It is important to also have conferences with family members so they can help support whatever strategy is being used with the students. It is important to keep good communication with the parents of the student. Parents can become very good support systems if told what is being accomplished with their sons/daughters. Parents know their children/youth better than any of us and they not only can provide information but can also be excellent supports for the persons working with them.

4. Have information available concerning the type of program you have as you are teaching the students with autism. Having the literature available on the type of program and students who are enrolled in the program will be helpful to the general public and other teachers in the school.

5. Educate the public about students with autism and help explain to as many community members what the goals are for the various members of the program. Educating the public will help bet-

ter support the research and work that is being accomplished with students with autism.

6. Have meetings with team members working with students in order to determine the progress being made with students is important. This will help team members realize what strategies are working with students and which ones are not.

7. Make sure parents understand all the different behavior intervention strategies that are being attempted with their sons/daughters.

8. Involve the students in as many meaningful and functional activities as possible in order to reduce the amount of inappropriate behavior that students may be engaged in. Idleness or inactivity often causes the student to act inappropriately (Kluth, 2003; La Vigna, 1980; Olley, 1985).

9. Educate the general education public about what autism is and also explain to the general school public the benefits of developing friendships with students with autism and other disabilities. Some of the best advocates can be students in general education if they know about the various students in the schools who are participating in regular classrooms in full inclusion sites. Often if students in general education know about their fellow classmates they will become more involved in welcoming them to the school and the various classes they are enrolled (Kluth, 2003; Koegel & Koegel, 2000; Meyer, 1995).

10. If possible, ask students about their behavior (Kluth, 2003). This writer has firsthand experience utilizing this strategy especially when she has worked directly with adolescent students with autism. One moderate student with autism was engaged in repeating what she was doing over and over. When this writer asked Sonia why she was doing this Sonia responded that no one listened to her first request. This writer then told her that if she asked over and over all the time no one would pay attention to her. She said that she would stop if people answered her the first time. We all talked about Sonia's request and we all attempted to respond to her the first time she asked a question. Communicating with Sonia about her behavior was positive in that we became aware of why she was repeating statements and questions during her time with us.

11. Positive behavior interventions must be attempted also with the students in job sites and in the community. Positive behavior

interventions have been discussed above. The entire area of management and or positive behavior support requires the teacher to be a skilled communicator with the public and, above all, requires the teacher to try a variety of positive programming in teaching the students with autism.

More information will be described on positive interventions in the chapter on transition.

INDEPENDENT SKILL TRAINING

The area of independent skill training is of continuing utmost importance in teaching the adolescent with autism. In fact, it takes a dedicated commitment to teach the students these skills, with reinforcement training repeatedly required from time to time over the years in order to maintain the desired skills (Kluth, 2003; Koegel & Koegel, 2000; Lovaas, 1981). Below are some suggestions of what can be accomplished with students with more moderate to severe disabilities. Many of these suggestions were implemented by this writer in a program she coordinated at a university and community-based program for students with autism and other learning difficulties.

SELF-HELP SKILLS

In order to teach students skills that involve learning to care for themselves, it is suggested that parents be asked what specifically their son or daughter needs to learn. After the parents provide this information, the individual's needed skills should be prioritized or rank ordered, with the important skills being labeled number one or two, while others will be labeled as of lesser importance. Some of the skills parents feel their son or daughter should learn are washing hands and face, brushing teeth, wiping their mouth while eating, chewing with their mouth closed, teaching them to comb and brush their hair, helping them keep their fingernails clean and trimmed, teaching them to put on clean and appropriate clothes for different occasions, and helping them learn to apply deodorant. Some of the specific strategies which help students learn these particular skills include letting them see a picture or photograph of what clean teeth look like, or what constitutes appropriate clothes to wear for different occasions.

A strategy which is helpful in teaching these students self-help skills is physically guiding their hands momentarily so they can become aware of the appropriate strokes to use when brushing their teeth, for instance. The trainer or teacher should also stand in back of the student as the student is trained to learn a particular skill. Standing in back of the student will not allow the student to keep following the teacher or trainer with his/her side vision and will teach him/her to focus forward on his/her own to get his/her task completed. Different instructors or trainers should have the student do the task. These same skills should be practiced under parental supervision in the student's home environment. All of these techniques help to bring about generalization of the skills. Parents especially should be encouraged to take the time to teach the student at home (Falvey, 1984; Koegel & Koegel, 2000). Home training accomplished with different members of the family is extremely important; otherwise skills taught to the student in other environments will not be generalized from one place to another.

It should be noted that some other important independent skills to teach the students are to have them learn to cook simple meals, clean their homes, cross streets, and take the city bus to and from their work and homes. In order to teach cooking skills, photographs should be taken of the different steps involved in making a sandwich or enchiladas, for example. The photographs cue the student to follow different steps in recipe sequences. With practice, students learn to cook independently by imitating actions in the photographs. Colored photographs should be glued to a large file folder and placed in a recipe file or file cabinet when not in use. All these recipe files should be titled according to the different recipes they represent, for example, "Making a sandwich" or enchiladas, for example. The photographs cue the student to follow different steps in recipe sequences. With practice, students learn to cook independently by imitating actions in the photographs. Thus, when the file folders are placed in the file cabinet, the title of each recipe will show for ease in having the student select recipes. A similar set of these photographs should be sent home so that parents will make use of the photographs to have their son or daughter cook at home. Picture icons from the PECS or Picture Exchange Communication System can also be used to help the students learn to follow sequences for recipes as well as the photographs. The more realistic the photograph is the easier it will be for the students to follow the picture sequences.

In order for the students to become independent in learning to perform some cleaning tasks, such as mopping and sweeping, they need to be given practice in performing these activities both at school and at home. A task analysis sheet which indicates the incorrect and correct steps they are performing, in the proper sequence of steps, should be kept on each student in order to see what areas they will need more assistance in, or to indicate that they are ready to move on to learn new skills. Again, learning to mop and sweep are important skills that must also be practiced wherever the student lives. Such practices will assist with generalization training for the student, who will need help practicing in various environments before he/she can learn to do the various skills independently. When the student is completing a task incorrectly, it is important to model for the student how to do various steps correctly for a particular task. Oftentimes, modeling different steps for the student can be helpful in teaching the student how to complete each step of the task correctly, and in the proper sequence.

During parent/staff conferences, it is necessary to ask parents how their sons or daughters are doing at home with the various independent training skills. If parents know that the staff will ask them questions about their son's or daughter's home training, they will more likely make an effort to have them do more training of different skills at home. During parent conferences, it is necessary to reevaluate what is being taught to students and, if necessary, help should be given to parents so they can reprioritize new skill areas. There should be constant feedback coming from the teacher and other staff persons and the parents. Only with open communication and constant feedback will the adolescent's programming improve satisfactorily.

LITERACY INSTRUCTION

This writer would like to refer the readers to her chapter on Literacy Instruction within this book. Because this area of instruction is so important and has often been very neglected in most of the literature and other textbooks for students with moderate to more significant intellectual disabilities this writer has devoted an entire chapter to the discussion of literacy instruction. Please refer to that chapter for information on what should be instructed to the students with autism and other moderate to significant disabilities.

INCLUSION AND SECOND LANGUAGE ACQUISITION OF STUDENTS WITH AUTISM: QUALITATIVE STUDY RESEARCH RESULTS

Pre and Post-Inclusion Data with Students with Autism at a School in Northern California

Even though this chapter emphasizes the adolescent student with autism, this writer would like to share this research which is still in progress because she cannot emphasize enough the importance of including students in general education classrooms as much as all people concerned with the student feel is possible. What follows is a summary of some of the beginning research results which have been collected and analyzed up to this date.

As more and more general education classrooms begin opening their doors to students with severe disabilities, the research data and information that is conducted will become increasingly important in order to see the long-term effects of full inclusion among all the students in the different classrooms. This investigator has collected data on five students who have been labeled as having autism and other autism spectrum disorders in their self-contained classroom and secondly in their fully-included site. The report will give accounts of self-contained and regular classrooms where the students were assigned.

PRE-TEST DATA IN SELF-CONTAINED SITE ON FIRST CAMPUS

In the self-contained classroom the five students were placed in a room with one special education teacher and two instructional aides. The teacher had a curriculum in the self-contained classroom which included oral language development activities, such as singing, nursery rhymes, stories enhanced with puppets, free play activities, and shared literature. The students also had speech development with a speech and language pathologist during the week. Also, as part of the curriculum, the students participated in art and music activities.

The instructional aides and teachers spent a considerable amount of time developing activities so the students could learn as much language or means of communication in order for some of their inappropriate behaviors to decrease. Research indicates (Durán, 1990, 2005; Durand, 1990; Kulth, 2000) that the more the student with autism and/or autism spectrum disorders can communicate, the more his/her inappropriate behaviors will decrease.

The curriculum of the students also included some physical exercise which was greatly encouraged by the teacher and instructional aides during recess.

This investigator collected data twice weekly for approximately two to two and a half hours each visit. The qualitative study was based on research collection information developed by Bogdan and Biklen (1992) using an alpha program to help the investigator visually see the various variables which were increasingly evident as the observations continued throughout the year.

The variables that repeatedly became evident in the various observations were a rich language environment; students with disabilities were talking and socializing with one another or the staff of the classroom. Additionally, some other behavior variables which were noted were some tantruming behaviors from the students with autism during the day. The students with autism also engaged in self-stemming and, at times, self-hitting behavior. Additionally, the students showed poor attending skills whenever any stimulus or modeling was done by the staff. Often inappropriate social skills were seen by the students as they pulled things from one another during free play and other more structured times. Much crying behavior was seen especially as the staff changed some of the activities for the students.

The one Hmong child with autism who was on a beginning level of English language development would frequently not respond to any of the curricular activities designed to enhance his English knowledge and language development. The Hmong student often tantrumed so one of the aides or the teacher would sit beside the student in order to offer him enough support so that he could attend for some of the time as the language activities were being presented. The Hmong student continued his inappropriate behavior and shouted words in his Hmong language.

The classroom teachers and the investigator conferred weekly as this writer presented the teachers with copies of the observation data. Both teachers and investigator shared weekly what the data was revealing and all concerned talked about how changes could be made in order to help improve some of the behaviors of the children. The students' behavior and language development remained the same. Data collection in this particular classroom stopped in June as the school year came to an end. Thus, the first year of predata was concluded.

Fully Included Site in Another School–Year II of Study

During the summer, the students with autism and other autism spectrum disorders participated in the regular activities of a regular kindergarten classroom. No data was taken by the investigator during the summer months, but the special education teacher noted verbally to the writer that much planning was done with the general education teacher in order to see how all the children would respond to each other. Full inclusion started with these students with special challenges. By the fall of the school year the students, teachers, and instructional aides were invited to fully participate in the kindergarten classroom with twenty regular kindergarten children and two regular education teachers.

The investigator obtained permission from the director of special education of the district and the principal of the new school site to continue the qualitative research study and follow the students of the general education classroom to see how their oral language development was progressing.

During the fall semester the investigator and the research assistant went twice weekly for two to two and a half hours each time to observe the progress of the students with special needs in the fully-included classroom.

Some of the variables or characteristics which started to evolve as the year progressed in the fully-included site were as follows:

1. Much oral language development was seen in evidence as the regular and special education teachers planned daily to add shared

literature units, finger plays, and riddles to the curriculum. Music and use of puppets and art activities were continued as part of the curriculum.

2. Centers or various group activities were planned in order for the students to sit beside one another and share materials and conversation.

3. The teachers placed general education students beside the students with special needs so the general education students could assist the children. The Hmong child with special needs increased his English vocabulary and socially did not require as much assistance as he had previously in the self-contained classroom, or the first site where the data was started.

Two of the general education students who were Asian imitated the Asian special education teacher and constantly offered assistance to the students with autism and other pervasive disorders. Buddies naturally evolved and developed as the year progressed.

One of the students with autism who had previously been assigned to a one-to-one intervention and home program started to attend to lessons and stood by the general education children and participated with other general education students. During circle time, which is a large part of the curriculum in this kindergarten classroom, the students with special needs sit beside the general education students and participate in all of the circle time activities. These circle time activities include shared literature units, singing, reading, math, and dancing. Outside at recess, or other free play activities, the students with special needs played with general education students, by themselves, and often observers commented that one could not tell which child had the disability.

Social relationships and friendships also developed among the general education children and the students with autism and other autism spectrum disorders. The students with autism tantrumed very little if at all in the new setting as the year progressed.

By the end of the school year in June, the students with special needs were reminded by the general education children that everyone had to participate and not make a lot of noise. Good modeling from the general education students was evident throughout the day.

Parents of both groups of children have commented on the benefits all the children have received. The parents further believe that more growth has taken place this school year than was ever imagined. The parents of the children with special needs and the general education students have commented to the teachers about how happy they are with the progress all the children have achieved.

Thus, the post-data results in the fully-included, general education classroom setting reveal that the students have grown socially, have developed language, and have learned to profit from much of the general education curriculum which is rich and varied in this kindergarten classroom. The general education students have also benefited as they are now more tolerant to people who are slower or less talkative than they may be. The extra help from the special education teacher and her staff has also enriched the children in the general education setting. The qualitative study continued for five years after the kindergarten and first-grade setting. Results indicate that the students now in sixth grade have continued to thrive from the general education classroom setting. One of the Asian students with autism spectrum disorder was given additional help during the fifth grade and was pulled from the general education classroom for an hour each day to work on comprehension reading skills. After the student grasped the comprehension skills new ones were presented to him. Each day the student returned after the hour of specific instruction in his tutoring session. The special tutoring was important in order for the student to keep up with a fast-paced reading curriculum that the school district has been using for several years. It is important to note that successful full inclusion classrooms do pull students either in the regular classroom setting or in a separate tutoring area in order to specifically assist students with specific skill instruction. The overall benefits of the inclusion study cannot be overemphasized as this writer has seen the progress these students have made through the years. Some observations will continue periodically with these students in order to determine the longitudinal effect of their progress in the fully-included classrooms.

DISCUSSION QUESTIONS

1. Define autism spectrum disorders.
2. What are some strategies you use in teaching language and/or communication with the adolescent with autism?
3. Explain some social skills you can teach adolescents with autism.

4. List at least three management strategies you can try with an adolescent with autism who acts inappropriately.

5. What are some independent living skills you can teach adolescents with autism?

6. What are positive effects of full inclusion with students with autism and other autism spectrum disorders?

REFERENCES

Bogdan, R., & Biklen, S. (1992). *Qualitative research for education: An introduction to theory and methods* (2nd Ed.). Boston: Allyn & Bacon.

Bondy, A. & Frost, L. (1985). *Picture Exchange Communication System.* Newark, DE: Pyramid Educational Products.

Brown, L. (1978). *A strategy for developing chronological age appropriate and functional curricular content for severely handicapped adolescents and young adults.* Paper published in cooperation with the University of Wisconsin, Madison & Madison Metropolitan School District, (pp. 1–11).

Carr, E. (1980). Generalization of treatment effects following educational intervention with autistic children and youth. In B. Wilcox & A. Thompson (Eds.), *Critical issues in educating autistic children and youth* (2nd Ed., pp. 118–134). Washington, DC: U.S. Department of Education Office of Special Education.

Durán, E. (1986). Developing social skills in autistic adolescents with severe handicaps and limited English competencies. *Education, 107*(3), 203–207.

Durán, E. (1987). Overcoming people barriers in placing severely aberrant autistic students in work sites and community. *Education, 107*(3), 333–337.

Durán, E. (1990). *Managing students with autism.* Lecture presented to transition class at California State University, Sacramento.

Durán, E. (2005). *Teaching students with autism.* Lecture presented to Education of Exceptional Children/Youth class at California State University, Sacramento.

Durand, M. (1990). *Severe behavior problems, a functional communication training approach.* New York: Guilford Press.

Gillberg, C., et al. (1990). Autism under age of 3 years: A clinical study of 28 cases referred for autistic symptoms in infancy. *Journal of Child Psychology and Psychiatry and Allied Disciplines. 31*, 921–934.

Kluth, P. (2003). *You're going to love this kid!: Teaching students with autism in the inclusive classroom.* Baltimore: Paul H. Brookes.

Koegel, R. L. & Koegel, L, K. (2000). *Teaching children with autism strategies for initiating positive interactions and improving learning opportunities.* Baltimore: Paul H. Brookes.

La Vigna, G. (1980). Reducing behavior problems in the classroom. In B. Wilcox & A. Thompson (Eds.), *Critical issues in educating autistic children and youth,* (2nd Ed., pp. 135–153). Washington, DC: U.S. Department of Education Office of Special Education.

Lovaas, I. (1980). *Child with developmental delays.* Conference paper presented at the meeting of National Autism Society, California.

Mesibov, G. B. (1984). Social skills training with verbal autistic adolescents and adults: A program model. *Journal of Autism and Developmental Disorders, 14*(4), 395–404.

Meyer, L. (1995). *Quality inclusive schooling for students with severe behavioral challenges.* Unpublished manuscript, Partnership for Statewide Systems Change, New York.

Olley, G. J. (1985). Current issues in school services for students with autism. *School Psychology Review, 14*(2), 166–170.

Schuler, A. (1990). Teaching functional language. In B. Wilcox & A. Thompson (Eds.), *Critical issues in educating autistic children and youth* (2nd Ed.). Washington, DC: U.S. Department of Education Office of Special Education.

Smith, M. D., Belcher, R. G., & Juhrs, P. D. (1995). *A guide to successful employment for individuals with autism.* Baltimore: Paul H. Brookes.

Wetherby, A. M., & Prizant, B. M. (2000). *Autism spectrum disorders: A transactional developmental perspective.* Baltimore: Paul H. Brookes.

Wing, L., & Gould, J. (1979). Severe impairments of social interaction and associated abnormalities in children: Emidemiology and classification. *Journal of Autism and Developmental Disorders, 9*, 11–29.

Chapter 6

STUDENTS WITH MULTIPLE DISABILITIES

Vivian L. Correa
AND
Joyce Targaguila-Harth

The problems of students with multiple disabilities are severe enough and probably frequent enough to warrant special consideration (Orelove, Sobsey, & Silberman, 2004), and the educational needs of this heterogeneous population are extremely varied. Typically, students with multiple disabilities have been defined as students having one or more impairments (Sacks & Silberman, 1998; Westling & Fox, 2004), and it is important for educators to become increasingly aware that students who evidence severe disabilities often have additional sensory impairments requiring diverse intervention programs (Downing, 2003; Orelove, Sobsey, & Silberman, 2004; Turnbull, Turnbull, Shank, Smith, & Leal, 2002; Utley, 1994). The definition of multiple disabilities specified in IDEA states, "Multiple disabilities means concomitant impairments (such as mental retardation-blindness, mental retardation orthopedic impairments, etc.), the combination of which causes such severe educational problems that they cannot be accommodated in special education programs solely for one of the impairments. The term does not include deaf-blindness" (IDEA, 34 C.F.R., Part 200, Sec. 300.7). This chapter presents information on the student with multiple disabilities who evidences sensory impairments, including blindness and deafness. Although IDEA creates a separate category for students who are deaf-blind, information on this disability will also be reviewed. It identifies the major aspects of visual and auditory impairments and discusses assessment and intervention procedures. Educational implications for working with students with multiple disabilities, who are also English Language Learners (ELL), will also be discussed.

PREVALENCE

It is difficult to delineate the numbers of students who evidence multiple disabilities. The U.S. Department of Education's Twenty-Fourth Annual Report to Congress (2003) revealed that 122,559 students ages six to twenty-one were served in 2000–2001 under IDEA's part B programs for students with multiple disabilities. Overall, the prevalence of severe and multiple disabilities are between one percent and 1.9 percent (Turnbull et al., 2002).

Although there exists a paucity of studies addressing this issue, researchers agree that students with severe disabilities often have sensory impairments. In general, two out of every five students with severe and multiple disabilities will have sensory impairments (Silberman, Bruce, & Nelson, 2004; Turnbull et al., 2002). For example, Cross, Spellman, DeBriere, Sizemore, Northam, and Johnson (1981) reported that as many as 75 to 90 percent of persons with severe and profound disabilities evidence visual impairments. Similarly, Ellis (1986) reported that the prevalence of visual impairments among mentally retarded persons was ten times higher than in the normal population, and Holden-Pitt and Diaz (1998) estimated that 34 percent of children with hearing impairments had additional handicapping conditions, with nine percent of those having two or more additional disabilities. The most common additional disabilities are mental retardation, learning disabilities, and autism (Gallaudet Research Institute, 2003). Karchmer & Allen (1999) warn that many children who have multiple disabilities are still undercounted due to definition problems and to the lack of valid diagnostic procedures. Schrimer (2001) reports that although the numbers of Rubella children in special education programs has decreased since the 1970s and 1980s, from 9,000 students in the 1982–1983 Annual Survey to less than 1,000 students in 1992–1993, the number of children who are non-Rubella, with multiple sensory defects and additional disabilities has increased. The most common causes of deafness are heredity, otitis media, meningitis, premature birth, and Cytomegalovirus (Gallaudet Research Institute, 2003; Holden-Pitt & Diaz, 1998).

There is almost no data available on the number of students with multiple disabilities who are English language learners. One source of information on the prevalence of Hispanic children with hearing impairments is the Annual Survey of Deaf and Hard of Hearing Children and Youth (2002–2003). This document shows that 17.9 percent of students with hearing impairments attending residential schools are of Hispanic descent. Furthermore, Hispanics are the fastest growing minority population in deaf culture (Christensen, 2000). In 2002–2003, 24.5 percent of all students receiving services for hearing impairments in the United States were of Hispanic descent (Gallaudet Research Institute, 2003). While the number of children with disabilities from diverse backgrounds increases, only five to ten percent of deaf education teachers are from cultural and linguistically diverse backgrounds (Johnson, 2004).

While the prevalence figures are inconsistent and difficult to obtain, it is evident there exists a higher incidence of sensory impairments among persons with severe disabilities than among other persons with mild disabilities. The growing concern that many students with severe disabilities evidence problems with visual and/or hearing is clearly indicated by these figures. Further, to compound the problem, there are a growing number of students with multiple disabilities whose primary language and cultural background is different from the majority Anglo population. For example, Kirchner & Peterson (1981) suggest that children from ethnically diverse backgrounds are statistically more likely to have severe visual impairments, due to premature births and prenatal care in women who are ethnically diverse and poor. To better understand this group of students, basic assessment and intervention information on sensory impairments is necessary, and educational implications for providing services to students from ethnically diverse backgrounds with multiple disabilities must be considered.

VISUAL IMPAIRMENTS

The leading causes of visual impairments among school-age children are due to congenital cataracts (opacity of the crystalline lens of the eye), retinopathy of prematurity (overgrowth of blood vessels from retina in premature infants), and cortical visual impairment (damage to the visual cortex of the brain) (Erin et al., 2002; Ward, 2000). For students to be diagnosed as legally blind, they must evidence vision of no better than 20/200 in the better eye after correction or a visual field of less than 200, and partially sighted children are defined as having vision of 20/70 to 20/200 after correction (Sacks & Silberman, 1998). The diagnosis of vision in children with multiple impairments requires a transdisciplinary approach.

There are many professionals working in the area of visual disabilities who can support the teacher of students with multiple disabilities. Ophthalmologists, optometrists, and clinical low-vision specialists are among the team of professionals that evaluate and prescribe optical lenses and aids. Teachers of students with visual impairments (TVIs), certified orientation and mobility specialists (COMS), and low-vision therapists (LVT) are professionals who assist in providing educational intervention in areas such as Braille, low-vision training, cane travel, and skills of daily living. For the student who has multiple disabilities, occupational and physical therapists serve an important role in developing programs for movement, posture, hand function, and oral-motor skills.

Furthermore, if students are from culturally and/or linguistically diverse backgrounds, professionals in bilingual education, English for speakers of other languages (ESOL) education, and migrant education can assist in developing appropriate educational programs for the students. Rainforth and York-Barr (1997) provided an excellent model for collaborative teamwork among professionals who work with students with severe and multiple disabilities and their families. The complex assessment and intervention needs of students with multiple disabilities require that professionals work within a transdisciplinary team model.

ASSESSMENT

There exists a paucity of psychoeducational assessment instruments available for use with students with visual and multiple disabilities. General guidelines for interviewing families, teachers, and other relevant professionals have been developed by Bradley-Johnson (1994) to help organize information obtained from various sources for students who are visually impaired or blind. Lewis & Russo (1998) propose an approach which is individually tailored, process-oriented, and includes the use of multiple assessment batteries along with informal observation. Several instruments have been recommended for students with visual and multiple impairments (Benoff, 2001). Some of the instruments suggested for use with this population are outlined in Table XV.

Table XV
ASSESSMENT INSTRUMENTS USEFUL WITH STUDENTS WITH
MULTIPLE DISABILITIES AND VISUAL IMPAIRMENTS

Instrument	*Author*
Assessment, Evaluation, and Programming System (AEPS®) for Infants and Children, Second Edition	Bricker (2002)
Brigance® Diagnostic Comprehensive Inventory of Basic Skills (Green), Student Braille Edition	Brigance (1983, revised 1999)
Callier-Azusa Scale (G) Scales for the Assessment of Cognitive Development	Stillman (1985)
Developmental Activities Screening Inventory (DASI-II)	Fewell & Langley (1984)
Griffiths Mental Development Scales [Revised]	Griffiths & Huntley (1996)
Informal Assessment of Developmental Skills for Visually Handicapped Students	Swallow, Mangold, & Mangold (1978)
The Oregon Project: For Visually Impaired & Blind Preschool Children - Skills Inventory - Fifth Edition	Brown, Simmons, Methvin, Anderson, Boigon, & Davis (1991)
Reynell-Zinkin Developmental Scales For Visually Handicapped Children	Reynell & Zinkin (1979)
Revision of the Reynell-Zinkin Scales For Young Visually Handicapped Children	Vervloed, Hamers, Van Mens-Weisz, & Timmer-van de Vosse (2000).
Uzgiris and Hunt Infant Psychological Development Scale (IPDS): Dunst Revision	Dunst (1980)
Vineland Adaptive Behavior Scales - Expanded	Sparrow, Balla, & Cicchetti (1984)
Vulpe Assessment Battery - Revised (VAB-R)	Vulpe (1994)

As discussed in previous chapters, assessment of students with severe disabilities must be ecological in its approach and result in functional curriculum planning (Browder, 2001; Orelove, Sobsey, & Silberman, 2004; Westling & Fox, 2004).

Additionally, the assessment of functional vision in students with multiple disabilities is difficult. Nevertheless, functional vision assessment is critical to the evaluation and intervention process for this population. Among the instruments most suggested for use with students with multiple disabilities is the Individualized Systematic Assessment of Visual Efficiency (ISAVE) (Langley, 1998); the STYCAR Battery (Sheridan, 1976); and a functional vision assessment developed by Topor, Rosenblum, & Hatton (2004). Additionally, Erin (1996) and Zambone, Ciner, Appel, and Graboyes (2000) provided excellent suggestions for assessment and intervention techniques appropriate for use with students who are multiply disabled and partially sighted.

For students who are English language learners, the dilemma of assessment has been well-documented (Baca & Cervantes, 2003; Correa & Heward, 2003; Figueroa, 2002; Ortiz & Yates, 2002). The implications for assessing students with visual and multiple disabilities are clear. Most instruments discussed in this chapter are not available in other languages, and unless the examiner is fluent in Spanish, for example, the ELL student must receive assessment instruction in English. To illustrate, let us look at the case of Ricardo, a student from the Dominican Republic, living in Miami.

At the age of seven, Ricardo, a student with multiple disabilities and limited English proficiency was given the STYCAR, functional vision assessment in English. He did not understand the instruction "find the same one," so the examiner concluded that Ricardo could not see from a distance and asked the parents to take him to an ophthalmologist. Ricardo's parents were very confused but followed through on the referral. After a very expensive office visit to an ophthalmologist, it was determined that Ricardo had no visual problems and refractive lenses were not prescribed. Ricardo's parents were relieved but also upset with the school examiner because of the cost of the visit. They also had to arrange for a interpreter to accompany them to the doctors' office. Additionally, in their native country going "outside" of the family to solve problems was not common which had made the family uncomfortable.

The case described above illustrates not only the potential damage that can occur due to language barriers but also the cultural barriers that must be understood by professionals working with English language learners with multiple disabilities and their families.

INTERVENTION

Intervention with students who are multiple and visually disabled should not be much different than intervention with students who have normal vision (Orelove, Sobsey, & Silberman, 2004). Currently, several texts provide effective practices for evaluating and educating students with visual disabilities (Bishop, 2004; Holbrook, 1996; Pogrund & Fazzi, 2002; Sacks & Silberman, 1998; Warren, 1994).

Noteworthy, there is a recent national effort to define essential educational services for students who are visually impaired and may have additional disabilities. The National Agenda (Huebner, Merk-Adam, Stryker, & Wolfe, 2004; Wolfe, 2001) outlines critical goals and strategies for achieving them and effective educational programs for children with visual and multiple disabilities.

Perhaps the most important aspect of intervention for students with multiple disabilities incorporates both the fields of vision and severe disabilities. Gee (2004) outlines the five major principles for developing curriculum and instruction for students with multiple disabilities. The principles include:

- Person-centered family-centered planning that seeks input from the family on key priorities for the individual related to quality of life, relationships, and access.
- Ecologically-based assessments and designs based on activities in the community, home, and school environments of same-age peers without disabilities.
- Functionally and socially relevant curriculum that represents areas of need that will truly have a significant impact on the student's life.
- Individualized, systematic, yet, responsive instruction that carefully evaluates instruction and modifications through data-based decision making, and utilizes critical "teachable" moments for growth and success.
- Active and informed participation that assures that students are given a meaningful way to contribute to social and academic activ-

ities or tasks, connecting students to functional learning environments.

For students with multiple disabilities and visual impairments, specific areas of concern for intervention include early intervention (Pogrund & Fazzi, 2002), inclusion in general education (Downing, 2003); maximizing residual vision (Silberman, Bruce, & Nelson, 2004), orientation and mobility (Blasch, Wiener, & Welsh, 1997), and providing positive behavioral supports (Gee, 2004).

Early intervention for young children with visual disabilities is a disabilities phase of the service delivery continuum. The focus of early intervention is to provide the infant with visual disabilities with appropriate and systematic sensory stimulation in order to facilitate maximum development, and provide the families with support to better understand the development and special needs of their child. A program developed by Ferrell (1985) provided parents and teachers with excellent suggestions for early intervention with young students with visual disabilities. The Reach Out and Teach materials also address the needs of children with multiple disabilities. Additionally, Gold (2002) provides information on how parents with the help of educators and medical professionals, can give children with visual impairments the necessary skills to lead active, independent lives.

Students with multiple and visual disabilities are best served in inclusive school environments with the appropriate school supports. Students in inclusive settings become members of their grade-level activities and "develop skills related to communication, socialization, and academics in natural and functional situations" (Gee, 2004, p. 73). Maximizing residual vision is also a major focus of educational programs for children with visual disabilities. Interventions include use of optical lenses and aids, electronic aids (e.g., Visualtek, Viewscan, Versabraille), and environmental modifications (e.g., lighting) (Spungin, 2002). For many students who are multiple disabled, the use of sophisticated electronic aids is difficult, and the focus of stimulating vision is more functional in nature. Systematic and age-appropriate visual stimulation should occur during functional daily routines (Silberman, Bruce, & Nelson, 2004). For example, training a student to visually track an object can be taught within the functional routine of eating with a spoon, in which the spoon becomes the object for tracking. Similarly, stimulation programs involving the other senses (tactile, auditory, olfactory, gustatory) should be taught systematically and within a student's functional routines. Sensory bombardment is no longer justified in programs serving students with multiple disabilities with sensory impairments. Erin, Fazzi, Gordon, Isenberg, & Paysse (2002) provide guidelines for promoting use of vision in students with cortical visual impairments. The strategies include:

- Using objects and toys that are bright red and yellow.
- Presenting objects in an uncluttered background or foreground.
- Try various body positions in order to find one that is most comfortable and engaging to the child.
- Pair tactile and auditory cues to help the child increase recognition of objects.
- Use familiar and real objects.
- Allow sufficient time for the child to interpret and respond to the visual stimuli.

Orientation and mobility (O&M) is yet another critical component of the service delivery package for students who evidence multiple disabilities. Today, O&M specialists are receiving extensive training in working with preschoolers and students with multiple disabilities. The idea of independent cane travel may not be realistic for many students with multiple disabilities, thus, the definition and parameters of O&M have broadened (Anthony, Bleier, Fazzi, Kish, & Pogrund, 2002; Perla & O'Donnell, 2002; Sacks & Silberman, 1998). The O&M training arena is not just teaching formal cane travel around schools and communities. Instead, the training occurs in daily living areas such as kitchens, bathrooms, and bedrooms. Furthermore, concept development (the process of utilizing sensory information to form ideas of space and the environment), sensory training, and motor development become a major part of the O&M curriculum for students with multiple disabilities. In addition, physical and occupational therapists are becoming more involved in the O&M process (Blasch, Wiener, & Welsh, 1997) by providing teachers with excellent guidance for early movement and posture development using techniques such as described in neurodevelopment treatment (Bobath & Bobath, 1984). Interestingly, Foy (1991) provides professionals with basics O&M guidelines in Spanish and English.

Lastly, intervention techniques for decreasing maladaptive behaviors (self-injury, self-stimulation, aggression, withdrawal) are often needed with students with multiple disabilities. Perhaps, due to the lack of sensory input, communicative function, or motivation, many of these students must be involved in behavioral treatment programs to decrease maladaptive behaviors. There is an abundance of literature on the use of positive behavior supports (PBS) with students with serious problem behaviors (see Sugai et al., 2000; Westling & Fox, 2004). PBS uses "proactive strategies that are focused more on teaching students positive ways to behave than what type of consequences will ensue if students misbehave" (Gee, 2004, pp. 73–74). A collaborative team is required to closely monitor PBS through individually-based and school-wide interventions. Attention should also be paid to the communicative function of challenging behaviors, and interventions that increase forms of communication are critical (Downing, 2004).

Clearly, the educational needs of students with multiple disabilities are diverse, and the roles of professionals working with them are varied. Students from language minority cultures will require added support. Intervention must meet the cultural expectations of the family from a diverse background (Milian, 2001; Milian & Erin, 2001). As described in the following situation, there is often conflict between the perceived needs of family and the educational system.

> Anita is a sixteen-year-old, Mexican American student who evidences multiple disabilities and blindness. The O&M specialist has requested that Anita's parents reinforce the use of cane travel for independent mobility during times when she is not in school. However, Anita's parents, and particularly her grandfather, oppose this request. They do not believe Anita should travel by herself, and should always be chaperoned by an older sibling or other family member.

Anita's situation is all too common. In this instance, Anita's family values dependence, particularly for a young woman like Anita; it is not proper for her to go places alone. Anita comes from a large extended family who will always be available to provide her with a sighted-guide. Independence and particularly the use of a cane (sometimes a stigma of blindness) are in conflict with the values inherent within Anita's Mexican American culture.

Whether the focus of an educational program is on early intervention, visual stimulation, O&M training, or teaching positive social behaviors, the professional working with the culturally diverse student with multiple disabilities needs the support of parents and other professionals in order to execute a quality program. However, as discussed, the program must be sensitive to the diverse needs and values of students and families from different cultures.

HEARING IMPAIRMENTS

According to Jones & Jones (2003) the leading causes of hearing impairments in school-aged children with multiple disabilities are otitis media (inflammation of middle ear occurring in the presence of chronic Eustachian tube dysfunction); viral infections (Rubella and cytomegalovirus-CMV); hereditary diseases (Norrie's disease and Usher's syndrome); Rh factor; and low birth weight.

Hearing impairments are traditionally classified into three categories: conductive hearing loss involving the sound conducting pathways of the outer and middle ear, sensorineural loss caused by problems involving the cochlea (inner ear) and the neural pathway from the inner ear to the brain stem (Marschark, Lang, & Albertini, 2002). In some cases, when both conductive and sensorineural losses occur in the same individual, it is regarded as mixed hearing loss (Schirmer, 2001). In conductive hearing loss, typical sounds are not loud enough to stimulate normal hearing, due to an impairment in the outer or middle ear. Conductive hearing loss is often caused by diseases that leave fluid or wax buildup in the middle ear. Amplification may improve the problem by increasing sound sufficiently to bypass the damaged area, and initiate reception by the cochlea and auditory nerve. Yet, with sensorineural loss, an increasing amplification of sound does not improve its clarity. In this case, the cochlea or the auditory nerve pathway is damaged and the brain does not receive the sound vibrations, receives very little of them or the sound is delivered in a distorted manner (Schirmer, 2001). Causes of sensorineural loss include maternal infections such as rubella, and childhood diseases such as meningitis (Downing, 2003).

Marschark, Lang, and Albertini (2002) present another way of understanding the typical classifications of hearing impairment. Table XVI outlines these classifications by the average amount of loss in frequencies or decibel.

Table XVI
CLASSIFICATION BY DEGREE OF HEARING LOSS

Class	Classification	Decibel	Characteristics
	Slight or Borderline	16-25 (dB)	Difficulty hearing faint speech in noisy environments
1	Mild	26-40 (dB)	Can hear most speech sounds in quiet environments
2	Moderate	41-55 (dB)	Problem with speech sounds. Can hear conversational speech only at a close distance.
3	Moderate/Severe	56-70 (dB)	Hear little speech range. Can only hear loud, clear conversational speech and has difficulty in group situations. Speech is impaired but intelligible.
4	Severe	71-90 (dB)	Problems with other environmental sounds. Cannot hear speech unless it is loud. Cannot recognize many words. Speech is not completely intelligible
5	Profound	>90 (dB)	Hear no speech and very little other sound. Relies on visual modes of communication

Adapted from Marschark, Lang, and Albertini (2002)

ASSESSMENT

As with the student with multiple and visual disabilities, assessment of the student with multiple disabilities and hearing impairments requires sophisticated procedures (Jones & Jones, 2003). Standardized nonverbal tests which may be used in the assessment of hearing impaired students include: WISC-R for the Hearing Impaired (Anderson & Sisco, 1976); Hiskey Nebraska Test of Learning Aptitude (Hiskey, 1966); Leiter International Performance Scale (REVISED) (LEITER-R) (Leiter, 1969; Roid & Miller, 1997); Columbia Mental

Maturity Scale (Burgemeister, Blum, & Lorge, 1972); Merrill Palmer Revised Performance Tests (Roid & Sampers, 2004) and Stanford Achievement Test Hearing Impaired Version (Gallaudet Research Institute, 1996). Since it is unlikely that any one test instrument will provide enough information to determine a student's strengths and weaknesses, the assessment of students with hearing impairments is best approached from an ecological, multifactor perspective that takes into account the individual needs of the student (Gallaudet Research Institute, 1998; Marschark et al., 2002; Westling & Fox, 2004). The emphasis of assessment and intervention for students with hearing impairments is on communication development. Ideally, the assessment of children with hearing impairments and multiple disabilities should be conducted by a team of examiners from a variety of disciplines ensuring a transfer of knowledge and skills across disciplinary boundaries (Gallaudet Research Institute, 1998; Folsom, 2000).

Assessment of functional hearing is also an important component to the complete assessment of the student with multiple disabilities and hearing impairments. Instruments such as the Auditory Behavior Index (Northern & Downs, 2002) can be adapted easily for students with multiple disabilities.

For the English language learner student with multiple disabilities and hearing impairments, assessment is not as difficult, since nonverbal assessment procedures are usually employed. Structured observations of the student performing daily life routines is the most valuable means of gathering data on students potential. Using materials and skills that are most common to the student's environment is recommended. For example, when evaluating object/picture matching with a Puerto Rican student with multiple disabilities and hearing impairments, the teacher must use objects that are familiar to the student, such as matching pictures with foods like mangos, pineapples, guavas, plantains, acerolas, and coconuts. Clearly, sensitivity to cultural differences during the assessment is necessary.

INTERVENTION

Intervention for students with multiple disabilities and hearing impairments is primarily focused toward the development of communication and the enhancement of auditory potential (Stewart & Kluwin, 2000; Strassel, 2003). Various communication systems, including oral, gestural, and symbolic modes are used with students who are hearing impaired. The most frequently used with students with multiple disabilities and hearing impairments include gestural, sign, augmentative communication systems and computers. Of course, if there is residual hearing, amplification is the desired treatment.

For students from language minority cultures, special sign systems may be employed. Although American Sign Language (ASL) is the most commonly used signing system, translation of those signs into Spanish have become necessary for families and students of limited English proficiency (Schirmer, 2001). Most bilingual/bicultural programs in deaf education introduce ASL as the first language and teach English as a second language (ESL) through the written form with little use of spoken English (Turnbull et al., 2002). Bilingual/bicultural programs emphasize the acquisition of two languages, ASL and English, and two cultures, deaf and hearing culture (Schirmer, 2001).

According to Schirmer (2001), most individuals with a hearing loss can benefit from some form of amplification due to technological improvements in the field. Hearing aids make sounds louder by converting the acoustic energy into an electrical signal, increasing the magnitude of the electrical signal and then converting the magnified electrical signal back into acoustic energy. There are many types of hearing aids available, including hearing aids worn behind the ear, in the ear, in the ear canal, and built into eyeglasses (Turnbull et al., 2002).

According to Marschark (2001), by 1997, more than 9,000 adults and 700 children worldwide had received cochlear implants. Unlike hearing aids, cochlear implants do not make sounds louder. These electronic devices compensate for damaged hair cells in the cochlea by stimulating the auditory nerve fibers which enables the person with a hearing impairment to perceive sound (Connor & Zwolan, 2004). Cochlear implants have an internal part that is surgically implanted under the skin with electrodes inserted into the cochlea and an external part that is worn like a hearing aid. Accumulating evidence suggests that cochlear implants hold significant promise for improving the speech perception skills, speech production and oral language development of children who derive no significant benefit from conventional amplification (Cheng, Grant, & Niparko, 1999; Connor &

Zwolan, 2004). The use of cochlear implants in children has generated much controversy given that many adults in the deaf community view deafness as a cultural difference and not as a disorder that needs to be cured (Schirmer, 2001).

DUAL SENSORY IMPAIRMENTS

Although most often referred to as students with deaf-blindness, it is important to note that deaf-blindness rarely means total loss of vision and hearing (Silberman, Bruce, & Nelson, 2004). It is far more common for individuals labeled deaf-blind to have some functional hearing and/or vision (Prickett & Welch, 1995). Further, the intellectual level of students with dual sensory impairments ranges from giftedness to profound mental retardation. According to federal legislation (IDEA, 34 CFR 300.7[c][2]) "deaf-blindness means concomitant hearing and visual impairments, the combination of which creates such severe communication and other developmental and educational needs that they cannot be accommodated in special education programs for children with deafness or children with blindness."

Furthermore, the Helen Keller National Center (n.d.) defines a student who is deaf-blind as an individual:

1. who has a central visual acuity of 20/200 or less in the better eye with corrective lenses, or a field defect such that the peripheral diameter of visual field subtends an angular distance no greater than 20 degrees, or a progressive visual loss having a prognosis leading to one or both these conditions;
2. who has a chronic hearing impairment so severe that most speech cannot be understood with optimum amplification, or a progressive hearing loss having a prognosis leading to this condition; and
3. for whom the combination of impairments described in clauses (1) and (2) cause extreme difficulty in attaining independence in daily life activities, achieving psychosocial adjustment, or obtaining a vocation.

Today, Rubella is no longer the leading cause of deaf-blindness. Rather, it occurs from prematurity in infancy, genetic syndromes (CHARGE, Usher), infectious causes (meningitis, cytomegalovirus, encephalitis, rubella), and multiple anomalies (asphyxia, trauma, fetal alcohol syndrome) (Silberman, Bruce, & Nelson, 2004).

ASSESSMENT

The assessment needs of students with deaf-blindness are similar to those of students with multiple disabilities and visual impairments or hearing impairments. Few instruments are available that are specifically designed for assessing students with dual sensory impairments. However, the Callier-Azusa (Stillman, 1985), the Callier-Azusa: H (Stillman & Battle, 1985), the INSITE Developmental Checklist (Morgan et al., 1989); and the Assessment, Evaluation, and Programming Systems Measurement for Birth to Three Years (Bricker, 2002) are the most frequently used scales for this population. Additionally, Nelson, van Dijk, McDonnel, and Thompson (2002) provide guidelines for assessing a child's behavioral or alertness states, including:

• orienting responses to outside stimuli;
• preferred sensory learning channels;
• like and dislikes;
• memory;
• social interactions; and
• communication.

Finally, assessments such as the *Dimensions of Communication* designed to meet the needs of children who communicate at the nonsymbolic and symbolic level should also be used in assessing students with deaf-blindness, and should be related closely to curriculum development (Marr & Sall, 1999).

Assessment of sensory intactness in deaf-blind students can be done by using functional vision instruments previously mentioned (Erin; 1996; Langley, 1998; Topor, Rosenblum, & Hatton, 2004; Zambone et al., 2000), and by using functional auditory assessment instruments designed for use with students with dual sensory impairments and multiple disabilities (Siegel-Causey, 1996).

INTERVENTION

Educational programs for deaf-blind students have been discussed in many books and articles (see Giangreco, Edelman, & Nelson, 1998;

Giangreco, Edelman, Nelson, Young, & Kiefer-O'Donnell, 1999; McInnes, 1999; Silberman, Bruce, & Nelson, 2004; van Dijk, 1986; Visser, 1998; Wyman, 2000). Similar to the program priorities for students with multiple disabilities and visual or hearing impairments, the student who is deaf-blind will require intervention in the areas of visual and auditory training (Sims-Tucker & Jensema, 1984), orientation and mobility (Geruschat, 1980), social and communication development (Bruce, 2002; Janssen, Riksen-Walraven, & van Dijk, 2003; Nelson, van Dijk, McDonnell, & Thompson, 2002).

Perhaps one of the most commonly used approaches to educational programming for deaf-blind students has been developed by van Dijk (1986). The major philosophy guiding the van Dijk approach is its emphasis on the attachment or bonding process between a child and an adult and the child's motivation for environmental exploration. The attachment component of the curricula includes three steps:

1. Co-active movements and responsiveness ("hands-on" method of shared movement with child and adult in as many daily living activities as possible);
2. Structuring the child's daily routine (structuring daily living routines and building a sequence of expectations);
3. Characterization (providing the child with the opportunity to develop an association with the adult through use of an "ear-ring" or recognizable such as a pipe for the father, a scarf for the mother, and a bowl for the sister) (van Dijk, 1986).

When students become aware of their control over the environment, the educational goal is the development of a formal system of communication. A variety of formal communication systems can be used depending on the degree of visual and auditory impairment evidenced by the deaf-blind student. Table XVII outlines the most commonly used communication systems used by persons who are deaf-blind. However, for more severely involved students with deaf-blindness, more concrete and pragmatic ways of communicating must be used.

Intervention strategies for culturally and linguistically diverse students who are deaf-blind have not been documented in the literature. If the student is non-English speaking, communication systems such as the alphabet glove method (see Table XVII) will have to be taught in

Table XVII
MOST COMMONLY USED COMMUNICATION SYSTEMS
FOR PERSONS WHO ARE DEAF-BLIND

System	Description
Palm Writing	Block letters printed on palm of hands
Fingerspelling	One manual sign for each letter of the alphabet
Morse Code	Dots and dashes signaled gesturally, transmitted to any part of the body
Braille Hand Speech	Reproduces Braille dots in palm
Sign System	Hand over hand in accordance to customary sign language, also used with spoken communication for total communication approach
Glove Method	Glove with letters and numbers imprinted upon surface of the palm, sender touches area of glove assigned to the letter
Tadom Method	Hand on face of person for sensing speech sounds
Braille	Traditional Braille system
Typing and Script Writing	Traditional typing and script-writing
Telephone Communication	TTDs or TTYs covert type input to an audio-frequency which is converted back to letter/Braille
Augmentative Communications Systems	Including symbol systems (e.g. Bliss, Rebuses); picture communication boards, electronic communication boards, speech-output communication systems, etc.

Adapted from Bullis (1986)

the student's native language. For students with more severe disabilities who are ELL and deaf-blind, functional signs and gestures can more easily be taught to the family with the use of a translator. For example, an ELL student who is taught a sign for "eat" can use that sign at home to represent the Spanish word "*comer*" even if the parents are non-English speakers. However, the syntax sequencing of two or more words does require the teachers to understand the basic elements of Spanish. To further illustrate, an ELL child who wants to communicate the phrase "hot water" during a dishwashing lesson, would sign "*agua caliente*," thus reversing the syntax.

The major role of the teacher is to communicate with the parent in their native language and instruct them in the use of signs. This instruction has been most successfully done in parent groups with other families of children who are deaf, and are instructed by a bilingual teacher using sign books printed in Spanish (McLean & Mendez, 1986).

For students who require a total communication approach (speech and sign) to language, the teacher will need to speak in basic Spanish phrases. Silberman and Correa (1989) have developed a list of common Spanish-English survival words and phrases to be used by non-Spanish-speaking teachers who work with Hispanic families and students with multiple disabilities. The list provides the teacher with vocabulary often associated with the education of students with multiple disabilities, such as medication (*medicina*), seizures (*convulciones*), and visual impairment (*impedimentos de vision*).

CONCLUSION

This chapter has reviewed a variety of assessment and intervention strategies used in educating students with multiple disabilities and sensory impairments. These students have typically been considered the most difficult population to educate, due to the severity and multiplicity of their impairments. The education of students with multiple disabilities requires teachers to not only have skills in generic teaching practices for educating students with severe disabilities but, also specific knowledge of sensory impairments, alternative communication systems and orientation and mobility techniques. Ideally, families and professionals should be involved in a collaborative effort to provide an optimal educational and home environment for developing independence and enhancing the quality of life of these individuals (Milian & Erin, 2001).

For students and families from culturally and linguistically diverse backgrounds, the educational process becomes more complex. The field of special education for culturally diverse students with severe disabilities is in its infancy. The future directions of research and personnel preparation must bring into focus the importance of cultural patterns associated with culturally and linguistically diverse populations and provide educators with the tools to most effectively intervene with diverse students with multiple disabilities and their families.

DISCUSSION QUESTIONS

1. List the causes and prevalence of sensory impairments among children.
2. Define the following terms: legally blind, partially sighted, conductive hearing loss, sensorineural hearing loss, mixed hearing loss.
3. List two assessment instruments appropriate for evaluating the following groups of students with multiple disabilities: (a) multiple disabilities/visually disabilities, (b) multiple disabilities/hearing impaired, and (c) deaf-blind.
4. What assessment instruments are available for assessing functional vision and hearing in students with multiple disabilities?
5. Provide three appropriate curricular objectives for each of the following groups of students with multiple disabilities: (a) multiple disabilities/visually disabilities, (b) multiple disabilities/hearing impaired, (c) deaf-blind.
6. Discuss the broadened definition of orientation and mobility for students with multiple disabilities.
7. Discuss the major components of the van Dijk approach for educating students who are deaf-blind.
8. Define the following terms associated with the van Dijk theory: (a) co-active movement, (b) ear-ring", (c) "hands-on" method.
9. List and describe the communication systems most often used with persons who are deaf-blind.
10. What special considerations must a teacher take into account when working with the families of culturally and linguistically diverse students with multiple disabilities?

REFERENCES

Anderson, B., & Sisco, F. H. (1976). *Standardization of the WISC-R performance scale for deaf children.* Washington, DC: Gaulladet University.

Baca, L. M., & Cervantes, H. T. (2003). *The bilingual special education interface* (4th Ed.). Columbus, OH: Merrill.

Benoff, K. (2001). *Compendium for assessing the skill and interests of individuals with visual impairments or multiple disabilities.* New York: Lighthouse.

Bishop, V. E. (2004). *Teaching visually impaired children* (3rd ed.). Springfield, IL: Charles C Thomas.

Blasch, B., Wiener, W., & Welsh, R. (1997). Foundations of orientation and mobility (2nd Ed.). New York: American Foundation for the Blind.

Bobath, B., & Bobath, K. (1984). The neurodevelopment treatment. In D. Stratton (Ed.), *Management of the motor disorders of the children with cerebral palsy.* Philadelphia: J. B. Lippincott.

Bradley-Johnson, S. (1994). *Psychoeducational assessment of visually impaired and blind students: Infancy through high school.* (2nd Ed.). Austin, TX: Pro-Ed.

Bricker, D. D. (2002). *AEPS measurement for birth to three years.* Baltimore: Paul H. Brookes.

Brigance, A. (1983). *Brigance diagnostic comprehensive inventory of basic skills* (Revised 1999). North Billerica, MA: Curriculum Associates.

Browder, D. M. (2001). *Curriculum and assessment for students with moderate and severe disabilities.* New York: Guilford Press.

Brown, D., Simmons, V., Methvin, J., Anderson, S., Boigon, S., & Davis, K. (1991). *The Oregon project for visually impaired and blind preschool children* (5th Ed.). Medford, OR: Jackson County Education Service District.

Bruce, S. (2002). Impact of a communication intervention model of teachers' practices with children who are congenitally deaf-blind. *Journal of Visual Impairment and Blindness, 96*, 154–169.

Bullis, M. (Ed.) (1986). *Communication development in young children with deaf blindness.* Monmouth, OR: Oregon State System of Higher Education, Deaf-Blind Communication Skills Center.

Burgemeister, B., Blum, L., & Lorge, I. (1972). *Columbia mental maturity scale.* New York: Harcourt Brace Jovanovich.

Cheng, A. K., Grant, G. D., & Niparko, J. K. (1999). Meta-analysis of pediatric cochlear implant literature. *Annals of Otology, Rhinology & Laryngology, Supplement 177*, 124–128.

Christensen, K. (2000). *Deaf plus: A multicultural perspective.* San Diego, CA: Dawn Sign Press.

Connor, C. M., & Zwolan, T. A. (2004). Examining multiple sources of influence on the reading comprehension skills of children who use cochlear implants. *Journal of Speech, Language, and Hearing Research, 47*, 509–526.

Correa, V., & Heward, W. (2003). Special education in a culturally diverse society. In W. Heward, *Exceptional children: An introduction to special education* (7th Ed., pp. 86–119). Upper Saddle River, NJ: Merrill/Prentice Hall.

Cross, P., Spellman, C., DeBriere, T., Sizemore, A., Northam, J., & Johnson, J. (1981). Vision screening for persons with severe handicaps. *Journal of the Association for Persons with Severe Handicaps, 6*, 41–49.

Downing, J. E. (2003). Accommodating motor and sensory impairments in inclusive settings. In D. Ryndak, & S. Alper, *Curriculum and instruction for students with significant disabilities in inclusive settings* (p. 411–430). Boston: Pearson.

Downing, J. E. (2004). Communication skills. In F. E. Orelove, D. Sobsey, & R. K. Silberman, *Educating children with multiple disabilities: A collaborative approach* (4th Ed., pp. 529–561). Baltimore: Paul H. Brookes.

Dunst, C. (1980). *Uzgiris and Hunt Infant Psychological Development Scale (IPDS): Dunst Revision.* Austin, TX: Pro-Ed.

Ellis, D. (1986). The epidemiology of visual impairment in people with a mental handicap. In D. Ellis (Ed.), *Sensory impairments in mentally handicapped people* (pp. 3–34). San Diego, CA: College-Hill Press.

Erin, J. (1996). Functional vision assessment and instruction of children and youths with multiple disabilities. In A. L. Corn & A. J. Koenig (Eds.), *Foundations of low vision: Clinical and functional perspectives* (pp. 221–245). New York: AFB.

Erin, J., Fazzi, D., Gordon, R., Isenberg, S., & Paysse, E. (2002). Vision focus: Understanding the medical and functional implications of vision loss. In R. Pogrund & D. Fazzie (Eds.), *Early focus: Working with young children who are blind or visually impaired and their families* (2nd Ed., pp. 52–106). New York: American Foundation for the Blind Press.

Ferrell, K. A. (1985). *Reach out and teach.* New York: American Foundation for the Blind.

Fewell, R. R., & Langley, M. B. (1984). *The developmental activities screening inventory II.* Austin, TX: Pro-Ed.

Figueroa, R. (2002). Toward a new model of assessment. In A. Artiles & A. Ortiz (Eds.), *English language learners with special education needs: Identification, assessment, and instruction* (pp. 51–64). McHenry, IL: Delta Systems.

Folsom, R. C. (2000). Interdisciplinary team assessment for young children with possible hearing loss. In M. J. Guralnik (Ed.), *Interdisciplinary clinical assessment of young children with developmental disabilities.* Baltimore: Paul H. Brookes.

Foy, C. J. (1991). *English/Spanish basics for orientation and mobility instructors.* New York: American Foundation for the Blind.

Gallaudet Research Institute. (1996). Stanford Achievement Test (9th ed.), Form S. *Norms Booklet for Deaf and Hard of Hearing Students.* Washington, DC: Gallaudet University.

Gallaudet Research Institute. (1998). *Considerations in evaluating deaf children and youth.* Retrieved December 5, 2004, from http://gri.gallaudet.edu/~catraxle/INTELLEC.html.

Gallaudet Research Institute. (2003, December). *Regional and national summary report of data from the 2002-2003 annual survey of deaf and hard of hearing children and youth.* Washington, DC: GRI, Gallaudet University.

Gee, K. (2004). Developing curriculum and instruction. In F. E. Orelove, D. Sobsey, & R. K. Silberman, *Educating children with multiple disabilities: A collaborative approach* (4th Ed., pp. 67–114). Baltimore: Paul H. Brookes.

Geruschat, D. R. (1980). Orientation and mobility for the low functioning deaf-blind child. *Journal of Visual Impairment and Blindness, 74*, 29–33.

Giangreco, M., Edelman, S., & Nelson, C. (1998). Impact of planning for support services on students who are deaf-blind. *Journal of Visual Impairment and Blindness, 92*(1), 18–30.

Gold, D. (2002). *Finding a new path: Guidance for parents of young children who are visually impaired or blind.* Toronto, Ontario, Canada: Canadian National Institute for the Blind.

Griffiths, R., & Huntley, M. (1996). *Griffiths mental development scales* (Rev. Ed.). England: Test Agency Limited.

Helen Keller National Center (n.d.). *Who we serve.* Retrieved December 6, 2004, from http://www.hknc.org/AboutUsWHOWESERVE.htm.

Hiskey, M. (1966). *Hiskey Nebraska test of learning aptitude.* Austin, TX: Pro-Ed.

Holbrook, M. C. (1996). *Children with visual impairments: A parents' guide.* Bethesda, MD: Woodbine House.

Holden-Pitt, L., & Diaz, J. A. (1998). Thirty years of the annual survey of deaf and hard of hearing children and youth: A glance over the decades. *American Annals of the Deaf, 143,* 72–76.

Huebner, K., Merk-Adam, B., Stryker, D., & Wolfe, K. (2004). *The national agenda for the education of children and youths with visual impairments, including those with multiple disabilities.* New York: American Foundation for the Blind.

Individuals with Disabilities Education Act Amendments (IDEA). (1997). Regs: Definitions of Term and Acronyms. Pub. L. No. 015-17, 20 U.S.C. § 1400 et seq. Retrieved December 6, 2004, from http://www.cec.sped.org/law_res/doc/law/regulations/glossaryIndex.php.

Janssen, M. J., Riksen-Walraven, M., & Van Dijk, J. P. M. (2003). Contact: Effects of an intervention program to foster harmonious interactions between deaf-blind children and their educators. *Journal of Visual Impairment & Blindness, 97,* 215–229.

Johnson, H. (2004). *Shortages and demographic changes require new approaches: The preparation of qualified deaf education teachers: What states should know. Special education workforce watch: Insights from research.* Retrieved December 3, 2004, from http://www.coe.ufl.edu/copsse/policyfiles/PB-03.pdf.

Jones, T. W., & Jones, J. K. (2003). Educating young deaf children with multiple disabilities. In B. Bodner-Johnson, & M., Sass-Lehrer, *The young deaf or hard of hearing child: A family centered approach to early education.* Baltimore: Paul H. Brookes.

Karchmer, M.A., & Allen, T.A. (1999). The functional assessment of deaf and hard of hearing students. *American Annals of the Deaf, 144,* 68–77.

Kirchner, C., & Peterson, R. (1981). Estimates of race-ethnic groups in the U.S. visually impaired and blind population. *Journal of Visual Impairment and Blindness, 75,* 73–76.

Langley, M. A. (1998). *Individualized systematic assessment of visual efficiency.* Louisville, KY: American Printing House for the Blind.

Leiter, R. G. (1969). *The Leiter international performance scale.* Chicago, IL: Stoelting.

Lewis, S., & Russo, R. (1998). Educational assessment for students who have visual impairment with other disabilities. In S. Sacks & R. Silberman (Eds.), *Educating students who have visual impairments and other disabilities* (pp. 39–72). Baltimore: Paul H. Brookes.

Marr, H., & Sall, N. (1999). *Dimensions of communication.* Paterson, NJ: Authors.

Marschark, M. (2001). Context, cognition, and deafness: Planning the research agenda. In M. D. Clark, M. Marschark, & M. Karchmer (Eds.), *Cognition, context and deafness* (p. 179–198). Washington, DC: Gallaudet Press.

Marschark, M., Lang, H. G., & Albertini, J. A. (2002). *Educating deaf students: From research to practice.* New York: Oxford University Press.

McInnes, J. (1999). *A guide to planning and support for individuals who are deaf-blind.* Toronto, Ontario, Canada: University of Toronto Press.

McLean, M., & Mendez, A. (1986, November). *Working with Hispanic parents of deaf children: Cultural and linguistic considerations.* Paper presented at the meeting of the CEC Symposia on Ethnic and Multicultural Concerns, Dallas, TX.

Milian, M. (2001). Schools' efforts to involve Latino families of students with visual impairments. *Journal of Visual Impairments and Blindness, 95,* 389–402.

Milian, M., & Erin, J. (2001). *Diversity and visual impairment: The influence of race, gender, religion, and ethnicity on the individual.* New York: American Foundation for the Blind.

Morgan, E. C., Watkins, S., Terry, B. G., Snow, P. S., Boyle, P., Watts, J., et al. (1989). *The INSITE developmental checklist.* Logan, UT: SKI-HI Institute.

Nelson, C., van Dijk, J., McDonnell, A. P., & Thompson, K. (2002). A framework for understanding young children with severe multiple disabilities: The van Dijk approach to assessment. *Research and Practice for Persons with Severe Disabilities, 27*(2), 97–111.

Northern, J. L., & Downs, J. P. (2002). *Hearing in children* (5th ed.). Baltimore: Williams & Wilkins.

Orelove, F. E., Sobsey, D., & Silberman, R. K. (2004). *Educating children with multiple disabilities: A collaborative approach* (4th Ed.). Baltimore: Paul H. Brookes.

Ortiz, A., & Yates, J. (2002). Considerations in the assessment of English language learners referred to special education. In A. Artiles & A. Ortiz, (Eds.), *English language learners with special education needs: Identification, assessment, and instruction* (pp. 65-86). McHenry, IL: Delta Systems.

Perla, F., & O'Donnell, B. (2002). Reaching out: Encouraging family involvement in orientation and mobility. *Review, 34*(3), 103–109.

Pogrund, R. & Fazzie, D. (2002). *Early Focus: Working with young children who are blind or visually impaired and their families* (2nd Ed.). New York: American Foundation for the Blind Press.

Prickett, J. G. & Welch, T. R. (1995). Deaf-blindness: Implications for learning. In K. M. Huebner, J. G. Prickett, T. R. Welch, & E. Joffee (Eds.), *Hand in hand: Essentials of communication and orientation and mobility for students who are deaf-blind* (pp. 289–312). New York: American Foundation for the Blind.

Rainforth, B. & York-Barr, J. (1997). *Collaborative teams for students with severe disabilities: Integrating therapy and educational services.* Baltimore: Paul H. Brookes Publishing Co.

Reynell, J., & Zinkin, P. (1979). *Reynell-Zinkin developmental scales for visually handicapped children.* Chicago, IL: Stoelting Co.

Roid, G. H., & Miller, L. J. (1997). *Leiter International Performance Scale-Revised* (LEITER-R). Wood Dale, IL: Stoelting.

Roid, G. H. & Sampers, J. (2004). *Merrill-Palmer-Revised* (M-P-R). Wood Dale, IL: Stoelting.

Ryndak, D., & Alper, S. (2003). *Curriculum and Instruction for Students with significant disabilities in inclusive settings* (2nd Ed.). Boston: Allyn & Bacon.

Sacks, S. & Silberman, R. (1998). *Educating students who have visual impairments and other disabilities.* Baltimore: Paul H. Brookes.

Schrimer, B. R., (2001). *Psychological, social and educational dimensions of deafness.* Boston: Allyn & Bacon.

Sheridan, M. D. (1976). *Stycar vision.* Windsor: NFER-Nelson.

Siegel-Causey, E. (1996). *Assessing Young Children with Dual Sensory & Multiple Impairments (Ages Birth-Five) Assessment Guidelines* Vol. 1. Columbus, OH: GLAR-CDB.

Silberman, R. & Correa, V. (1989). Survival words and phrases for professionals who work with students who are bilingual and severely/multiply handicapped and their families. *Journal of the Division of Physically Handicapped, 10,* 57–66.

Silberman, R. K., Bruce, S. M., & Nelson, C. (2004). Children with sensory impairments. In F. E. Orelove, D. Sobsey, & R. K. Silberman, *Educating children with multiple disabilities: A collaborative approach* (4th Ed., pp. 425–527). Baltimore: Paul H. Brookes.

Sims-Tucker, B. & Jensema, C. (1984). Severely and profoundly auditorially /visually impaired students: The deaf-blind population. In P. Valletutti & B. Sims-Tucker (Eds.), *Severely and profoundly disabilities students: Their nature and needs* (pp. 269–317). Baltimore: Paul H. Brookes.

Sparrow, S. S., Balla, D. A., & Cicchetti, D. V. (1984). *Vineland Adaptive Behavior Scales -Expanded.* Circle Pines, MN: American Guidance Service.

Spungin, S. (2002). *When you have a visually impaired student in your classroom: A guide for teachers.* New York: American Foundation for the Blind.

Stewart, D. A., & Kluwin, T. N. (2000). *Teaching deaf and hard of hearing students. Content, strategies, and curriculum.* Needham Heights, MA: Allyn & Bacon.

Stillman, R. (1985). *Callier-Azusa Scale (G) Scales for the assessment of cognitive development.* Dallas:, TX: University of Texas, Callier Centre for Communication Disorders.

Stillman, R., & Battle, C. (1985). *Callier-Azusa Scales (H): Scales for the assessment of communicative abilities.* Dallas, TX: University of Texas.

Strassel, G. L. (2003). The role of the early interventionist. In B. Bodner-Johnson, & M. Sass-Lehrer, *The young deaf or hard of hearing child. A family centered approach to early education.* Baltimore: Paul H. Brookes.

Sugai, G., Horner, R. H., Dunlap, G., Heineman, M., Lewis, J. J., Nelson, C. M., et al., (2000). Applying positive behavioral supports and functional behavioral assessments in schools. *Journal of Positive Behavioral Interventions, 2*(3), 3–27.

Swallow, R., Mangold, S., & Mangold, P. (1978). *Informal assessment of developmental skills for visually handicapped students.* New York: American Foundation for the Blind.

Topor, I., Rosenblum, L., & Hatton, D. (2004). *Functional vision assessment and age appropriate learning media assessment.* Chapel Hill, NC: Early Intervention Training Center for Infants & Toddlers with Visual Impairments. FPG Child Development Institute, University of North Carolina.

Turnbull, R., Turnbull, M., Shank, M., Smith, S., & Leal, D. (2002). *Exceptional lives. Special education in today's schools.* Upper Saddle River, NJ: Merrill Prentice Hall.

U.S. Department of Education. (2003). *Twenty fourth annual report to congress on the implementation of the Individuals with Disabilities Education Act*. Washington, DC: Author.

Utley, B. L. (1994). Providing support sensory, postural, and movement needs. In L. Sternberg (Ed.), *Individuals with profound disabilities: Instructional and assistive strategies* (3rd Ed., pp. 123-192). Austin, TX: Pro-Ed.

van Dijk, J. (1986). An educational curriculum for deaf-blind multi-disabilities persons. In D. Ellis (Ed.), *Sensory impairments in mentally handicapped people* (pp. 374–382). San Diego, CA: College-Hill Press.

Vervloed, M. P. J., Hamers, J. H. M., Van Mens-Weisz, M. M. & Timmer-van de Vosse, H. (2000). Revision of the Reynell-Zinkin scales for young visually handicapped children. In C. Stuen, A. Arditi, A. Horowitz, M. A. Lang, B. Rosenthal, & K. R. Seidman (Eds.), *Vision rehabilitation, assessment, intervention and outcomes* (pp. 161–165). Lisse, The Netherlands: Swets & Zeitlinger.

Visser, T. (1998). Educational programming for deaf-blind children: Some important topics'. *Deaf-Blind Education, 2,* 4–7.

Vulpe, S. G. (1994). *Vulpe Assessment Battery-Revised* (VAB-R). East Aurora, NY: Solosson Educational Publications.

Ward, M. E. (2000). The visual system. In M. C. Holbrook & A. J. Koenig (Eds.), *Foundations of education: Instructional strategies for teaching children and youths with visual impairments* (Vol. I, pp. 325–337). New York: American Foundation for the Blind Press.

Warren, D. (1994). *Blindness and children: An individual differences approach*. Cambridge, England: Cambridge University Press.

Westling, D. L., & Fox, L. (2004). *Teaching students with severe disabilities* (3rd Ed.). Upper Saddle River, NJ: Pearson/Merrill.

Wolfe, K. (2001). National agenda implementation in action. *Journal of Visual Impairment & Blindness, 95*(5), 308–310.

Wyman, R. (2000). *Making sense together*. London, England: Souvenir Press.

Zambone, A., Ciner, E., Appel, S., & Graboyes, M. (2000). Children with multiple impairments. In B. Silverstone, M. A. Lang, B. P. Rosenthal, & E. E. Faye (Eds.), *The lighthouse handbook on vision impairment and vision rehabilitation* (Vol. 1, pp. 451–468), New York: Oxford University Press.

Chapter 7

CULTURALLY AND LINGUISTICALLY DIVERSE FAMILIES

RACHEAL A. GONZÁLES

CREATING PROACTIVE PARTNERSHIPS BETWEEN FAMILIES, SCHOOLS AND COMMUNITIES

Of all man's group memberships, the family is the most important because it is the initial and primary vehicle for assessing the group's cultural heritage to the child (Diggs, 1974, p. 583). Family plays a basic role in shaping and developing social values in children. After the family, Berger (2000) points out that school is the most important agent of socialization for the child. While the involvement of families in the education of their children with disabilities has been a goal for professionals since the initial passage of special education legislation, families from culturally and linguistically diverse (CLD) backgrounds continue to face major obstacles in becoming recognized as key stakeholders in the special education process. For effective partnerships to occur, the culture, history, and values of the individual child with disabilities and the parents must be taken into consideration. In this chapter, the following topics will be addressed:

- Legislative landmarks.
- Defining families.
- The family's understanding of disability.
- The impact of having a child with a disability on the family.
- Deterrents to culturally and linguistically diverse parent participation and advocacy in schools.

- A paradigm shift: Moving away from traditional parent involvement
- Strength-based approach to family, school and community partnership

LEGISLATIVE LANDMARKS

The issue of team partnership and parental rights was first introduced into special education with the passage of The Education for All Handicapped Children Act in 1975 (EAHCA), (P.L. 94-142). This comprehensive legislature act initiated on behalf of individuals with disabilities specified a provision that legally ensured parents the right to participate in the special education process (Yell, 1998). The six principles of the law are:

1. **Free Appropriate Public Education (FAPE)**–for all children with disabilities that include "specially designed instruction, at no cost to the parents, to meet the unique needs of the child with a disability" and the related services the student needs in order to benefit from specially designed instruction (Bateman & Bateman, 2001, p. 9).
2. **Appropriate Evaluation**–multidisciplinary team to determine whether the child needs special education and related services and a written notice to the parents in their native language. Tests and other procedures must be selected and administered so as not to be discriminatory on a racial or cultural basis.
3. **Individualized Education Program (IEP)**–an individually tailored educational plan written for a child with a disability that is developed, reviewed and revised by a team which includes the parents and student when appropriate.
4. **Least Restrictive Environment (LRE)**–educational placement that will best meet the child's needs; presumption that it should be with nondisabled peers.
5. **Parent and Student Participation in Decision Making**–involving parents and students as partners in the decision-making process gives them the opportunity to have an active voice in the special education process. Parents participate on issues of evaluation, eligibility and placement. Students can participate by expressing his/her preferences and interests, particularly during the transition-planning meeting (Turnbull & Turnbull, 1998).
6. **Procedural Due Process**–provides procedures to resolve disagreements between parents and schools; ensures that information is provided for parents and student to make a decision regarding the child's educational program (Bateman & Bateman, 2001).

Every ten years the original intent of The Education for All Handicapped Children Act (EAHAC) has been reviewed in order to see what has worked well and what needs to be changed. The first reauthorization of EAHAC was in 1986, with The Education of the Handicapped Amendments (P.L. 99-457), which added services to children from birth through five years of age with developmental delays. The regulation states that the multidisciplinary teams must consider not only the concerns and preferences, but also the service and support needs, of parents and others family members as well as those of the infant or toddler receiving services. Under this law the Individualized Family Service Plan (IFSP) was designed to give parents an equal voice in planning and deciding their child's education (Yell, 1998).

In 1990, Congress changed the name of the original law to Individuals with Disabilities Education Act (IDEA). Provisions in IDEA (P.L. 101-476) continued to strengthen parental rights while adding provisions for transitional services for youth as well as adding autism and traumatic brain injury to the categories of special education. Another significant change to this legislation was changing all references from "handicapped children" to "children with disabilities" thus identifying children with disabilities as "people first" (Smith, 2004).

The 1997 reauthorization of IDEA (P.L. 105-17) further strengthened parent and student participation in the decision-making process by specifying that parents give consent for evaluation and initial placement of their child, be instrumental in designing the IEP and to provide information to the school about their child. The reauthorization also encouraged students to participate in designing their IEP by expressing their goals and interests, particularly during the transition-planning meeting (Turnbull & Turnbull, 1998).

IDEA 97 also ensured that children with disabilities would have access to the general education core curriculum and that parents would receive regular reports during the school year regarding the progress their child was making toward meeting their IEP goals. Another key element of the IDEA 97 encouraged parents and educators to work out their differences by using nonadversarial dispute resolution (Bateman & Linden, 1998, p. 3).

The reauthorization of the Elementary and Secondary Education Act, which is now known as No Child Left Behind Act (NCLB) was instituted across the nation in 2001 (U.S. Department of Education, 2002). Besides stating that children with disabilities must be full participants in state and district testing with accommodations or modifications as determined by the individualized education program team, NCLB also requires schools to involve families in ways that will help their children achieve success in schools by communicating to them their children's academic progress. NCLB defines parental involvement as regular, two-way, and meaningful communication between parents and schools to ensure that parents are full partners in their children's educational experience (Yell & Drasgow, 2005).

IDEA was again reauthorized in 2004 as Individuals with Disabilities Education Improvement Act (IDEIA), (P.L. 108-446). While IDEIA 2004 presents many changes, the basic six principles remain the same. One of the major changes in the 2004 reauthorization is the removal of benchmarks and short-term objectives that are used to measure progress toward the annual IEP goals. Only those students with the most significant cognitive disabilities and who take alternative assessments will be allotted the benchmarks and short-term objectives. Even if short-term objectives are not mandated by law, parents can still request their child's IEP team to identify them as a means to measure their child's progress. Another critical issue facing parents is that they now must state any concerns they may have about possible emotional and behavioral issues related to their child during the IEP meeting. Parents will need to make sure that their concerns are documented if support services are necessary in the future. The burden of proof whether the child's disability affects the ability to understand his/her actions has also been shifted to the parents where previously it was the responsibility of the school to prove that the behavior was not manifested by the student's disability. Parents will also need to be attentive about asking for procedural safeguard notice as that information will no longer be automatically distributed with the IEP team notice or upon reevaluation (IDEA, 2004; Mandlawitz, 2005).

With the passage of IDEA 2004, calling on parents to take more of an initiative in the decision-making process, schools must be sure to provide culturally and linguistically diverse parents the opportunities to learn about the new changes and the expectations that are being placed on them. This calls on school districts to act responsible by providing opportunities for families to become engaged in learning about the changes in the language that is understood by them and within the cultural context of the families.

DEFINING FAMILIES

The changing demographics of schools from predominantly mono-lingual English speaking to one of diverse cultures and languages calls for schools to view parental involvement different from the tradition-al Anglo-Saxon middle class perspective. As the demographics of schools are changing so is the makeup of families. One of the issues educators need to take into consideration is not only how the com-munity defines family but also how do families from diverse back-ground define family (Cartledge, Kea, & Ida, 2000).

The 2000 U.S. Bureau of the Census composed a legal definition of family as two or more persons related by birth, marriage, or adoption who reside in the same household, a relationship they clarified as determined by blood or contact. For many families from culturally and linguistically diverse backgrounds that definition does not describe their living situation. Their view of family is a dynamic social system which includes the people who think of themselves as part of the family, whether related by blood or marriage or not, and who sup-port and care for each other on a regular basis (Lian & Aloia, 1994; Turnbull & Turnbull, 2001).

In many communities, churches of various denominations and com-munity agencies that provide support to families living with a child with a disability are considered a part of the extended family. Fiesta Educativa, a support group for Spanish-speaking families with special needs children plays a critical role in the everyday challenges the immediate and extended family face. As a support group Fiesta Educativa relies on parent advocates to develop supportive networks and formulate strategies for intervening in schools (Rueda & Martinez, 1992). Another example of an excellent supportive organization is SPRED, Special Religious Education Department in the Diocese of Oakland, California (2005), which reaches out to parish communities to welcome children, teens and adults with special needs into parish life. Organizations such as Fiesta Educativa and SPRED are examples of how the definition of family grows and the impact they have in each other's lives.

This expansion of what makes up a family may cause some schools difficulty in that they do not know how to work with multiple mem-bers of a family. In the same light, families may not understand why individuals they consider as family members may not be welcomed in school meetings such as the IEP. Schools would benefit greatly by acknowledging the cultural make-up of families and respecting how these extended family members help the family cope with the demands of raising a child with disabilities. Extended members of a family unit provide invaluable support to families that range from economic, emotional, and spiritual support to the much-needed respite support (Dunst, Trivette, & Deal, 1994; Salend & Taylor, 1993).

THE MEANING OF DISABILITY

Across society parents from culturally and linguistically diverse cultures interpret or apply their own meaning to their child's disability, ideas of family, and decision-making techniques, in addition to using languages other than English (Policy Research Brief, 2001). Every family has its own unique beliefs and values about disabilities, illness and health (Gartner, Lipsky, & Turnbull, 1991; Hansen, Lynch, & Wayman, 1990; Kalyanpur & Harry, 1999; Linan-Thompson & Jean, 1997). How a parent interprets the terminology used in describing their child's behavioral or learning disabilities is seldom if ever considered when planning and providing services for the child (Harry, 1992b; Hendricks, 1997; Kalyanpur & Rao, 1991).

Educators need to understand that families from diverse backgrounds may have an understanding of the term *disability* from a different cultural context than the mainstream, middle class, North American standards (Hendricks, 1997, p. 40). Not understanding this position puts families again in the receiving end of information instead of being viewed as an essential contributing member of the decision-making team (Smith, 1990). To provide culturally appropriate family support calls for educators to recognize that the perspectives and interests of family members are different and that educators need to have an understanding of both the meaning of the disability and the nature and roles of families and ways in which families can be supported (Gartner, Lipsky, & Turnbull, 1991). Instead of simply assuming that families are in denial when they question the terms and labels being applied by the educational and medical systems, educators must make an effort to understand the families' cultural context of what makes up a disability (Mosert, 1998; Salend & Taylor, 1993; Thorp, 1997). A family may explain a disability as a family idiosyncrasy such as "Uncle Jose has always acted that way but look he has a good job and he is a good member of the community." Professionals (Correa, 1989; Ferguson & Ferguson, 1987; Hansen, 1992; Harry, 1992a; Lynch & Stein, 1987) working with families can make a difference in building relationships with them if they explore and understand the family's beliefs and practices regarding their child's disability. Alper, Schloss, and Schloss (1995) state that having the knowledge and understanding about a family's decisions on childrearing, their utilization of social services, the search for medical care and their views of their child's role in society can assist educators in reaching out to the families and making culturally appropriate recommendations for the child and family.

The process in which a parent comes to an understanding of their child's disability is an individual experience that will have a significant impact on how they are involved in making decisions for the child's well-being. Understanding the make-up and dynamics of a family can help schools develop parent partnerships that are positive learning experiences for both family and school (Epstein & Salina, 2004). A step in that direction is for educators to listen respectfully without making any judgments on parents' experiences and views of their child's disability and work together to provide the best educational program and services for the child.

IMPACT ON A FAMILY

The impact on a family when a child is born with a disability or a child is diagnosed with a disability is a significant life stressor that has a profound affect on all members of the family (Berger, 2000; Doberman, 1998; Hurtig, 1994; Lynch & Stein, 1987; Poston, Turnbull, Park, Hasheem, Marquis, & Wang, 2003; Turnbull & Turnbull, 2001). For families dealing with issues of homelessness and poverty the impact of having a child with a disability places the family at a greater disadvantage (Fuller, 2003; Olson & Pavetti, 1996). Ferguson and Asch (1989, p. 108) claim that as children are labeled the parents are often associated with the disability of their child and not seen as a separate individual.

Research (Gartner, Lipsky, & Turnbull, 1991; Hanson, Lynch, & Wayman, 1990; Turnbull & Turnbull, 2001) has shown when a parent is informed that their child has been diagnosed with a disability they need time to assimilate, understand and adjust to the information they have been presented. Sources of stress include financial problems, emotional ties within family, limitations of family activities/social life and nurturing children who may require skilled medical care. Families with children with disabilities often face serious financial difficulties so they may stay on a job, giving up career decisions for reasons of insurance and stability or they lose their job due to absences related to taking care of their child. Living in a home with a child with disabilities requires parents to have detailed plans of the day's activities, leaving little time to take care of personal needs causing parents to feel over-committed, stressed and guilty for not taking care of the whole family (Bauer & Shea, 2003; Turnbull & Turnbull, 2001).

In conversations with families, Gonzáles, Johnson, and Suitor (2003) found that parents often felt a sense of being violated by professionals such as doctors, therapists and educators who have total access to the lives of their children and subsequently, every aspect of their family life because of the nature of the disabilities involved. Parents also felt that by having their homes open to the various specialists there was a complete lack of privacy, as their lives appeared to be under a microscope for everything they did and said. The parents also stated that most professionals had little understanding of how carefully they had to plan their daily routine to meet the many challenging needs of a child with a disability from juggling appointments to various medical specialists to searching for information on education, health services, day care programs or simply a "child friendly" place to eat. Parents also commented that the responsibility of taking care of their child was not over at 3:00 p.m. but that it was a 24-hour, 7 days a week responsibility. Thus, an issue such as homework was not necessarily a priority for them. The parents stated that it wasn't that they didn't care about the homework their children had to complete but they were often physically exhausted from trying to balance taking care of the special needs of their child and the rest of the family. The Spanish-speaking parents involved in these conversations commented that they wanted to help their children with homework but they were not able to because all of the work was in English.

The matter of siblings can also (Alper, Schloss, & Schloss, 1995; Bauer & Shea, 2003; Powell & Gallagher, 1993) add stress to the family interaction if siblings feel the need to compete for their parent's attention due to the care and time the brother or sister with the disability requires from the parents. Depending on the interrelationships within the family, siblings can either have a negative reaction to having a brother/sister with special needs or they can play a positive and critical role in the family by modeling appropriate behavior, coaching their brother or sister in daily activities, and being a source of power and inspiration (Meyer, Vadasy, & Fewell, 1985).

Every aspect of a family's life is affected to different degrees when a diagnosis of disability is given to a child. For families from diverse backgrounds the impact and stress is compounded by issues of cultural differences, language issues, available resources and the lack of experience with an educational system that requires them to be active participants in their children's educational planning (Hassan & Gardner, 2002; Lynch & Stein, 1987; Winzer & Masurek, 1994).

DETERENTS TO CLD PARENT PARTICIPATION AND ADVOCACY IN SCHOOLS

The Meeting

One of the key factors blocking parent participation in the special education process is the language and professional jargon used by educators (Hendricks, 1997; Kalyanpur & Harry, 1999). There are many conflicting interpretations of diagnostic categories, labels and technical terms used in special education that do not always translate accurately or sensitively to a family's culture and language (Bauer & Shea, 2003; Bennett, 1988). Not only do parents have to deal with the language of special education itself but must also deal with the material and meetings being conducted in English, which is often the language of the school and teacher, not of the parent.

The structure of IEP meetings often place the parents as passive recipients of information instead of equal partners while the educational jargon used by professionals gives them the status and authority (Mehan, 1983; Nieto, 2000; Smith, 1990). These types of meetings result in parents feeling intimidated and alienating them even more from the school activities (Calabrese, 1990; Harry, Allen, & McLaughlin, 1995).

Although special education procedures state that schools should make every effort to hold meetings at a time that fit the parents schedule, parents frequently complained to Gonzáles, Johnson, and Suitor (2003) that IEP meetings were determined by the school personnel with little or no regard to their ability to meet at that time and day. Meetings between parents and professionals are often scheduled on the basis of what works best for the professionals instead of what works best for the family. Parents who are working at one or two low-level jobs may risk losing those jobs to attend a school meeting scheduled in the middle of the day (Bernheimer, Weisner, & Lowe, 2002; Harry, Allen, & McLaughlin, 1995). Educators may interpret a parent not attending a meeting as the family not making their children a priority instead of reevaluating their procedures in setting up meetings.

It is also critical to recognize how unequal family resources can influence parental involvement and therefore, student placement and achievement opportunities (Hansen & Carta, 1995; Lynch & Stein, 1987; Olson & Pavetti, 1996). The lack of a telephone or access to a regular mailbox easily adds stress to families and breaks down the line of communication between them and schools (Sherman, Amey, Duffield, Ebb, & Weinstrin, 1998). The issue of where IEP meetings are held can be problematic for parents who live a distance from their child's school. Parents who take public transportation often endure long trips, several bus transfers and unpredictable bus schedules to get to school at a time that was determined by the school personnel. Parents may live in an area where public transportation is not even available or easily accessed. For many educators, the idea that a parent could not find some form of transportation to get to their child's school is not within their realm of reality. Once parents finally arrive to the meeting they may face a group of professionals who want to move quickly to their reports, allowing little or no time for discussion or questions from parents. At this point, due to the climate of the meeting, many of the parents forego any contribution to the IEP process. The attitude in which parents are welcomed to a meeting can play a positive step in helping families not only feel at ease but also reinforce that their role in the meeting is indeed essential.

When parents are asked during the meeting to report on progress regarding previous recommendations given to them at an IEP, they may feel embarrassed or guilty about not having been able to follow through with the recommendations but do not feel at ease in sharing the reason with the school (Harry, 1992b). Teachers who do not understand the possible cultural implications of the parent's lack of follow-through may, in fact, have their perceptions of parents not being capable enough to participate in the decision-making process reinforced and thus place the parent in a lesser role (Thorp, 1997; Utley, Delquadri, Obiakor, & Mims, 2000).

As educators we must reserve judgment on families and follow the advice of a group of parents who stated that professionals need to "walk a mile in our shoes" before passing any judgment on parents (Gonzáles, Johnson, & Suitor, 2003).

Cross-Cultural Communication Styles

Interpersonal communication style differences and language barriers can lead to misunderstandings between culturally and linguistically diverse families and school personnel (Hendricks, 1997; Kalyanpur & Harry, 1999; Winzer & Masurek, 1994). For schools to have effective partnerships with families they must become aware of the level of cultural context that families use in their communication with non-family members (Lynch & Hansen, 1992; Misra, 1994; Salend & Taylor, 1993). Anthropologist Edward T. Hall (1976) identified cultures on a continuum ranging from high context to low context according to the way individuals in that culture communicated.

The structure of most IEP meetings do not allow for families to have a "platica" or small talk about family matters, to tell the story about events in their life. Instead, the meeting is pretty straightforward; assessment reports, progress and recommendations are generally directed by school staff leaving the parent out of the process. Observing the interactions in an IEP meeting between families from a high context culture and school personnel from a low context culture exemplifies the misunderstandings that can occur when communication styles are not understood or appreciated. Nonverbal communication, such as eye contact, facial expression, gestures, and posture, is considered more important than words in the high context cultures. A parent may nod their head out of respect to what the professional is saying and not necessarily that they are agreeing with what is being said. For families from this group interpersonal relationships are emphasized. They see developing trust as an important first step to taking any kind of action such as signing an IEP. High context cultures prefer group harmony and consensus to individual achievement. Families within the high context culture would not think of interrupting a meeting by asking questions or they may defer questions or recommendations to the teacher as they see him/her as the expert and would not consider disrespecting the profession by questioning their abilities or recommendations (Inger, 1992). On the other spectrum, low context cultures emphasize presenting information in a concise, direct manner with discussions based on fact rather than intuition. Low context cultures expect discussions to be straightforward with the end result being some type of action taken place such as parents signing the IEP or agreeing with the school on recommendations for their child. Low context cultures "may be uncomfortable with long pauses and silences, cryptic sentences, and indirect modes of communication such as storytelling . . . feeling they are time-wasters or signs of resistance" (Lynch, 1992, p. 45).

In any type of meeting where communication styles are not understood, the family's communication may be seen as uncooperative, noninterested or taking too much time while the school personnel may be viewed by the parents as being too impersonal and out-of-step with their child's needs (Hall, 1976; Lawrence-Lightfoot, 2003). To have a better understanding of communication styles and behaviors, it would benefit the school to contact a cultural informant who could be a resource liaison to both the parents and the school as a means to ease the confusion and frustration that arises when individuals do not understand each others' communication style.

Unqualified Interpreters and Translators

Schools often feel that they are indeed communicating effectively with parents who do not speak English simply by providing an interpreter/translator. IDEA clearly states that schools must do everything possible to provide information to families in their native language if one is needed or requested. Often individuals being used as interpreter/translator have had little or no training as to the role and responsibilities they play in an IEP meeting. Schools often make the assumption that anyone that speaks the language of the parents will be able to step in and facilitate the presentation of information in the parents' native language. While an individual may be used as both a translator and interpreter, it is important for school personnel to understand that both require strong technical skills. A translator is one who changes written information from the primary language to the second language. An interpreter changes the spoken message from the primary language to the second language (Langdon, 1994). The basic qualifications needed by an individual who will serve as interpreter/translator include effective communication skills in English, the ability to function in the cultures of the two languages, and native or near native language skills in the target language (Fradd, 1993, p. 163). The individual should also have an understanding of the United States culture, the culture of the non-English-speaking community, the culture of the school, and finally, a participant level understanding of the culture (Fradd, 1993, p. 173). Another key factor to consider when looking for an interpreter/translator is that the individual should have competent knowledge of the field of special education and the language encompassing the field. Schools should be careful in choosing who will act as the interpreter as often critical and confidential information will be presented that families may not want to have shared. Not only should schools make every effort to never place a child in the role of interpreter, caution should also be taken when placing family members in that role as doing so could place the entire family into a stressful and insecure situation (Lynch, 1992).

If an interpreter/translator is going to be used in a meeting, it is important to inform all members of their presence. It is critical to understand that any type of interpretation will require more time thus it is imperative that individuals not lose patience or become frustrated at the process by making comments or displaying negative facial gestures or body language regarding how long the meeting is taking. For a more effective meeting all translated reports should be shared with the interpreter before the meeting for a smoother transition between speakers. School personnel need to keep in mind that speaking too fast, having more than one conversation at the same time, or speaking directly to the interpreter instead of the parents can make the job of the interpreter very difficult leading to a nonproductive school meeting where both parties are frustrated with the process. If schools truly want parents' input into the decision-making process then the use of qualified interpreters or translators must be given the respect and time required to communicate effectively with parents who need this service.

Fathers—A Neglected Resource

One group that is often overlooked in parental involvement is the role fathers play in forming partnerships with schools, as they generally are not seen as part of the big picture of parent involvement. Until recently, the school community discounted the value and importance of how a father's involvement benefited their children's schooling instead causing fathers to feel like they were being treated like second-class citizens in educational settings (Gallagher, Cross, & Scharfman, 1981; Hennon, Olsen, & Palm, 2003; Lamb & Meyer, 1991). Society has overwhelmingly accepted fathers as being the economic providers and mothers as the nurturers and caretakers within the family structure. The new focus is not to lessen the role of the mother in children's lives, but rather to highlight the fact that fathers being actively involved in their children's lives play a critical part in their overall development (Bauer & Shea, 2003; Turnbull & Turnbull, 2001). The National Center on Fathers and Families (1997) stressed that if society is truly interested in changing the culture of fathers being involved in schools then it must reach out to fathers of color, low income, and working class. The Center went on to report that fathers from African American and Latino populations are currently overrepresented in studies of father absences and underrepresented in studies of father presence and involvement.

Research conducted by the National Household Education Survey (U.S. Department of Education, 1997) looked at the extent to which fathers were involved in their children's K-12 grade school. The results of the research confirmed that children whose fathers were positively involved in their school activities completed more school and had stronger emotional and cognitive developments. Schools, families and communities would greatly benefit from tapping into the tremendous knowledge and skills fathers could bring with their involvement in their children's schools. In order to have fathers from diverse backgrounds involved in school, the schools must embrace a cultural understanding of their parental role, which may not be typical of the Anglo middle-class father (Hennon, Olsen, & Palm, 2003).

Los Compadres, a group of Latino fathers in Northern California have been meeting for several years to discuss and put into action how they can become more involved in their children's education, school and community. These fathers have taken part in literacy programs in their children's schools, attended seminars to better understand their rights and responsibilities within the IEP process and have been active members in planning and implementing family/community-based activities. When asked why they had never volunteered in their children's school before the fathers responded that "they had never been asked" and when they did attend school functions, they were "never made to feel welcomed."

Hennon, Olson, and Palm (2003) suggest that "engaging fathers to learn their strengths, hearing their stories, taking advantage of their stock of knowledge, participating in their lives, and appreciating their family themes and parenting strategies" is a step in recognizing fathers as positive role models (p. 315). Schools and communities working together would both gain from having fathers actively engaged in meaningful activities that could result in their children developing a stronger sense of learning, reaching higher achievement and leading a productive independent life. A father of a child diagnosed with multiple disabilities shared that his involvement in his daughter's life had given him the opportunity to be an active participant in the decision-making process instead of being on the sidelines always waiting for others to tell him what was going on with his daughter. When the author asked him how he became involved, the proud father replied, "I was invited."

A PARADIGM SHIFT

Moving Away from the Traditional Parental Involvement

Parental involvement has long been pictured, as a mother who does not have to work, is able to stay at home to take care of the children and is available to meet the schedules and needs of her child and the school (Berger, 2000). Schools have used various terms such as school partnerships, parent-teacher association (PTA), and parent empowerment to describe parents participating in their children's school activities. Regardless of what term is used, the involvement of parents in a child's education has long been recognized as a critical component to the child's school readiness and success regardless of family income, education or cultural background (Berger, 2000; Epstein & Salina,

2004; Henderson, 1987; Turnbull & Turnbull, 2001). Research has found that parents, who create a positive learning home environment for their children, demonstrate a sincere interest in their children's education and follow through with school requirements, such as homework, increase their children's opportunities for academic success (Epstein, 2001; Henderson & Berla, 1994).

Parents from diverse backgrounds may not respond to traditional methods for establishing parental partnership. The level of parent involvement being asked of by schools is a new experience to many of the families who may hold different views about schooling, their role in their child's education and the educational meaning and impact of disability (Harry, Kalyanpur, & Day, 1999; Linan-Thompson & Jean, 1997). Too often schools expect families and community members to become involved in schools as a natural process of having their child in school. For families who do not understand this expectation their nonparticipation in school activities are often seen as not caring about education. Harry's (1992b) and Chavkin's (1989) research state that culturally and linguistically diverse parents have a strong interest in their child's school yet may feel awkward when approaching school personnel. Families from other countries may not have any school experience in their home countries in order to base what schools in the United States are asking of them (Lynch & Stein, 1987). In fact, the schools their children attended may not have had any type of special education services available to them. The growing population of families from diverse backgrounds in schools has produced a growing disparity between the background of school personnel, the student body and parents (Calabrese, 1990). In de Valenzuela, Baca, and Baca's (2004) research, they found that "programs aimed at lower social economic status (SES) and culturally and linguistically diverse families have historically been based on a deficit model of family abilities and functioning" (p. 366). The work of Osterling, Violand-Sanchez, & von Vacano (1999) emphasize that "the persistent portrayal of the diverse family as deficient in the knowledge, skills and abilities necessary to prepare their children for school present enormous barriers to active parental participation" (p. 206). This type of thinking only serves to widen the distance between schools and families from culturally and linguistically diverse backgrounds participating in the special education process (Perez, 1991).

Families from diverse backgrounds often practice forms of parent involvement that mainstream school personnel may not always recognize. A parent participating with their child in a church function or simply sending their child to school daily is seen by the parent as involvement in their child's life. Schools need to capture those experiences as a means to make the connection with culturally and linguistically diverse families instead of trying to get families to adopt more dominant cultural approaches to school involvement (Moles, 1996). For an inclusive parent involvement to be effective (Correa, 1989; Delgado-Gaitan, 1991; Kalyanpur & Rao, 1991; Nieto, 2000), it is essential for schools and teachers to recognize and value the diversity of student and family beliefs, attitudes, cultural customs and values in the planning and implementation of an appropriate educational program.

A question that many schools ask is: Why is it so difficult to engage parents from diverse backgrounds into the special education process? The answer may lie in how schools think and act in relationship to these parents and school-community engagements (Inger, 1992; Nicolau & Ramos, 1990). Schools often interpret the culture of families through food, music, holidays, folklore, traditional dress and art as they are easily identified and observed. Building a relationship with families from diverse backgrounds requires that we have an understanding of the deeper levels of culture, which are generally not easily accessed and understood by members outside of the particular group. Besides family beliefs, attitudes, cultural customs, and values previously stated, deep levels of culture also includes ways of establishing relationships and interacting with others, concepts of time, sex roles, family organization and ways of conducting everyday business (Fradd, 1993, p. 99). If a teacher does not understand the dynamics of the deep culture he/she may project to a family that the information they offer about their child has little or no educational value or they treat the family as part of the disability, the opportunity to engage in the building of a respectful relationship is lost (Fradd, 1993; Marzoas, 1988). The special education process in itself is often difficult for families to understand but for those families who are newly immigrants, or non-documented, non-English speakers living in poverty with little or limited educational experience in their native country, the special education process is intimidating and unfriendly (Fuller, 2003; Hansen & Carta, 1995). If we truly believe that parents are the key stakeholders in their children's life then it is essential that we "begin by laying a foundation built of teachers engaging in activities that communicate sensitivity, trust, respect and acceptance to parents" (Rock, 2000, p. 32).

STRENGTH-BASED APPROACH TO FAMILY, SCHOOL AND COMMUNITY PARTNERSHIP

The first goal in establishing a parent partnership is to recognize parents from culturally and linguistically diverse backgrounds as more capable, supportive and responsible for making important and informed decisions about their child's education (McCaleb, 1997; Nieto, 2000). As schools are asking parents to become more directly involved in school activities, educators need to keep in mind the cultural patterns and beliefs which may impact how the family participates in the decision-making process (Delgado-Gaitan, 1991; Rodgers-Adkinson, Ochoa, & Delgado, 2003). A new model of partnership must be based on viewing a parent as a valuable resource not as a problem or another responsibility added to the teacher's workload or school's program (Bauer & Shea, 2003; Dunst, Trivette, & Deal, 1994).

Partnerships can be built when there is mutual respect, trust, open communication, shared responsibility and collaboration between families, schools and communities (Bauer & Shea, 2003; Davis, Brown, Bantz, & Manno, 2002; de Valenzuela, Baca, & Baca, 2004). Effective family support programs should aim to strengthen and protect the integrity of the family unit by emphasizing and promoting the unique strength of each individual family member (Dunst, Trivette, & Deal, 1994; Kalyanpur & Rao, 1991) while promoting the development of leadership within their community. The work of Harry, Allen and McLaughlin (1995, p. 106) point out that schools and communities should also assist families in identifying available resources that meet their specific needs instead of trying to fit families into existing programs and services that have been ineffective.

A prerequisite to effective family, school and community partnerships is reaching out to know and understand the family and the community in which they live. Both teachers and parents would gain from incorporating strategies built on knowledge gained from interacting with each other. Building cultural reciprocity with families asks that educators set aside their perceptions of the family until they have an opportunity to learn about the family's strengths, cultural values and practices (Davern, 1996; Harry, Kalyanpur, & Day, 1999; McCaleb, 1997; Turnbull & Turnbull, 2001). The following recommendations are presented as a means for educators to get to know the children and families in their schools.

Conversations with Families

The first step in cultural understanding is a willingness to be open to new perspectives and new views of the world (Lynch & Stein, 1987, p. 110). For this to be effective, Diggs (1974, p. 578) points out that there must be a common belief among parents and educators that there should be a close relationship in the child's growth and progress in the home and in his/her development through his/her years in schools.

Every parent has a story to tell about his or her experiences living with a child with a disability. Having a conversation can provide the opportunity for two people to make themselves understood through language by talking together. It requires that one truly considers the weight of the other's opinions, thoughts or beliefs without arguing the person down (Gadamer, 1992; Nicolau & Ramos, 1990). Conversations provide an opportunity for educators to gain a better understanding of the family system by providing parents the opportunity to ask questions, to articulate their thoughts and reach an understanding on a child's disability. Hearing stories from families about how various actions or inactions have affected the family can assist the educators in understanding their reluctance in becoming involved with the school system (Dennis & Giangreco, 1996). Having conversations with parents outside of the IEP process provides an opportunity for parent and teacher to engage in an informal dialogue without the time constraints and stress generally present in an IEP meeting. The purpose of a conversation is not to tell a parent what is wrong with their child instead it is an opportunity to listen to the parent, to hear their story. Gadamer (1992) states that one must also be prepared to suspend any preconceived thoughts or comparisons of his/her life to that of the family, only then can the possibilities of new understanding occur.

The author has found that parents are generally open to speaking about their children with a simple, "tell me about your child." Conversations held by the author with families from diverse cultural and linguistic backgrounds have allowed her to gain valuable insights into the strength and resiliency these families have in living with a child with a disability.

Understanding the pressure that educators have in meeting state standards and other school district responsibilities, having a conversation with a family may seem as a burden, but if schools are truly interested in including families from diverse backgrounds as decision-makers, they must also be open to truly learning about the family. Lawrence-Lightfoot (2003) states that "teacher and parents must work extra hard not to let . . . prejudice, ignorance, fear and social and economic hierarchies . . . obscure their clear sight of one another and distract them from focusing on the well being of the child" (p. 221).

Learning from Households through Home Visits

All families have strength and they should be recognized for what they are doing and have been able to accomplish. Home visits provide an opportunity to get to know and discover what educators and parents may have in common (Ascher, 1988; Davis, Brown, Bantz, & Manno, 2002; Dunst, Trivette, & Deal, 1994; Harry, Torguson, Katkavich, & Guerrero, 1993; Lynch & Hansen, 1992). Awareness of a child's home environment can help the teacher create learning activities that can be integrated into what is being taught in the school.

While early intervention programs have educators that typically make home visits in support of the child and family, other special education programs do not emphasize home visits as an integral part of their educational program. It is critical for professionals who develop programs for children to get input from the family and to have direct knowledge of the home setting when making recommendations for services or programs. When a teacher asks a student to perform certain activities at home and those activities are not carried out, the teacher may interpret the student's action as a lack of support or commitment on the part of the family where in fact the student was not able to complete the task because the materials, tools, resources, even physical space were not available to him/her. A home visit by the teacher can provide him/her with the necessary information to design an appropriate program that can be implemented by the student and family (Chang, Lai, & Shimizu, 1998; Rodgers-Adkinson, Ochoa, & Delgado, 2003).

Assumptions are often made about families who are homeless or living in lower economic communities as not caring for their children or having lower expectation of them (Berger, 2000; Harry, Torguson, Katkavich & Guerrero, 1993; Salend & Taylor, 1993). A research project carried out by Moll, Amanti, Neff, and González (1992) explored the social and intellectual resources surrounding Latino families. The researchers found that families had various types of experiences and knowledge capable of providing their children opportunities to learn. Moll et al. defined *Funds of Knowledge* as "the essential cultural practices and bodies of knowledge and information that households use to survive, to get ahead, or to thrive" (p. 21). The information gathered in this research was used to develop and implement instruction based on the knowledge and skills that the students brought with them to school directly from their families and community.

A home visit would allow professionals to view the world of his/her students from their perspective not to make judgments but to look at the strengths of the family and what they value as a family unit. Having those insights and understanding could certainly produce a different type of IEP meeting where family concerns are put into perspective with the end result being a more productive parent-teacher relationship.

A Field Trip through your Students Community

How can teachers who live outside of their teaching assignment get to know the community of their students? Elba Maldonado-Colón (1999, p. 22) contends, "When teachers do not understand the community and cultural background of the children they teach, their efforts to reach them by referring to the community and background can reveal cultural gaps between teachers and their students."

Many children in special education are bused outside of their home school into a community that is often very different from their own. Oftentimes teachers do not really know or are even aware of their student's experiences—what happens in the homes and in the communities of the children they teach (Thorp, 1997). Teachers may have stereotypes or make assumptions about the student and parents based on what he/she has heard from others but not from direct personal contact with the community. Those assumptions can lead the teacher to consciously or unconsciously lower her expectations of her students and their families.

Fradd (1993) reports that "examining the differences and similarities between the interactional styles and cultures found in students' communities and the performance expectations of the school can be insightful in understanding why some students may be having difficulty" (p. 131). McCaleb (1997) claims that it is the teacher who must be responsible for initiating and fostering a home-school partnership by recognizing and accepting the strengths that students and families have already developed from within their community. A field trip to a student's community can yield valuable information that can be incorporated into conversations with the student and parents as a means to gain a better understanding and appreciation of the family and community.

A community field trip can be held on any day that the educator has time to be an observer. One of the best ways to carry out this community field trip is to have a student or a member of the community act as a guide. By visiting the community during different times of the day one has the opportunity to observe a variety of activities and the ways the community changes throughout the day (Fradd, 1993). Points of interests to observe can be the type of print noted in the community; where it is located; what kinds of colors are noted; what services are found within or nearby this community; what type of special events occur in the neighborhoods; what type of businesses are located in the community; what kind of public transportation is available; is there a bank or public library located in the area; are the sidewalks accessible for wheelchairs; is the presence of a police force more visible than other public agencies; is there a park with vegetation in the community, is there easy access to the community? The list is endless of what one could observe and learn by taking a walk around the student's community.

Educators who have taken the time to observe the community of students they work with reported that their assumptions about the community changed as they gained a new appreciation and respect for their students, their families, and the community they call home. Several teachers reported to this author that they never realized the effort it took in order for their students to arrive at school every day.

One special educator described the route her students had to go through to get to school as "a combat zone something that I never imagined." Another special education teacher noted that several of her students knew the procedures of sending money through Western Union to family members outside of the United States. She in turn not only developed Math and Social Studies lessons around that experience but also invited the Western Union personnel who happened to be members of the community to speak about their experiences during Career Week.

With the stress on all educators to improve student performance based on scripted programs, one might wonder how they could possibly integrate community information into an already tight structured teaching day. The integration of such observations into the routine of a classroom asks teachers to scaffold and bridge new learning paradigms not only for the students but also for themselves. Simple actions such as using a community calendar to count numbers in math, taking pictures of different print in the community to help students with letter recognition or having quality literacy books in different languages in the classroom can be steps in furthering the relationship between teachers, students, and their community. The genuine integration of the strengths of a community into the daily activities of a classroom validates the existence of the family and student as members of that unique community.

KOREAN AMERICAN FAMILIES OF CHILDREN WITH DISABILITIES: PERSPECTIVES AND IMPLICATIONS FOR PRACTIONERS
HYUN-SOOK PARK

Introduction

A partnership between parents and schools has long been regarded as essential in the education of students with disabilities (Kroth, 1987; Park, Turnbull, & Park, 2001). As our schools serve more students from culturally and linguistically different backgrounds, it is inevitable that teachers and other professionals will deal with diverse cultures which are often unfamiliar to them. In such cases, parents and families can become valuable resources to teachers and other professionals in conducting culturally sensitive educational assessment and developing programs.

Despite the importance of family involvement, however, professionals have failed to establish a successful partnership with families from nonmainstream cultural backgrounds (Delgado-Gaitan, 1991; Harry, 2002; Turnbull & Turnbull, 2001). This is probably because these families may have not responded to the traditional methods for establishing family-school partnerships (Harry, 1993; Kalyanpur & Harry, 1999). Our current programs to involve parents have targeted mainly English-speaking middle-class families (Lynch & Stein, 1987; Salend & Taylor, 1993). Harry (1993) found that parents from culturally diverse backgrounds possessed cultural perspectives and expectations that were different from mainstream families, which prevented them from collaborating with educational professionals. Fortunately, literature dealing with perspectives of families from diverse cultural backgrounds has increased over the past decade (e.g., Delany-Barmann, Prater, & Minner, 1997; Harry, 1992; Herbert, Mayhew, & Sebastian, 1997; Heller, Markwardt, Rowitz, & Farber, 1994; Lo, 2005; Shapiro & Simonsen, 1994; Sileo & Prater, 1998).

Yet, there is little information available on the families of Korean American students with disabilities. Ironically, Korean American families and students have received fair amount of attention as model immigrants and high achievers. On the other hand, Korean American students with disabilities have been obscured by this well-publicized stereotype. Professionals, including teachers, need to have a better understanding of the Korean American families of children with disabilities if they are to provide better service and education to such children.

The following section discusses information that will help professionals understand better where Korean American families come from when dealing with the educational system in the U.S. It will primarily focus on recently immigrated Korean American families and their children. However, this section, by no means, characterizes all Korean Americans or their families. Rather, the information should serve as background information which may help professionals seek explanations of certain behaviors in Korean American families (Park & Yount, 1994). In other words, professionals should view the following cultural perspectives as a set of framework that families may apply when interacting with others (Anderson & Fenichel, 1989; Salend & Taylor,

1993). In addition, implications for teachers and professionals are described.

CULTURAL TRADITION AND DISABILITY

Confucian values are among the cultural traditions that may affect perceptions and behaviors of many Korean American families both toward a disability and toward their participation in the education of their children with disabilities. The following section discusses the influences of Confucian values on the families and its implications for professionals, including teachers.

Confucian Values

Description

Confucian values are the principles observed in Confucianism which developed from the teaching of Confucius (551–479 B.C.) and his disciples in China. Confucianism is concerned with the principles of good conduct, practical wisdom, and proper social relationships (Yutang, 1994). This system of thought influenced people's attitude toward life, and set the standard of social values and social order from China to Korea, Japan, and Indochina. Confucianism is not considered a religion, but is a philosophy and ideology. The principles of Confucianism are explained in the nine ancient Chinese works handed down by Confucius and his disciples. Confucian virtues include love (or translated as humanity), righteousness, propriety, integrity, and filial piety (Yutang, 1994). These virtues set a system of well-defined social relationships with one another.

> These mean love in the parents, filial piety in the children, respect in the younger brother, friendliness in the elder brothers, loyalty among friends, respect for authority among subjects, and benevolence in the rulers. (Yutang, 1994, p. 209)

A person who observes these social rules is supposed to do everything with "propriety." A person who possesses all these virtues becomes a "perfect gentleman" who achieves a perfect balance in life.

The "perfect gentleman" is also supposed to achieve the "universal moral order" (Chung-yung), usually translated as "the Mean." Chung-yung places an entire "harmony" in the life of a "perfect gentleman" who finds the true central harmony and balance in his moral being (Yutang, 1994). In education, Confucius advocated "education for all without class distinction", which is remarkable for the feudal period in which he lived (Yutang, 1994).

Influences and Implications

Influenced by these Confucian virtues (social rules), many Koreans follow strict social and behavioral codes when interacting with others. These social rules are defined by a person's gender, age, and relative status. For example, a person who observes the Confucian social rules would first identify his/her position in relation to another person considering gender, age and status. For example, a person would ask the following questions: "Who is the authority figure?" "Who is older?" "Is there difference in gender?" Then a person would behave strictly according to the proper rules assigned to the structure of a relationship (cf., Fiske, 1992). For example, a person would interact with an authority figure with respect and with no confrontation. He/she may not give eye contact because eye contact is considered a sign of disrespect.

It is common for many Korean American parents of children with disabilities to follow the behavioral code given in the example above when they interact with professionals because they would regard the professionals as authority figures. They may be reluctant to express their disagreement because they consider disagreement as disrespectful confrontation. Their best purpose is to show respect and to preserve the harmony in the relationships. Therefore, it might be necessary for the professional to state that it is acceptable for the parents to express their disagreement. The professionals may also ask questions to the parents rather than expecting them to ask. It would be also important for professionals to create nonintimidating, yet respectful environments in order to encourage parents to share their input into educational programming. Professionals may ask the parents if they prefer to be addressed as Mr. _____ or Mrs. _____ rather than as their first names. In addition, using basic social phrases in Korean such as "Hello" and "thank you" would serve as ice breakers and may make the parents feel less intimidated.

In addition, Confucianism mandates that Koreans retain strong ties with families and extended families. Kinship and extended families can serve as strong support networks to families of children with disabilities. On the same token, however, Park (1995) found, in her ethnographic interviews with three Korean American families, that immigrant families of children with disabilities who did not have extended family members in the U.S. experienced more social stress than those families with extended family members in their communities. In addition, people experienced more severe social stress when they did not receive enough support from their own family members, particularly when the fathers of children with disabilities did not provide such support. Confucianism mandates distinct gender roles within the family. Therefore, the mothers of children with disabilities bear the whole responsibility for educating such children. Korean American mothers in these situations may experience more frustration when they do not have an access to external resources available due to their cultural and language barriers (Park, 1995). Similar findings on greater stress levels with Latino immigrant families were made (Heller, Markwardt, Rowitz, & Farber, 1994).

A large number of Korean American families expand their circles of extended families beyond their kinship and relatives, through participation in community organizations (e.g., church). Recently, these community organizations have taken leadership roles of providing resources to families with disabilities. Professionals may need to utilize these community organizations more effectively. For example, professionals may provide in-service training to the community organizations in order to connect the families with more resources. Teachers may include relevant members of these organizations as well as family members and significant relatives when developing an educational plan (e.g., by interviewing significant members for input and including them in the intervention plan for social-relationship building).

EXPECTATIONS FOR EDUCATION AND SOCIAL RELATIONSHIPS OF CHILDREN WITH DISABILITIES

Although many Korean American families have high academic expectations for their children's education, the families of children with disabilities were found to have realistic views toward their children's education (Park, 1992; Cho, 1993). When they were asked about their preferences in school curricular areas, most of these families responded that functional life skills were more important than academic skills. This pattern of parental preference was parallel to findings by Hamre-Nieptuski, Nieptuski, & Strathe (1992) who surveyed Caucasian families of children with severe disabilities. In addition, Korean American parents of lower grade elementary school children emphasized social goals than academic goals as a second priority to functional skills, whereas parents with such children in upper grade levels considered academic goals as the second most important priority (Park, 1992). Korean American parents of children with disabilities were also found to expect their children to work as hard as children without disabilities (Cho, 1993). This conflicts with Chan's (1986) previous findings that Asian parents were more permissive and had low expectations for children with disabilities. This incongruence implies that professionals may need to be cautious when attempting to apply the findings of studies with Asian families to Korean American families.

Many Korean American parents seem to expect their children to have friends both with and without disabilities (Cho, 1993; Park, 1995). They expect their children to have as many friends as possible to help the children socialize better and prepare them for future normalized environments. This provides important implications for teachers when facilitating socialization for Korean American students with disabilities. Teachers may need to consider facilitation of various types of socialization including children with and without disabilities. Our profession has paid too much attention to friendships only between children with disabilities and those without disabilities despite the fact that some children with disabilities develop valuable friendships with peers with disabilities (Harry, Park, & Day, 1998).

In addition, Korean American children with disabilities seemed to develop their friendships with nondisabled peers at churches while developing friendships with peers with disabilities at schools (Cho, 1993; Park, 1995). Therefore, it seems that churches can provide normalized social opportunities for some Korean American children. This finding provides teachers and other professionals with valuable implications when developing a plan for social opportunities for Korean American children with disabilities. Teachers and other professionals may need to encourage families who attend churches, to utilize the environment for outside-of-school social opportunities for their children with disabilities. This may be practical because the families do not then need to seek often unfamiliar social clubs, which are designed mostly for mainstream English-speaking families and take extra time away from their work and other responsibilities.

PARTICIPATION IN EDUCATIONAL SYSTEMS

Many Korean American families of children with disabilities agree that there are more services and educational opportunities available in the U.S. than in Korea for their children with disabilities (Cho, 1993; Park, Turnbull, & Park, 2001). Many Korean American families state that they immigrated to the U.S. for their children's education. Yet, their participation in the educational services seems very limited mainly because of cultural and language barriers (Cho, 1993; Park, 1995; Park, Turnbull, & Park, 2001). Another reason for not participating in the service system includes a lack of time due to inflexible and long work hours and other responsibilities as well as a lack of connection, information and advocacy skills (Cho, 1993; Park, 1995; Park, Turnbull, & Park, 2001). These findings, however, do not agree with previous findings in this area with other Asian American families. The reasons explained in the previous studies were the stigma attached to accepting services, emphasis on self-control, and subordination of self (Ishisaka, Nguyen, & Okimoto, 1985; Kinzie, 1985; Owan, 1985; Tung, 1985).

This new finding provides an important implication for the planning and coordination of services for Korean American families. More practical assistance and considerations should be made. For example, agencies may provide child care during meetings. There is a need to train more direct professionals to work closely with families and empower families by sharing information and resources. These professionals may include case managers, teachers, or parent advocacy group coordinators. It is more culturally appropriate and practical for professionals individually to converse with Korean American parents about their children rather than having the parents participate in support group meetings or seminars.

Korean American parents may have different expectations for professionals than other mainstream English-speaking families do. They may expect the professionals to provide guidance in helping their children's education. When information is shared by the professionals, they are more likely to implement the educational strategies and pursue the services more actively. In fact, some Korean American families said that they wanted teachers to tell them what to do at home in order to help their children's progress (Cho, 1993; Park, 1995). Teachers may need to work closely with Korean American families in order to facilitate the generalization and maintenance of appropriate skills taught to students.

TOWARD UNBIASED COLLABORATION

Although the information discussed so far helps professionals better understand the families of Korean American children with disabilities and facilitates collaboration with such families, there is a need for a framework which professionals can refer to when working with the families. The following guidelines are to serve that purpose (refer to Table XVIII). These guidelines would be helpful to professionals working with families from other different cultural backgrounds as well as with Korean families.

Step 1. Be familiar with information related to the culture, but do only use it as background information. Some behavioral codes and communication styles related to a particular culture (e.g., Korean culture) may help professionals stay open-minded when encountering behaviors that are not common to the mainstream culture. However, never use such behavioral codes and communication styles as a universal approach to all people fitting a certain profile. Judge each person as an individual.

Step 2. Begin communicating with the families. In discussions with families, ask direct questions rather than expecting the families to ask. This is the best way to obtain unbiased and valid input from the families. Explore explanations for their decisions and input. Respect their reasons and decisions. Acknowledge that you heard the information they provided.

Table XVIII
STEPS INVOLVED IN THE UNBIASED COLLABORATION PROCESS
WITH CROSS-CULTURAL FAMILIES

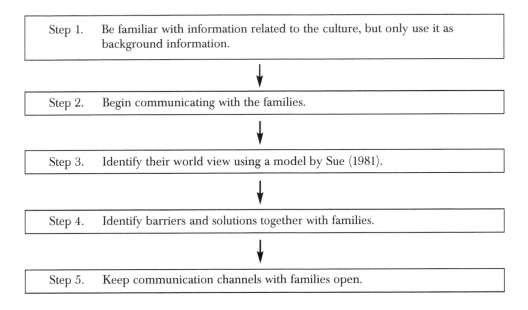

Step 1. Be familiar with information related to the culture, but only use it as background information.

↓

Step 2. Begin communicating with the families.

↓

Step 3. Identify their world view using a model by Sue (1981).

↓

Step 4. Identify barriers and solutions together with families.

↓

Step 5. Keep communication channels with families open.

Step 3. Identify their worldview using a model by Sue (1981). The world view model helps one to understand how an individual thinks and behaves in making decisions and interpreting events. This world view consists of attitude, value, and opinions, and it is influenced by cultural heritage, life experiences, socioeconomic factors, religious belief, and gender. Sue's world view model (1981) consists of two psychological orientations: locus of control (C) and locus of responsibility (R). Each orientation has two directions of force: internal (I) and external (E) force. Therefore, there are four different types of world views when combining two orientations with two different directions of force (2 x 2 = 4): Internal locus of control–Internal locus of responsibility (IC-IR); Internal locus of control–External locus of responsibility (IC-ER); External locus of control–internal locus of Responsibility (EC-IR); and External locus of control–external locus of responsibility (EC-ER).

Individuals who have an IC-IR world view believe that success is the result of one's own efforts and has a strong sense of control over what happens. These individuals rely heavily on personal resources for solving problems. While many western cultures encourage this type of world view, it is not surprising to see someone from Korea that would have this type of world view also. For example, Changho's family has been very active utilizing community resources (e.g., church) and available support network (e.g., relatives) to help Chris participate in a normalized environment as much as possible. They believe that what they do for Changho will make a difference in his life. They have a very positive view for Changho.

Individuals with an IC-ER world view realize that they are able to affect their children's lives if given a chance. They are well aware that external barriers such as discrimination or prejudice might still hinder their ability to succeed. Therefore, they do not participate in their children's education. For example, Sujin's parents clearly see the value of getting more involved in the educational process and they want to do so. However, they have not previously participated because they felt they did not have enough of a support system in their lives (e.g., lack of support from family). But they hope to get involved in the process in the future, which might never be possible. They tend to blame external sources rather than themselves for their lack of participation.

Individuals with an EC-IR world view accept the dominant culture's definition of self responsibility, but do not have any control over what is happening around them. These individuals live on the margins of two cultures, not freely partaking of either (Sue, 1981). For example, Jemin's parents understand it is their responsibility to use services and to participate in the educational process for the sake of their child's welfare. However, they are not motivated to do so probably because of their unsuccessful past experiences. They hope to regain confidence and actively participate in the system, but they are waiting to be motivated by somebody else. They take full responsibility for the outcome. They may not be aware of some external barriers that can be removed so that their participation can be more easily made successful. They are frustrated with themselves for not overcoming the difficulties. They may be too harsh on themselves.

Individuals with an EC-ER world view feel that they have no control over what is happening and feel that such obstacles are not their responsibility either. They feel helpless. For example, Tesoo's family has low self-confidence, and they do not take any responsibility either. They feel that they are the victims of the system.

Professionals can identify the world view that the families have by asking questions related to their experiences about the educational system. Examples of the questions include: What are the things you have tried in terms of working with schools? What were the outcomes? How did you feel about the outcome? Why? How do you perceive yourself participating in your child's education? What kinds of things can you think of doing? Why?

Step 4. Identify Barriers and Solutions Together with Families. Once professionals understand how families view their participation in their children's education and their world view, then they need to identify the barriers that prevent the families from actively participating in the education of their child. Each world view might suggest different types of solutions and collaborations. The types of solutions may vary depending on the kind of barriers that the families identify. If we take families mentioned above as an example, professionals may share related information with families only for Changho's family and may not need any substantial follow-up with them. Soojin's family, on the other hand, may need tangible supports such as linking them with other community resources where they can utilize child-care services during meetings. With Jemin's parents, professionals probably need to convince the families that external variables, not parents themselves, may be responsible for the unsuccessful experiences. They may want to identify the barriers as an initial task. Then, they can either provide tangible support if identified, or they can start with concrete action that is feasible and has a high probability of leading to success. For Tesoo's family, professionals may share many successful stories of children of similar functioning levels and may focus on a simple and concrete activity that would lead to success. It is often valuable for teachers to invite parents to the school and have them observe their children performing tasks that they might never have thought the children could do. In this way, the families can gain confidence and be motivated to continue the participation. At times, it might be necessary for professionals to refer the families to other professionals or networks in order to provide tangible support.

Step 5. Keep Communication Channel with Families Open. Professionals need to send a clear message to families that their feedback and input are always welcome and appreciated. This communication channel should be always open throughout the collaborating process even after whatever the solution was implemented. The following communication tips are derived from the literature (Anderson & Fenichel, 1989; Brower, 1986; Gallegos & Gallegos, 1988; Finders &

Lewis, 1994; LaFromboise & Graff, 1989; Nagata, 1989; Ramirez, 1989; Salend & Taylor, 1993) and from the ethnographic interviews by Park (1995):

1. Greet family in its native language, if possible.
2. Address parents by Mr. _____ or Mrs. _____.
3. Arrange seating so that every one is in close proximity to everyone else (e.g., round table over rectangle table)
4. Respect the thoughts of parents.
5. Be patient.
6. Allow enough time for parents and family members to express themselves openly and freely.
7. Provide, when necessary, an interpreter who understands the family's culture and needs, e.g., an individual from the same community as the family. Avoid asking young children to translate for their parents. It may create dysfunction within the family hierarchy.
8. Use humor and share your own similar experiences to establish trust and personal relationships.
9. Don't be afraid to ask questions.
10. State what you expect of the parents.
11. State what you expect of the child.
12. Realize the parents live with the child and can't go home at the end of day.
13. Avoid the standard clichés such as "I understand how you feel," "What I hear you saying is . . . ," or "This must be difficult for you but . . ."
14. Provide a structure for the meeting and explain the agenda.
15. Agree on the goals.
16. Define roles.
17. Meet parents on their own level and treat them with respect.
18. Be sensitive to parents and have a working knowledge of the grief cycle.
19. Accept your own feeling and limitations when working with parents and children with disabilities.
20. Recognize that parents are experts about their children.
21. Take into consideration of family activities and home experiences when developing programs.*

Endnote: The author wishes to thank Beth Harry for her input in the analysis and interpretation of ethnographic interviews with Korean American families. This work was supported in part by Cooperative Agreement No. H086A20003, the consortium for Collaborative Research on Social Relationships, awarded to Syracuse University, by the U.S. Department of Education, Office of Special Education Programs. However, the opinions expressed herein are not necessarily those of the Department of Education, and no official endorsement should be inferred.

FINAL THOUGHTS

The original intent of special education legislation was to have parents involved in the decision-making process of planning for their child's education. While much progress has been made in that area, families from culturally and linguistically diverse backgrounds still find barriers in place that keep them from being true partners when it comes to the decision-making process involved in special education. As educators we must first take a look at our own beliefs and values and how they may influence our interactions with individuals from another culture. Educators need to move away from the traditional ways of connecting with parents to a more proactive approach in bridging the gap between culturally and linguistically diverse families, schools and communities by recognizing the strength of our student's families and the communities they live in; celebrating their everyday accomplishments; integrating knowledge of the community into classrooms and embracing the richness of diversity. Schools are not alone in needing to create a paradigm shift to address the needs of parental involvement; teacher-training programs must also take a look at the way they train future special educators to collaborate with families from diverse backgrounds. Building an alliance with families based on respect and culturally responsive practices is a vital first step in demonstrating to parents that they are indeed critical members of the educational process.

DISCUSSION QUESTIONS

1. Describe the barriers that keep parents from participating in school activities. Provide your solutions in breaking down those barriers.
2. Explain why a family's understanding of their child's disability could have an impact on the types of services provided.
3. Discuss the benefits of having a conversation with a parent outside of the classroom.
4. Plan a field trip to your student's community. What preparations would you make? Ask a student to be your community tour guide. Report on your observations.

REFERENCES

Alper, S., Schloss, P. J., & Schloss, C. N. (1995). Families of children with disabilities. In elementary and middle school: Advocacy models and strategies. *Exceptional Children, 62*(3), 261–270.

Anderson, P. P., & Fenichel, E. S. (1989). *Serving culturally diverse families of infants and toddlers with disabilities.* Washington, DC: National Center for Clinical Infant Programs.

Ascher, C. (1988). Improving the home school connection for the poor and minority urban students. *The Urban Review, 20,* 109–123.

Bateman, B. D., & Linden, M. A. (1998). *Better IEPs: How to develop legally correct and educationally useful programs* (3rd Ed.) Longmont, CO: Sopris West.

Bateman, D., & Bateman, C. F. (2001). *A principal's guide to special education.* Arlington, VA: Council for Exceptional Children.

Bauer, A. M., & Shea, T. M. (2003). *Parents & schools: Creating a successful partnership for students with special needs.* Upper Saddle River, NJ: Merrill Prentice Hall.

Bennett, A. T. (1988). Gateway to powerless: Incorporating Hispanic deaf children and families into formal schooling. *Disability, Handicap and Society, 3*(2), 119–151.

Berger, E. H. (2000). *Parents as partners in education: Families and schools working together* (5th Ed.). Upper Saddle River, NJ: Merrill Prentice Hall.

Bernheimer, L. P., Weisner, T. S., & Lowe, E. D. (2002). Impacts of children with troubles on working poor families: Mixed-method & experimental evidence. *Mental Retardation: 41*(6), 403–419.

Brower, D (1986). *The rubber band syndrome: Family life with a child with a disability.* Project report. (ERIC Document Reproduction Service No. ED280255).

Calabrese, R. L., (1990). The public school: A source of alienation for minority parents. *Journal of Negro Education, 59,* 148–154.

Cartledge, G., Kea, C. D., & Ida, D. J. (2000). Anticipating differences celebrating strengths: Providing culturally competent services for students with serious emotional disturbance. *Teaching Exceptional Children, 30*(3), 30–37.

Chan, S. (1986). Parents of exceptional Asian children. In M. K. Kitano & P. C. Chinn (Eds.), *Exceptional Asian children and youth* (pp. 36–53). Reston, VA: Council for Exceptional Children and Youth.

Chang, J. M., Lai. A., & Shimizu, W. (1998). Linking what they know with school intervention assisting APA English-language learners to succeed in school. *National Association of Bilingual Educators News, 22*(1), 21–24.

Chavkin, N. F. (1989). Debunking the myth about minority parents. *Educational Horizons, 67*(4), 119–123.

Cho, E. M. (1993). Korean-American parents' attitudes toward their children or youth with disabilities and their education in the U.S.A. Unpublished master's thesis, California State University, Sacramento. California.

Correa, V. I. (1989). Involving culturally diverse families in the educational process. In S. H. Fradd & M. J. Weismantel (Eds.). *Meeting the needs of culturally and linguistically different students* (pp. 130–144). Boston: College Hill.

Davern, L. (1996). Listening to parents of children with disabilities. *Educational Leadership, 53*(7), 61–63.

Davis, C., Brown, B., Bantz, J. M., & Manno, C. (2002). African American parents involvement in their children's special education process. *Multiple Voices, 5*(1), 13–27.

Delany-Barmann, G., Prater, G., & Minner, S. (1997). Preparing Native American special education teachers: Lessons learned from the rural special education project. *Rural Special Education Quarterly, 16*, 10–15.

Delgado-Gaitan, C. (1991). Involving parents in schools: A process of empowerment. *American Journal of Education, 100*(1), 20–46.

Dennis, R. E., & Giangreco, M. F. (1996). Creating conversations: Reflections on cultural sensitivity in family interviewing. *Exceptional Children. 63*(1) 103–116.

de Valenzuela, J. S., Baca, L., & Baca, E. (2004). Family involvement in bilingual special education: Challenging the norm. In L. M. Baca & H. T. Cervantes (Eds.). *The Bilingual Special Education Interface* (4th Ed., pp. 360–381). Upper Saddle River, NJ: Pearson.

Diggs, R. (1974). Education across cultures. *Exceptional Children, 40*(8), 578–583.

Doberman, F. J. (1998). Meeting the challenge. *Exceptional Parent, 28*(12), 38–40.

Dunst, C. J., Trivette, C. M., & Deal, A. (Eds). (1994). *Supporting and strengthening families: Vol. 1 Methods, strategies and practices.* Cambridge, MA: Brookline Books.

Epstein, J. L. (2001). *School, family and community partnership: Preparing educators and improving schools.* Boulder, CO: Westview Press.

Epstein, J. L., & Salina, K. C. (2004). Partnering with families and communities. *Education Leadership, 61*(8), 12–18.

Ferguson, P. M., & Asch, A. (1989). What we want for our children: Perspectives of parents and adults with disabilities. In D. Biklen, D. Ferguson & A. Ford (Eds.), *School and Disability* (pp. 108–140). Chicago: The University of Chicago Press.

Ferguson, P.M., & Ferguson, P. (1987). Parents and professionals. In P. Knoblock (Ed.), *Introduction to Special Education* (pp. 181–203). Boston: Little Brown.

Finders, M. & Lewis, C. (1994, May). Why some parents don't come to school. *Educational Leadership*, 50–54.

Fiske, A. P. (1992). The four elementary forms of sociality: Framework for a unified theory of social relations. *Psychological Review, 99*, 689–723.

Fradd, S. H. (1993). *Creating the team to assist culturally and linguistically diverse students.* Tucson, AZ: Communication Skill Builders.

Fuller, M. (2003). Poverty. In G. Olsen & M. L. Fuller (Eds.), *Home School Relationship: Working Successfully with Parents and Families* (pp. 273–289), Boston: Allyn & Bacon.

Gadamer, H. G. (1992). *Philosophical hermeneutics.* (D. E. Linge, Ed. and Trans.) Berkeley, CA: University of California Press.

Gallagher, J. J., Cross, A., & Scharfman, W. (1981). Parental adaptation to a young handicapped child: The father's role. *Journal of the Division for Early Childhood, 3*, 3–14.

Gallegos, A., & Gallegos, R. (1988). *The interaction between families of culturally diverse handicapped children and the school.* Lubbock, TX: Texas Tech Press. (ERIC Document Reproduction Service No. ED316044).

Gartner, A., Lipsky, D. K., & Turnbull, D. (1991). *Supporting families with a child with a disability: An international outlook,* Baltimore: Paul H. Brookes.

Gonzáles, R., Johnson, K., & Suitor, S. (2003). Conversations with parents of children with moderate severe disabilities: Lessons learned. *10th Annual Building on Family Strengths Conference Proceedings.* Research and Training Center on Family Support and Children's Mental Health (pp. 115–118). Portland, OR: Portland State University.

Hall, E. T. (1976). *Beyond culture.* Garden City, NY: Doubleday.

Hamre-Nieptuski, S., Nieptuski, J. & Strathe, M. (1992). Functional life skills, academic skills, and friendship/social relationship development: What do parents of students with moderate/severe/profound disabilities value? *The Journal of the Association for Persons with Severe Handicaps, 17,* 53–58.

Hansen, M. (1992). Ethnic, cultural and language diversity in intervention settings. In E. Lynch & M. Hansen (Eds.), *Developing cross cultural competence: A guide for working with young children and their families* (pp. 3–18). Baltimore: Paul H. Brookes.

Hansen, M. J., & Carta, J. J. (1995). Addressing the challenges of families with multiple risks. *Exceptional Children, 62*(3), 201–212.

Hansen, M. J., Lynch, E. W., & Wayman, K. I. (1990). Honoring the cultural diversity of families when gathering data. *Topics in Early Childhood Special Education, 10*(1), 112–131.

Harry, B. (1992a). Making sense of disability: Low-come, Puerto Rican parents' theories of the problem. *Exceptional Children, 59*(1), 27–40.

Harry, B. (1992b). *Cultural diversity, families and the special education system: Communication and empowerment.* New York: Teachers College Press.

Harry, B. (1992c). An ethnographic study of cross-cultural communication with Puerto Rican-American families on the special education system. *American Educational Research Journal, 29,* 471–494.

Harry, B. (1993). *Cultural diversity, families, and the special education system: Communication and empowerment.* New York: Teachers College Press.

Harry, B. (2002). Trends and issues in serving culturally diverse families and children with disabilities. *The Journal of Special Education, 20*(3), 134–138.

Harry, B., Allen, N., & McLaughlin, M. (1995). Communication vs. compliance: African American parents' involvement in special education. *Exceptional Children, 61,* 364–377.

Harry, B., Park, H. S., Day, M. (1998). Friendships of many kinds: Valuing the choices of children and youth with disabilities. In L. Meyer, H. S. Park, M. Grenot-Scheyer, I. Schwartz, & B. Harry (Eds.), *Making friends: The influences of culture and development* (pp. 393–402). Baltimore: Paul H. Brookes.

Harry, B., Torguson, C., Katkavich, J., & Guerrero, M. (1993). Crossing social class and cultural barriers in working with families. *Teaching Exceptional Children,* 48–51.

Hassan, Suba-Al, & Gardner, R. III (2002). Involving immigrant parents of students with disabilities in the education process. *Teaching Exceptional Children, 35*(5), 52–58.

Heller, T., Markwardt, R., Rowitz, L., & Farber, B. (1994). Adaptation of Hispanic families to a member with mental retardation. *American Journal on Mental Retardation, 99*(3), 289–300.

Henderson, A. T. (Ed.) (1987). *The evidence continues to grow: Parent involvement improves student achievement.* Columbia, MD: National Committee for Citizens in Education.

Henderson, A. T., & Berla, N. (1994). *A new generation of evidence: The family is critical to student achievement.* Washington, DC: National Committee for Citizen in Education.

Hendricks, C. O. (1997). The child, the family, and the school: A multicultural triangle. In E. P. Congress (Ed.), *Multicultural perspectives in working with families* (pp. 37–60). New York: Springer Publishers.

Hennon, C. B., Olsen, G., & Palm, G. (2003). Fatherhood, society and school. In G. Olsen & M. L. Fuller (Eds.), *In home-school relations: Working successfully with parents and families* (pp. 290–323). Boston: Allyn & Bacon.

Herbert, M. A., Mayhew, J. C., & Sebastian, J. P. (1997). The circle of life: Preparing teachers to work with American Indian students with disabilities. *Rural Special Education Quarterly, 16*, 3–9.

Hurtig, A. L. (1994). Chronic illness and developmental family psychology. In L. L. Abate (Ed). *Handbook of Developmental Family Psychology and Psychopathology* (pp. 265–283). New York: Wiley.

IDEA 2004: A new law. (2005, Winter). *PACESETTER, 28*, (1). Minneapolis, MN: PACER Center, Inc.

Inger, M. (1992). Getting Hispanic parents involved. *Education Digest, 58*, 32–34.

Ishisaka, H. A., Nguyen, Q. T., & Okimoto, J. T. (1985). The role of culture in the mental health treatment of Indochinese refugees. In T. C. Owan (Ed.), *Southeast Asian mental health: Treatment, prevention, services, training, and research* (pp. 113–135). Washington, DC:U.S. Department of Health and Human Services, National Institute of Mental Health.

Kalyanpur, M., & Harry, B. (1999). *Culture in special education: Building reciprocal family-professional relationships.* Baltimore: Paul H. Brookes.

Kalyanpur, M., & Rao, S. S. (1991). Empowering low-income black families of handicapped children. *American Journal of Orthopsychiatry, 61*(4), 523–532.

Kinzie, J. D. (1985). Overview of clinical issues in the treatment of Southeast Asian refugees. In T.C. Owan (Ed.), *Southeast Asian mental health: Treatment, prevention, services, training, and research* (pp. 113–135). Washington, DC: U.S. Department of Health and Human Services, National Institute of Mental Health.

Kroth, R. L. (1987). Mixed or missed messages between parents and professionals. *Volta Review, 89*(5), 1–10.

LaFromboise, T. D., & Graff, L. K. (1989). American Indian children and adolescents. In J. Taylor-Gibbs & L. Nahme-Huang (Eds.), *Children of color: Psychological interventions with minority youth* (pp. 114–147). San Francisco: Jossey-Bass.

Lamb, M. E., & Meyer, D. J. (1991). Fathers of children with special needs. In M. Seligman (Ed.), *The family with a handicapped child* (pp. 151–179). Boston: Allyn & Bacon.

Langdon, H. W. (1994). *The interpreter/translator: Process in the educational setting.* Sacramento, CA: Resources in Special Education (RiSE), California Department of Education.

Lawrence-Lightfoot, S. (2003). *The essential conversation: What parents and teachers can learn from each other.* New York: Random House.

Lian, M-G. J., & Aloia, G. F. (1994). Parental responses, roles and responsibilities. In S. K. Alper, P. J. Schloss, & C. N. Schloss (Eds.), *Families of students with disabilities: Consultation and advocacy* (pp. 51–93). Boston: Allyn & Bacon.

Linan-Thompson, S. & Jean, R. E. (1997). Completing the parent participation puzzle: Accepting diversity. *Teaching Exceptional Children, 30*(2), 46–50.

Lo, L. (2005). Barriers to successful partnerships with Chinese-Speaking parents of children with disabilities in urban schools. *Multiple Voices, 8*(1), 84–95.

Lynch, E. W. (1992). Developing cross-cultural competence. In E. W. Lynch & M. J. Hanson (Eds.), *Developing cross cultural competence: A guide for working with young children and their families.* (2nd ed., pp. 35–59), Baltimore: Paul H. Brookes.

Lynch, E. W. & Hansen, M. J. (Eds.) (1992). *Developing cross-cultural competence: A guide for working with young children and their families.* (2nd Ed.) Baltimore: Paul H. Brookes.

Lynch, E. W., & Stein, R. C. (1987). Parent participation by ethnicity: A comparison of Hispanic, Black & Anglo families. *Exceptional Children, 54*, 105–111.

Maldonado-Colón, E. (1999). Through the eyes of children: A model project for spanning cultural gaps. *Reaching Today's Youth.* National Educational Service, *3*(2), 21–24.

Mandlawitz, M. (2005). *What every teacher should know about IDEA 2004.* Boston: Allyn & Bacon.

Marzoas, D. S. (1988). Parental involvement in special education: Focus on the special child. *Perceptions, 23*, 2–22.

McCaleb, S. P. (1997). *Building communities of learners: A collaboration among teachers, students, families, and community.* Mahwah, NJ: Lawrence Erlbaum Associates.

Mehan, H. (1983). The role of language and the language of role in institutional decision-making. *Language in Society, 12*, 187–211.

Meyer, D. J., Vadasy, P. F., & Fewell, R. R. (1985). *Sibshops: A handbook for implementing workshops for siblings of children with special needs.* Seattle: University of Washington Press.

Misra, A. (1994). Partnership with multicultural families. In S. K. Alper, P. J. Schloss, & C. N. Schloss (Eds.), *Families of students with disabilities: Consultation and advocacy* (pp. 143–179). Boston: Allyn & Bacon.

Moles, O. C. (Ed.). (1996). *Reaching all families: Creating family-friendly schools.* Washington, DC: U.S. Department of Education. Office of Educational Research & Improvement.

Moll, L. C., Amanti, C., Neff, D., & Gonzalez, N. (1992). Funds of knowledge for teaching: Using a qualitative approach to connect home and classrooms. *Theory into Practice, 31*(2), 132–141.

Morrow, R. D. (1987). Cultural differences-Be aware! *Academic Therapy, 23*(2), 143–149.

Mosert, M. P. (1998). *Interpersonal collaboration in school.* Boston: Allyn& Bacon.

Nagata, D. K. (1989). Japanese American children and adolescents. In J. Taylor-Gibbs & L. Nahme-Huang (Eds.), *Children of color: Psychological interventions with minority youth* (pp. 114–147). San Francisco: Jossey-Bass.

National Center on Fathers and Families. (1997). Father Lit Database. Retrieved May 31, 2003, from http://www.ncoff.gse.upenn.edu.

Nicolau, S., & Ramos, C. L. (1990). *Together is better: Building strong relationships between schools and Hispanic parents.* Washington, DC: Hispanic Policy Development Project.

Nieto, S. (2000). *Affirming diversity: The social-political context of multicultural education.* (3rd Ed.). New York: Longman.

Osterling, J. P., Violand-Sanchez, V. E., & von Vacano, M. (1999). Latino families learning together. *Educational Leadership, 57*(2), 64–68.

Olson, K., & Pavetti, L. (1996). *Personal and family challenges to the successful transition from welfare to work.* Washington, DC: Urban Institute.

Owan, T. C. (Ed.). (1985). *South East Asian mental health: Treatment, prevention, services, training, and research.* Washington, DC: U.S. Department of Health and Human Services, National Institute of Mental Health.

Park, H. S. (1992). *Korean American parents' perceptions toward educational priorities for their children with severe disabilities.* Paper presented at the International Conference of the Association for Persons with Severe Handicaps (TASH). San Francisco: CA.

Park, H. S. (1995a). *A preliminary report on ethnographic interviews with three Korean families.* Consortium for Collaborative Research on Social Relationships of Children and Youth with Diverse Abilities. Syracuse, NY: Syracuse University.

Park, J., Turnbull, A. P., & Park, H. S. (2001). Quality of partnerships in service provision for Korean American parents of children with disabilities: A Qualitative inquiry. *Journal of Association for Persons with Severe Handicaps, 26*(3), 158–170.

Park, H., & Yount, M. (1994). *Helping English language learners socially adjust at both school and work settings.* Paper presented at the Symposium for Second Language Learners in Regular and Special Education. Sacramento, CA: California State University, Sacramento.

Perez, S. M. (1991). Parental involvement and low socio-economic status children in New York City: An assessment of Camp Liberty. *Journal of Hispanic Policy, 5,* 31–57.

Policy Research Brief (2001). *Family support for families of persons with developmental disabilities in the U. S.: Status and trends.* Published by the Research and Training Center on Community Living, Institute on Community Integration (UCEDD). College of Education and Human Development, University of Minnesota, 12(2).

Poston, D., Turnbull, A., Park, J., Hasheem, M., Marquis, J., & Wang, M. (2003). Family quality of life: A qualitative inquiry. *Mental Retardation, 41*(5), 313–328.

Powell, T. H., & Gallagher, P. A. (1993). *Brothers and sisters: A special part of exceptional families* (2nd Ed.), Baltimore: Paul H. Brookes.

Ramirez, O. (1989). Mexican American children and adolescents. In J. Taylor-Gibbs & L. Nahme-Huang (Eds.), *Children of color: Psychological interventions with minority youth* (pp. 114–147). San Francisco: Jossey-Bass.

Rock, M. L. (2000). Parents as equal partners: Balancing the scales in IEP development. *Teaching Exceptional Children, 32*(6), 30–37.

Rodgers-Adkinson, D. L., Ochoa, T. A., & Delgado, B. (2003). Developing cross-cultural competence. *Focus on Autism and Other Developmental Disabilities. 18* (1).

Rueda, R., & Martinez, I. (1992). Fiesta Educativa: One community's approach to parent training in development disabilities for Latino families. *The Association for Persons with Severe Handicaps, 17*(2), 95–103.

Salend, S. J., & Taylor, L. (1993). Working with families: A cross-cultural perspective. *Remedial and Special Education, 14*(5) 25–32, 39)

Shapiro, J., & Simonsen, D. (1994). Educational/support group for Latino families of children with Down syndrome. *Mental Retardation, 32*(6), 403–415.

Sherman, A., Amey, C., Duffield, B., Eff, N., & Weinstein, D. (1998). *Early findings on family hardship and well-being.* Washington, DC: Children's Defense Fund and National Coalition for the Homeless.

Sileo, T. W., & Prater, M. A. (1998). Creating classroom environments that address the linguistic and cultural backgrounds of students with disabilities. An Asian Pacific American perspective. *Remedial and Special Education, 9*, 323–337.

Smith, D. D. (2004). *Introduction to special education: Teaching in an age of opportunity.* Boston: Pearson.

Smith, S. W. (1990). Individualized educational programs (IEPs) in special education from intent to acquiescence. *Exceptional Children, 57*(1), 6–14.

SPRED: A special ministry for special friends. (2005). *The Diocesan Digest, 11*(2), Diocese of Oakland: Development Office.

Sue, D. W. (1981). *Counseling the culturally different: Theory and practice.* New York: Wiley & Sons.

Thorp, E. K. (1997). Increasing opportunities for partnership with culturally and linguistically diverse families. *Intervention in School and Clinic, 32*(5), 261–269.

Tung, T. M. (1985). Psychiatric care for South East Asians: How different is different? In T. C. Owan (Ed.), *Southeast Asian mental health: Treatment, prevention, services, training, and research* (pp. 113–135). Washington, DC: U.S. Department of Health and Human Services, National Institute of Mental Health.

Turnbull, A. P., & Turnbull, H. R. (2001). *Families, professionals, and exceptionality: Collaborating for empowerment* (4th Ed.). Upper Saddle River, NJ: Merrill/Prentice-Hall.

Turnbull, H. P., & Turnbull, A. P. (1998). *Free appropriate public education: The law and children with disabilities* (5th ed.). Denver, CO: Love Publishing.

U.S. Bureau of the Census. (2000). Poverty in the U.S. (Current Population Series P60-185). Washington, DC: U.S. Government Printing Office.

U.S. Department of Education. (2002). *No Child Left Behind Act*, Volume 67 (Number 231) of the Federal Register. Washington, DC: Author.

U.S. Department of Education, National Center for Education Statistic. (1997). *Fathers' involvement in their children's school.* NCES 98–091 by C. W. Nord, D. Brimhall, & J. West. Washington, DC.

Utley, C. A., Delquadri, J. C., Obiakor, F. E., & Mims, V. A. (2000). General and special educators' perceptions of teaching strategies for multicultural students. *Teacher Education and Special Education, 23*, 34–50.

Winzer, M. A., & Masurek, K. (1994). *Special education in multicultural context.* Upper Saddle River, NJ: Merrill.

Yell, M. L. (1998). *The law and special education.* Upper Saddle River, NJ: Merrill Prentice Hall.

Yell, M. L., & Drasgow, E. (2005). *No child left behind: A guide for professionals.* Upper Saddle River, NJ: Pearson Prentice Hall.

Yutang, L. (1994). *The wisdom of Confucius.* New York: The Modern Library.

Chapter 8

THE EDUCATION OF LATINOS AS LINGUISTICALLY AND CULTURALLY DIVERSE STUDENTS: A SOCIOCULTURAL PERSPECTIVE

PORFIRIO M. LOEZA

INTRODUCTION

This chapter addresses the education of Latinos as linguistically and culturally diverse students. Similar to other ethnic groups in the United States, Latinos are far from being a homogeneous group. The heterogeneity of the group ranges from issues of class, race and ethnicity to ideological, religious, and world views. It is given this complexity that this chapter will subsume and posit a sociocultural perspective on Latinos in the United States. This chapter is divided into three broad sections covering preliminary and demographic issues, followed by a discussion on sociocultural perspectives on Latinos, and concluding with a presentation of effective instructional practices for the education of Latino students.

SECTION I: WHO'S A LATINO?: CIRCUMSTANCES OF LATINOS IN THE UNITED STATES

What's in a name? In the 1980s the term "Hispanic" gathered national momentum as a referent for Latinos. Unlike the immigration experience of other Western European groups, Latino migration to the

U.S. has been a continuous experience. This migration originates from every conceivable country in Latin America and has profound implications for Latinos in the U.S. As a member of the group, I opted to use the term Latino since it is generally preferred within members of the group. However, the reader is reminded that Latinos indeed make use of other self-referents including, Hispanic, Latin American, Mexican, Mexican American, Chicano, as well as their respective country of origin. Each of the self-referents are grounded in the particular historical continuum where Latinos find themselves. For example, Chicano is used by Mexican origin individuals that were born and raised in the U.S. Notwithstanding the naming variations of the group, Latinos continue to change and thrive as the sociocultural landscape as the group flourishes. This section provides an overview of the demographic characteristics of Latinos in the U.S. Demographic data from the U.S. Census Bureau will be used to provide a demographic overview of Latinos in the U.S. The author makes the disclaimer that "Latino" will be used in this chapter to refer to what the Census calls "Hispanics." The choice is deliberate and conscious since Latino is the overwhelmingly preferred umbrella self-referent for members of this group.

General Demographic Characteristics

Latinos, similar to other ethnic groups in the United States, are not a homogeneous group. There is extensive diversity within the group as well as vis-à-vis the general U.S. population. Census data from March, 2002 holds that there were 37.4 million Hispanics in the civilian population of the United States. This figure comprises 13.3 percent of the U.S. population as being Latinos. As seen in Figure 7, people of Mexican origin comprise 66.9 percent of the population. Thus, most Latinos in the U.S. are of Mexican origin. By no means does this simplify an understanding of Latinos since there are multiple complexities in understanding individuals of Mexican origin. Until recently, Latinos in the U.S. have been overwhelmingly of Mexican origin.

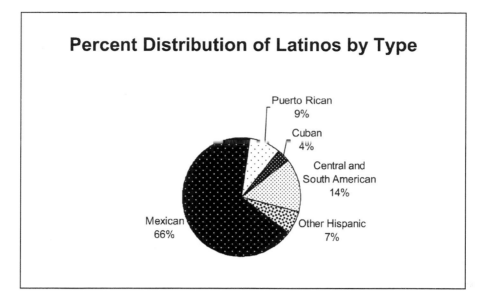

Figure 7. Percent Distribution of Latinos by Type. Source: Current Population Survey, U.S. Census Bureau.

The next largest group consists of Central and South Americans. This is a subgroup that has seen a dramatic rise in immigration beginning in the late 1970s. There are 14.3 percent of Latinos in the U.S. originating from either a Central or South American country. Puerto Ricans, in turn, comprise the third largest subgroup. As a U.S. protectorate, Latinos of Puerto Rican origin are able to move freely to the U.S. mainland. Figure 8 provides the same breakdown for the Latino population by type.

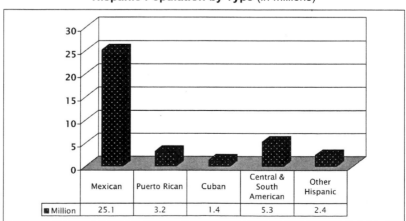

Figure 8. Hispanic population by type (in millions). Source: U.S. Census Bureau, Current Population Survey, March 2002, PGP-5.

Age is a critical demographic characteristic for understanding Latinos (see Figure 9). One-third of all Latinos in the U.S. are under age eighteen. Additionally, among Latinos, Mexicans have the largest proportion of people under age eighteen (37 percent). The implications for educators are significant in that individuals under eighteen comprise the K-12 population and an increasing percentage of the Latino population is likely to be in school. Even outside the group, the Latino population is younger than the non-Latino white population, for example.

Percentage of Population Under 18 by Latino Origin

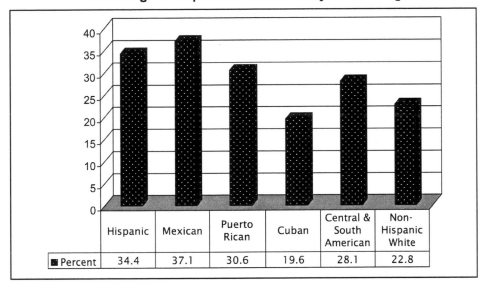

	Hispanic	Mexican	Puerto Rican	Cuban	Central & South American	Non-Hispanic White
■ Percent	34.4	37.1	30.6	19.6	28.1	22.8

Figure 9. Percentage of population under 18 by Latino origin. Source: U.S. Census Bureau, Current Population Survey, March 2002, PGP-5.

A major issue for Latinos is their educational attainment. There are profound policy implications not only for the group but for maintaining the democratic and pluralistic values that U.S. society espouses. As seen in Figure 10, the educational attainment of Latinos lags behind that of non-Latino whites. Among Latinos, Mexicans twenty-five years and older had the lowest proportion of people with at least a high school diploma. In higher education, Mexicans twenty-five years and older also had the lowest proportion of Latinos with a bachelor's degree or more.

Educational Attainment by Latino Origin

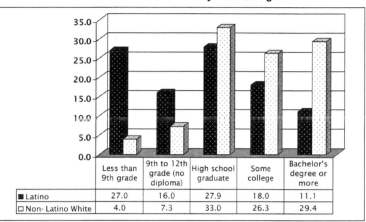

	Less than 9th grade	9th to 12th grade (no diploma)	High school graduate	Some college	Bachelor's degree or more
■ Latino	27.0	16.0	27.9	18.0	11.1
□ Non- Latino White	4.0	7.3	33.0	26.3	29.4

Figure 10. Educational attainment by Latino origin. Source: U.S. Census Bureau, Current Population Survey, March 2002, PGP-5.

Whereas roughly one in ten Latinos has an undergraduate college degree, one in three non-Latino whites has an earned degree. There may appear to be some relative parity for high school graduation. This is, however, misleading given that a higher percentage of Latinos do not actually make it to high school. Tragically, twenty-seven percent of the Latino population has less than a ninth-grade education. The social, economic and policy implications are considerable when one out of every four Latinos has less than a ninth grade education (see Figure 11).

Percent of Population with a Bachelor's Degree

or Higher by Hispanic Origin

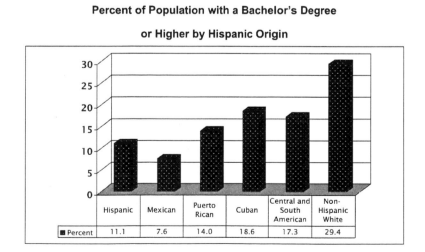

	Hispanic	Mexican	Puerto Rican	Cuban	Central and South American	Non-Hispanic White
■ Percent	11.1	7.6	14.0	18.6	17.3	29.4

Figure 11. Percent of Population with a Bachelor's Degree or Higher by Hispanic Origin. Source: U.S. Census Bureau, Current Population Survey, March 2002, PGP-5.

Family households and marital status provide other indices of vulnerability. Latino family households are more likely than non-Latino white family households to be maintained by a female with no spouse present. Among Latino family households, Puerto Ricans have the largest proportion of households maintained by a female with no spouse present. About half of Latinos aged fifteen years and older are married.

Poverty is another major index of vulnerability for this population. Latinos are more likely to be living in poverty than non-Latino whites. Over one-quarter of Latino children under age eighteen live in poverty (see Figure 12).

Percent of Population Below the Poverty Level in 2001

by Age and Latino Origin

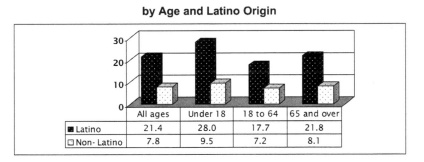

	All ages	Under 18	18 to 64	65 and over
■ Latino	21.4	28.0	17.7	21.8
□ Non- Latino	7.8	9.5	7.2	8.1

Figure 12. Percent of population below the poverty level in 2001 by age and Latino origin. Source: U.S. Census Bureau, Current Population Survey, March 2002, PGP-5.

Residence and economic characteristics are two additional demographic markers that help us obtain an understanding of Latinos in the U.S. In terms of residence, slightly less than half of the population in the United States lives inside central cities of metropolitan areas. Latinos are less likely to reside in nonmetropolitan areas than non-Latino whites. Latinos are more likely to reside in the West than non-Latino whites. Economically, Latinos were more likely than non-Latino whites to be unemployed in March 2002. Among employed Latinos in March 2002, the most common occupations were in service work, precision production, craft, repair, and transportation (see Figure 13).

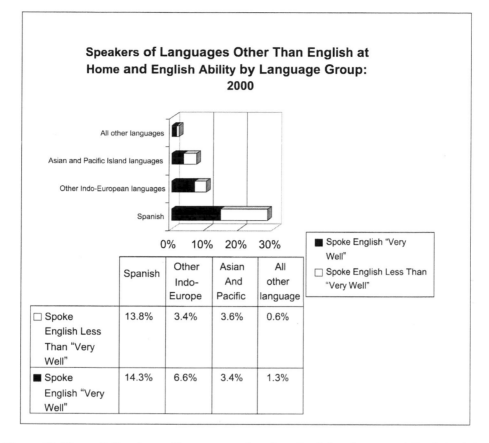

Figure 13. Figure 7. Speakers of languages other than English at home and English ability by language group: 2000. Source: Shin & Bruno, (2003).

SECTION II: LATINOS AND SOCIOCULTURAL PERSPECTIVES ON TEACHING AND LEARNING

This section provides an overview on the education of Latinos from a sociocultural perspective. A sociocultural perspective on learning challenges the conception of teaching and learning as isolated and decontextualized activities. Sociocultural theorists posit, for example, that reading and writing are not skills that are separate from a specific content, context, or communicative space. Hence, from a sociocultural perspective reading and writing are seen as a central part of a social setting and full of all the complexities of any cultural context. This same understanding would be given to other facets of learning. Sociocultural theorists see educational processes as being organized within social practices. In turn, these practices are further embedded in and inextricable from language and Discourse (Gee, 1996; Perez, 1998). August and Hakuta (1997) declare that the research on literacy forms a continuum between a focus on the individual (psycholinguistic processes) and a focus on learning in a social setting. Research on psycholinguistic processes includes such components as letter recognition, lexical access, and computation of sentence meaning. Since language is central to an understanding of sociocultural perspectives, the emphasis in this section will be on language and literacy practices that consider learning in a social context, henceforth referred to as a sociocultural perspective.

Sociolinguistic Considerations for the Education of Latinos

Language is central to an understanding of Latinos. August and Hakuta (1997) state that research on literacy forms a continuum. On one side of this continuum literacy is defined as a psycholinguistic process involving component subprocesses. These subcomponents include what may be regarded as "technical" aspects of written language such as letter recognition, phonological encoding, and word recognition. On the other side of the continuum, literacy is defined as a social practice. August and Hakuta define the social practice perspective on biliteracy as "participation in a community that uses literacy communicatively" (p. 54). Participation is the critical precondition on this side of the continuum for becoming literate. Given this, Perez (1998) cites several major significant implications for the education of Linguistically and Culturally Diverse (LCD) students. According to Perez (1998), these major findings are:

- Children acquire the foundations of literacy within their native language and culture (Cummins, 1989; Purcell-Gates, 1993, 1995; Wells, 1986; Wong Fillmore, 1991; as cited in Perez, 1998);
- There is a social nature to literacy learning (Au & Mason, 1981; Heath, 1983; Scribner & Cole, 1981; Vygotsky, 1978; as cited in Perez, 1998);
- Background knowledge plays a significant role in meaning making (Bruner, 1996; Goodman, 1992; Langer, 1984; Pritchard, 1990; as cited in Perez, 1998);
- Reading and writing are interrelated (Clay, 1979; Edelsky, 1986; Harste, Woodward, & Burke, 1984; as cited in Perez, 1998); and

• Becoming literate in a second language requires time, from five to seven years depending on the individual, strength of native literacy, type of second language instruction, and status of second language (Cummins, 1989; Ramirez, Yuen, Ramey, & Pasta, 1991; Tucker, 1986; as cited in Perez, 1998).

Since context is central to an understanding of sociocultural education, there are a number of ethnographic studies that incorporate sociolinguistic and anthropological perspectives (e.g., Cook Gumperz, 1986; Heath, 1983; Moll, 1990; Vasquez, Pease-Alvarez, & Shannon, 1999). In addition to linguistic and cognitive resources, the communicative needs and sociocultural environments determine the literacy practices that take place in a given community (Heath, 1983; Wong Fillmore, 1979). What appears from these studies is that distinct *ways with words* (Heath, 1983) influence literacy instruction, learning, and literate practices (Gee, 1996; Heath, 1983; Moll, 1990; Perez, 1998). It is a view of literacy and education that is based on social and cultural practices, and actions (Perez, 1998; Street, 1984). The implication from this body of work is that literacy is a culture-shaping tool, and that contextual and cultural contributions cannot be overstated in what and how learning occurs (Perez, 1998).

Hornberger (1994; as cited by Perez, 1998) attempts to account for the complexity of monolinguism versus bilingualism and orality versus literacy by placing them in a continuum rather than as bipolar conditions. There are several successful studies of literacy practices based on Hornberger's continuum of biliteracy development (e.g., Carrell, 1987, Hadaway, 1990; Langer, Bartolome, Vasquez, & Lucas, 1990; Miramontes, 1990; Pritchard, 1990; Smitherman, 1994). These studies offer insight into the sociocultural situatedness of literacy practices. These studies guided Perez (1998) in determining her findings which I referred to earlier, and they suggest literacy practices that improve or impede literacy development along this continuum, leading to full biliteracy.

When thinking about sociocultural perspectives on teaching and learning, it is very important that educators consider the notion of development. How is development defined either implicitly or explicitly? What develops and under which circumstances? In her study of writing in a bilingual program, Edelsky (1996) considers the notion of development in the education of bilingual students. Her conception of development deals with a general movement toward adult norms

(Edelsky, 1996). Within this movement there is the possibility of what she calls regressions and spirals. Similar to Edelsky, the famous Russian theorist, Lev Vygotsky, sees development as change-in-action of some higher order intellectual process (Vygotsky, 1978; see also Edelsky, 1996). This is what is famously known as the Zone of Proximal Development (ZPD). Vygotsky defines development as the difference between actual development and potential development. Conceptions of development are always embedded within any theory of learning.

Community Literacy

There is a diversity of community literacy practices that create variable contexts for the development of literacy (Perez, 1998). Paulo Freire stressed, for example, the importance of reading the world before reading the word (Freire, 1970; Freire & Macedo, 1987). Teaching and learning, Freire and Macedo (1987) would argue, are dialogic in character and as such provide an exchange of ideas and opinions. This is an attitude that he calls conscientization (*conscientizacao*). In this sense, education is much more than merely extending the teacher's knowledge to the uneducated. Education, *à la* Freire, de- pends on the awareness of oneself as a knower.

The basis of Paulo Freire's pedagogy is the idea that you change the world by naming it (Freire & Macedo, 1987). The mere act of naming the world transforms reality from "things" in the present to activities that are in the process of *becoming* (Freire & Macedo, 1987). Freire and Macedo (1987) consider the capacity for language as innate but acknowledge that it can only be realized in a social setting. For Freire, education plays a role in the development of critical consciousness though is does not substitute for political action. The ultimate goal of education according to Freire is liberation. In turn, liberation can only be attained through political action. Hence, political action lies at the core of an understanding of Freire's pedagogy. Macedo (Freire & Macedo, 1987) views Freire's conception of writing as a figure for *transforming the world* that could certainly be "salutary and prophylactic."

In her now classic work, *Ways with Words*, Heath (1983) describes the language and literacy practices of two culturally diverse communities. She called them Trackton and Roadville. She examined how children learned to use language and literacy within their respective social group (Heath, 1983). Both groups developed literacy from the oral to the written language, and the African American children from Trackton did indeed develop literacy before entering school. Yet, contrary to the White rural children from Roadville, reading was done aloud as a performance and there were multiple open-ended interpretations (Heath, 1983). African American children from Trackton were not expected to interpret a text, nor were they expected to answer text-related factual questions. In turn, the White rural children from Roadville were taught to interpret texts as a set of facts. In sum, Heath's research shows that language and literacy are part of a group's culture (Heath, 1983; Perez, 1998).

Moll (1990), in what he calls *funds of knowledge*, examined and documented the origin, use and distribution of knowledge and skills in the Latino community. His underlying principle is that "the student's community represents a resource of enormous importance for educational change and improvement." *Funds of knowledge* consists of the "cultural practices and bodies of knowledge and information that households use to survive, to get ahead or to thrive," for example, information about the cultivation of plants, seeding, water distribution and management, animal husbandry, veterinary medicine, ranch economy, mechanics, carpentry, electrical wiring, midwifery, biology, and mathematics.

Vasquez et al. (1994) proposes that bilingual children do indeed cross cultural borders. In their study of a Latino community in the San Francisco Bay Area, they found that becoming bilingual and biliterate is a natural part of growing up in that community. Eclectic knowledge and skills contribute to a bilingual/biliterate child's ability to act as a valuable resource for their families by helping them to negotiate an unfamiliar language and culture. Bilingual children's literacy practices include acting as cultural brokers or translators. In what they call the Eastside, the children they studied were actively involved in their own and others' learning as they negotiated multiple languages and cultures.

Survey data on the language preferences of Latino groups indicate that there is a rapid shift from Spanish to English occurring in many communities and that Spanish seldom lasts beyond the second or third generation (Veltman, 1988). Sanchez (1983) argues that the presence of a large concentration of Latinos is not sufficient to explain or predict Spanish and English use patterns. Rather, economic, historical, social, and political factors determine these patterns. Indeed, Vasquez et al. (1994) found that biliterate children use their second language for a variety of purposes outside of school. Their excerpts provided insight into the benefits of and process involved in becoming bilingual and biliterate in a community like Eastside. Bilingual children used both languages interchangeably.

Vasquez et al. (1994) identify the question of translating as a fourfold problem in two directions. A translator must comprehend the vocabulary and the message. In turn, the message must be reformulated and the translator must judge the reformulation's accuracy. This occurs in two directions: Spanish and English, for example. This ability to translate promotes, according to Vasquez et al. (1994) a metalinguistic awareness of both languages for bilingual students. They define metalinguistic awareness as the ability to use language as a tool and to focus consciously on language. This is one such ability or skill that can be realized through the knowledge and use of two languages (Malakoff, 1991). Bilingual children translators learn about the underlying meanings conveyed through the use of language. They not only learn to convey meaning using two different modes of expression, but they learn that some meanings defy a simple linguistic translation. Novice translators learn that they must draw upon extralinguistic information, for example, cultural knowledge, and situational cues.

There are several implications to Vasquez et al.'s study. Contrary to the common misconception that linguistic and cultural isolation are prevalent in ethnic communities, the community they studied was not confined to a single realm of linguistic and cultural activity. Those bilingual children reaped the special benefits from participating in and negotiating their multiple worlds. Their role as cultural broker may contribute to their cognitive development by providing them with an occasion to treat language, and possibly culture, as abstract entities. For these children, being bilingual and bicultural and being part of a Mexican immigrant community like Eastside has its advantages.

The bilingualism and multiculturalism manifested in these children are resources that are ignored or systematically destroyed in this country. Bilingual and multicultural education may help reverse this state of affairs if children's native and second languages and cultures are given equal value throughout the curriculum, and if moving between languages and cultures, a necessary and practical activity for those of us who live multiple cultures, is emphasized. For this to happen, schools should recognize and incorporate the multiple and varied modes of bilingual and multicultural activity practiced by students, their families, and members of their communities.

To meet the challenges of diversity, Vasquez et al. (1994) have several suggestions. Simply grounding the program in one aspect of student experiences is no guarantee that it will function smoothly. A recognition perspective to schooling, at least theoretically, opens the possibility for students and teachers to view students' background experiences as an integral and valued component of the learning milieu in schools. Consequently, teachers and administrators need in-depth knowledge of their students and their students' communities.

Vasquez et al. (1994) offer two final points. The first deals with a recognition perspective for all students. Education that emphasizes only one set of experiences or one learning context is insufficient for preparing students to become active and informed citizens in a culturally and socially diverse society. Second, as shown in their study, ways to achieve a multiplicity of perspectives are available to minority students in and out of school. Educators must gain access to these perspectives, and find ways to help all students understand and respect one another.

Sociocultural Perspectives in the Classroom

There are several school biliteracy studies that have begun to explore literacy development within the classroom. For example, in studying how Mexican American students construct meaning when reading in Spanish and English, Langer, Bartolome, Vasquez, and Lucas (1990) found that a major difference in comprehension related to the student's use of good *meaning making strategies* and the ability to relate the text to prior experience or learning. Other studies also suggest that students develop elaborate coping strategies for biliteracy and schooling in general (Miramontes, 1990). In this section I will review two school biliteracy studies: Edelsky (1996) and Jimenez, Garcia, and Pearson (1996).

Edelsky (1996) also takes on a social practice approach to biliteracy. She posits that the question of "how people write?" from a social practice perspective should be interpreted as how are "ideological and cultural conditions" a part of the writing that is done in a society. Thus, in her view, the technical aspects of written language and knowledge of socially shared conventions cannot be taken for granted. Edelsky (1996) cites Dyson's (1989) research on young public school children's reliance on each other as they talked and collectively drew their way into text creations. Instead of becoming more isolated as writers and creating increasingly decontextualized texts, Dyson's children's writing became more socially "embedded."

In her study, Edelsky (1996) also found direct and indirect influences on children's writing. She found that a teacher's assignment had a direct impact on the genres children wrote. Thus, what children wrote was directly affected by teacher's preference (Edelsky, 1996). Indirectly, the teacher's assignments have an effect on the organizational structure of writing. For example, Edelsky found that many children organized their pieces according to a chronology (first, then).

As a biliteracy practice, Edelsky (1996) found that the print environment available in both the classroom and in the community is a critical resource for learning where writing is used, what it is used for, and how it works. In the particular district where she conducted her study, Edelsky found that one particular lesson that was indirectly coming from the classroom biliteracy practices was that code-switching rarely appeared in writing, despite being ubiquitous in talk. A further lesson that the children were indirectly receiving had to do with the materials available in the classroom: More of the Spanish print was homemade, while English print was overwhelmingly commercially produced. Edelsky thus concludes that Spanish print could well look informal while English print may have looked authoritative (Edelsky, 1996). For children growing up in a print-saturated popular culture, Edelsky sustains English print may have been more "real."

Similar to earlier literacy theorist (e.g., Goody & Watt, 1968; Olson, 1977; Ong, 1982; Scribner & Cole, 1981), Edelsky (1996) found that bilingual children were not only surrounded by multiple literacies, but were agents in their own biliteracy practices. This "practice" for the children in her study included both the notions of writing as a tool and the social uses of writing in a biliterate environment. In order for children to invent stable unconventional spellings and punctuation patterns, they must be actively creating new hypotheses. This is what

Edelsky (1996) calls writing as a tool, a system that works to do other work, and that deals with how writing works, what its parts are like, and how they fit with different social uses.

In another study, Jimenez, Garcia, and Pearson (1996) investigated the reading knowledge and strategic processes of bilingual Latino/a students. Becoming biliterate or achieving native-like proficiency in second-language reading is often difficult (Weber, 1991; as cited by Jimenez, Garcia, & Pearson, 1996). Garcia (1991b) cites a variety of factors that affect bilingual students' development of biliteracy. For example, bilingual students differed in the level and type of background knowledge they brought to a text. They also differed in their interpretation of a text and their knowledge of English vocabulary. Bilinguals produce more elaborate protocols when they use their dominant language to demonstrate comprehension of texts written in their second language (Jimenez, Garcia, & Pearson, 1996).

There were several interesting findings in the Jimenez, Garcia, and Pearson (1996) study. First, successful Latino/a readers have a unitary view of reading. They viewed learning to read in another language as simply learning a new set of vocabulary and maybe learning another phonological system. Second, successful Latino/a readers had meta-cognitive knowledge of bilingual strategies. They were capable of describing these strategies. This includes knowledge of cognates, using translation as a strategic activity.

The students in Jimenez, Garcia, and Pearson's (1996) study use a variety of strategies while reading. They paid more attention to resolving unknown vocabulary than did monolingual students. This activity, according to these researchers, did not radically interfere with their overall comprehension. There was a strong determination on the part of these students to resolve unknown vocabulary. Second, these students carefully monitored their comprehension by identifying comprehension obstacles. Often, these obstacles were overcome by simply rereading a portion of a passage. A critical third strategy was connecting prior knowledge to a text. Anderson and Pearson (1984; as cited by Jimenez, Garcia, and Pearson, 1996) found that integrating prior knowledge with textual information is crucial for comprehending text. Fourth, successful Latino/a students made a large number of inferences and drew conclusions while reading in both Spanish and English. In fact, this was the predominant activity in which these students engaged in either language. Finally, these students only occasionally exploited the strategy of questioning to aid their comprehension. This strategy was used less frequently than the others.

The Jimenez, Garcia, and Pearson (1996) study provides evidence that successful Latino/a readers possess an enhanced awareness of the relationship between their primary literacy and their biliteracy. Bilingual strategies, such as searching for cognates, transferring, and translating, are a reflection of this. A further awareness that reading in either language is a unitary phenomena can enhance comprehension, according to Jimenez, Garcia, and Pearson. A unitary view of reading means that bilingual children fully understand that learning to read occurs only once and that reading in a second language largely means transferring their knowledge of reading from their first language. A major obstacle for bilingual students in this study was dealing with unknown vocabulary. In contrast to less successful readers, successful bilingual readers faced this problem in many ways. Searching for cognates was one such way. Jimenez, Garcia, and Pearson finally conclude that less successful Latino/a readers did not know how to use knowledge of Spanish to enhance their comprehension of English text. The opposite was also true: Knowledge of English was not used to enhance their comprehension of text in Spanish.

SECTION III: EFFECTIVE INSTRUCTIONAL PRACTICES FOR THE EDUCATION OF LATINO STUDENTS

There are several implications for classroom research. At the center of a social perspective on biliteracy is the social world of school-aged children. What instructional and social practices take place in a classroom that are likely to lead to an authentic biliteracy practice? Alternatively, the opposite question also provides part of the answer. When an authentic biliteracy practice does not exist, what classroom practices lead to this precious language loss? Literacy and biliteracy theory give credence to the notion that literacy is much more than a neutral or technical tool, or simply a series of discrete elements of reading and writing skills that are independent of context, as Street (1993) maintains. Garcia (1991b) concludes that linguistic and culturally diverse students can indeed be served effectively and can achieve academically at or above national norms. The instructional strategies that work best are those that acknowledge, respect, and build upon the language and culture of the home (Garcia, 1991b). In the early grades,

Garcia (1991b) concludes that teachers are the significant players and that native language instruction is key.

In his studies on effective instructional practices for the education of Latino students, Garcia (1991a) identified a number of common attributes in the instructional organization of the classrooms. These studies included examination of preschool, elementary, and high school classrooms. The primary focus was on Latino students who were successful academically. Garcia's findings included the following:

- Functional communication between teacher and students and among fellow students was emphasized.
- The instruction of basic skills and academic content was consistently organized around thematic units.
- Instruction was organized in such a way that students were required to interact with each other utilizing collaborative learning techniques.
- Students progressed systematically from writing in the native language to writing in English, making the transition without any pressure from the teacher to do so.
- Teachers were highly committed to the educational success of their students and served as student advocates.
- Principals were highly supportive of their instructional staff and supported teacher autonomy while maintaining an awareness of the need to conform to district policies on curriculum and academic accountability.
- Both Anglo and non-Anglo parents were involved in the formal parent support activities of the schools and expressed a high level of satisfaction with and appreciation for their children's educational experience in these schools.

Lois Meyer and Barriers to Meaningful Instruction for English Learners

"Every teacher must be a language educator." These are the words that I would often hear from my former professor, Lily Wong Fillmore, an educational linguist at the University of California at Berkeley. In fact, she summarized this idea in a popular article entitled "What Teachers Need to Know About Language." This piece, coauthored with Catherine Snow, is readily available on the web and is highly recommended to all educators. In the spirit of Wong Fillmore and as language educators, this section is provided. The focus of this section is on the intellectual work of Lois Meyer and her "Barriers to Meaningful Instruction for English Learners." I will conclude this section with two specific strategies that focus in turn on analyzing vocabulary (lexicon) and discourse.

Several years ago, as I was completing my doctoral coursework, I had the good fortune of hearing Lois Meyer, then professor of education at San Francisco State University. As an educational linguist, Dr. Meyer posits that language educators must focus on what she calls "barriers to meaningful instruction" when considering the education of English Learners. These barriers are eclectic and embrace a range of considerations. In particular, Meyer (personal communication, 1998) suggests that educators of English Learners must consider five factors, including cognitive, cultural, language, learning and yearning factors. She links each of these factors with the notion of "load." I would briefly define "load" as the burden that a person must unpack in order to have comprehensible access within each domain. Here is a summary of Meyer's barriers to meaningful instruction for English Learners (see Table XIX). There is a focused series of questions that go along with each domain.

Although each of these factors is discussed discretely, educators must consider them as a whole. Teachers should constantly ask themselves these questions as they prepare, deliver and modify their lessons. Learning is such a complex and dynamic process that educators must be well-versed on many aspects of the learning process. In the following two subsections, I will provide a couple of analytical tools for looking at language. The first strategy for analysis deals with lexical factors (i.e., vocabulary) and the second one addresses discourse aspects.

Considering Lexical Factors in the Education of English Learners

When considering the education of English Learners, educators do well to focus on language. This focus on language, however, must range from analyzing the smallest unit of language to larger aspects of discourse. In traditional linguistics, the study of language is broken down into phonology (including phonics), morphology, syntax, semantics and pragmatics. Whereas phonology studies the sounds and their relationships with each other in a language, pragmatics is the study of the practical application of a language by its speakers. The lexicon of a language is the vocabulary and words that make up that language. This is also part of the study of linguistics and language educators benefit from understanding ways to analyze lexicon. Once

Table XIX
MEYER'S BARRIERS TO MEANINGFUL INSTRUCTION
FOR ENGLISH LEARNERS

Issues to Consider as Educators of English Learners:	Relevant Questions to Ask When Considering Each of These Domains:
Cognitive load	How much decontextualized, factual, academic knowledge is conveyed in an academic text or activity, and how complex or detailed is that knowledge?
Cultural load	How much culture-specific, experienced-based, context-specific knowledge is assumed by a text or activity, and how general or universal is that knowledge?
Language load	How many and how complex are the linguistic features used (e.g. amount of text or talk; number and complexity of lexical items; length and complexity of sentence and discourse structures)?
Learning load	How appropriate are the text, the instructional talk, the learning tasks, and the teaching strategies, for promoting students' second language acquisition and their cognitive development?
Yearning load	How much motivation and enticement to learn is sparked by the lesson or activity, or how much intrinsic energy or "yearning" does the learner bring to the task of learning?

Reference: Lois Meyer, Personal Communication (1998).

again, Meyer (personal communication, 1998) provides the following recommendations when considering lexical factors in the education of English Learners:

- number of different lexical items
- "everyday" vs. "academic" vocabulary
  Examples:
  hidden vs. camouflaged
  save vs. conserve
  feathers vs. plumage
- 1-or-2 syllable words vs. 3-or-more syllable words
  Examples:
  throat vs. esophagus
  hen vs. whippoorwill
  nesting vs. environment

- General experience vocabulary vs. cultural/situation specific vocabulary
  Examples:
  bird vs. bald eagle vs. quetzal
  stairs vs. escalator
  write vs. e-mail
- Active vs. passive vocabulary
  Examples:
  fluids vs. secretion
  grasshopper vs. katydid
  breastbone vs. sternum
- Simple vs. compound words (true or false compounds)
  Examples:
  grass vs. grasshopper
  bug vs. ladybug
  ship vs. courtship

Considering Discourse Factors in the Education of English Learners

In contrast to lexicon, discourse refers to broader aspects of language use. Although a basic definition of discourse would refer to it as a linguistic unit larger than a sentence, discourse entails much more sophisticated and complex language usage that are bound by social constructions and embedded in cultural practices. Despite this complexity, when considering discourse factors, Meyer (personal communication, 1998) provides the following recommendations in the education of English Learners:

- length of text
- number of sentences
- mean length of sentences
  (average number of words per sentence)
- number of sentences with more than one clause
  Example: "When barbules become unhooked, the smooth surface of the feather is ruffled and less suited for flying."
- pronomials and subject deletions
  Example: "Using their beaks, they apply this oil to their feathers."
- Passives
  Example: "A bird's feathers are called its plumage."
- number and complexity of different lexical items
- key linguistic emphases
  Example: "In trees and in bushes, at the edge of a brook, in the ground, and in the air, birds are flying, singing, calling, bathing, nesting."
- focal linguistic structure (key linguistic frames)
  Example: "Is it a bird if it...?

In sum, it is very important that all educators consider the language load that their students encounter when attempting to make sense of the world and as they grapple with the content in their classrooms. Educators can indeed facilitate the learning process for their students by their ability to understand how to analyze lexicon (i.e., vocabulary) as well as discourse. It is only in this manner that we will be able to collectively begin to break down the barriers to meaningful instruction for English Learners.

CONCLUSION

Much has been written about the education of language minority students, including Latinos. Studies have ranged, for example, from issues of methodological approaches to diverse learning styles within different communities. Undoubtedly, our understanding of Latinos and their education continues to expand. After a lifetime dedicated to the success of all language minority students, I can fairly say that we know one thing for sure: The teacher is the pivotal player in the success (or failure) of all children. In particular, teachers of language minority students have a duty to expand on their knowledge of effective approaches to the education of Latinos and other language and cultural minority students.

REFERENCES

August, D., & Hakuta, K. (1997). *Improving schooling for language-minority children.* Washington, DC: National Academy Press.

Carrell, P. L. (1987). Content and formal schemata in ESL reading. *TESOL Quarterly, 21,* 461–481.

Cook-Gumperz, J. (Ed.) (1986). *The social construction of literacy. Studies in international sociolinguistics.* Cambridge, England: Cambridge University Press.

Dyson, A. H. (1989). *Multiple worlds of child writers: Friends learning to write.* New York: Teachers College Press, Columbia University.

Edelsky, C. (1996). *With literacy and justice for all: Rethinking the social in language and education.* Bristol, PA: Taylor & Francis.

Freire, P. (1970). *Pedagogy of the oppressed.* New York: Herder & Herder.

Freire, P., & Macedo, D. (1987). *Literacy: Reading the word and the world.* Westport, CT: Bergin & Garvey.

Garcia, E. (1991a). Effective instructional practices for the education of linguistically and culturally diverse students. Retrieved on July 7, 2005, from http://www.help-forschools.com/ELLKBase/practitionerstips/EffectiveInstructionalPracticess.html.

Garcia, E. (1991b). *Education of linguistically and culturally diverse students: Effective instructional practices.* Washington, DC: National Center for Research on Cultural Diversity and Second Language Learning, Center for Applied Linguistics.

Gee, J. P. (1996). *Social linguistics and literacies: Ideology in discourse.* Bristol, PA: The Falmer Press.

Goody, J., & Watt, I. (1968). The consequences of literacy. In J. Goody (Ed.), *Literacy in Traditional Societies* (pp. 27–68). Cambridge, England: Cambridge University Press.

Hadaway, N. L. (1990). Reading and writing for real purposes in the English as a second language classroom. *Reading Education in Texas, 6,* 67–73.

Heath, S. (1983). *Ways with words: Language, life, and work in communities and classrooms.* Cambridge, England: Cambridge University Press.

Jimenez, R., Garcia, G., & Pearson, P. (1996, February/March). The reading strategies of bilingual Latina/o students who are successful English readers: Opportunities and obstacles. *Reading Research Quarterly.* International Reading Association.

Langer, J. A., Bartoleme, L., Vasquez, O., & Lucas, T. (1990). Meaning construction in school literacy tasks: A study of bilingual students. *American Educational Research Journal, 27,* 427–471.

Malakoff, M. & Hakuta, K. (1991). Translation skills and metalinguistic awareness in bilinguals. In E. Bialystok (Ed.), *Language processing in bilingual children* (pp. 141–166). New York: Cambridge University Press.

Miramontes, O. (1990). A comparative study of English oral reading skills in differently schooled groups of Hispanic students. *Journal of Reading Behavior, 22,* 373–394.

Moll, L. (1990). *Vygotsky and education: Instructional implications and applications of sociocultural psychology.* New York: Cambridge University Press.

Olson, D. (1977). From utterance to text: The bias of language in speech and writing. *Harvard Educational Review, 47,* 257–281.

Ong, W. J. (1982). *Orality and literacy: The technologizing of the word.* (pp. 31–57, 78–116). New York: Routledge.

Perez, B. (1996). *Learning in two worlds: An integrated Spanish/English biliteracy approach.* White Plains, NY: Longman.

Perez, B. (1998). Language, literacy and biliteracy. In B. Perez, *Sociocultural contexts of language and literacy.* Hillsdale, NJ: Lawrence Erlbaum Association.

Pritchard, R. (1990). The effects of cultural schemata on reading processing strategies. *Reading Research Quarterly, 25,* 273–295.

Sanchez, R. (1983). *Chicano discourse: Socio-historic perspectives.* Rowley, MA: Newbury House Publishers.

Scribner, S., & Cole, M. (1981). *The psychology of literacy.* Cambridge, MA: Harvard University Press.

Shin, H. B. & Bruno, Rosalind. (2003). Language use and English-speaking ability. U.S. Census Bureau. Issued October 2003.

Smitherman, G. (1994). "The blacker the berry the sweeter the juice": African-American student writers. In A. H. Dyson & C. Genishi, *The need for story: Cultural diversity in classroom and community.* Urbana, IL: National Council of Teachers of English.

Street, B. (1984). *Literacy in theory and practice.* New York: Cambridge University Press.

Street, B. (1993). *Cross-cultural approaches to literacy.* Cambridge, England: Cambridge University Press.

U.S. Census Bureau. (2000). Census 2000 Summary, File 3.

U.S. Census Bureau. (2003). Current Population Survey.

Vasquez, O., Pease-Alvarez, L, & Shannon, S. (1994). *Pushing boundaries: Language and culture in a Mexicano community.* Cambridge, MA: Cambridge University Press.

Veltman, C. (1988). *The future of the Spanish language in the United States.* New York & Washington, DC: Hispanic Policy Development Project. (ERIC Document Reproduction Service No. ED 295 485).

Vygotsky, L. (1978). *Mind in society.* Cambridge, MA: Harvard University Press.

Wong-Fillmore, L. (1979). Individual differences in second language acquisition. In C. J. Fillmore, D. Kempler, & W. S. Y. Wang (Eds.), *Individual differences in language ability and language behavior.* New York: Academic Press.

Wong-Fillmore, L. (1992, Fall). When learning a second language means losing the first. *Educator.* Berkeley, CA: The Graduate School of Education, University of California at Berkeley.

Chapter 9

TEACHING ASIAN AMERICAN CHILDREN

MING-GON JOHN LIAN

Asians/Pacific Islanders are in one of the fastest growing populations in the United States. During the years of 1996–2003, there was a 28.9 percent increase in this group, second to the Hispanic/ Latino group with a 37.6 percent increase, and followed by African Americans and Caucasians with a 14.3 percent and 0.4 percent increase, respectively (see Table XX). It is predicted that, by the year of 2050, the number of Asians/Pacific Islanders will increase from the current four percent up to 10 percent of the nation's total population (Chen, 1989; Kim, 1993). This prediction may come true sooner than expected, especially in the Asian/Pacific Islanders-populated communities. DuPage County in the Greater Chicago Area, for example, has been reported to have eight percent of Asian Americans in its population (DuPage Mayors & Managers Conference, 2003), while specific urban areas and local communities such as Schaumburg, Westmont, Glendale Heights, and Oak Brook in Northern Illinois, each have already had more than 10 percent of Asian/Pacific residents. Similar statistics may occur in other states including California, New York, Massachusetts, Texas, and so on (T. W. Wang, Inc., 2004).

Regarding the total number of Asian American school-age children, Ong and Hee (1993) reported that there were over three million Asian/Pacific American students in the United States. They predicted that the number of these students would become twenty million by the year of 2020. Since the past thirty years, school practitioners have noticed the increase and paid much more attention about teaching this special population of learners.

Table XX
INCREASE IN RACIAL/ETHNIC POPULATIONS (1996-2003)

	1996		2002		Increase
	n	%	*n*	%	1996-2003
African American	33,500,000	17.3	38,300,000	13.5	14.3%
Asian/Pacific Islander	9,700,000	3.7	12,500,000	4.4	28.9%
Caucasian	194,000,000	73.1	194,822,000	68.5	0.4%
Hispanic/Latino	28,200,000	10.6	38,800,000	13.6	37.6%
Total	265,400,000	100.0	284,422,000	100.0	14.4%

Source: U.S. Census Bureau (1997a, 1997b, 2003).

Asian Americans are frequently identified as a unified group, despite the great variation among Asian and Pacific ethnic groups in culture, language and experience (Lian, 1996, 1999; Lian & Poon-McBrayer, 1998). Actually, members in the Asian American population may represent diverse familial and cultural backgrounds, including those from Bangladesh, Cambodia, China, the Hmong territory, Hong Kong, India, Indonesia, Japan, Korea, Laos, Malaysia, Pakistan, Singapore, Sri Lanka, Taiwan, Thailand, the Philippines, Vietnam, and many other Asian countries and areas. A broader classification of the Asian American population also includes Pacific islanders from Guam, Hawaii, Micronesia, Okinawa, Polynesia, Saipan, Samoa, Tonga, and other islands and areas in the Pacific Ocean (Lian, 1994; U.S. Census Bureau, 1997a, 1997b, 2003). Even within a specific racial or ethnic group, such as the Chinese American population in any states, there are members who speak different dialects and have their own subcultures and traditions (e.g., Mandarin Chinese, Cantonese, Fujianese, Shanghainese, and Taiwanese).

Asian Americans were previously referred to as "Orientals," a term that may critically disadvantage Asian American children. Through the years, a stereotype of the "Orientals" has existed (Nahm, 2004). Consequently, many people relate Asian Americans to illegal aliens or criminals, peculiar living style, habits, and speaking mannerisms, thinking of them as different from persons of "the Western World" or the mainstream society. As a result, Asian American children identified as "Orientals" in the school and community may have suffered from cultural and social discrimination and racism (Blau, 2003; Luke,

1987). Outside the school campus, prejudice, segregation or isolation, and even hostile responses or treatment may still exist at the present time (Ming Pao, 2004a, 2004b; Shiao, 2001).

"Asian American" has been a more preferred term and identification over the past fifteen plus years, originating during the last two decades (Lian, 1996, 1999). Just like African Americans, European Americans, Latin Americans, and Native Americans, many persons with Asian descent are also Americans. Bangladesh Americans, Cambodian Americans, Chinese Americans, Filipino Americans, Hmong Americans, Indian Americans, Indonesian Americans, Japanese Americans, Korean Americans, Laotian Americans, Malaysian Americans, Pakistani Americans, Thai Americans, Urdu Americans, and Vietnamese Americans represent a portion of the subpopulations of Asian Americans.

CHARACTERISTICS OF ASIAN AMERICAN CHILDREN

Asian American children may include individuals who have recently immigrated to the United States as well as those who were born or raised in this country as the second, third, fourth, or fifth generation (Lian, 1996). Some Asian American children may have limited English proficiency (LEP) or speak English as a second language (ESL), while others may speak only English. Some children may speak only one of the numerous Asian languages, while others may be bilingual, trilingual, or multilingual (e.g., English, Vietnamese and French). Even students who speak the same Asian language may use different dialects. Any of these linguistic factors could add to the complicated multicultural experience of school-age Asian American children (Lian, 1999).

In the future, there will be more students who come from biracial (e.g., Asian American and European American, or Asian American and Latino) or multiracial (e.g., Asian American, African American and Native American) families (Hu-DeHart, 1999; Lian, 1996, 1999).

Also, there have been new families and communities with new kinds of Asian American children who were adopted from Asian countries such as Korea and China into American home environments. In 1993, for example, 93 Chinese children were brought to the U.S., and the number has gone up to 5,053 in 2002. There have been a total of 33,637 Chinese children adopted within the 10 years of October, 1983 through September, 2002 (Hume, 2003).

For many years, Asian Americans were ignored in American literature on ethnic relations, resulting in the general public knowing very little about this population (Lian, 1999). Wakabayashi (1997) described Asian Americans as the "least acknowledged of the national minorities" (p. 430). Many Americans developed their awareness and knowledge of Asian Americans based on false or stereotypic information eventually leading to prejudice, negative attitudes and discriminatory responses. Kim (1993) pointed out that, in the mid-19th to the mid-twentieth century, Asian Americans were often perceived to be "inassimilable," "inscrutable," "cunning," or "filthy." Because of the **exclusion legislation** enacted in 1882, most Asian Americans were not allowed to become U.S. citizens until 1952 (Chang, 2000). Even today, Asian American children may be perceived by their teachers or peers in schools as foreigners or refugees (Cheng, Ima, & Labovitz, 1994) and many Asian Americans, who are U.S. citizens, have had the experience being asked about their nationality or when they plan to go back to their own country or "where they belong" (Lian, 1999).

Since the 1960s, a new stereotypic image of Asian Americans has developed. Asian Americans are now often classified as diligent, hardworking, and high educational and economic achievers (Lian, 1999). Such overgeneralizations may cause the public to overlook hidden issues and concerns among this population including poverty, limited health care, family violence, child abuse and neglect, parent-child conflicts and confrontations, and increased school failure and dropping out of Asian American children. As indicated by Sadker and Sadker (1994):

> Despite outstanding accomplishments, the statistics hide problems that many of the new immigrants from Southeast Asia and Pacific Islands face. Cultural conflict, patterns of discrimination, lower educational achievement, and the diversity of the Asian/Pacific Americans are all hidden by the title "model minority." (p. 411)

Similar situations occur in the classroom setting. As Pang (1997) indicated:

> . . . Asian/Pacific American or APA] students are often overlooked or misunderstood in schools. Many teachers do not feel pressured to attend to the needs

of APA children since they are not discipline problems and do not seem to need special attention; however, many students may feel invisible and forgotten. Many APA students are seen and never heard. It happens in the classrooms of the best teachers and in classrooms where teachers have little interest in their students. (p. 149)

Chen (1989) expressed the concern about the potentially lower self-concept among general Asian American students. He listed a great number of positive characteristics of Asian American students which can be suggested as a way to enhance self-concept in these students, including bilingual and bicultural experiences, long cultural history, respect within the culture for each other, strong family bonding, assertiveness, trustworthiness, higher expectations, hardworking, strong work ethics and moral values, flexibility, and adaptability. For example, Asian American students need to be aware that they actually have unique "inner strength" or persistency, that is, being flexible to bend but hard to break, especially during hardships.

In addition, the "melting pot" concept tends to force culturally and linguistically diverse students to assume the Caucasian culture and language as a priority for learning and living (Lian, 1992, 1999). If the student does not learn well, he or she may be labeled as a slow learner or even removed from the mainstreamed classroom and placed in a self-contained class for students with cognitive or learning disabilities (Chang, 1999). Such students may thus have lower self-esteem and expectations for educational achievement (Chen, 1989; Lian, 1994, 1999).

Leung (1990) indicated six major concerns related to educating Asian American students: (1) physical differences, (2) linguistic differences, (3) culture-based differences, (4) acculturation dilemma (e.g., adjustment problem), (5) identity crisis, and (6) uninformed and insensitive significant others. According to Leung, an example is provided when Asian American students speak their native language at school and other children laugh. It is not unusual for a child in this situation to say, "Mom, don't speak Chinese! It's embarrassing" (Lian, 1999, p. 369).

Like adults, students in the schools may face cultural differences and conflicts between the Asian American community and other ethnic populations. Lian and Poon-McBrayer (1998) described that "Asian American youth may struggle with a number of issues such as racism and conflicts with traditional values" (p. 18). In a survey by Poon-McBrayer (1996), teachers overwhelmingly reported that students from Asian American families tended to concentrate more on academic subject matters in school than did their non-Asian peers. However, Feldman and Rosenthal (1990) noted that Asian American children may often be torn by pressures associated with demands to conform to diametrical values: the Western notion of individualism and the traditional Asian value of collectivism. According to Rick and Forward (1992), Asian children and adolescents perceived themselves to be less connected to parental value systems as they become more acclimated to American norms. This phenomenon is logically more apparent between the first-generation immigrant parents and the U.S.-born, second generation children. Cultural conflicts and linguistic differences between these parents and youth are more frequently found and severe than if the parents themselves were also born in the United States. Other variables that may affect the severity of conflicts and differences between Asian parents and children may include the education of parents, where they received their education, parents' length of stay in the U.S., and level of acculturation (Lian, 1999).

In the classroom setting of an American school, maintaining eye contact with the teacher during instructional activities is often emphasized whereas Asian American students might be told at home that it is rude to stare at or to look into the eyes of an adult whom they respect (Lian, 1994, 1999). Direct eye contact may give Asian American parents or teachers the impression that the child disagrees or wants to argue with them, or is showing disrespect or hatred toward them. Such a response from an adult perspective, represent serious behavioral problems. At the same time, teachers may find that Asian American students show politeness by: (a) standing while parents, teachers, or elderly persons sit, (b) remaining quiet or silent when adults are talking, and (c) avoiding direct eye contact and debate with adults.

Asian American children may exhibit learning and response patterns that appear to be unusual in American schools. In the classroom, Asian American children may feel more comfortable answering yes-no questions instead of open-ended questions. Also, in addition to "yes" and "no" answers, children may choose the third way of response silence, which may mean yes, no, agree, disagree, no answer, no comment, didn't understand the question, or waiting for the answer to emerge by itself (e.g., the teacher or other children eventually would answer the question). Heward and Orlansky (1992) stated that "the toughest thing a teacher of Asian students must deal with is the silence; its reasons are complex" (p. 510). Teachers should try to get to understand the child, and avoid labeling him or her as difficult or uncooperative.

Instead of showing and telling to his or her classmates, an Asian American child in the classroom may define "sharing" as listening quietly (Lian, 1999). In addition, teachers may find it difficult for Asian American children to talk about their own achievement, to ask for or offer help, to ask questions in class, or to answer a teacher's question, or to express their own opinion (Brower, 1983). Teachers definitely need to avoid the conclusion that Asian American children are less active in classroom learning activities. This is especially true for a new, non- or limited-English-speaking child who may exhibit a great deal of silence in class.

Asian American children may show one type of passive resistance. When an Asian American child is selected to represent his or her class in an activity, the child may feel that his or her friends are more deserving of the honor and decline. This passive resistance should not be interpreted as a lack of willingness to participate and volunteer.

A general autonomy issue also exists among Asian American children. Research has indicated that Asian American children may take a few more years than European American children to become independent (Lian, 1999). For example, a fifteen-year-old Asian American student may repeatedly ask for an adult or his/her parent to give directions for the next step in a routine activity such as setting up a dining table for a regular meal. Asian American parents, especially mothers, tend to provide their children with tender, loving care, which often means doing as many things for them as possible. For example, a mother of a child with physical disability or cognitive impairment said that cleanliness and tidiness were more important than teaching her child independent self-feeding. Asian American children may also rely heavily on adults for decision-making. Many Asian American parents may expect that their child's major responsibility is to concentrate on academics, to study and to get nothing else but good grades in school (Lian, 1994, 1999).

UNIQUENESS IN EDUCATING ASIAN AMERICAN CHILDREN

Asian American children have unique cultural and linguistic backgrounds. Families of these children have special traditions and values affecting their daily life, including education (Lian, 1996, 1999). Members of Asian American families generally have a strong respect for parents, the elderly, teachers, scholars, tradition, and the educational system, thinking of them as authorities. Asian American children are usually taught to be obedient and cooperative, to be dependent at home and in school, and to express unconditional loyalty to their ethnic community. As stated by Arakawa (1981), "In Western culture, individuality is praised, [while] in Asian culture, anything that breaks homogeneity is troubling" (p. 1). Among the Asian American population, there may be an extended family orientation and a strong family-central focus and tie.

Education, in the eyes of Asian American parents, is of extremely high value and is perceived to be the vehicle for upward mobility. Heward and Orlansky (1992) described the influence of such perception of education:

> For many years, teachers and scholars have been revered in China and other Asian countries. For parents influenced by their traditional cultural heritage, no sacrifice is too great to obtain a good education for their children. From the child's view point, scholastic achievement is the highest tribute one could bring to his or her parents and family. . . . This philosophy and work ethic has helped many Asian American students excel in schools (p. 507).

Most Asian American parents and families value and support the education of their children. In fact, Chen (1989) identified Chinese parental support and commitment as two of the major strengths and assets in the education of Chinese American children. However, educators need to be aware of the incongruencies between non-Asian teachers' expectations and Asian American parents' expectations (Cheng, 1987). In the American school, students are encouraged by teachers to participate actively in classroom discussion and activities, while Asian American students may be told by their parents to "behave," that is, to keep quiet and obedient at school (Lian, 1999). Students may be encouraged by non-Asian teachers to be creative, while Asian American parents may think that students should be told about what to do. In the American school, students learn through inquiry and debate, while Asian American students may prefer to study and place their trust in what the teacher says and what is written in the textbooks, i.e., to learn through memorization. For example, Asian American parents may send their children to academic summer camps, expecting that their children would learn and achieve accelerated course contents for the gifted and talented. To their surprise and disappointment, they may find that their children are actually taught mainly how to find a problem or ask a question and, then, develop a way to generate optional answers by self.

American teachers may believe that Asian American students generally do well on their own, while Asian American parents may think that teacher's role is to teach and the student's job is to "study." In the American school, critical thinking and analytical thinking are perceived to be important, while Asian American parents may believe that it is more important to deal with the real world. Students' creativity and fantasies are encouraged by American teachers, while Asian American parents may perceive factual information to be much more practical and important than fantasy. Problem-solving skills are emphasized in American schools, while Asian American parents may want their children to go to school to be taught the exact steps required to solve a problem. In American classrooms, students need to ask questions, while Asian American parents and their children may try not to ask questions, thinking that teachers should not be challenged. The teacher may think of reading as a way of discovering, while Asian American parents may think of reading as the decoding of information and facts.

Many Asian Americans believe and follow the thoughts of Confucianism, Buddhism, Christianity, and/or Muslim, in which moral behaviors and a sense of forgiveness can be strictly emphasized. An extensive number of Asian Americans also tend to rely on the **Yin-Yang philosophy**. Yin-Yang means a contrast between two extremes such as darkness and brightness, femininity and masculinity, interior and exterior, fast pace and slow pace, and happiness and sadness. Thus, they tend to seek equilibrium between two distinct phenomenon, feelings, or theories. In other words, Asians Americans may avoid either extreme or criticism of the opposite point of view. They may try to stay at the neutral-point in a controversial issue and attempt to make both sides in an argument happy, that is, to avoid competition, conflict, confrontation, and the related debate, and to work out a compromise (Lian, 1996, 1999), to which a number of the general or mainstream Americans may happen to disbelieve due to recent racial tension and terrorist events in the world.

Asian Americans may try to avoid conflict with nature. Many tend to accept their fate and do nothing to change it or create a "new" fate. This contrasts with the fighting-for-rights effort which is prevalent in the United States. When facing the challenge of having a child with a disability, for example, Arakawa (1981) described, "The Asian perspective is to minimize the handicap. The emphasis is on adapting and doing as little out of the ordinary as possible. This even means you avoid legal action against discrimination. To get employment, you tough it out. If buses are inaccessible, you say it doesn't matter" (p. 1).

An Asian American official in the U.S. Department of Education, M. J. Chang reminded Asian American parents not to overlook the right to nondiscriminatory individual support and language remedial or enrichment programs for LEP students through the "No Child Left Behind" legislation (Lin, 2004).

While differences between Asian American and the majority culture may create educational obstacles, Asian American traditions and values actually have positively and significantly contributed to diversity in American schools and society. As Heward and Orlansky (1992) stated, a great strength of the United States is cultural diversity. Our society is made up of immigrants from many lands, and we have all benefited from the contributions of the many ethnic groups (Chang, 2000; Lian, 1996, 1999). It is the responsibility of American educators to attend to the Asian American heritage and the unique educational needs of children from the Asian American population.

PARENTS OF ASIAN AMERICAN CHILDREN

Asian American parents play a significant role in education of their children. Most parents of Asian American children tend to treasure education and respect teachers and scholars highly, expecting high standards and academic achievement from educators (Lian, 1996, 1999). A Thai-American parent, for example, may wish that his or her child is educated to become an "ideal student" with the following virtues (Sriratana, 1995):

1. values
    • to be well-rounded and honest,
    • to have confidence,
    • to be trustworthy with integrity,
    • to have courage and dare to attempt difficult tasks and challenges,
    • to be peaceful, calm, and serene when dealing with conflict, and
    • to be self-reliant and well-disciplined;
2. giving
    • to be dependable and loyal to family,
    • to respect life, property, and nature,
    • to love friends and neighbors,
    • to be sensitive to others' needs and feelings and to be unselfish,
    • to be kind and friendly, and
    • to have justice and mercy.

However, Asian American families are generally reluctant to tell when they are in need of help. Dao (1994), for example, reported that

> Hmong, Cambodian and Lao parents tend not to speak up . . . because of a cultural politeness and respect toward the professional, who is seen as the expert. They don't want to insult him or her by asking too much—even though they have a right and even though the question or observation might help the professional. (p. 15)

Heward and Orlansky (1992) indicated that Asian American families may be reluctant in sharing information about their children's disabilities and individualized needs, especially when the disability is cognitive or emotional rather than physical. Unless the disability is severe, Asian American families may not seek special services or attention. Parents in the Asian American communities may rely on family units and totally assume the obligations of managing disordered or challenging behaviors within the family. Agencies often are the last resort. Asian American families may try not to go through governmental agencies and procedures, including due process hearing, courts or other education and judicial systems, to fight for their children's basic rights to appropriate education and related services.

Consumerism and advocacy may be difficult for Asian American families to understand and engage in for a person with disabilities. These families may also seek to avoid underscoring a disability and focusing public attention on it. To do otherwise would be discomforting. As indicated by Arakawa (1981), "In the last few years, attitudes about disability in the Asian community have become more Western. But the basic values remain: be a high achiever and transcend your disability. Asians want to excel. They want to be the best" (p. 1).

In addition, Asian American parents may actually be unaware of how to actively participate in PTA/PTO or other school activities. Instead of concluding that these parents are less willing to volunteer for school activities, it may be more appropriate to perceive and assume that they need more time to get warmed-up or to get acquainted with the American school system, or that they might need to be informed or provided with information and opportunities before they become active volunteers to support school programs.

In the Asian American community, there is also general concern for "face." To challenge the educational system, for example, may not be acceptable because it causes trouble and, even worse, causes school administrators and teachers to lose "face." It is not unusual that parents and other family members of a child with a disability happen to apologize repeatedly, worrying that they have bothered or caused too much trouble to the school.

Dao (1994) provided a more complete list of potential barriers which may prevent Southeast Asian American parents from accessing services:

1. fear of persecution as a result of the experience in the war against the communists in Vietnam, Laos, and Cambodia;
2. self-reliance which may cause Asian American families to be the main caregivers of children with special education needs, to solve educational problems, and to fulfill needs within the families;
3. limited English proficiency which may slow the assessment process and cause delay of service;
4. tendency to trust the psychoeducational system and authority and try not to question them;
5. perception and expectation out of a disabling condition, e.g., feeling of guilt;
6. lack of training and experience in evaluating their child's progress and achievement;
7. cultural and custom difference, e.g., trying not to be demanding or not to advocate and trying to prevent court actions; and
8. general misunderstanding of the Asian American families.

School practitioners need to teamwork with Asian American parents in an attempt to remove or overcome these barriers for their increased and active access to special education programs and related services.

Asian American parents may have different perceptions of school failure as compared to parents from other ethnic or cultural groups. Lynch (1994) compared the three educational failure paradigms perceived by Asian American parents:

1. **children deficit orientation** as in the medical model—the cause of failure resides within the child's physical body;
2. **environmental deficit orientation** as in the behavioral model—since behavior is learned, children fail as a result of inappropriate or inadequate environmental circumstances in which they learn;
3. **contextual or sociological paradigm**—learning and behavioral problems are not a result of within-child deficits or environmental inadequacies, but the product of inappropriate child-environment interactions.

School practitioners may need to try to achieve further communication with Asian American parents regarding their perception and interpretation of their children's failure in the classroom and, therefore, increase better understanding and mutual home-school partnership.

Asian American parents may also misunderstand English-as-a-second-language (ESL) programs and other resource or educational support systems for limited-English-proficient (LEP) students, thinking that these programs and resource or support systems are a type of pull-out special education projects for slow or developmentally disabled learners and, thus, it is shameful and unnecessary for their children to be involved. In addition, parents may be concerned that their children are missing classes in other subject areas because of the pull-out for ESL instruction or other resource/support services. Actually, ESL program or other services may provide significant benefits for LEP students through individualized assistance to enhance their English language skills and general study skills as well as multicultural experiences (San, 1992).

Professionals need to be sensitive to each family's values and must not judge the family based upon social status-poor or rich, educated or not (Angell & Edwards, 2003). Nor, should they assume that the family knows the law or the educational system. Lian and Aloia (1994) recommended that teachers utilize internal and external resources of each individual and unique family to support parents with specific needs related to the education of their children. Significant **internal re-sources** of parents include the degree of perceived control of the parenting situation, the extended family, parental relationships, health, energy, morale, and spiritual perspectives, problem-solving skills, and available financial and related resources. School practitioners may also utilize **external resources** of parents, such as friends, neighbors, professionals, and community agencies and organizations, to support parental concerns and fulfill their needs in their children's successful involvement in the school program.

SUGGESTIONS FOR TEACHERS

Being in a culturally and linguistically diverse environment, teachers and students should try not only to prevent stereotypes and prejudice, but also to utilize more appropriate and less restrictive approaches in their teaching and learning activities (Lian 1990a, 1990b). In the school setting, as well as general local community, three different approaches may be implemented when teachers and culturally and linguistically diverse children interact with each other: the aggressive, assertive, and passive approaches among which all members in the setting are recommended to adopt the assertive approach which is neither overaggressive nor overpassive (Lian, 1999, pp. 374–375).

1. The **aggressive approach** tends to be used by teachers and students who consider certain things to be for themselves only. For example, an aggressive teacher may view a culturally and linguistically diverse student as a burden on the class or a mismatch with other students. The teacher may determine that this student should go back to where he or she belongs. Or, the student deserves a lower grade in classroom evaluations. An aggressive non-Asian student may perceive Asian American students to be followers instead of leaders. Other aggressive statements made by some members of the non-Asian populations include: "Orientals are not good at sanitation," "They are always late for their appointments," and "They speak broken English or 'Chinglish'." Asian American students and their parents may also be aggressive. For example, parents might tell their children who are attacked by non-Asian peers that, "The only way for you to survive in this country is to fight back."
2. The **passive approach** is the opposite of the aggressive approach. A passive teacher or student may decide that there is no need to deal with the issue because "everything is going to be all right." Persons using a passive approach may think totally for others and blame themselves—to "swallow" the complaint or the unfair situation.

3. The **assertive approach** represents an effort to consider both sides—self and the counter part. Persons utilizing the assertive approach may conduct rational thinking and find the balance point to perceive and to handle issues. They engage a thoughtful evaluation of the situation, find each individual's needs and concerns, and fulfill as many personal and group considerate goals as possible.

The following are general suggestions for teaching Asian American students:

Accept Asian American Students as They Are A teacher needs to understand, accept, and appreciate students who are from diverse cultural and linguistic backgrounds (Angell & Edwards, 2003; Lian, 1999). Efforts must be made to develop an awareness of these students' specific needs, learning styles, and response patterns (Nash, 1996). Teachers must let the students work at their own pace and assure that major learning objectives are mastered. The major concepts for children to learn may be presented in different ways and then followed by the teacher giving repeated review. Teachers should avoid frustration, while encouraging students to think things out instead of supplying answers too quickly. Overall, teachers need to create a learning environment which fits the student, and not to simply ask the student to fit the school (Lian, 1999; Voltz, 1995).

Nonbiased Assessment Asian American students may be at-risk for socially, culturally, and linguistically biased assessment, educational placement, and instructional activities which may lead to misunderstandings, closed doors (e.g., less opportunity), and lower expectations of school achievement. School administrators and teachers need to help these students by providing better opportunities for them to learn and realize their maximum potential (Lian, 1999). Cheng (1991) suggested that Asian American students be observed over time by the teacher in multiple contexts, which includes various interactants, to obtain a better understanding of their response patterns to different individuals and situations. Maker, Nielson, and Rogers (1994), for example, suggested the use of the approaches of *multiple intelligence assessment* to prevent underestimates of culturally and linguistically diverse children's giftedness and problem-solving abilities. A *portfolio assessment* system, as well as the student-centered assessment and instructional approaches, is highly recommended for limited-English-proficient students (Lian, 1999; Tam & Gardner, 1997). Examples of various types of student's work completed at different times are collected, such as art work, creative writing, math exercise, and book reports, to provide a more reliable evaluation of their ability, performance, and learning progress.

Promote Meaningful Communication Teachers of new Asian American students should enunciate clearly, avoid speaking too quickly or too slowly, and use gestures to reinforce oral language, but not to replace it (Lian, 1999). Teachers should not introduce too much new information in one sentence; they should write on the chalkboard or paper frequently to reinforce key terms and concepts. Also, the experiences they incorporate into lessons should be familiar to the students. Teachers should start out by asking yes-no questions and, then, work up to "wh" questions (i.e., what, when, where, why, and how). Teachers should not assume that a "yes" necessarily means that the student has understood. They should praise the student's efforts and model the correct forms in both written and oral language.

In addition, meaningful communication should be facilitated and enhanced between Asian American students and their parents, for them to have more consensus upon an appropriate value system and mutual expectations for each other (Lian, 1995, 1999; T. W. Wang, Inc., 1997). As indicated by Lian and Poon-McBrayer (1998), "The fact that more than half of the youth expressed a wish for parents to listen to them and trust them more while 90% of parents expressed that they trusted their children may confirm the need for better communication" (p. 20).

Advance Language Ability Lack of language proficiency may cause frustration, learned helplessness, lower self-esteem, and even compensation or disordered behaviors. Campbell, Campbell, and Dickinson (2004) suggested the use of multilingual and multicultural programs for enhancing students' cultural experiences and spoken and written language skills; these programs can be accomplished through a variety of musical and literature-oriented activities (e.g., songs, folklores, pictures, poems, riddles, and puzzles from various cultures). Specific receptive and expressive language abilities can also be enhanced by alternative and augmentative communication techniques and devices, especially those which are Asian as well as English language based (Lian, 2004; Poon-McBrayer & Lian, 2002).

Develop New Curricula Kim (1993) suggested that teachers should develop new curricula which will focus on life experiences of Asian Americans and their structural position in the United States.

Major issues such as immigration patterns, ethnic diversity among Asian American or other racial and cultural groups, socioeconomic diversity within groups, language and communication issues, high and low educational achievement, experiences of discrimination and civil rights violations, and the complexity of family life and traditions, should be addressed (Kim, 1993; Liu, 2001a, 2001b).

Many local schools are still at the stage of emphasizing Asian foods and festivals as the major elements of Asian culture to which students are exposed. The multicultural education curriculum in an understanding and supporting classroom environment should include in-depth discussion of Asian as well as other ethnic families' traditions and values. It should be directed toward helping all students in developing more positive attitudes toward diverse cultural, racial, ethnic, and religious groups and considering the perspectives of other groups (Banks, 1989; Lian, 1999, Tam & Gardner, 1997).

Cooperative Learning Children learn quickly and effectively from each other. Teachers need to facilitate opportunities and encourage learning through cooperation. Cooperative learning assignments start with concrete and simple game-oriented projects. In such projects, an Asian American student will have the chance to take the role at which he or she feels competent and comfortable. Gradually, the teacher moves onto more complicated and abstract projects by which an Asian American student can increase his or her participation, contribution, and leadership (Lian, 1999), as well as enhanced problem-solving skills, social competency and interpersonal skills, and self-esteem/self-confidence (Harriott & Martin, 2004; Tam & Gardner, 1997).

Collaborative and Effective Teaching Sadker and Sadker (1994) suggested that teaching be done in collaboration. Contemporary schools are more complicated than ever before, dealing with such issues as bilingual and multilingual special education services, limited English proficiency, low self-esteem, family crisis, and poverty. A teacher cannot stand alone. He or she needs to be assisted and supported by experienced educators and professionals from various disciplines, e.g., social work, counseling, nursing, and teacher education (Farra, Klitzkie, & Bretania-Schafer, 1994). In addition, through collaborative teaching, more culturally responsive teaching ideas, strategies, and activities can be developed and implemented, such as "Looking Inside Yourself," "A Community Chain," and so on (Harriott & Martin, 2004, pp. 49–51).

Enhance Home-School Cooperation Parents and other family members are valuable assets for supporting and promoting school programs for students with special education needs (Angell & Edwards, 2003; Lian & Yeh, 2002). A teacher needs to try to find factors that are influencing parents' involvement in their children's learning and teaching activities at home as well as in the classroom settings. Arrangements can be carried out to remove potential barriers and encourage participation based on the understanding of existing factors such as parental perception, concerns, preference, and effective approaches for successful home-school partnership (Angell & Edwards, 2003, Chang, 1999).

Utilize Community Resources There are many agencies and organizations that provide school practitioners with helpful suggestions and support for more effective approaches in teaching Asian American students. These agencies and organizations disseminate useful information and related materials through traditional brochures and booklets as well as online set-ups, e.g., websites and listserv. Teachers are encouraged to find a lot more resources in today's national or local communities. For example, the Division for Culturally and Linguistically Diverse Exceptional Learners (DDEL) of the Council for Exceptional Children (CEC), the Family Support Network, the Multicultural Committee and International Committee of the TASH: Equity, Opportunity and Inclusion for Persons with Disabilities, the National Opinion Research Center (NORC), which provides results of the General Social Survey (GSS), and the Asian American Writers Workshop (AAWW), Chinese American Service League (CASL), Organization of Chinese Americans (OCA), and a great number of local Asian American weekday and weekend schools as well as the Asian scholar and student associations in higher education institutions, which would support school practitioners' daily teaching of children who come from culturally and linguistically diverse background (Chang, 2000; Lian, 1999). Besides, international organizations or agencies in Asian countries or areas, such as the Japanese Institute for Special Education (JISE), Korea National Institute for Special Education (KISE), and the Centre for Advancement in Special Education (CASE) of the University of Hong Kong, are potential resources for contact and inquiry for information and support.

SUMMARY

Asian American children are a special group of learners who bring unique cultural and linguistic backgrounds to American schools. They have special traditions and values as well as learning styles which may significantly enrich school programs and society in general. These students may also have unique educational needs. Teachers of Asian American students will need to understand each individual student attributes and learn to implement instructional strategies and contents, which provide the optimal benefits and educational outcomes for these special learners.

DISCUSSION QUESTIONS

1. What are some stereotypes we often have of Asian American students?
2. What are some uniquenesses of Asian American students which we have to keep in mind when teaching the students?
3. What are some potential barriers which may prevent Asian American parents from accessing services for their children?
4. Discuss some suggestions for teachers that the writer makes in order to work successfully with Asian American students.

REFERENCES

Angell, M. E., & Edwards, E. L. (2003, December 11). *Factors that influence African American parents' involvement in their children's special education programs.* Paper presented at the TASH Conference, Chicago.

Arakawa, J. (1981). Minority voices: Neither part of a double disability is the whole person. *Disabled USA, 4,* (8), 1.

Banks, J. A. (1989). Multicultural education: Characteristics and goals. In J. A. Banks & C. A. M. Banks (Eds.), *Multicultural education: Issues and perspectives* (pp. 2–26). Boston: Allyn & Bacon.

Blau, J. R. (2003). *Race in the school.* London: Lynne Rienner Publishers.

Brower, I. C. (1983). Counseling Vietnamese. In D. R. Atkinson, G. Morten, & D. W. Sue (Eds.), *Counseling American minorities* (2nd Ed.) (pp. 107–121). Dubuque, IA: William C. Brown.

Campbell, L., Campbell, B., & Dickinson, D. (2004). *Teaching and learning through multiple intelligences.* Boston: Pearson Education.

Chang, F. (2000, May 7). The 180 years of Chinese in New England, *World Weekly, 842,* 14–18.

Chang, H. Y. (1999, August 15). Fighting for children: Confrontations between Chinese parents and schools. *World Weekly, 804,* 18–21.

Chen, V. L. (1989). Know thyself: Self-concept of Chinese American youths. *Asian Week,* 8–9.

Cheng, L. L. (1987). *Assessing Asian language performance: Guidelines for evaluating limited English-proficient students.* Rockville, MD: Aspen Publishers.

Cheng, L. L. (1991). *Assessing Asian language performance: Guidelines for evaluating LEP students* (2nd Ed.). Oceanside, CA: Academic Communication Associates.

Cheng, L. L., Ima, K., & Labovitz, G. (1994). Assessment of Asian and Pacific Islander students for gifted programs. In S. B. Garcia (Ed.), *Addressing cultural and linguistic diversity in special education* (pp. 30–45). Reston, VA: Council for Exceptional Children.

Dao, X. (1994). More Southeast Asian parents overcoming barriers to service. *PACE-SETTER,* 15.

DuPage Mayors & Managers Conference. (2003, November). *Diversity in DuPage-2000.* Chicago: Author.

Farra, H. E., Klitzkie, L. P., & Bretania-Schafer, N. (1994). Limited English proficient, bilingual, and multicultural special education students: Implications for teacher education and service delivery. *International Journal of Special Education, 9*(2), 128–134.

Feldman, S. S., & Rosenthal, D. A. (1990). The acculturation of autonomy expectations in Chinese high schoolers residing in two western nations. *International Journal of Psychology, 25,* 259–281.

Harriott, W. A., & Martin, S. S. (2004). Using culturally responsive activities to promote social competence and classroom community. *Teaching Exceptional Children, 37*(1), 48–54.

Heward, W. L., & Orlansky, M. D. (1992). *Exceptional children: An introductory survey of special education* (3rd Ed.). Columbus, OH: Merrill.

Hu-DeHart, E. (1999, April 20). *How to recruit and retain Asian American students at American colleges and universities.* Keynote speech at the MECCPAC Workshop, Illinois State University, Normal, IL.

Hume, E. (2003, November 15). *Chinadopt: Adopting children from China.* [Online] http://www.pshrink.com/chinadopt.

Kim, S. (1993). Understanding Asian Americans: A new perspective. In J. Q. Adams & J. R. Welsch (Eds.), *Multicultural education: Strategies for implementation in colleges and universities* (pp. 83–91). Springfield, IL: Illinois Staff & Curriculum Developers Association.

Leung, E. K. (1990). Early risk: Transition from culturally/linguistically diverse homes to formal schooling. *The Journal of Educational Issues of Language Minority Students, 7,* 35–49.

Lian, M-G. J. (1990a). Book Review on E. Durán: Teaching the moderately and severely handicapped student and autistic adolescent. *Journal of the Association for Persons with Severe Handicaps, 15*(2), 118–119.

Lian, M-G. J. (1990b). Enhancing ethnic/cultural minority involvement. *TASH Newsletter, Vol. 16*(5), 1–2.

Lian, M-G. J. (1992, Fall). *Project TCLDSD: Teaching culturally and linguistically diverse students with disabilities.* Paper presented at the Illinois Council for Exceptional Children Fall Conference, Chicago, IL.

Lian, M-G. J. (1994). Teaching Asian American students. In E. Durán (Ed.), *Symposium for second language learners in regular and special education* (pp. 75–85). Sacramento, CA.

Lian, M-G. J. (1995, September). Education of Chinese American students: Trends, issues, and recommendations. In A. M. Hue, C. Hwang, J. Huang, & S. Peng (Eds.), *The 3rd annual national conference program proceedings of the Chinese-American educational research and development association,* (pp. 155–169).

Lian, M-G. J. (1996). Teaching Asian American children. In E. Durán (Ed.). *Teaching students with moderate/severe disabilities, including autism* (2nd Ed., pp. 239–253), Springfield, IL: Charles C Thomas.

Lian, M-G. J. (1999). Educating Asian American students: Past, present, and future. In J. Q. Adams & J. R. Welsch (Eds.), *Cultural diversity: Curriculum, classroom, and climate* (pp. 367–378). Macomb, IL: Illinois Staff & Curriculum Developers Association.

Lian, M-G. J. (2004). *Alternative and augmentative communication: New opportunities for persons with communication disabilities.* Hong Kong: INSTEP.

Lian, M-G. J., & Aloia, G. (1994). Parental responses, roles, and responsibilities. In S. Alper, P. J., Schloss, & C. N. Schloss (Eds.). *Families of persons with disabilities: Consultation and advocacy* (pp. 51–93), Boston: Allyn & Bacon.

Lian, M-G. J., & Poon-McBrayer, K. F. (1998, June). General perceptions of school and home among Asian American students and their parents. *New Wave - Educational Research and Development, 3*(3), 18–20.

Lian, M-G. J., & Yeh, C. C. (2002, March). Parents' perceptions of their children with disabilities, inclusive education, and related services in Taiwan. *Journal of Asia-Pacific Special Education, 2*(1), 75–91.

Lin, B. C. (2004, January 13). No Child Left Behind: Chinese Americans should not overlook their rights. *World Journal,* A1.

Liu, A. J. (2001a, April 1). New force in the United States: Marching forward of Latino descendents. *World Weekly, 889,* 14–18.

Liu, A. J. (2001a, April 1). Education makes them more competitive. *World Weekly, 889,* 18.

Luke, B. S. (1987). *An Asian American Perspective.* Arlington, WA: REACH Center for Multicultural & Global Education.

Lynch, J. (1994). *Provision for children with special educational needs in the Asia region.* Washington, DC: World Bank.

Maker, C. J., Nielson, A. B., & Rogers, J. A. (1994). Giftedness, diversity, and problem-solving. *Teaching Exceptional Children, 27*(1), 4–17.

Ming Pao. (2004a, July 3). Rapid increase of number of Asian descendents being inspected by British police. [Online] http://www.mpinews.com.

Ming Pao. (2004b, July 24). *Female merchants from Mainland China beaten up by American police.* [Online] http://www.mpinews.com.

Nahm, H. Y. (2004). *Susie Wong revisited.* [Online] http://goldsea.com/Personalities.html

Nash, R. (1996). *Relationships between learning styles and disability, culture origin, and gender of elementary-aged students.* Unpublished doctoral dissertation, Illinois State University, Normal, IL.

Ong, N. T., & Hee, S. (1993). The growth of the Asian Pacific American population: Twenty million in 2020. In *The state of Asian Pacific America: A public policy report: Policy issues to the year 2020.* Los Angeles: LEAP Asian Pacific American Public Policy Institute & UCLA Asian American Studies Center.

Pang, V. O. (1997). Caring for the whole child: Asian Pacific American students. In J. J. Irvine (Ed.), *Critical knowledge for diverse teachers and learners* (pp. 149–189). Washington, DC: American Association of Colleges for Teacher Education.

Poon-McBrayer, K. F. (1996). Profiles of Asian American students with learning disabilities. *Dissertation Abstracts International, 58*(01), 65. (University Microfilms No. 9719430).

Poon-McBrayer K. F., & Lian, M-G. J. (2002). *Special needs education: Children with exceptionalities.* Hong Kong: The Chinese University Press.

Rick, K., & Forward, J. (1992). Acculturation and perceived intergenerational differences among youth. *Journal of Cross-Cultural Psychology, 23*(1), 85–94.

Sadker, M. P., & Sadker, D. M. (1994). *Teachers, Schools, and Society* (3rd Ed.). New York: McGraw-Hill.

San. (1992, June 14). Don't misunderstand ESL. *World Journal,* 25.

Shiao, W. (2001, April 22). Perceptions held by Americans toward Asian descendents. *World Weekly, 892,* 6–8.

Sriratana, P. (1995). *Education in Thailand: Past, present and future.* Paper presented at the Thailand Culture and Heritage Night, Illinois State University, Normal, IL.

Tam, B. K. Y., & Gardner, R. (1997). Developing a multicultural and student-centered educational environment for students with serious emotional disturbances. *Multiple Voices, 2*(1), 1–11.

T. W. Wang, Inc. (1997, July 23). How much do parents understand their children? *The World Journal,* B1.

T. W. Wang, Inc. (2004, January 9). Over 70,000 Asian descendents in DuPage County as leading in the Mid-Central area of America. *World Journal,* B1.

U.S. Census Bureau. (1997a). *Statistical Abstract of the United States* (117th Ed.). Washington, DC: U.S. Government Printing Office.

U.S. Census Bureau. (1997b, March). *The Asian and Pacific Islander population in the United States* (Document #P20-512). Washington, DC: U.S. Government Printing Office.

U.S. Census Bureau. (2003, March). *Current population survey.* [Online] http://www.census.gov/population.

Voltz, D. (1995). Learning and cultural diversity in general and special education classes: Framework for success. *Multiple Voices, 1*(1), 1–11.

Wakabayashi, R. (1997). Unique problems of handicapped Asian Americans. In *The Whitehouse Conference on Handicapped Individuals*, Vol. 1, (pp. 429–432), Washington, DC: U.S. Government Printing Office.

Chapter 10

EDUCATION AND THE ACADEMIC ACHIEVEMENT FOR AFRICAN AMERICAN STUDENTS

BEVERLY E. CROSS

This chapter addresses educating African American children and youth in K-12 school settings. Strengthening how schools improve school achievement for this group of students could well represent one of the most significant moments in the evolution of the United States of America. This is true due to the historical development of this Nation and the relationship of African Americans to the remainder of U.S. society, particularly to the dominant group. The debates about education and the academic achievement of African American students are essentially as long-standing as the notion of America itself, particularly America as a free democracy because "Race and freedom evolved together" (Adelman, 2003). Banks (1991) suggests that "Africans have been in America for many centuries . . . and were with the first Europeans who explored America" (p. 194). Thus in a real sense, the history of the U.S.A. is also the history of African Americans and their relationship to all groups (i.e., indigenous, white settlers, immigrants).

The history of the United States is too rarely linked to academic achievement as a means to understand contemporary issues related to African Americans. While this history is too enormous and significant to summarize here, this chapter would be too historical without addressing it at all. This history is necessary to understand the role of the master narrative and its insidious, invisible role in shaping educational achievement of African Americans. Further, the predilection toward viewing the conditions of African Americans as novel thwarts not only deepens the understanding of persistent issues in educational achievement but also any meaningful determinations of solid improvements. When "we appreciate less often the considerable historical continuity between the failures of schools in relation to African American children and families, today, and such failures throughout the history of the African American presence in the United States" (Lee & Slaughter-Defoe, 1995, p. 349), we limit our abilities to make worthwhile progress. We further ignore that "There have been essential relationships between popular education and the politics of oppression. Both schooling for democratic citizenship and schooling for second-class citizenship have been basic traditions in American education" (Anderson, as cited in Lee & Slaughter-Defoe, 1995, p. 349). For this reason, I suggest from the outset of this chapter that providing education that result in high-academic achievement for African Americans is so critical to the question of whether America is a democracy. Stated another way, educational achievement for African Americans challenges whether the U.S. is the Nation it claims to be in values, practices, and history or if it is living a lie much as it did when pressures from around the world regarding the contradictions of slavery forced the move toward the end of overt, legalized, racialized slavery practices within U.S. borders.

Lomotey (1990) suggests, "Despite virtuous aims and copious oratory with regard to equal educational opportunity, America has frequently failed to educate African American children effectively" (p. 2). Myrdal (1944) contextualizes this educational failure within the larger sociopolitical climate when he refers to the American Dilemma as the immense inconsistencies between the democratic ideals of the U.S. and its practices. This inconsistency between its ideals and its lack of equity in educational opportunities is an important element of the dilemma considering that education is believed to be the great equalizer in U.S. society. In fact, Haberman (2003) suggests that the failure to educate African American and other racial minority children and youth is a "predictable, explainable phenomenon not a series of accidental, unfortunate, chance events" (p. 2).

In this chapter I resist the typical approach in addressing education and academic achievement of African Americans in the U.S. by outlining a series of issues such as demographics on poverty, crime, dropout rates, special education overrepresentation, and low academic achievement. I rather approach the chapter from the standpoint of analyzing the nature of schooling and education that African Americans have access to and how this shapes their academic achievement. This chapter will participate in an enduring dialogue about education and academic achievement for African American students through three sections that allow for exploring: (1) The Dominant Debates, (2) Minority Perspectives, and (3) A Practical Case. This framework for the chapter was chosen to honor the necessary start with a historical context that then moves into more contemporary challenges and possibilities. For sure, both are tantamount to a discussion of educating African Americans.

THE DOMINANT DEBATES AND DOMINANT NARRATIVES

The dominant debates around education and academic achievement of African Americans are dominant in at least two ways: They are dominant in that they are produced, circulated and controlled by the *dominant* white society and they are thusly *dominated* by beliefs of racial and intelligence inferiority about African Americans. Many old debates are inextricably linked to the history of the subordinated status of African Americans in the U.S. and are controlled by dominant discourse and power. This suggests that the debates are linked either explicitly or inexplicitly to racialized oppression and white supremacy.

> Since the beginning of public education in the United States, African American children have been labeled, and even misclassified and tracked, relative to educational standing, as a combined result of inequitable resource allocations; the application of inadequately developed and normed intelligence and achievement tests; disproportionately inappropriate placements in special educational classrooms and settings; and insufficient attention to the learning styles evidenced by many of the children (Lee & Slaughter-Defoe, 1995, p. 348).

The inability of African Americans to define and represent themselves and their realities to the larger society or even within their own communities operates against this historical backdrop that empowers the dominant white society to produce, circulate and control their representation in society based in labeling, misclassifications, testing and placements. Such an act of power to represent the "truth" about African Americans is at least traceable back to the founding fathers of the U.S. For it was Thomas Jefferson who produced some of the early work that defined African Americans as racially inferior (Adelman, 2003). His belief of inferiority was then "proven" by the scientists who he invited to prove his theory true. And they did. They constructed the truth at the invitation of the Nation's leader, and that constructed belief along now powered by scientific validation is as old as the history of the Nation itself.

With this strong link between Jeffersonian-type racist beliefs and the scientific community, African American inferiority became viewed as "natural" and academic underachievement became not only natural but also generational. The basic premise became that "a given African American child cannot perform well intellectually because his or her parents could not perform well: the inability has been passed on due to racial genetic inferiority" (Lomotey, 1990, p. 3). The large scale acceptance of racial inferiority led to educators and policymakers being persistently grounded in educating the "disadvantaged" which became a euphemism for African Americans and the poor (Jones-Wilson, 1990, p. 31). Consistently casting African Americans as disadvantaged, deficit, the underclass, and low academic achievers has created quite an image of intellectual and racial inferiority. The creation of this image is then used to justify inequity in virtually all forms of life, including access to high performing learning conditions. This accepted story not only grossly misrepresents African Americans and their abilities but it also misrepresents the story for all of America by distorting academic achievement for everyone and creating invisible normalcy for white Americans against which all groups get measured and defined as normal or aberrant. This logic gets further extended into defining the quality of education provided in individual classrooms, schools and educational systems that serve African American students. Educational opportunities, expectations, curriculum and teaching are all too often fitted to this deficit thinking. Thus, the entire society becomes one where everyone is invisibly and insidiously measured against invisible white norms while equity and pluralism struggle to exist.

Over the years, various educational efforts have been used to transfer the myth of racial inferiority into a produced reality. Countless tests, intelligence measures, brain size calculations, and other ability calisthenics have been invented to transfer the racial inferiority belief into the master narrative—one to which many assent without thought. It is important to note that the standards and instruments by which educational achievement have been measured have changed in response to the expansion of mandatory public education, the educational requirements of the labor market, and the development of formalized instruments for measuring proficiency in basic school subject matters, for example. Thus, the data for achievement reflect the historical era during which they were collected, and any broad conclusions to be drawn from such data must be considered tentative (Lee & Slaughter-Defoe, 1995, p. 353). Anderson (2004) illustrates how African Americans have been "overcoming one achievement gap after another, each succeeding generation building on the strengths and possibilities created by the previous generations" (p. 3). He outlines these gaps as the literacy gap, the elementary school attendance gap, the high school completion gap, and now the test score gap.

As illustrated repeatedly by Loewen (1995), white America exercises the power to define a group as inferior or aberrant once it is necessary to justify the injustices they have leveled against them and to frame inequity as natural. Thus in education, standardized testing measures have been used to categorize (as inferior or aberrant) and limit (then justify) educational access for African American students (Lee & Slaughter Defoe, 1995, p 354). While this has been true across the history of education for African Americans, the notion of disadvantaged and inferiority plays out in particularly damaging ways through the ideology of special education. As suggested by Harry, Kalyanpur and Day (1999), "Special education in the United States is a product of American culture" (p. 3). They go on to clarify that certain core American values underpin current policies and practices in special education and that these values are mainstream values. These values are too frequently cloaked in the mask of psychology, standardized tests, IQ measures, and the overall ideology of racial superiority of whites. Avoiding peeling back these layers preserves the image of African Americans as intellectually inferior and of low academic ability. Further, the misguided policies and reforms common in education today (test score requirements in high-stakes testing, school vouchers, school charters, commercial programs, bureaucratizatizing parts of the educational process, especially remedial and special education, Individualized Education Plan teams) constitute the virtual totality of our response of low performance of African American children and are fundamentally flawed (Hilliard & Amankwatia, 2003, p. 160).

It is clear that these traditional debates are grounded in deficit thinking and have little to do with equity. It is not a stretch to suggest that these deficit theories to explain African American academic achievement complement one another. The power to represent African Americans positions the dominant society to secure their image of superiority. Perhaps it is reassuring to dominant society to imagine that there is a group consistently worse off them they are—a group who makes the dominant society appear intelligent, possibly more intelligent than they really are. Poor education, not African American intelligence or ability, is the source of low achievement in this group.

This dominant thinking along with its themes and interests have been maintained into the present for it works against the interest and master narrative of the dominant society for African Americans to be high achieving. In fact, this system of unequal power represents a complete, circle of control in that it allows the dominant society to blame African Americans for their lack of educational achievement. "In death by miseducation, the blame . . . is placed on the victims and their families who are accused of perpetrating their own demise" (Haberman, 2003, p. 3).

This preoccupation with deficit thinking and representing African Americans as inferior has obscured in the public arena, but not made impossible, high achieving educational environments in which many African Americans thrive. Such environments have been proven to exist and to facilitate African American high achievement. Thinking more in terms of equity reframes the debates, practices and policies and can build on these successes. It is important to explore minority perspectives to understand what is possible for educating African Americans.

MINORITY PERSPECTIVES AND COUNTERING NARRATIVES

Converse to the dominate debates about the academic achievement of African Americans, are those produced by various African American scholars in particular, that have challenged the deficit representation. These debates are nondominant and, in a sense, are minority debates. They are minority in at least two ways: They are produced largely by African American minority group members and the ideology that undergirds them is minority because it counters outright the seemingly intractable deficit views. A long history exists of countering the prevailing dominant views of African American as deficit and intellectually inferior. In terms of education, "African-American parents and community leaders have been pacesetters, in the forefront of calling for educational improvement" (Jones-Wilson, 1990, p. 35) that does not come out of deficit thinking, for they know the promise for the future of their children and community members rests in the strengths of their own communities.

The debates arising from within African communities have been immensely important in disrupting the dominance of the old oppressive dialogue that has directly and indirectly shaped the education that African Americans have had access to. "There are clear examples of environments that have, over long periods of time, been successful in educating large numbers of African American students" (Lomotey, 1990, p. 9). Perry, Steele and Hilliard (2003) are clear that it is not a great mystery to close "the gap" between African American student achievement and their other counterparts. Although there is healthy debate about the ideas emanating from these minority perspectives, they all counter the old debates in that they assert, "We should not begin with a search for student deficiencies as the explanation for their academic failure or success. Language and cultural diversity, poverty, crime, drug-ridden neighborhoods, and single-parent mostly female-headed households may determine opportunity to learn, not capacity to learn" (Hilliard & Amankwatia, 2003, pp. 133–134). These scholars remind us that the real gap is not in intelligence between African Americans and white Americans and that the gap in intelligence beliefs are grounded in "the legacy of slavery, segregation, and the ideology of white supremacy and in large measure allows us to be satisfied with mediocrity for the elite" (p. 138). They suggest the real gap is a "gap in quality of service and opportunity to learn" (p. 140). To reframe the debate in this way, leads to dramatically oppositional views of African Americans and their academic achievement. Thinking from deficit views leads to solutions grounded in natural inferiority while thinking from high achievement views leads to solutions designed for high expectations and high abilities that assure equity in the opportunity to learn. As Anderson (2004) reminds us:

Probably the most important lesson throughout the history of minority student achievement is that the opportunity to learn and real investments in the education of minority students are the keys to closing various achievement gaps. A second important historical lesson is that all successful reforms to date have tapped into and relied heavily on the strengths inherent in minority communities, families, students and teachers. This capacity should be developed and relied on, not ignored or dismissed as pathological. (p. 33)

Despite the lack of real investments in the education of African Americans over time in the United States, many successful educational efforts have emanated from the strengths of African American communities as Anderson suggested above. The following brief descriptions represent some of the nondominant theories and practices in educating African Americans that are essential to counter the old myths and bring about sound opportunities to learn. They illustrate the ability and dedication of African Americans to constantly struggle against educational and racial barriers while simultaneously building on their histories of achieving academically despite systems to mediate their success. Anderson (2004) states,

In vital respects the history of African American achievement in America has been like a '110 Meters Hurdles' race, as soon as you cross one hurdle its time to gear up for the next one that is just as demanding and even more important for reaching the finish line. The history of African American education . . . is a remarkable record of overcoming one achievement gap after another, each succeeding generation building on the strengths and possibilities created by the previous generation. (p. 2)

African Americans communities and scholars are researching more and disrupting more the master narrative. Nothing less than this work is essential to high advancing academic achievement for African Americans. The selected descriptions that follow represent voices and perspectives from within African American communities on how to improve education and academic achievement. Understanding them is essential to countering deficit perspectives and replacing them with practices that advance education and academic achievement for African Americans. This overview is incomplete, but gives a good glance into some of the key elements forming the basis for high academic achievement (see Table XXI).

Table XXI
KEY MINORITY PERSPECTIVES ON EDUCATION AND
ACHIEVEMENT FOR AFRICAN AMERICANS

Major Approach	Key Characteristic	What These Characteristics Mean Inside Your Classroom
Culturally Relevant Teaching	Uses student culture in order to maintain it and to transcend the negative effects of dominant culture and to prepare students to effect change in society (Ladson-Billings, 1992, p. 17). Also read J. Irvine (2001) and G. Gay (2000) to further understand Culturally Relevant Teaching	Present and develop multiple perspectives in the curriculum; Assure that teaching and learning is meaningful, relevant, important and intellectually simulating; Build on the students' experiences and knowledge; Unlearn the negative effects of deficit views of African American students even if you did not seek to learn these deficit views; Ask yourself frequently if you are holding high academic expectations for African American students; Connect the academic content to preparing students of effect change rather then merely using academic preparation for low-wage work; Use cultural referents to impart knowledge, skills and attitudes; Develop personal bonds with students and avoid viewing them as the other
Multicultural Education	Aims to reform the school and other educational institutions so that students from diverse racial, ethnic, and social groups will experience educational equity (Banks, 1995, p. 3). Also read C. Grant (1995), B. Gordon (1990), and C. Bennett (2001) to learn more about multicultural education	Examine achievement along racial lines and assure that pedagogy is diverse and multiple to meet various learning needs and styles; Employ a system to constantly examine yourself for your ability to genuinely respect a diverse student body and to understand your own identity in the context of society; Work to diversify the teaching staff; Help students to view and interpret events, situations, and conflict from diverse ethnic and cultural perspectives and points of view; Help students to imagine alternatives to current racial relationships in the U.S.; Explicitly teach about school practices that contribute to the reproduction of inequity and deal with the inequities in your classroom; Advocate for multiple voices in school decisions

Table XXI–*Continued*

Major Approach	Key Characteristic	What These Characteristics Mean Inside Your Classroom
Black Pedagogy	Rooted in acquiring knowledge not only of the world, but also specifically about African American history and culture in order to empower students to succeed in an antagonistic world and society (Foster, 1995). Also read more about Black pedagogy and knowledge from C. Lee (1990) and B. Gordon (1990)	Promote social justice, democracy and equity; Teach about the political history of African Americans; Help students connect history to current realities and lived experiences; Connect teaching to the African American community, Value learning that occurs inside and outside of schools; Build on caring that is ground in African American ideology; Be relentless in achieving academic success; Teach to empower students; Oppose rigidity and favor intellectual and creative learning; Learn from successful African American teachers
Engaged Pedagogy	Aims at risk taking that results in self-actualization, challenging conformity and existing systems of domination, making life and academic connections, and valuing student voices and expressions. Read B. Hooks (1994) to become more grounded in engaged pedagogy	Facilitate students asking where knowledge comes from and what does it mean for me to know it; Foster curiosity and question posing and inquiry; Use a framework that develops inquiry skills; Engage in processes to examine the construction of knowledge; Utilize the varied strengths in African American communities to teach; Create authentic caring environments essential to cognitive and emotional development; Avoid rote learning disconnected from African American communities; Critique white dominance; Resist ideology of African American inferiority; Engage students in attaining self-actualization; Use student voice; Take risks and teach against conformity; Hold a vested interest in African American communities
Critical Race Teaching	Based in the study of the relationship between race, racism and power; questioning liberal order, activism, and questioning	Study your own privilege, status, and its relationship of groups other than your own; Study how you wish to remake yourself differently than the way that society has made you; Use

Table XXI–*Continued*

Major Approach	Key Characteristic	What These Characteristics Mean Inside Your Classroom
	how society organizes itself along racial lines and hierarchies and how to transform it for the better (Delgado & Stefancic, 2003)	an oppositional pedagogy that challenges race, racism and power; Teach students to resists white superiority; Teach students about activism and how they can be participants; Teach students to acquire, use and share power; Take critical attitudes toward inequality, racism and discrimination in any of its forms; Seek appropriate actions against inequity
Afrocentric Teaching	Legitimates African stores of knowledge, reinforces community ties and idealizes service, promotes positive social relationships, promotes critical consciousness, imparts a world view that idealizes positive relationships, self-sufficiency, self worth, and self determination (Lee, Lomotey, & Shujaa, 1990). Read also B. Gordon (1990) and A. Hilliard III (2003) for more on Afrocentricity	Consistently engage students with their communities in ways that facilitate their understanding of "giving back" and advancing their communities; Promote self-worth through community and cultural centered classrooms; Use African American knowledge as integral to teaching and learning; Teach about unity; Legitimize elders; Respect the world views and values of the African American communities; Simulate the strengths in the climate of the African American community in the classroom; Model social relations as they exists in the African American community; Collaborate with members of the community in order to learn of its strengths

This sampling of significant perspectives to attaining high academic achievement for African Americans can be useful to teachers and other educators in dismantling the seemingly intractable belief systems that maintain the old, dominant ideology. There is a rich scholarly and practical knowledge base for each of them and further explorations of each beyond the snapshots presented here is essential to implementing them in a meaningful way in classrooms. Each perspective alone is significant, but combining some of these approaches create even more powerful, integrative ways to improve the academic achievement of African Americans.

Utilizing several of these major perspectives on achieving successful academic performance for African Americans is not as challenging as it may first appear. This is due largely to some significant overlap in what makes these approaches appropriate and exceptional. For example, they value the culture of African Americans. They value connecting to the African American community. They evolve from the strengths of African Americans and require a critical consciousness. They focus on equity and justice. They foster inquiry and investigation or even interrogation. They require an analysis of history and the construction of knowledge. They require that students experience academic success. In the following case, I make an attempt to profile a teacher who takes advantage of the integrative nature of these major approaches to high achievement for African Americans.

Martha Goes For Broke as an Achievement Gap Closer

Martha teaches in a large urban school district where the teaching population if over 80 percent white and the student population is over 80 percent non-white, where the graduation rate for African Americans is under 50 percent, where the achievement gap between African American children and youth and their white counterparts has slowly and persistently widened since the Civil Rights Era and where the number of African American children labeled as special education is reaching 25 percent. Martha never accepted the story that this situation is "natural" and represents the ability or intellectual distribution in U.S. society. She wanted to illustrate that when teachers chose to go for broke they can be gap closers. Let's take a glimpse into her teaching.

Martha describes herself as a "student of her students and their communities." By this she means that she is constantly going for broke to learn more about her students and the strengths and values in their communities. She does this despite warnings from her fellow teachers and principal that the communities where her students live are dangerous and that she should not go there alone or for field trips. She has resisted these admonitions and retorts with "I can't teach those I am afraid of." Instead she forges ahead. For example, Martha conducts interviews with her students at various intervals throughout the year–the interviews are conducted at some location within their community not in the school. The aims of these interviews are to find out what her students are interested in and curious about, how they are articulating their learning, what types of things they are involved in within their communities and how to bridge what she learns about her students to the district's curriculum. She actually videotapes these interviews and studies them in a manner similar to the way that sports coaches study films of previous games to plan strategies for future success.

She conducts similar interviews with parents and various members of the community who others say, "If you want to teach our children well, you have to be connected to . . . they know our community and culture well." She calls these people her community scholars because they teach her about a community she has had no long history with. From these interviews she has learned a great deal about African American culture, values, knowledge, ancestry, learning styles and heritage. This knowledge now informs her pedagogy and helps make her curriculum culturally relevant, more multicultural and more based in Afrocentric knowledge integration. Her intent in these interviews is to further learn more about the children she teaches. She also wants to learn how the parents can help her be a better teacher rather than viewing parents as the problem or someone to support her as the colleagues do. Instead she has learned from them how to make the curriculum and her teaching culturally relevant, how to integrate meaningful service learning projects into her curriculum, how parents and community members can help her teach the curriculum, and how she can be more authentically a member of the community although she does not live geographically in the community and suffers from various gaps between her and her students and their communities (e.g., class gaps, education gaps, status gaps). In addition, she has learned how the community holds high expectations for its children and how her expectations and teaching can build on the community values and how she can move toward cultural solidarity with the community.

The curriculum, Martha believes, is hers. That is, she does not view the curriculum as something developed by others during a summer meeting or by textbook publishers or by high-stakes test designers. Yes, she is very familiar with all of these expectations but has studied them to identify the key ideas, concepts, and theories inherent in the academic content. She is thoroughly familiar with the content enough to "play" with it. This means she has a sophisticated enough understanding of what she teaches so that she can teach in different pedagogical and learning style approaches, she can make it culturally relevant, she can bridge it to the communities of the students, she can make it practical and meaningful. She values the knowledge, skills, inquiry processes, and world views inherent in each academic discipline. Equally important, she knows how to create interdisciplinary, project-based learning that engages students. They are frequently posing problems, solving problems, and working with the community to solve social issues, and develop a consciousness about issues of race and class that negatively impact on their communities. For example in their last integrated unit of study, Martha and her students examined the idea of "privilege" as a curricular theme. While the students formulated interesting questions to study around the topic (because Martha believes the curriculum is more interesting when students problem pose, question, draw patterns and participate in solutions), Martha developed the unit to assure that it aligned with the educational and performance standards expected of her and her students. Her young students explored the ideas of privilege as related to class, race, health and gender during the unit. It culminated with a forum sponsored by the students at their local city council meeting on how the disparities created by the structure of privilege in our society are particularly harmful for children. The students acquired signature of the city council members on a resolution to honor and care for all children in their communities not just the already privileged one. A few city council members now check with Martha's student on various issues. They see her class as a reality check for policies and issues. Martha always designs such culminating events to her teaching units to assure that what students study engages them understanding themselves and their own communities, problems and possibilities.

Martha takes the notion of teaching each child and believing that all children can learn seriously because she has grown tired of empty platitudes. She is constantly examining achievement data for her students to determine any individual, racial or gender nuances that she needs to address. Her eyes are on the prize of closing the achievement gap. Any patterns around these categories catapult Martha into a flurry of study to decrease any inequities in student achievement. For example, if she detects any troubling achievement problems, she studies the child, the content area, her pedagogy, the resources available, and her community resources to directly target what students need. In addition, she queries all the content that she teaches to determine if it is intellectually, socially, experientially, developmentally appropriate. She works to assure that the curriculum is imaginative, intellectual, and creative. Further, she is working with other teachers to challenge district policies that interrupt or limit the learning and achievement of her students.

Yes, Martha is a very busy and an often exhausted teacher. But few teachers are not. But she feels she is exerting her energy in a way that more directly and explicitly makes her a good teacher of African American students. Her energy is well spent because her students are high achievers. She states, "I am happiest when I am exhausted because the African American students I teach are excelling and because I do not have an achievement gap in my classroom. I recall being exhausted when a gap still existed. This is a good tired." She challenges other teachers to be tired in this way.

This is an interesting case to discuss with other teachers or members of the community. Some important points of dialogue include: (1) What do you perceive the race of the teacher to be; (2) What type of community do you think she grew up in; (3) What can you imagine she learns from her community engagement; (4) How can she have time to be as engaged as she is; (5) How do her fellow teachers respond to her; (6) What keeps her going; (7) What does it mean to develop curriculum in the way that she does; (8) Will her efforts really work for students with disabilities; (9) Won't she burn out; and (10) Can she sustain this intensity of work? There are, of course, other questions that can derive from the case that can be used for fruitful dialogue about this case. They should be identified and explored as meaningful learning opportunities.

CONCLUDING WITH A THOUGHT FOR TEACHERS

Here I intentionally adapt the title of a speech to teachers by James Baldwin called "A Talk to Teachers." This is particularly important because in that statement he calls for teachers "to go for broke" in regards to the education of African Americans. Although he published this statement in 1963, it is still time to go for broke because the teaching and academic achievement of African Americans children is still critical and we still need to go for broke—that is we need to take risks, think counter to what appears "normal" to think, and in the process take U.S. society closer to its values and democratic state. As illustrated in this chapter, African Americans are high achieving academically and their achievement can be realized with good opportunities to learn and achieve utilizing the now minority perspectives that should come to dominate in time.

Educators should be vigilant in questioning education for "market interests and the interests in maintaining the existing racial hierarchy" (Anderson, as cited in Lee & Slaughter-Defoe, 1995, p. 350). Market interests may appear more visible now while, for some, racial hierarchies are less visible. Anderson reminds us to that both exists together and shape educational decision making, models, and reforms. It is clear to me that both represent real dangers for African Americans alone, but combine to create a particularly heinous condition for "learning while Black." But "gap closers" (Perry, Steele, Hilliard III, 2003) or those who "go for broke" (Baldwin, 1963) are the types of educators who can produce high academic achievement in African American students and who should be studied and modeled. Their successes can become tomorrow's new normalized or natural perspectives on African American achievement if they will follow the know-how that is illustrated within this chapter.

REFERENCES

Adelman, L. (Executive Producer). (2003). *Race - The power of an illusion.* [Film Series]. California: Public Broadcasting Service. [http://www.newsreel.org/nav/title.asp?tc=CN0149].

Anderson, J. D. (2004, November). *The historical context for understanding the test score gap.* Unpublished paper distributed at the Mississippi State Conference on

Dismantling the Achievement Gap: A Gathering of the Stakeholders to Assess Where We Have Been, Where We Are, and to Determine Where We Need to Go, Mississippi State, MS.

Baldwin, J. (1963, December 21). A talk to teachers. *Saturday Review*.

Banks, J. A. (1991). *Teaching strategies for ethnic studies* (5th Ed.). Boston: Allyn & Bacon.

Banks, J. A. (1995). Multicultural education: Historical development, dimensions and practices. In J. A. Banks & C. A. McGhee Banks (Eds.), *Handbook of research on multicultural education*. New York: Simon & Schuster Macmillan.

Delgado, R., & Stefancic, J. (2003). *Critical race theory: An introduction*. New York: New York University Press.

Foster, M. (1995). African American teachers and culturally relevant pedagogy. In J. A. Banks & C. A. McGhee Banks (Eds.), *Handbook of research on multicultural education*. New York: Simon & Schuster Macmillan.

Gay, G. (2000). *Culturally responsive teaching: Theory, research and practice*. New York: Teachers College Press.

Haberman, M. (2003). *Who benefits from failing urban school districts? An essay on equity and justice for diverse children in urban poverty*. Houston: Haberman Educational Foundation.

Harry, B., Kalyanpur, M., & Day, M. (1999). *Building cultural reciprocity with families: Case studies in special education*. Baltimore: Paul H. Brookes.

Hilliard III, A. G., & Amankwatia II, N. B. (2003). No mystery: Closing the achievement gap between Africans and excellence. In T. Perry, C. Steele, & A. G. Hilliard III (Eds.), *Young, gifted and black: Promoting high achievement among African-American students*. Boston: Beacon Press.

Hooks, B. (1994). *Teaching to transgress: Education as the practice of freedom*. New York: Routledge.

Irvine, J. J., & Armento, B. J. (2001). *Culturally responsive teaching: Lesson planning for elementary and middle grades*. Boston: McGraw-Hill.

Jones-Wilson, F. C. (1990). The state of African-American education. In K. Lomotey (Ed.), *Going to school: The African American experience*. Albany, NY: State University of New York Press.

Ladson-Billings, G. (1994). *The dreamkeepers: Successful teachers of African American children*. San Francisco: Jossey-Bass Publishers.

Lee, C. D., Lomotey, K., & Shujaa, M. (1990). How shall we sing our sacred song in a strange land? The dilemma of double consciousness and the complexities of an African-centered pedagogy. *Journal of Education, 172*(2), 45–61.

Lee, C. D., & Slaughter-Defoe, D. T. (1995). Historical and sociocultural influences on African American education. In J. A. Banks. & C. A. McGhee Banks (Eds.), *Handbook of research on multicultural education*. New York: Simon & Schuster Macmillan.

Loewen, J. W. (1995). *Lies my teacher told me: Everything your American history textbook got wrong*. New York: Touchstone Publishers.

Lomotey, K. (Ed.) (1990). *Going to school: The African American experience*. Albany: State University of New York Press.

Myrdal, G. (1944). *An American dilemma: The Negro problem with modern democracy.* New York: Harper Press.

Perry, T., Steele, C., III, A. (2003). *Young, gifted and Black: Promoting high achievement among African-American students.* Boston: Beacon Press.

ADDITIONAL SUGGESTED READINGS

Banks, J. A. (1991). *Teaching strategies for ethnic studies.* Boston: Allyn & Bacon.

Bennett, C. (2001). *Genres of research in multicultural education Review of Educational Research. (71)*2,171–217.

Foster, M. (1997). *Black teachers on teaching.* New York: New Press.

Gay, G. (2000). *Culturally responsive teaching.* New York: Teachers College Press.

Gordon, B. M. (1990). The necessity of African American epistemology for educational theory and practice. *Journal of Education,173*(3), 88–107.

Grant, C. A., & Tate, W. F. (1995) Multicultural education through the lens of multicultural education research literature. In J. A. Banks & C. A. McGhee Banks (Eds.), *Handbook of research on multicultural education.* New York: Simon & Schuster Macmillan.

Irvine, J. J., & Armento, B. J., (2001). *Culturally responsive teaching.* Boston: McGraw-Hill.

Ladson-Billings, G. (1994). *The dreamkeepers: Successful teachers of African American children.* San Francisco: Jossey-Bass Publishers.

Watkins, W. H., Lewis, J. H., & Chou, V. (2001). *Race and education: The roles of history and society in educating African American students.* Boston: Allyn & Bacon.

Chapter 11

PROACTIVE EVALUATION AND ASSESSMENT TO FACILITATE INSTRUCTIONAL DATA-BASED DECISIONS

Elba Maldonado-Colón

Evaluation that responds to the needs of the student produces useful information. Subsumed in evaluation is the assessment process that every teacher must follow to determine how effective has been his/her teaching. Daily and/or weekly teachers use multiple means to assess students' performance—for example tests, observations, and rubrics. Based on the results of the process they select, they proceed to draw inferences about teaching and learning. When working with students with exceptionalities, these decisions must be tempered by the nature of the student's disability, or degree of ability (giftedness). Questions teachers must ask as they review and evaluate data collected include:

- Has the student learned as expected?
- What has the student done well (strengths)?
- What does he/she need to continue working on (academic, social, emotional areas)?
- How successful was the teaching?
- Does the student have the background and/or linguistic competence necessary to learn what he/she is supposed to learn?
- Is there a need to reteach? Is there a need for further evaluation?

These reflective questions are of greater importance when teachers work with culturally and/or linguistically diverse learners (CLD) with exceptionalities.

300

Today, more than ever, diversity prevails in most classrooms across America. Every student brings to school different experiences (background and/or levels of language development and abilities) and expectations. Thus, it behooves educators and evaluators to take into consideration the multiple aspects of diversity when they interpret individual student performance in the classroom and/or in standardized local and/or state measures. The more skilled you become in evaluation and assessment, the greater could be the impact of your efforts on the education of students who are not learning as expected, or who need to be instructed through different approaches than those prevailing in the mainstream school setting. Such data helps you to differentiate instruction and to develop more meaningful plans for intervention.

To support you, in this chapter you will read about: (1) the distinctions between evaluation and assessment, (2) the legal mandates and safeguards for children and youth with disabilities concerning assessment and instruction, (3) procedures and tools that could be used in data collection, (4) considerations on interpreting data, and (5) moving onto data-based instructional planning.

Questions for you to consider as you read into the chapter include:

- What is the difference between assessment and evaluation?
- What factors influence referrals for comprehensive assessment?
- What guidelines do legal mandates provide?
- Why is it important to distinguish between difference and disability?
- What processes and tools could be used to collect information?
- How does one use multiple data sources to learn more about the student?
- What must one consider in utilizing evaluation results for instructional planning?

CHALLENGES AND CONCERNS IN ASSESSMENT

As cultural and linguistic diversity increase among the school populations across the nation (Abedi, 2004; Baca, Baca, & de Valenzuela, 2004), teachers and evaluators need to be prepared to: follow mandates, understand the issues and challenges related to teaching and learning, work on the best educationally appropriate practices, and be ready to draw nonbiased interpretations and recommendations for intervention. Because diversity and exceptionality can and do coexist, it behooves teachers to attend to sociocultural and/or linguistic background as they interpret student performance data. Remember that a comprehensive approach is necessary to strengthen informed educational planning for a diverse population.

Before delving into issues, concerns and practices, it is important to clarify the distinction between assessment and evaluation. In practice these terms are used to substitute each other, however, a distinction exists between the two. Assessment is a process which requires gathering information on what a person can and cannot do. Salvia & Ysseldyke (1998) consider it broadly as, ". . . the process of collecting data for the purpose of making decisions about individuals and groups . . . " (p. 5). On the other hand, evaluation involves the interpretation of data, that is, making a judgment about the student's development based on "available information."

It is important to remember that "available information" does not imply sufficient information, or even essential information. For example, old language proficiency test scores could be the available and essential yet not sufficient information. We would need to gather additional more current information to make a better judgment of the actual needs of the student. I will elaborate on this later on in the text.

Evaluation includes the analysis of the results of the efforts of an assessor to draw out the child/youth's strengths and needs, and requires that he/she use his/her professional judgment to develop recommendations and/or a plan to improve instruction. An example of the evaluation and assessment processes in action would be when teachers collect data about students' writing competence through samples of their written work, and study them in order to draw conclusions about strengths and needs observed in the patterns of usage, strengths and challenges.

Hence, in this chapter assessment will refer to data collection, and evaluation will refer to interpretation of data for application purposes.

On working with culturally and/or linguistically diverse children/ youth with and without disabilities, a conscientious evaluator will require multiple data points (assessments) from multiple sources to be able to draw realistic conclusions (evaluation) about the students' competencies and needs. I concur with de Valenzuela and Baca (2004a) and O'Malley and Valdez Pierce (1996) that comprehensiveness yields significant data for educational planning, which is the ultimate purpose of assessment and evaluation. Triangulation of data points is critical. Comprehensiveness is necessary to be able to distinguish whether the child/youth has or does not have a disability or significant degree of giftedness, and later on to elaborate meaningful recommendations for sound instructional intervention. Furthermore, it is necessary to prevent misidentification as de Valenzuela and Baca so aptly state, "Assessments are heavily biased against students from cultural, linguistic, and economic groups other than the mainstream, and there is good evidence that limited English proficient (LEP) students, Spanish speaking or otherwise, have been and continue to be misplaced with regard to special education services" (p. 164).

Comprehensiveness also tempers intentionality. When best intentions override best practices in professional judgment, we encounter a plethora of cases of overidentification of second language learners (English language learners) and black students who are referred and placed in special education programs to provide them additional or individual academic support. Good intentions to help the students or to respond to accountability demands such as those grounded in No Child Left Behind (2000), lead to poor professional decisions (evaluations) based on limited data or on misinterpretations of the data available (Abedi, 2004; Ortiz & Yates, 2002).

SAFEGUARDS IN ASSESSMENT AND EVALUATION

This section addresses safeguards provided by legislation, mandates, and recommendations for meaningful evaluations and assessments. Throughout this book you will notice that we are concerned with promoting instructional effectiveness in inclusive classrooms. As stated in previous chapters, inclusive classrooms embrace all children/youth and support them in their efforts to benefit from the educational opportunity schools afford them. The teachers in these classrooms must be effective assessors and evaluators, seeking to draft appropriate interventions for all their students. In classrooms where a team composed of the general educator and the special educator collaborate, teachers must strive to understand the requirements and limitations of the law and mandates related to children/youth with and without exceptionalities to be able to serve them well.

For exceptional students, Public Law No. 10-476 known as IDEA (Individuals with Disabilities Education Act) and its subsequent amendments (1997 and 2004) require that in order to identify children/youths with exceptionalities a comprehensive assessment process must be conducted by a multidisciplinary team in a timely manner. In addition, at the point of evaluation (elaborating a judgment based on data collected), the team must ensure that the interpretation and recommendations are free of bias and appropriate for the individual. Hence, multiple perspectives in assessment and evaluation are required to support instructional recommendations (e.g., programming, long- and short-term goals, instruction) that are in consonance with students' strengths and needs.

Salvia and Ysseldyke (2001) identify the following elements as essential to the evaluation process according to legal mandates (P.L. 94-142):

- Nondiscriminatory measures
- Assessment through native or primary language
- Valid tests
- Standardized application
- Inclusive assessment that attends to all areas affected by suspected disability
- Tests that yield information appropriate for instructional planning
- Decision-making based on multiple data sources
- An evaluation process that includes multiple perspectives by including several professionals, and at least one which is familiar with the child/youth's suspected disability, or ability (like giftedness)

For students who are second language learners the evaluation process becomes more complex given the diversity that exists among this population (Ortiz & Maldonado-Colón, 1984; Ortiz & Yates, 2002). One must document the student's history not only in terms of academic progress and health, but also in terms of language development and dual language competence, because we know that strong language skills underlie academic progress and academic English language competence. This process might prove burdensome to professionals, however, if one seeks instructional effectiveness, it must be done. One must collect data beyond what is typical "available information" (e.g., old test scores, comments in students' permanent records, old individualized educational plans [IEP's]). Ample data is what enables the evaluator to distinguish between difference and disability (Salend, 2001). For a synthesis of legislation on litigation related to the rights of students of limited English proficiency, see Applewhite (1979); Baca and Baca (2004); and Fernandez (1992).

For students without disabilities, common professional practice endorses periodic assessments to monitor academic performance in terms of growth/improvement or lack of it. Statewide laws like California's Proposition 227 (1998) and federal legislation like the No Child Left Behind Act (2002) require annual assessment and monitoring of ALL students to determine their degree of educational effectiveness. Mandates of Proposition 227 among other things require monitoring progress toward English language competence for English Language Learners (including students of limited English proficiency or LEP's) (Crawford, 2004). Today, both assessment and evaluation are strong components of the educational programming available to all students. Hence, current accountability requires that teachers develop strong skills in collaboration, assessment and evaluation in order to draft appropriate educational interventions.

PROCEDURES AND TOOLS FOR DATA COLLECTION

An understanding of the background, or development of a learning problem merits careful study of the factors which might have influenced or promoted the students' current patterns of performance. Two ecologies are critical to this understanding, the home's and the school's. Actions and expectations in the home environment impact on school and vice versa. Each sphere of influence affects the students' learning opportunities.

The Ecology of the Home

The child/youth that arrives at school does not live in a vacuum. Regardless of the severity of a disability, every child/youth functions in a world outside school which can be quite different from or quite similar to the world of the school. Knowledge of his/her language models, socioeconomic conditions and the family's expectations is important to the interpretation of problems/challenges in school and assessment outcomes. Case studies of several students should be developed to assist professionals later on as they reflect while interpreting data. Essential elements of these cases/profiles follow.

Language

Language proficiency is a critical variable in the interpretation of many problems for which students are referred (Ortiz & Maldonado-Colón, 1984). Sociolinguistic heterogeneity characterizes the group profile of culturally and/or linguistically diverse children in our schools (Abedi, 2004). While some children come from homes where a language other than English and another language coexist in varying functions and proportions, others come from monolingual homes. In some homes for example, English is used by siblings, the other language by adults; or English is used for daily communication among nuclear family members while the other language is used when older relatives and/or relatives and friends not proficient in English visit the family; or English would be used to scold and the native language to love.

Other children reside in English-speaking environments where the language proficiency of models available ranges from limited to full competence; for example, the father barely speaks it while the mother is proficient in basic communication, and the oldest siblings are in the process of developing it. There are also homes where academic English is the norm. Understanding the students' language experiences and challenges help to interpret difficulties with learning and related behaviors, and guides the instructor in developing meaningful instructional programs. Evaluators and teachers should recognize and document such variations in background and learning opportunities, and most importantly, use that information to triangulate data when interpreting prior learning and current test performance. For example, absence of models of academic English in a home represents a socio-cultural difference not a disability in the students' speech: It requires intensive language development at school. Understanding this reduces the possibility of developing low expectations and inaccurate professional evaluations as well as inappropriate interventions.

What about children with moderate to severe disabilities? While some professionals hold the perspective that in cases of students with moderate to severe disabilities the presence of the disability overrides issues related to dual language or the promotion of non-English language use. Such a perspective limits a full appreciation of the child/youth's potential (Greenlee, 1981; Rueda, 1983). Evaluators need to consider the nature of optimal learning opportunities for the student (Ruiz, 1989) and an openness to untapped potential. At home, he or she might be immersed in a non-English primary language (L1), or in L1 language and English (L2), but neither condition precludes him/her from learning through two languages.

Hence, efforts to assist the student need to include attention to his/her most meaningful linguistic environments in order to gain the understanding and support needed to facilitate academic progress. Unlike educating students without disabilities, the education of students with disabilities must respond to a mandate that indicates that students must be taught through their native or primary language, for many students that language is not English. Therefore, this calls for the development of an extensive linguistic profile regardless of the suspected disability.

At the prereferral stage, professionals should take time to study and analyze the linguistic environments in which the child/youth lives, gathering specific information to assist with interpretation. De León (1990) developed several surveys related to language usage, within an advocacy-oriented process which seeks information about how the first and second languages are used within the home. These surveys are useful data collection tools.

Experiential Background

Organization for learning includes sociocultural attitudes, behaviors and expectations which affect the processing and assimilation of new information. While many children arrive at school prepared to tackle new learning challenges with organization strategies geared for success, others do not. Some children by virtue of restricted socioeconomic conditions and/or other circumstances arrive at school without the organization necessary to succeed in academic-related learning. Another group of children enters school with a disability which affects their potential to learn and succeed in school. Among these groups are some second language learners, who in addition to a biologically-based disability, bring limited language skills and experiential backgrounds to the classroom (Baca & Cervantes, 2004; Salend, 2001).

Hence, while conducting prereferral screenings and/or later interpreting results of diagnostic assessments, it is important to distinguish between: (1) students whose experiential and linguistic background reveal patterns of limited academic performance due to linguistic and/or socioeconomic difference who do not have a disability, and (2) students whose intrinsic disability interferes with their opportunities to learn regardless of their linguistic and/or socioeconomic background.

Reduction of inappropriate referrals is essential. Also, support for children/youths at risk of academic failure, and increased teacher knowledge and intervention competence are desirable goals at the prereferral stage.

Perspectives about Disabilities

Regardless of socioeconomic level, parents all over the world have the potential of having a child with a disability. Cultures differ in their perspectives on, and their expectations concerning the potential of children with disabilities (Harry, 1992; Lynch & Hanson, 1998). Hence, attitudes toward a disability are going to impact on the availability and quality of the child/youth's opportunities to learn. The family's attitude toward such issues as promoting readiness to learn and patterns for independent living (such as feeding, greeting, dressing, engaging participation with others) can be critical to the success of the student and important in understanding problems that arise in schools. Investigation of perceptions about disability and genuine efforts to understand them make teachers and parents active partners in the assessment and evaluation processes (Harry, 1992). Such collaboration improves the quality of data available to interpret the problem/challenge(s) the child/youth faces at school and to draft appropriate recommendations for meaningful interventions.

The Ecology of the Classroom

Lack of academic progress as well as the presence or suspicion of a mild, moderate or severe disability triggers referrals to special education. These referrals are often motivated by teachers' attempts to seek assistance and/or support in promoting changes in student learning. They want to facilitate transformations in students' learning patterns which can result in leaps in learning, increased motivation, adoption of helpful strategies to learn and ultimately, improved academic performance. In an age of accountability this attitude is very important. Thus, assessments of the ecology of the school are also critical to develop knowledge needed to support the students in processing new academic experiences and learning. A discussion of the elements of language, experience, intervention and expectations within the classroom follows.

Language

Most children with and without disabilities who are second language learners (English Language Learners) receive instructional services through what is often their emerging and weakest language (English) (Crawford, 2004; Ortiz & Yates, 2002). The presence of a mild, moderate or severe disability often triggers a set of arbitrary assumptions concerning the language of instruction (Ortiz & Yates, 2002). Evaluators and teachers often feel that given the presence of a disability, the child should be taught through the school's preferred language (English). However, to ignore the influence of the native language severely limits the usefulness of the evaluation. This in turn may affect the students' learning opportunities and ultimately extend negatively to affect the parent-child or family-child relations at home. Dire consequences of such attitude result in a reduction or ineffectiveness of critical home support for school interventions. For example, parents who are in the beginning stages of English language learning will barely interact with the child on meaningful topics, since their language is still very limited. Teachers insist that they use English to communicate with the student, and the parents cannot do it. Tremendous learning opportunities are lost through this severing approach. This discrepancy between home and school needs to be documented to interpret the student's performance.

Determination of the student's ability to use language to communicate within his/her immediate community at school and at home is critical to evaluation. In search of meaningful data, previous efforts to facilitate language acquisition and development are of particular interest. The assessor must document efforts to reduce communication barriers, their effects, and the level of the child/youth's functional language. Knowledge of language competence is essential for instructional planning since language is the foundation of learning, the bricks of the knowledge structure.

Experiential Background

Many culturally and/or linguistically diverse (CLD) children come from homes where experiences directly related to the school curriculum can vary significantly from those of non-CLD children. When these children begin school, they have to work with and manage the linguistic and curricular demands of a classroom environment not tailored to their sociocultural and linguistic profiles. The lack of knowledge, or limited familiarity with routines, habits, and expectations of the school can lead to confusion and eventual academic-related failures, placing the student within a zone of high risk regardless of having or not having a disability. While many children share common experiences that make schooling familiar to them, others don't. These experiences include opportunities to interact with adults and toys, as well as to engage in some form of pretend play, or to visit places like libraries and museums. Such taken-for-granted experiences might be absent from the lives of many CLD children. It could be also that the experiences are similar for both groups but their quality varies. Yet, CLD students may have other equally valuable experiences that are rarely included in the curriculum (Moll, Amanti, Neff, & Gonzalez, 1992).

Understanding such difference in experiences can enhance the interpretation of problems/challenges related to academic performance as well as assessment outcomes. Most important, it helps to differentiate between individual difference and specific disability (Salend, 2001). Further, this background information can assist the professional evaluator to distinguish between level of needs and between degrees of severity, something which test scores alone cannot do, particularly standardized test scores (Popham, 2003). One must remember that sociocultural experiences exert a strong influence in the learning process (Shapiro, 2004).

Previous and Current Interventions

It is useful to determine what has been done, if anything, to assist the child in transitioning from native language to English language.

- Have the English and home language proficiencies been evaluated recently?
- How do they compare to proficiencies at school entry?
- Is there a gap between the level of language used at home and at school for instruction? What has been done to bridge such gap?
- Has the child participated and benefited from a specialized language development program (e.g., English Language Development)?
- What instructional methodologies or approaches have been used with the child/youth? How effective were they? Why?

Thorough attention to the collection of these types of data will enhance interpretation of testing outcomes and reduce misidentification of learners. De León (1990) developed a survey that promotes understanding of the relationship of students' sociolinguistic experiences to literacy development.

Expectations

Teachers' expectations are powerful determinants of students' progress. Expectations impact attitudes, behaviors, and the availability and quality of learning opportunities. Classroom observations should include both the student and the teacher-student interactions as well as the instructional modifications, appropriateness of materials, and teacher's expectations concerning the culture of the student and his/her first language (or the language of the home).

Summarizing, in order to become familiar with the conditions underlying an apparent or real disability among culturally and/or linguistically diverse individuals, teachers and evaluators need to study both, home and classroom ecologies. They should focus on language use, quality and type of experiential background, perspective of disabilities and giftedness, and teachers' expectations. Such an approach would enable them to make changes to increase transformations (learning) in the mainstream, or to proceed with greater and stronger confidence to the diagnostic stage. Data gathered at this point, as well as the insights developed, are essential for interpretation at all stages of the evaluation and instructional planning processes.

CONSIDERATIONS IN THE INTERPRETATION OF DATA

This section presents a framework for examining the process of assessment and features that constitute the backbone of a proactive program. When a student is not progressing as expected, whether at home or school or both, a referral for additional evaluation can be helpful to determine the cause and nature of the problem(s). Finding the best fit between the youth's needs and research-based interventions can promote strengths and ameliorate weaknesses. To facilitate the quest for information, scholars and researchers (Barona & Barona, 1987; Cummins, 1984; Durán, 1989; Ortiz & Wilkinson, 1991) have proposed various models of intervention which roughly include three stages: modification, diagnosis and prescription. Special features of these models are examined briefly in the following sections in an effort to assist professionals in understanding the conditions that interfere with the academic development of CLD students and to derive sound instructional recommendations.

Modifications Stage

At the modifications stage information is sought about the home and school ecologies in an attempt to understand the degree of alignment between the curriculum, its delivery, and the child/youth's current characteristics and needs. This prereferral stage is considered a preventive stage (Ortiz & Wilkinson, 1991) since it is the point when significant improvement (modifications) can eliminate the need for further study or advanced referral to special education.

Before a student is referred for special education evaluation and services, every effort should be made to assist him/her within the framework of the regular classroom (Adelman in Ortiz & Wilkinson, 1991). At this point inclusion in everyday classroom activities ensures exposure to same-age/grade models, authentic interaction with grade-level materials and routines, and most important, the development of positive self-esteem. Ortiz and Yates (2002) propose that when a students' academic performance falls below expectations, it is more beneficial to study the child's background (linguistic and experiential) as well as previous and current interventions and to provide alternatives within the regular curriculum and placement. They believe that planned modifications to existing conditions can improve the opportunity to learn and increase the learning rate (transformations) of the student. For example, if a student is struggling with beginning reading in first grade, an intensive period of Reading Recovery (Hiebert & Taylor, 2000) intervention might help him/her overcome the challenge.

Making prevention a first priority, both Ortiz and Yates (2002) endorse teacher support teams in practice known as multidisciplinary teams. Their function is to focus on exploring and suggesting alternatives or adaptations. This approach provides opportunities for teacher consultation as well as for specialized support such as experts in the education of second language learners, personnel familiar with the language and culture of the student, and personnel conversant with instructional modifications for students with disabilities. Multidisciplinary teams can provide strong support to the teacher, and help increase appropriate learning opportunities for students. Therefore, a proactive evaluation program should plan to build culturally and linguistically diverse expertise into its capacity plan.

At the modification stage consideration should be given to De León's (1990) "Survey of factors which might affect test performance [of CLD students] and [its] implementation." It addresses language and cultural mismatches, as well as gaps between the students' preacademic experiences and the expectations of the curriculum. The survey's twenty-seven items are divided into issues related to the family/home background, the child's most immediate community, the school's ecology (overall and classroom), and the student (self-image and language competence). A companion instrument, De León's "Student First and Second Language Oral and Literacy Skills," enables evaluators to gather informal data on the student's "language proficiency and classroom language demands" (p. 65).

A critical question to be considered at this stage was raised by Fradd and Hallman (1983): Has the child had the opportunity to develop competencies appropriate to the school's learning environment (e.g., academic English)? A question to follow-up must be: What has been the quality of such experiences?

Also of particular concern with CLD children is transfer of knowledge, skills and strategies from one context to another (application). Greenlee (1981) suggests that checking for transfer must become an automatic habit in teachers of CLD learners; therefore, it should also be considered during the modification stage–How did teachers plan and check for transfer? This information is helpful to the interpretation of previous limitations in academic performance, to future instructional planning, and to the selection of alternative instructional approaches. The instruments and questions suggested can be part of an ecological assessment plan, reserved for youth with limited success in learning the academic curriculum.

Ecobehavioral Assessment (EA) is an emerging and promising alternative to traditional assessment. Both ecobehavioral assessment and the assessment of instructional environments promote inclusion of qualitative data to enhance interpretation of the problem/challenge students face. Ecobehavioral assessment involves the collection of data to substantiate how students spend their time in school, with particular attention to the learning environment, the nature of opportunities to learn and academic engaged time. EA studies the school focusing on the presence and quality of the components of effective instruction (Salvia & Ysseldyke, 1998, p. 231). Currently, according to Salvia and Ysseldyke, a software version of the procedure and data collection aspect is available under the rubric of Ecobehavioral Assessment System Software (EBASS) (Greenwood, Carta, Kamps, & Delquadri, 1995).

Several researchers and evaluators (Ambert & Dew, 1982; Barona & Barona, 1987; Braden, 1989) endorse observation and interviewing as processes that enable observers to identify both facilitative and blocking teaching and learning behaviors. These processes of data collection inform the evaluator and/or assessor on: what the student knows and can act upon, what seems to be effective enabling strategies, what promotes learning in a linguistically and/or culturally different environment, what reduces blockages to learning, and what explains unexpected behaviors such as significant progress or lack of progress.

Gaining information through observation is an ongoing practice in the teaching profession, but consistently and systematically recording such observations is different (Guerin & Maier, 1983). Behaviors to be observed have to be defined in terms of its "observable attributes"– duration, latency, frequency, and amplitude (Salvia & Ysseldyke, 1998, p. 205). Once behavior, goals, context(s), procedures and caveats have been identified then teachers, evaluators and parents may conduct systematic observations which can be supplemented with informal and less structured notes such as those kept by teachers on Post-its® or index cards. The purpose for collecting observational data determines the method that is selected.

Ongoing systematic observation with multiple perspectives should be habitual in cases where students are not progressing as expected or when children have moderate to severe disabilities. Observations of CLD children should address the classroom ecology, particularly delivery of instruction, as well as the student's behavior(s)/response(s). The ecobehavioral model would be an appropriate tool. Readers interested in conducting quantitative behavioral observations should review Alberto and Troutman's (1990) and Guerin and Maier's (1983) texts.

The reader should recall that language, background experiences and educational interventions have special relevance at the modifications stage.

Language Evaluation

In spite of a disability, every child is immersed in a language milieu. Questions about usage, modeling, and proficiency are critical at this level since they can guide in the selection of alternative instructional approaches. Key aspects to consider among CLD children include: amount and quality of exposure to English, dialectal variations, the influence of one language (L1) on the other (L2), language loss, reasons for code-switching, interference, motivation to learn, self-image, and reason(s) for referral or teacher consultation. For specific suggestions on studying the child's language proficiency, see Ambert and Dew (1982); Barona and Barona (1987); Damico, Secord, and Wiig (1992); Ortiz and Garcia (1990); Peña, Quinn, and Iglesias (1992); Ruiz (1995); and Umbel, Pearson, Fernandez, and Oller (1992).

A promising practice for evaluating language skills that are in process of development is the portfolio–a collection of student's language and work samples. Portfolios enable professionals to gather data directly related to the student's performance in specific areas (e.g., oral and written language proficiencies). They are "intended to facilitate judgments about student performance . . . [being] collections of products used to demonstrate what a person has done and, by inference, what a person is capable of doing" (Salvia & Ysseldyke, 1998, p. 271). Data collected in portfolios is considered to be a better representation of the student's abilities and limitations because it is based on the student's actual classroom performance. Portfolio material can support or challenge standardized data garnered through tools such as the California English Language Development Test (CELDT) and thus provides a broader base for educational decision-making. Application is essential to academic performance and portfolios can be the compendium of growth and challenges as students work on applying new learning to different academic tasks defined by state standards and/or local benchmark materials.

According to Salvia and Ysseldyke (1998, p. 271), portfolios can be used to:

- document student effort
- document student growth and achievement
- augment information from other assessment methods
- provide a public accounting of the quality of educational programs

The content of a portfolio should respond to a specified purpose. For example, a language and literacy portfolio for an English Language Learner (ELL) may include materials documenting progress or lack of it in English language acquisition and competence. It could include:

- oral and written language samples
- creative writing
- responses to dictation
- cloze tests developed from narratives
- informational texts and/or poems
- written or oral interpretations of stories or information texts read or heard.

Part of the portfolio could be a collection of taped natural conversations, interviews and/or retelling samples. It could also include written samples (if youth can write or draw), or videotapes of the student sign-ing (if the child can sign). This collection of materials can be used to assess language and other previously identified aspects of academic language development, once rubrics are developed to ensure consistency and reduce bias. For more specific ideas on contents of portfolios, see O'Malley and Valdez Pierce (1996), and Salvia and Ysseldyke (2004).

Salvia and Ysseldyke (2004) recommend that professionals should work on resolving issues related to the development and content of the portfolios to increase their effectiveness and reduce bias. Portfolios represent a promising practice for academic English evaluation por-traying specific information that reflect students' strengths and needs in daily academic life.

Sociocultural Background

Orientation to learning is culturally bound. Learning is facilitated when the student's learning style, language and culture are taken into consideration (Ladson-Billings, 1995). De León (1990) proposes that information about how these factors have impacted on the student's learning opportunities be gathered during this stage since they are important for the identification of mismatches and later on for deter-mining instructional modifications. For example, language impacts on literacy development, thus, expectations and attitudes toward lan-guage and literacy development at home and at school should be com-pared to determine the student's unmet needs. The outcome could be a more meaningful program for support at home and at school.

Previous Academic Interventions

The construction of knowledge is incremental. Thus, underachieve-ment needs to be investigated to determine whether poor achievement resulted from poorly structured instructional opportunities or inherent problems with learning. Studying instructional opportunities includes both, exposure to content, and to language models. In addition, qual-ity of opportunities to practice and develop skills must be factored into the evaluation of academic progress. Modifications to instructional delivery must be considered in relation to the students' status, that is, whether he/she is a non-English speaker, a second language learner, a dialectal speaker, and culturally diverse. For example, if the student is an English language learner of limited English proficiency, one must study the quality of modifications that were made to enhance reading comprehension, particularly because the weakest language for learning (English) was used as the medium for instruction and to promote some learning.

Another aspect for analysis requiring documentation would be the child's experiential background in relation to classroom curriculum. For example, how did the teacher handle culturally-biased readings given the youth's limited exposure to certain sociocultural experiences critical to the understanding of such stories? Previous efforts to assist students with learning English both at school and at home must also be thoroughly documented. If he/she was a non-English or limited English speaker, or dialectal speaker, at the time of enrollment in school, documentation of the quality of efforts to assist the student augment linguistic competence must be sought. Have his/her teachers understood the difference between Cummins' (1984) dual linguistic competence dimensions of BICS (Basic Interpersonal Communication Skills) and his advanced concept of CALP (Cognitive Academic Language Proficiency)? Do teachers understand Cummins' (1980) Common Underlying Proficiency (CUP) model? If affirmative, did they adjust their planning, teaching and expectations accordingly in order to facilitate communication, comprehension, academic learning, and transfer of knowledge and skills?

According to Cummins (1980), language proficiency is more than an ability to communicate socially at interpersonal levels. It involves the application of linguistic knowledge and intuition, developed through experiences in meaningful contexts and through higher order thinking skills such as generalization, analysis, synthesis and abstraction. To distinguish between these two dimensions which affect academic performance, Cummins (1980) utilized the analogy of an iceberg. Like it, in language there is a perceivable, contextualized, more concrete dimension which can be readily noticed by those involved in the exchange. This perceptible dimension, or Basic Interpersonal Communication Skills (BICS), relies on a highly interactive context and is usually supported by other aspects of language such as nonverbal and paralinguistic cues. Like the submerged part of the iceberg, there is another aspect of language that is not readily perceived. It is hidden within itself, in a context that is much reduced in comparison with BICS. It is the abstract dimension of formal conceptualization, abstraction, higher order cognitive processing, advanced reading and writing, and oral expression.

Cummins (1980) named it Cognitive Academic Language Proficiency (CALP). He used it to refer to the competence that learners need to develop to successfully meet the more decontextualized demands of schooling. Examples would be, the language of the textbooks from second grade on, the style of short stories, novels, and advanced poetic forms; the language of debate, oral discussions and explanations in content area classes, particularly where no visual referents are used to guide learning; the language encasing word problems (applications) in mathematics; and the language of deep questions in science. In each of these fields the message is encoded in complex syntactical constructions and abstract language, forcing the reader to go beyond the printed language. When one operates through CALP, one must integrate, analyze, summarize, critique, reflect, question and recreate new texts in the process of responding to daily academic questions and challenges.

In studies reported by Cummins (1980, 1984), instructors do not understand these dimensions of language, as well as the time these require to be developed, or the conditions which favor their development. Ultimately, they refer second language learners for psychological evaluations believing that a disability exists in the learner which prevents him/her from achieving higher levels of academic performance (Cummins, 1984).

A promising approach to assessment and interpretation of academic achievement for CLD students might be curriculum-based evaluation, since the analysis of patterns of strengths and weaknesses can be cross-validated with information available on language proficiency, experiential background and previous interventions. Curriculum-based measures can be locally developed tools comparing the student's behavior samples to established performance standards (Howell, Fox, & Moorehead, 1993). Confidence in evaluation emerges from the authenticity of the material or tasks selected by relating it to the curriculum taught in the school, and to the standards promoted by the district and/or state. When curriculum-based assessments are conducted, specific skills and deficits are readily identifiable providing material for educational planning. Simplicity, practicality and flexibility characterize this type of assessment. For specific suggestions and models, see Howell, Fox and Moorehead (1993).

The process of instructional modifications should be continuous and consistent in classrooms and particularly in those situations where cultural diversity exists. Longitudinal monitoring (follow-up) is essential when working with students learning English as their second language (Cummins, 1987). For example, students who are succeeding in acquiring academic English for second grade might need additional instructional support as they begin to navigate the third-grade texts, or the fourth grade. This is because the linguistic and cognitive demands of the textbooks' language, organization and content increase as students advance through the upper grades. The assessment approaches suggested in the preceding sections of this chapter make periodic monitoring viable and fruitful. Such considerations are in tune with the central theme proposed in this chapter, that evaluators need to study the child/youth in all his/her ecologies in order to learn about his/her strengths and challenges, and to become familiar with the nature of the problem. Alternative ways should be explored to resolve or ameliorate the learning gap that these learners face in their classrooms.

Diagnostic Stage

When the repertoire of strategies appropriate to an inclusive environment have been exhausted, showing limited evidence of academic progress, or the severity of the disability consistently interferes with learning, an in-depth, or diagnostic evaluation is appropriate. Barona and Barona (1987) propose that careful consideration be given to the evaluation stages. At the diagnostic stage, three aspects need to be investigated and cross-referenced with the extensive information gathered in the modifications stage. Both formal and informal assessment should focus on communication, intelligence, and academic achievement, and if appropriate, on other specific behaviors contributing to the problem. Comprehensive approaches are necessary at this stage. Assessment profiles should include, "data that are representative of student performance across time, contexts, subjects and skills . . . [and across languages]" (Ortiz & Wilkinson, 1991, p. 41). Selective administration of subcomponents, modification of instruments, testing the limits, dynamic assessment, and other appropriate measurement strategies for CLD children are critical at this stage in order to obtain non-biased or limited-bias profiles (Cummins, 1984).

Before discussing approaches and tools in the following section, it is essential to review the case law that supports the recommendations made in this chapter pertaining to evaluation and assessment. As mentioned before, the right to an appropriate and meaningful education requires special considerations in cases involving English Language Learners. The legal support for such considerations emerges from several litigation cases, three of which involved California.

Diana v. State Board of Education (1970) established the precedent of testing in native or primary language, using nonverbal tests as part of intellectual assessment, collecting and using extensive supporting data in cases where students are not performing as expected.

Larry P. v. Riles (1971) dealt with assessment practices to identify students with mental retardation; however, it was a landmark case in that it strongly brought to light the consequences of misidentifying students through poor assessment and evaluation practices.

Lau v. Nichols (1974) promoted the development of guidelines to identify and evaluate all children having limited English skills (proficiency) in order to provide them with a meaningful educational program (access to the curriculum).

Jose P v. Ambach (1979) reinforced the timely evaluation and placement of children of limited English proficiency in appropriate educational programs. A later case dealt with the same goals for preschoolers.

Communication Assessment

Communicative competence is judged by the effectiveness of exchanges of information. In cases involving CLD children, the identification of language dominance is critical (Maldonado-Colón, 1984; Ortiz, 1984). Language dominance needs to be established from analysis and comparison of profiles in both the first (L1) and the second (L2) language. A profile of abilities and skills must be developed before the administration of intellectual and academic tests, since it will enable the evaluator to make necessary adjustments to assure reliable and valid results and interpretations (Cummins, 1984). Effective verbal communication throughout the assessment process is necessary in order to obtain an accurate profile of the student's potential, strengths, and developing competence, as well as frustrations with the learning process.

Both receptive and productive aspects of language competence need to be determined in evaluating communication. Specific suggestions on how to approach this process and/or strategies to use can be found in Ambert and Dew (1982), Barona and Barona (1987), Damico (1991), De León (1990), Hernández (1994), O'Malley and Valdez Pierce (1996), Pike and Salend (1995), and de Valenzuela & Baca (2004b).

Analysis of data gathered in the modifications stage suggests areas to pursue with diagnostic procedures at this stage.

Intellectual Assessment

The ability to learn (intellectual ability) is critical to the educational process. While the paradigm of intelligence continues to evolve (Cummins, 1984; de Valenzuela & Baca, 2004b; Drapeau, 2004; Gardner, 1985; Vygotsky, 1978), the procedures and measures to evaluate it and the learning potential remain static, restricted and limited in perspective, particularly for CLD children. Formal standardized measures continue to be required by most state agencies as part of the evaluation process to identify exceptionalities with very few local exceptions. These exceptions are windows of opportunity for a meaningful education of English Language Learners (de Valenzuela & Baca, 2004a). However, since traditional assessment practices continue to prevail in the field, careful use and cautious interpretation of testing outcomes are recommended. Approaches that rely solely on standardized verbal or nonverbal measures are not fully endorsed since they have been found consistently to be culturally biased (Popham, 2003; Salvia & Ysseldyke, 1998).

Salvia and Ysseldyke (1998) conclude that, ". . . intelligence is an inferred entity, a term or construct we use to explain differences in present behavior and to predict differences in future behavior" (p. 331). While predictions on intellectual potential have proven erroneous often in cases involving CLD youth (Artiles & Ortiz, 2002; Cummins, 1984; Durán, 1989; Figueroa, 2002; Garcia & Yates, 1986), professionals continue to measure discrete aspects like general knowledge and/or receptive vocabulary to predict these youths' potential. To remediate these limitations, several options to traditional intellectual assessment practices have emerged.

Dynamic assessment processes that invite and engage the student and incorporate observation, intervention and guidance followed by evaluation are the most promising options (Cummins, 1984; de Valenzuela & Baca, 2004b; Duran, 1989) in spite of the criticism leveled at them because of their demands on time. Rate of learning, quality of learning, and effort to learn are critical variables in the evaluation of intelligence. The estimation of potential to learn and to accomplish must be cross-referenced with cultural and linguistic abilities and demands in the classroom and at home. Standardized measures cannot yield such individualized profiles to guide instruction.

While tests of intellectual ability or functioning might indicate weaknesses in general information and/or in processing information, other criticisms endorsed by Durán (1989) include, providing limited information on the most pressing concerns of teachers and parents. In addition, they are not able to identify what the student is ready to learn which is a necessary condition for teachers to draft meaningful instructional plans (Abedi, 2004; Popham, 2003; Yates & Ortiz, 2004).

Cummins (1984) and Holtzman, Jr. and Wilkinson (1991), for instance, propose alternative interpretations of the WISC-R subtests and testing the limits as avenues to gain additional information necessary for interpretation to draft instructionally related recommendations. Additionally, Cummins underscores the evaluator's cultural sensitivity as critical to the intellectual assessment process since many test items and procedures included in the measures might appear unnatural to children from diverse sociocultural groups. For example, picture completion and/or picture arrangement might be a challenge for many culturally diverse students. Thus, data gathered during the diagnostic stage needs to be cross-referenced with instruments such as De León's surveys, in order to reduce bias in interpretation and to increase the possibility of appropriate placement and interventions.

Specific Assessments

Once the influence of culture, language and the intellectual potential have been estimated, an evaluation for disabilities requires assessment of academic-related knowledge. Combinations of formal and informal assessments are common (de Valenzuela & Baca, 2004b). Today's professionals have access to a gamut of informal evaluation strategies (see Pike & Salend, 1995). Currently, approaches such as curriculum-based assessment (CBA), portfolio assessment, and the development of curriculum-based frameworks for authentic literacy assessment that include informal reading inventories, locally developed rubrics, and portfolios seem to promise more accurate information of what the students know, and what they are ready to learn than national or state mandated standardized assessments (Artiles & Ortiz, 2002; de Valenzuela & Baca, 2004b; Salvia & Ysseldyke, 2004).

Informal strategies enhance the holographic image. They include interviews, work sample study, analysis of performance on teacher-developed tests, and comparative performance analysis on measures such as informal reading inventories. In addition, norm-referenced and standardized test results continue to be required in most programs. A blend of the local and statewide standardized measures such as the CELDT (California English Language Development Test) are more informative for teachers than a set of scores or averages on performance. Remember that, experienced evaluators attempt to gather a variety of data from multiple sources in order to increase accuracy and to facilitate data-based instructional decision-making.

Certain students, in addition to, or in lieu of measures of achievement, require evaluation of other aspects of individual functioning, such as motor, social, functional, and attitudinal behavior (Barona & Barona, 1987; Chamberlain & Medeiros-Landurand, 1991). For these students, selection of procedures and/or instrumentation, and interpretation of assessment outcomes requires cross-validation with knowledge about norms within the student's sociocultural group to prevent errors in interpretation of behaviors/performance. Evaluation of social and motor behaviors should be done from a multiple perspective approach in order to benefit from the expertise that several fields can contribute (e.g., physical therapy, occupational therapy, and developmental diagnostics). For example, observations, frequency counts, and time samplings are important in determining and interpreting the importance of behaviors of some children with autism. Functional analysis provides the opportunity to replace negative behaviors with more positive and efficient ones. Ecological inventories can be culturally and linguistically relevant tools to identify and plan for functional needs (Durán, 1989).

Specific suggestions made by de Valenzuela and Baca (2004, pp. 184–203) include:

- interview many different people
- consider the use of problem-solving and information seeking activities during interviews
- seek parents' input on students' behaviors and performances at home
- document conditions that elicit best performance at home along with those that prove challenging
- incorporate information provided by parents into suggestions for curricular modifications

Summarizing, the process of assessment should yield data that enable special educators and evaluators to identify and plan for functional needs as Ortiz and Wilkinson (1991) and Yates and Ortiz (2004) propose. Simultaneously, the evaluator should address the type and severity of disability while considering the interaction of these factors with the background (linguistic and social) of the student. In the hands of professionals such process remains open to learning, limiting bias, and yielding an increased understanding of the youth under study. Fragmentation and compartmentalization might be appropriate for administrative and accountability purposes; however, they have no place in the evaluation of a CLD student.

An organized, integrated and collaborative approach among professionals is necessary to optimize the learning opportunity of CLD youth (Gersten, Brengelman, & Jimenez, 1994). Potential bias must be monitored because of its impact on the generation of various hypotheses and eventually in the selection or design of appropriate interventions. A case study approach proposed by Barona and Barona (1987) would facilitate organization, data collection, data interpretation and evaluation as well as recommendations for instructional planning.

The previous sections of this chapter aimed at raising consciousness and directing professionals to considerations, caveats, instrumentation and procedures to promote greater understanding of CLD youth. Table XXII summarizes key aspects of a proactive approach to assessment and evaluation of CLD youth. The next section succinctly suggests considerations for instructional planning given the scope of this chapter. More detailed suggestions are found in other chapters of the book.

Table XXII
A PROACTIVE MODEL FOR THE ASSESSMENT OF CLD YOUTH

Stage	Information Needed or to be Utilized
Pre-referral Modification(s)	• Language abilities and background profile • Socio-cultural profile • Experimental profile (pre-academic and academic experiences, record of performance in relation to local curriculum) • Cross-validation analysis
Referral Diagnostic	• Multidimensional profile developed in previous stage (Includes results of all three profiles plus the text of the deliberations) • Stronger analytical profile of challenges the student is facing • Intellectual or learning potential assessment • Other assessments • Cross-validation analysis
Placement Prescriptive	• Multidimensional profile • Diagnostic profile

PRESCRIPTIVE STAGE: DATA-BASED INSTRUCTIONAL PLANNING

Teachers seek support in effecting transformations (learning) when they initiate referrals. They expect the outcome of the process to yield an educational plan that identifies what has originated the learning challenge and suggestions on how to reduce or eliminate the learning gap. According to IDEA (1998) the individual educational programs (IEP's) emerging from the data collected through multiple approaches that permeate the modifications and diagnostic stages should be the blueprint for instruction.

Thorough and appropriate assessments of the strengths and weaknesses of CLD youth, cross-validated with informal data on language and sociocultural background as well as previous interventions, yield robust data for evaluation and planning of educational programs for CLD students. Annual goals and short-term objectives flow from carefully interpreted critical data and specially from curriculum-based assessments, and in cases of mild to moderate disabilities, from students' portfolios. The evaluator uses the available information to formulate interpretations necessary for the development of goals and objectives, and the recruitment of supportive services. Ortiz and Yates (2002) as well as Salvia and Ysseldyke (2004) underscore that appropriate goals and objectives direct the selection of instructional opportunities, methods and materials. Alignment of the student's needs with state standards would vary depending on the individual profile. Thus, modification of age/grade level standards might be necessary to align the instructional program with the student's competence. Therefore, the IEP should reflect goals aimed at reducing the existing gap as the student works within his/her zone of proximal development (Vygotsky, 1978); that is, the level at which he/she indicates he/she is ready to learn something more advanced with appropriate scaffolding.

Transformation from a noneffective to an effective learning opportunity must be the ultimate goal of the assessment and evaluation processes in schools. Identification of strategies which promote high functioning and challenge the underdeveloped potential of the student must capitalize on his/her strengths. Strengthening weak areas is an expected outcome of the assessment and evaluation processes. It is what parents and teachers expect, too.

In summary, today's intervention approaches are characterized by higher expectations for students, highly interactive learning opportunities as well as integrated instruction and holistic perspectives concerned with the whole child. The most important current foci on intervention include methods such as interactionist (Cummins, 1984), collaborative and integrative (Ortiz & Yates, 2004; Ruiz, 1989). These approaches are aimed at increasing communication, motivation, and improving self-esteem (empowerment). Ultimately, they are intended to improve the students' academic performance.

Instructional planning should also take into consideration what is known about language acquisition and development (both L1 and L2) of English Language Learners, how skills transfer and the most effective modifications to instruction for these students. Today's teachers must strive harder to promote those abilities that enable students to generate their own knowledge. For appropriate adaptations for CLD children, see Ortiz and Wilkinson (1991), Ortiz and Yates (2002), Ruiz (1989), and Salend (2001).

CONCLUSION

Today's schools focus on identification and development of appropriate curriculum frameworks that enable all students to advance in their learning. A comprehensive assessment framework facilitates the match between the curriculum framework and the CLD student's profile. This chapter provides suggestions on how to facilitate this effort in consonance with Johnston's suggestion (Allington, 1994) that the evaluation of student learning, or exploration of their learning difficulties, become a personalized process relying on close, and careful examination of a student's work, background and previous efforts.

The essence of this chapter is to emphasize that a broader assessment of the abilities of English Language Learners is a necessary process, and not an optional one. Teachers and evaluators must seek as much information as possible to be able to understand the behaviors and limitations they observe in these learners. The richer the database, the sounder the interpretation of observed behaviors and performance will be. Heterogeneity of the population requires it, and professional ethics demand it.

Thoughts to take with you as you close this chapter: Best practices are expected of professionals who are involved in assessing and evaluating as well as planning educational programs for culturally and linguistically diverse youths. Best practices include a search and use of most effective procedures and instruments to gather comprehensive information for informed decision-making.

Best practices incorporate a concern for the students' self-image and cultural background in the selection of procedures and interventions. Best practices consider the degree of the students' language proficiency and dominance under varying conditions and environments. Best practices always link assessment with instruction. Best practices also require professionals to give consideration to variation of instructional opportunities and methods of instruction as they conduct instructional planning.

REFERENCES

Abedi, J. (2004). The No Child Left Behind Act and English language learners: Assessment and accountability issues. *Educational Researcher, 33*, 4–14.

Alberto, P., & Troutman, A. (1990). *Applied behavior analysis for teachers* (3rd Ed.). Columbus, OH: Merrill.

Allington, R. L. (1994). The schools we have. The schools we need. *The Reading Teacher, 48,* 14–29.

Ambert, A. & Dew, N. (1982). *Special education for exceptional bilingual students: A handbook for educators.* Milwaukee, WI: Midwest National Origin Desegregation Assistance Center.

Applewhite, S. R. (1979). The legal dialect of bilingual education. In R. V. Padilla (Ed.), *Bilingual education and public policy in the U.S.* Ypsilanti, MI: Eastern Michigan University.

Artiles, A. & Ortiz, A. (Eds.). (2002). English Language Learners with special needs: Identification, assessment, and instruction. McHenry, IL: Center for Applied Linguistics, Delta Systems.

Baca, L. M., & Cervantes, H. T. (Eds.). (2004). *The bilingual special education interface.* Upper Saddle River, NJ: Pearson.

Baca, L. M., & Baca, E. (2004). Bilingual special education: A judicial perspective. In L. M. Baca & H. T. Cervantes (Eds.), *The bilingual special education interface* (pp. 76–99). Upper Saddle River, NJ: Pearson.

Baca, L. M., Baca, E., & de Valenzuela, J. S. (2004). Background and rationale for bilingual special education. In L. M. Baca & H. T. Cervantes (Eds.), *The bilingual special education interface* (pp. 1–23). Upper Saddle River, NJ: Pearson.

Barona, A., & Barona, M. S. (1987). A model for the assessment of LEP students referred for special education services. In S. H. Fradd & W. J. Tikunoff (Eds.), (pp. 183–209). Boston: College-Hill.

Braden, J. P. (1989). Organizing and monitoring databases. In S. H. Fradd & M. J. Weismantel (Eds.), *Meeting the needs of culturally and linguistically different students: A handbook for educators* (pp. 14–33). Boston: College-Hill.

Chamberlain, P., & Medeiros-Landurand, P. (1991). Practical considerations for the assessment of LEP students with special needs. In E. V. Hamayan & J. S. Damico (Eds.), *Limiting bias in the assessment of bilingual students* (pp. 111–156). Austin, TX: Pro-Ed.

Crawford, J. (2004). *Educating English language learners: Language diversity in the classroom.* Los Angeles: Bilingual Education Services.

Cummins, J. (1980). The construct of language proficiency in bilingual education. In J. E. Alatis (Ed.), *Georgetown University Roundtable on languages and linguistics.* Washington, DC: Georgetown University Press.

Cummins, J. (1984). *Assessment of bilingual exceptional students: Issues in assessment and pedagogy.* Clevedon, England: Multilingual Matters.

Cummins, J. (1987). The role of assessment in the empowerment of minority students. In E. Bayardelle et al. (Eds.), A*ssessment: From policy to program* (pp. 2–3). Rochester, NY: New York State Education Department.

Damico, J. S. (1991). Descriptive assessment of communicative ability in limited English proficient students. In E. V. Hamayan & J. S. Damico (Eds.), *Limiting bias in the assessment of bilingual students* (pp. 157–217). Austin, TX: Pro-Ed.

Damico, J. S., Secord, W. A., & Wiig, E. H. (1992). Descriptive language assessment at school: Characteristics and design. *Best Practices in School Speech Language Pathology, 2,* 1–8.

De León, J. (1990). A model for an advocacy oriented assessment process in the psychoeducational evaluation of culturally and linguistically different students. *The Journal of Educational Issues of Language Minority Students, 7*, 53–67.

de Valenzuela, J. S., & Baca, L. (2004a). Issues and theoretical considerations in the assessment of bilingual children. In L. M. Baca & H. T. Cervantes (Eds.), *The bilingual special education interface* (pp. 162–183). Upper Saddle River, NJ: Pearson.

de Valenzuela, J. S., & Baca, L. (2004b). Procedures and techniques for assessing the bilingual exceptional child. In L. M. Baca & H. T. Cervantes (Eds.), *The bilingual special education interface* (pp. 184–203). Upper Saddle River, NJ: Pearson.

Drapeau, P. (2004). *Differentiated instruction: Making it work* (pp. 12–17). New York: Teaching Resources.

Durán, E. (1989). Functional language instruction for the handicapped or linguistically different students. *Reading Improvement, 26*, 265–268.

Fernandez, A. T. (1992). Legal support for bilingual education and language-appropriate related services for Limited English Proficient students with disabilities. *Bilingual Research Journal, 16*, 117–140.

Figueroa, R. (2002). Toward a new model of assessment. In A. Artiles & A. Ortiz (Eds.), *English language learners with special education needs: Identification, assessment, and instruction.* McHenry, IL: Center for Applied Linguistics, Delta Systems.

Fradd, S. H., & Hallman, C. L. (1983). Implications of psychological and educational research for assessment and instruction of culturally and linguistically different students. *Learning Disabilities Quarterly, 6*, 468–478.

Garcia, S. B., & Yates, J. R. (1986). Policy issues associated with serving bilingual exceptional children. *Reading, Writing, and Learning Disabilities, 2*, 123–137.

Gardner, H. (1985). *The mind's new science: A history of the cognitive revolution.* New York: Basic Books/Harper Collins.

Gersten, R., Brengelman, S., & Jimenez, R. (1994). Effective instruction for culturally and linguistically diverse students: A reconceptualization. *Focus on Exceptional Children, 27*, 1–16.

Greenlee, M. (1981). Specifying the needs of a "bilingual" developmentally delayed population: Issues and case studies. *NABE Journal, 6*, 55–76.

Greenwood, C., Carta, J., Kamps, D., & Delquadri, J. (1995). *Ecobehavioral assessment system software.* Kansas City, KS: Juniper Gardens Children's Center.

Guerin, G. H., & Maier, A. S. (1983). *Informal assessment in education.* Palo Alto, CA: Mayfield.

Harry, B. (1992). *Cultural diversity, families, and the special education system: Communication and empowerment.* New York: Teachers College.

Hernández, R. D. (1994). Reducing bias in the assessment of culturally and linguistically diverse populations. *The Journal of Educational Issues of Language and Minority Students, 14*, 269–300.

Hiebert, E. H., & Taylor, B. M. (2000). Beginning reading instruction: Research on early interventions. In M. L. Kamil et al. (Eds.), *Handbook of reading research, Vol. III* (pp. 455–482). Mahwah, NJ: Lawrence Erlbaum.

Holtzman, W. H., Jr., & Wilkinson, C. Y. (1991). Assessment of cognitive modifiability. In E. V. Hamayan & J. S. Damico (Eds.), *Limiting bias in assessment of bilingual students* (pp. 247–280). Austin, TX: Pro-Ed.

Howell, K. W., Fox, S. L., & Moorehead, M. K. (1993). *Curriculum-based evaluation: Teaching and decision-making* (2nd Ed.). Pacific Grove, CA: Brooks/Cole.

Ladson-Billings, G. (1995). Towards a theory of culturally relevant pedagogy. *American Educational Research Journal, 32,* 465–491.

Lynch, E. W., & Hanson, M. J. (Eds.). (1998). *Developing cross-cultural competence: A guide for working with children and their families.* Baltimore: Paul H. Brookes.

Maldonado-Colón, E. (1984). Assessment: Considerations upon interpreting data of linguistically/culturally different students referred for disabilities or disorders. In A. C. Willig & H. F. Greenberg (Eds.), *Bilingualism and learning disabilities: Policy and practices for teachers and administrators* (pp. 69–77). New York: American Library.

Moll, L. C., Amanti, C., Neff, D., & Gonzalez, N. (1992). Funds of knowledge for teaching: Using a qualitative approach to connect homes and classrooms. *Theory into Practice, 31,* 132–141.

No Child Left Behind Act, Pub. L. No. 107–110, 115 Stat. 1425 (2002).

O'Malley, J. M., & Valdez Pierce, L. (1996). *Authentic assessment for English Language Learners: Practical approaches for teachers* (pp. 1–8). Palo Alto, CA: Addison-Wesley.

Ortiz, A. (1984). Choosing the language of instruction for exceptional bilingual children. *Teaching Exceptional Children, 16,* 208–212.

Ortiz, A. A., & Garcia, S. B. (1990). Using language assessment data for language and instructional planning for exceptional bilingual students. In A. Carrrasquillo & R. Baecher (Eds.), *Teaching the bilingual special education student* (pp. 24–47). Norwood, NJ: Ablex.

Ortiz, A. A., & Maldonado-Colón, E. (1984). Reducing inappropriate referrals of language minority students in special education. In A. C. Willig & H. F. Greenberg (Eds.), *Bilingualism and learning disabilities: Policy and practices for teachers and administrators* (pp. 37–50). New York: American Library.

Ortiz, A. A., & Wilkinson, C. Y. (1991). Assessment and intervention model for the bilingual exceptional student (AIM for the Best). *Teacher Education and Special Education, 14,* 35–42.

Ortiz, A. A., & Yates, J. R. (2002). Considerations in Assessment. In A. Artiles & A. Ortiz, *English language learners with special education needs: Identification, assessment, and instruction.* McHenry, IL: Center for Applied Linguistics, Delta Systems.

Peña, E., Quinn, R., & Iglesias, A. (1992). The application of dynamic methods to language assessment: A nonbiased procedure. *Journal of Special Education, 26,* 269–280.

Pike, K., & Salend, S. J. (1995). Authentic assessment strategies: Alternatives to norm-referenced testing. *Teaching Exceptional Children, 28,* 15–20.

Popham, W. J. (2003). *Test better, teach better: The instructional role of assessment.* Alexandria, VA: Association for Supervision and Curriculum Development.

Rueda, R. S. (1983). Metalinguistic awareness in monolingual and bilingual mildly retarded children. *NABE Journal, 8,* 55–67.

Ruiz, N. T. (1989). An optimal learning environment for Rosemary. *Exceptional Children, 56,* 130–144.

Ruiz, N. T. (1995). The social construction of ability and disability: II. Optimal and at-risk lesson in a bilingual special education classroom. *Journal of Learning Disabilities, 28,* 491–502.

Salvia, J., & Ysseldyke, J. E. (1998). *Assessment.* Boston: Houghton Mifflin.

Salvia, J., & Ysseldyke, J. E. (2001). *Assessment.* Boston: Houghton Mifflin.

Salvia, J., & Ysseldyke, J. E. (2004). *Assessment.* Boston: Houghton Mifflin.

Salend, S. J. (2001). *Creating inclusive classrooms: Effective and reflective practices* (4th ed.). Upper Saddle River, NJ: Merrill-Prentice Hall.

Shapiro, A. M. (2004). How including prior knowledge as a subject variable may change outcomes of learning research. *American Educational Research Journal, 41,* 159–189.

Umbel, V. M., Pearson, B. Z., Fernandez, M. C., & Oller, O. K. (1992). Measuring bilingual children's vocabularies. *Child Development, 63,* 1012–1020.

Vygotsky, L. S. (1978). *Mind in society.* Cambridge, MA: Harvard University.

Yates, J. R., & Ortiz, A. A. (2004). Developing Individualized Educational Programs for exceptional language minority students. In L. M. Baca & H. T. Cervantes (Eds.), *The bilingual special education interface* (pp. 204–229). Upper Saddle River, NJ: Pearson.

Chapter 12

LITERACY DEVELOPMENT

ELVA DURÁN

This chapter will give information on literacy development for students with and without disabilities. There will be a review of the literature presented on all the different components that are useful and necessary when teaching students to listen, speak, read, and write. Many of these components presented in this chapter which are necessary to teach reading are found in various English language arts standards and are research based. The more one strives to teach students who are English learners and those who have and do not have disabilities, the more these students will learn and will be capable of reaching major goals in all they are wanting to and are on their way to accomplishing.

PHONOLOGICAL AWARENESS

Phonological awareness is defined as the ability to perceive spoken words as a sequence of sounds. It also refers to the awareness of and access to the sounds of language (Adams, 1990; Ball & Blachman, 1991; Lyon, 1995). Many differences between good and poor readers can be explained by phonological processing of which phonological awareness is a component (Smith, Simmons, & Kame'enui, 1995). Because of overwhelming research support for the hypothesis that phonological awareness plays a central role in reading acquisition, Smith et al. concluded that phonological awareness instruction is obligatory and is not optional. Because of the overwhelming research support for the hypothesis that phonological awareness plays a central awareness instruction is obligatory and is not optional. Phonological awareness refers to aspects of sound such as rhyming and manipulating sounds. Phonemic awareness refers only to awareness of phonemes, the smallest meaningful parts of spoken language (Carnine et al., 2004).

Some of the skills that need to be taught as part of phonemic awareness include phoneme isolation, auditory discrimination, sound manipulation, segmenting, blending and rhyming. An example of phoneme isolation would be having the students say a phoneme or sound in a word as the teacher calls out a particular sound; for example, the teacher says *cat* and then tells the students to say the sound in the middle position. The students would say *aaaaa*. Phoneme isolation is especially helpful if the students cannot recall a phoneme in a word and the extra practice or review with this sound or any sound the students cannot distinguish will be most helpful when practicing phonemes in isolation.

Other phonemic awareness skills that need to be taught would include sound segmentation and blending. When students segment sounds an example of what might follow in this activity would be when the teacher says, "We are going to see how well we can listen to the sounds in the word I tell you. The word is c-a-t." The students at this point repeat each phoneme in the word cat without stopping in-between sounds. The teacher now tells the students to say the entire word and the students say *cat*. This would be an example of blending. Utilizing the same word the teacher can call out the word *cat* and the students can pick up a finger for each sound heard in the word. In this example, the teacher will ask the children how many phonemes or sounds in the word *cat* and the children will say three. Such practice is critical because the students will be able to recognize that there are three phonemes in the word *cat*.

Additionally, the students can rhyme words with the teacher. For instance, the teacher can say *fat, bat, car*. "Which words rhyme?" the teacher may ask the students. The students will say *fat* and *bat* rhyme.

Other activities in phonemic awareness include sound manipulation. In sound manipulation the students can get practice substituting the first sound in each word; for example, the teacher may say, "The word is *bat*. Take the *b* away from *bat* and add an *m* what do you have?" The students will say the new word is *mat*. Now the middle sound can be substituted and the teacher can say, "The word is *mat.*" The students repeat after the teacher and say, *mat.* The teacher will now say, "Take the *a* away from *mat* and add an *e* what do you have?" And the students will say *met.* Another sound substitution will be to have the children indicate what is the new word when we take the *t* away from *met* and add an *n* what do we have and the students will say, *men.* Sound substitutions in the beginning, middle and final position in words is difficult for many students to grasp initially and will take review and practice to help the students learn these skills. Like with all phonemic awareness skills, practice must be given daily so these auditory discrimination skills will become automatic.

Phonemic awareness activities should be a big part in the teaching of reading curriculum. Such activities will assist the students to learn a strong foundation in sound awareness and help them as they begin reading words in a more systematic, explicit manner.

Persons with severe disabilities can learn to rhyme especially if they are learning to read utilizing a systematic reading program. The teacher of these students will need to decide if he/she will teach all the skills in phonemic awareness. Further, the teacher of persons with severe disabilities will need to decide if he/she will teach all the phonemic awareness skills or some of the phonemic awareness skills to their students. Also, another consideration for teachers of students with moderate/severe disabilities is that the teachers will need to decide if this is functional for their students to learn.

Teachers who teach students with disabilities who are also English learners will need to consider the student's first language and their level of proficiency in their native and second language. Since phonological skills transfer from Spanish to English for example, a teacher who knows the student's first language may want to teach her student some of these phonemic awareness activities to the students first in their native language, especially if the students are learning to read in their first language. In the book written by Durán et al. (2003) entitled, *Systematic Instruction in Reading for Spanish-Speaking Students*, also published by Charles C Thomas Publishers, there are several phonemic awareness activities that a teacher can utilize with their students in order to have them learn these critical activities.

CONCEPTS ABOUT PRINT

Another critical area in teaching reading to students in general and special education classes are the concept about print skills. Concept about print can be defined as the relation between the letters and the sounds the children have learned, and having them associate these relationships between letters and the sounds is symbolic: letters stand for sounds (Bialystok, 1995). Some of these skills include having students learn left to right, top and bottom of a book; how to turn a page; learn that there is an author's page, front and back of a book; and having students learn where to locate the page numbers in a book. Also, some concept of print skills include having students learn that print provides information; having students recognize that sentences in print are made up of separate words; identify the title and author of a reading selection; and identify letters, words and sentences. These are important skills that are usually taught to students before they learn to read. Their earliest concepts grow out of the interactive routines of reading story books (Snow & Ninio, 1986) and develop into formal awareness of print, sounds, and words. According to Bialystok, this concept of print, graphic awareness, phonemic awareness, and phoneme-grapheme correspondences predict children's later success with reading (Brady & Shankweiler, 1991). Additionally, the importance of exposure to print remains relevant and has even been linked to reading and spelling ability for children in the third and fourth grades (Cunningham, 1998). Cunningham suggests that because the purpose of reading is intertwined with its technique (namely, the representation of language), children must have a clear understanding of the basic concepts of print before learning to read. Adams (1990) further notes that children must induce that print symbolizes language.

When deciding what to teach students with disabilities, this is an area that is very important and should be taught as it will have a direct effect on how children will learn to read. English learners will need to learn all of these skills as these skills transfer from Spanish to English for example. Students with more severe disabilities need to understand the concept of left to right as this will be helpful to them in the community and when they do their jobs and read words to complete their job-related tasks. Again, how much of these concepts students with severe disabilities understand and learn will depend on the teacher and the student's family members. If students with severe disabilities will need these skills in home, school and community, then those concepts about print skills should be taught to the students.

DECODING AND WORD RECOGNITION

In decoding and word recognition, the students understand the basic features of reading. They select letter patterns and know how to translate them into spoken language by using phonics, syllabication, and word parts. By applying the skills the students are learning with phonological awareness and developing the alphabetic principle, the students progress to learning to read to develop fluency by first reading decodable texts that contain phonic elements and sight words that have been taught. The text should be unfamiliar to students so that they are required to apply word-analysis skills and not simply reconstruct text they have memorized. Even the number of irregular words and high frequency or sight words should be controlled so that students will have their own high frequency words or words that appear over and over in many of the stories and printed text for that particular basal series. Examples of high frequency words may be "is," "the," and "this." Students in beginning reading also learn to read common irregular sight words for example, "have," "said," and "give." According to Shefelbine (personal communication, January, 2006), students should have at least five minutes daily instruction with sight words. This practice is crucial to help students develop fluency which is a critical part of decoding and comprehension development. Some of the practice with sight words can involve having the students say the word, spell the word out as the teacher touches each letter on the card and having the student spell the word from memory. The student should also define the word being taught by using the word in a sentence. Following the oral spell-out and using the word in a sentence, the student will spell the word from memory (Durán, 2006).

Students learning sight words need multiple exposures to the words in order to learn them without hesitation. The practice they will get with the spelling dictation explained above and the practice that will come from reading the words in decodable texts will help them become better readers.

Additionally, in beginning reading the students will need to have knowledge of *r*-controlled letter sound associations such as "car" and "far." Also, the students will need practice with compound words and contractions. Some examples of compound words would be "pancake" and "escape." Examples of contractions may include: "I've" (I have) and "we've" (we have). Other words that students learn in beginning reading (grades first through third) include learning inflectional forms such as "s," "ed," and "ing." These inflected forms include such examples as, "look," "looked," and "looking." The students in learning the inflected forms of the words "looked" and "looking" will also learn the root words in this example which is "look." Again, the students will need to have practice with all of the above words in decodable texts so they can develop fluency in order to read in such a way that sounds like natural speech.

Decoding of multisyllabic words continues in second and third grades. It is important for students to get practice learning to decode words of more than one syllable. It is highly recommended that students practice seeing the syllables in the words so they can become familiar with the entire word once they begin reading multisyllabic words in decodable text. Many low readers do not know how to read multisyllabic words thus, it will be necessary to break the word into syllables or meaningful units. For example, if the students cannot decode the multisyllabic word "remake," the teacher will need to put his/her fingers under "re" and then "make" and have the students then read the entire word "remake." Also, in this word (remake) the students learn that "re" is a prefix and this will be helpful information for other words that have "re" in the word.

Phonic Analysis

Phonic analysis is defined as having the students learn the relationship between units of letters and their sounds (Carnine et al., 2004). Phonic analysis includes teaching students some of the common sound(s) represented by several consecutive letters (referred to as letter combinations). According to Carnine et al. (2004), a letter combination is a group of consecutive letters that represents a particular sound(s) in the majority of words in which it appears. If students know common sounds, this will greatly expand their abilities to decode new words. In order for students to learn letter combinations, the students must first know the most common sounds of single letters, at least twenty common sounds, and be able to decode passages made up of regular words at a speed of twenty words per minute (Carnine et al., 2004). This speed indicates that students are no longer laboriously sounding-out but are beginning to perceive words as units, which makes decoding words that contain letter combinations much easier (Carnine et al., 2004). The various reading rates per grade level (K-3) will be further discussed when we begin our section on fluency. Averages based in research will be given at that time for each grade level in kindergarten through third grade.

According to Carnine et al. (2004), there are some important considerations to make when students are learning sounds and combinations. Some of these include that students need to practice the vowels at least four times each when any new vowel is introduced. This becomes especially important so the students will not confuse vowel sounds with each other as they are learning new vowels and are trying to put other sounds together to make new words. Consonant sounds should be practiced at least three times each also as the students are learning new consonants along with vowels to make new words (Carnine et al., 2004). In teaching vowels and consonants it is important to discover how the reading program is teaching the vowels and consonants. If more practice is needed on the various components, it is important to make sure the students get the needed practice so they will recognize these sounds in words with ease and automaticity.

Additionally, other considerations which need to be made in phonic analysis is that the students need to see the sounds in isolation, then in words and connected or decodable text, and when students become proficient, they need to recognize the sounds in words in trade books. It is also important to model each new letter and letter combination, prefix, or word ending so that the students can learn the sounds, combinations and blend the word and then read the whole word (California State Board of Education, 1999). Also, it is important to separate auditorily and visually similar letter combinations in the instructional sequence. For example, it is important to separate the "i" and "e" sounds because these sounds look and sound similar when given to the students initially (Carnine, 2004). Students with reading disabilities are especially confused with sounds that sound the same and are visually similar.

Additionally, it is important that students learn the individual sounds before they are introduced to larger orthographic units such as "ill" or "end." Such practice with individual sounds then combinations will help them become proficient readers especially when they see the sounds in combinations then in words. Students should get repeated opportunities to read words in contexts where they can apply their advanced phonic skills with a high level of success. As has already been noted earlier it is very important for students to get practice with the sounds and combinations or larger orthographic units in decodable text. Later the students can advance to trade books. All of this practice helps the students to transfer their knowledge of sounds, combinations and words to the printed material in order to help them develop fluency.

As the students learn sounds, combinations and read these combinations in words in connected text they should be corrected on any errors they make so they can apply the correct word information whenever they are presented the word with the combinations and or sounds once again. For example, if the student does not know a sound or a combination in a word, the teacher should model the correct sound or combination and have the student repeat the combination or sound found in the word. To illustrate this important principle the student does not know how to say the word, "repack." The teacher says and points to the first part of the word, "This part (re) of the word is *reeee*. Say it." The student says *reeee*. The teacher now points to *pack* and says, "Pack. Say it." The student says *pack*. The teacher now says, "Repack. What word?" The student responds *repack*. Now the student should read the word within the sentence so that the student can see how the word is correctly used in the sentence.

When teaching students with moderate to severe disabilities it is often asked if the students should learn to read by phonics. This writer has had experience with this area and she would like to say that the teacher should take several things into consideration when deciding if their students with moderate to severe disabilities should learn to read by a phonic approach. If the students can retain the sounds and combinations presented to them when they see these sounds and combinations in words, this could be a reason to consider such an approach to teaching the students how to read. Also, if they can transfer the knowledge they learn of sounds and combinations when reading a decodable or connected text then this can also be taken into consideration when deciding if they can learn to read by a phonetic approach.

Parents of the students should be involved in the decision-making process because they will need to become partners in helping their children/youth receive the much needed practice they will need at home in order to continue learning more sounds, combinations, and words in connected text. They will additionally be teaching their sons and daughters long after they leave the public school system.

Further, when deciding whether to use a phonic approach with students with moderate to severe disabilities, it is important to consider their work and life skills in the community environments where they will be placed once they transition from the public school to the world of work. What words or reading skills will the students need to know to do their jobs? Also, what reading skills or words will they need to know to live and do various skills in the community? There are no easy answers but time should be taken to see how a phonic reading program fits with the students and his/her learning styles as they are learning in their present environment. Also, consideration should be given to what they will be doing in the community or world of work as to whether they will need a phonics approach to learning to read.

This should be constantly kept in mind because students with severe disabilities have great difficulty transferring and/or applying their learning to other environments and reading material. Thus, making a good decision about the student's reading will be one of the most important decisions that can be made for the student. Once the decision is made to include a phonics reading program there are several which can be used and which are scientifically researched based which can be helpful to the students. One of these programs that this writer recommends is *Reading Mastery* (Engelmann & Bruner, 1995). Another that might be considered but the rate of instruction is much faster is *SIPPS* (Shefelbine & Neuman, 2003). This writer would recommend that the teacher who is considering teaching the student with more severe disabilities to read by utilizing a phonic approach look at these two programs and other programs which may be systematic and explicit. These two reading programs, for example, will help the students learn because they are designed to teach the students with mastery learning. In mastery learning the students learn because they review the material they have missed in additional lessons until they know the information without making additional errors.

Sight Word Reading

Sight words are those words which have not been introduced as part of the reading lesson when the students encounter new sounds and syllables as part of the lesson. Sight words can also be those words which are highly irregular and do not have good letter sound correspondence. For example, the words "the" and "said" become sight words if they have not been introduced in the lesson as part of the new vocabulary or reading vocabulary section of the lesson. These words are also irregular or do not have good letter sound correspondence. Sight words are also common in word lists such as the "Dolch" basic sight words and there are numerous other words that make up commonly used words (that are highly irregular) and are also found in reading material. The more practice students have with sight words the more fluent they will become as readers when they encounter these words in decodable or connected text and or trade books. Thus, as has already been mentioned earlier giving students practice with sight words daily is important to help them recognize the words automatically in their reading material (Durán et al., 2003).

When presenting sight words included in a story, it is important to limit the number to one or two words per story. It is also necessary to preteach the sight words prior to having the children read the connected or decodable text. Additionally, a cumulative review of important sight words as part of daily reading instruction (two to three minutes) should be also provided.

Because sight words are difficult for some students to learn, the teacher may have to describe some of the sight words by modeling a sentence using the word(s) the students are learning. For example, if the word is "the," the teacher can say, "The dog is happy to be home." When teaching sight words it is important for the teacher to select words that have high utility; that is, words that are used frequently in grade-appropriate literature and informational text. Also, it is important to sequence high-frequency irregular words to avoid potential confusion. For example, high-frequency words that are often confused by students should be strategically separated for initial instruction. Additionally, it is also important to limit the number of sight words to five or seven when giving the students practice on these words. Sight words should also be pretaught prior to having students read connected text. Finally, it is important to provide a cumulative review of important high frequency sight words as part of daily reading instruction (two to three minutes) (Kame'enui & Simmons, as cited in California State Board of Education, 1999).

Students with more severe disabilities should be taught sight words that they will use in home, school, and community. By keeping home, school, and community in mind when discovering the words that should be taught to the students, a more functional and age-appropriate group of words will be presented to the students. These words should be made meaningful to the students by using photographs or pictures of the objects the words are representing. The sight words which are functional can be written under the photo or picture so that students with severe disabilities who can learn the sight words will also become proficient at recognizing the printed word when shown the word with or without the photo or picture. This writer has worked with several students with autism and other developmental disabilities and some were able to learn the sight words when shown with the pictures while others learned the sight words with and without the pictures or photos. Communication booklets can also be developed by the teacher which have photos and/or pictures of the actual items with the words written under the photos or pictures, and these booklets can be taken to the community when the students go to work or to eat. The photos and/or pictures can be changed as the students learn more and more functional sight words. It is also important that once the students learn to recognize the sight words that the teacher also show the students the different words in the community; for example, the word "exit" is found in the community above different doors in different buildings. Such practice will help the students generalize their learning to other environments.

Sight word reading will need to be part of the reading instruction for many years because it is a skill that needs attention for a long time since students with reading difficulties and those who have moderate to severe disabilities will need review until they learn the many sight words automatically.

VOCABULARY DEVELOPMENT

Vocabulary development is another important area in reading development. Vocabulary knowledge helps the students learn to understand what they are reading. With vocabulary knowledge students are able to write and also communicate orally. English learners and special need students are able to know what they are reading if they understand vocabulary. More time needs to be devoted to helping students grasp the vocabulary and the concepts presented in various reading material. Content material is especially hard for English learners and special needs students to understand because these students are behind in English development and communication and they do not have the background and the experiences to understand difficult vocabulary found in their reading material.

Another important reason for teaching vocabulary or word knowledge to children is that there is strong relationship for beginning readers with word knowledge and phonological awareness (Lehr et al., 2004). Young children who have a large number of words in their oral vocabularies may more easily analyze the representation of the individual sounds of those words (Lehr et al., 2004). Also, vocabulary knowledge helps beginning readers decode or map spoken sounds to words in print. If children have the printed words in their oral vocabulary, they can more easily and quickly sound out, read, and understand them and comprehend what they are reading. If the words are not in children's oral vocabulary, they have trouble reading the words and their comprehension is hindered (National Reading Panel, 2000). Therefore, an extensive vocabulary is the bridge between the word-level processes of phonics and comprehension. It has been determined that students in early grades learn anywhere from 2,500 to 26,000 words in the vocabularies (Lehr et al., 2004). There is considerable consensus among researchers that students add approximately 2,000 to 3, 500 distinct words yearly to their reading vocabularies.

How do students acquire new vocabulary? Many students acquire new vocabulary through incidental learning, that is, through exposure to and interaction with rich oral language and encountering new words in text, either through their own reading or being read to (National Reading Panel, 2000). We do know that such encounters cannot ensure that students will acquire in-depth meanings of specific words (Fukkink & de Glopper, 1998). If students are expected to learn words from a literature selection and/or words from content instruction they must be taught this vocabulary explicitly. We also know that no one single instructional method is sufficient for optional vocabulary learning. We also know that we must use a variety of methods to help students acquire new words and increase the depth of their word knowledge over time. Students will need direct instruction and incidental word learning in order to learn new vocabulary.

It is important to note that children who come from homes where they have fewer experiences speaking interactively and hearing oral language rich with new vocabulary words, especially as are found in literature stories, do not have the same vocabulary advantage that students have who are from the more advantaged homes where parents do speak to the children interactively and discuss with their children about the various stories they are reading to them. Research also reports that children in classrooms where the teacher consistently engages in interactive teacher-child talk and storybook reading ended up with larger vocabularies than children who did not participate with the text interactively. Children need exposure to all kinds of vocabulary that are found in literature stories.

Further, students need explicit instruction on specific word meanings and word learning strategies (National Reading Panel, 2000). There are many words that textbooks include for teachers to teach their students. Some of these include rare words and too many for teachers to attempt to teach directly. Still, there will need to be instruction in many vocabulary words or the various groups of words that students need to have knowledge about as they learn to read. For example, Beck et al. (2002) as noted in Lehr et al. (2004) propose that teachers should place major consideration on words' usefulness and frequency of use. To help in this endeavor, they categorized words into three tiers:

> **Tier One** consists of words such as *clock*, *baby*, and *happy* whose meanings students are likely to know (Lehr et al., 2004).
> **Tier Two** is made up of words such as *fortunate*, *maintain*, and *merchant* that are "likely to appear frequently in a wide variety of texts and in the written and oral language of mature language users" (Lehr et al., 2004), but whose meanings students are less likely to know.
> **Tier Three** is made up of words such as *irksome*, *pallet*, and *retinue* that appear in text rarely. Although these rare words are often unknown to students, their appearance in texts is limited to one or two occurrences, and because the vocabulary is often specific to particular content, students can use the context of texts to establish their meaning (Lehr et al., 2004).

Students will need instruction that is direct and incidental on all of these types of vocabulary words. Students who are English learners will need direct instruction practice on many of these vocabulary words because the students have had little background and experience with any of the words from Tier One, Two and Three. Students who are special needs and have difficulty with reading will also need direct instruction on Tier One, Two and Tier Three words. Since it is not possible to teach all the vocabulary to English learners and students with special reading and learning needs, the teacher will need to follow the guidelines set by the publishers and do as much as he/she can to ensure that the lessons being presented to students are full of instruction that is direct and explicit on the various vocabulary words that carry the main ideas of the lesson or literature story that is to be presented to the students. For example, if the students are learning about green plants and how green plants make their food, the teacher can discover which words will help the students understand this main concept or big idea of the chapter on green plants and photosynthesis. The teacher will need to look at the entire chapter on "photosynthesis/green plants" and will need to discover the vocabulary words that are important for the students to understand and reach comprehensible input with the big idea about green plants making their food.

Students are at different levels in classrooms and have had different experiences but the more the teacher asks this question, "What vocabulary do my students need to know in order to learn the big idea(s) related to what we are studying?" Once the teacher asks this important question he/she will be able to decide what are the critical vocabulary in order to teach the students and will help convey the big ideas of the chapter.

Additionally, teachers also need to remember that once he/she has selected the vocabulary related to the big idea(s) of any chapter he/she must keep in mind that students who have not had a lot of exposure to being read to at home or have background information on the material they are learning and reading will need to orally say the vocabulary words they are learning as part of any lesson. The students can chorally say each of the words out loud when the vocabulary is first introduced or as they work in groups after they have had discussions about the definitions of the words. This will help the students get much needed practice in seeing the vocabulary words visually, saying the words orally and also saying the definitions orally as they work to complete various activities to help them understand the various vocabulary of the lesson(s). The more exposure the students have with the words and their meanings, the better they will understand the vocabulary once they see the words in context or as they reread the chapter or literature material to themselves. It is also a good idea for the teacher to walk around as the students are working in their cooperative groups or in pairs and reinforce the students and tell them the vocabulary word orally once again so they can hear the word being modeled by the teacher. Students need multiple exposures to learning vocabulary. This is especially true for English learners and special needs students who often do not get enough practice saying the vocabulary words orally or getting enough practice with the vocabulary in various activities.

There are other instructional strategies to keep in mind when teaching vocabulary words to students. Students can be presented synonyms of words they already know (Lehr et al., 2004). Students can also learn that words have multiple meanings and students can learn that there are vocabulary words that represent concepts that may be new to them such as *liberty* and *photosynthesis* (Lehr et al., 2004). The teacher can additionally help students organize semantic maps of some of the vocabulary words so that they can better remember the various vocabulary words they are learning. For example, if the students are learning the vocabulary that is part of the big idea or concept in the word "movement," the teacher can organize other related vocabulary under "toys" (and place words that move under toys). These words would be: "bounce," "twirl," "buzz," and "tick." Lehr et al. (2004) notes that such organization can help the students better recall what the words mean if they are trying to learn providing they are organized around meaningful groups of vocabulary and their definitions or synonyms.

Students with special reading needs and English learners will need help to organize the groups of vocabulary under meaningful groups and will need help saying the various words orally until they get the necessary exposures to all of the words that are found in the different groups.

The students can learn the vocabulary also by utilizing the dictionary and reading the text and learning to utilize context as they are reading from the textbook and as they read their literature stories. There should be some words of caution when teaching students with special reading needs and English learners to use the dictionary to discover word meanings. First of all, a good teacher will teach the students how to use a dictionary by helping them understand the reason we have guide words and how to make use of guide words in discovering new words. Also, a good teacher will give the students the definitions of the words that are part of the big ideas so that students can spend productive time learning the meanings of words and not spending the entire reading period or content instruction to find the meanings of the various vocabulary words. Also, it is important for teachers to remember that learning vocabulary words in context may not always give the students the meaning of the vocabulary words, and it may be necessary to model and guide students as they read to help them understand the meaning of the vocabulary words that are used in context. Thus, the teacher will guide the reading and help the students find all the synonyms or word clues that will help the students discover what the unknown vocabulary words mean in the story or reading material.

Other vocabulary strategies that may be useful is having English learners, for example, Spanish speakers learn that cognates or words that are spelled the same and sound similar in both languages can be helpful in teaching the students the vocabulary in English. For instance, "chocolate" in Spanish is "chocolate" and is the same word with the same meaning in English. Another important way the students can learn vocabulary is to have them learn vocabulary through morphology. Morphology is the study of word formation which includes the origin and function of inflections, or changes made to words to show such things as tense, case or number (e.g., *looked, looking,* and *looks* from *look*) and derivates or words that are formed from other words (e.g., *sadly* and *sadness* from *sad*) (Lehr et al., 2004).

Students can further learn vocabulary by utilizing root words. It has been suggested that having students who acquire root words effectively learn to address the large number of words that students must learn each year (Lehr et al., 2004). According to some researchers students acquire 1,200 root word meanings a year during the elementary school years (Anglin, 1993). Also, the students can be taught to recognize prefixes since nine prefixes account for 75 percent of words (White, Sowell, & Yanigihara, 1989). Additionally, prefixes tend to be spelled consistently (Lehr et al., 2004). There is less agreement on whether we should teach suffixes. Lehr et al. (2004) contends that many suffixes have vague or unhelpful meanings; they can often confuse more than help students. Some suffixes are more useful than others; for example, "ful" meaning full of and "less" meaning without are more useful and stable in meaning and students can apply these suffixes to other words. A suffix like "ious" which means "state or quality of," may not help students learn meanings or much about words except for words like *ambitious* or *gracious* (Lehr et al., 2004). When teaching word parts it is most important to teach students the meanings of particular word parts as well as a strategy for when and why to use the word parts (Lehr et al., 2004).

When the word parts are encountered in reading material the teacher should teach students the meanings of particular word parts as well as a strategy for when and why to use them (Lehr et al., 2004). The National Reading Panel (2000) also has found computer-assisted instruction in vocabulary to be helpful than some traditional approaches in a few studies.

Having students learn a variety of ways to discover the meaning of words will help the students because there are many different ways available for students to learn meanings of the words they encounter in their curriculum. As Lehr et al. (2004) notes there is no single method to learn vocabulary but rather many different ways to learn such a complex and most crucial area.

FLUENCY

According to Carnine et al. (2004), fluency is reading smoothly, quickly, and with expression. In order for the students to become fluent readers, they must be accurate readers–fluency and accuracy go hand in hand. And in order for students to become good comprehenders, they must go beyond accuracy to automaticity in decoding. Carnine et al. (2004) also indicate that the progression from accurate to fluent reading makes sense when viewed from a beginning reader's perspective. At first, the student carefully inspects and sounds out each word. The student must remember the sound of each letter, be able to blend sounds, and then transform the blended sounds into a word (e.g., the written word *man* is sounded out *mmmmaaan* and then it becomes man). According to Carnine et al. (2004), if the student is given ample time at the beginning stages of learning to sound out words, the student will not guess at words when learning to sound out and will become a more accurate reader with time and practice. Also, this author notes it is much easier to increase reading rate with students who have appropriate decoding strategies since the teacher can concentrate solely on rate. As rate increases, accuracy stays high. Carnine et al. (2004) go on to say that for students who develop strong guessing behavior in early training, rate training is difficult since guessing tends to increase.

Carnine et al. (2004) indicate further that just as stressing fluency too soon causes problems, so can stressing fluency too late. Their research indicates that if students are required to sound out every word for months and months, they may become word by word readers which, in turn, may cause serious comprehension problems or may result in students not being able to complete assignments since they are reading too slowly.

According to Fuchs (1993), first graders increase their reading fluency approximately 2.10 correct words per minute per week. After an estimated 30 weeks of instruction, students should leave the first grade reading approximately 60 words per minute correctly. Practice in fluency is most appropriate when students are accurate word readers. One technique that has been used to increase fluency is repeated readings of the same text to develop familiarity and automaticity (Carnine et al., 2004).

The benchmark of fluent readers in the second grade is the ability to read grade-level material aloud and accurately in a manner that sounds like natural speech. Research studies indicate that students reading at the fiftieth percentile in spring in the second grade orally read 90 to 100 words per minute correctly (Kame'enui & Simmons, cited in California State Board of Education, 1999) and that, on average, they increase their reading fluency approximately 1.46 correct words per minute per week (Fuchs, 1993).

Extended word-analysis and ample opportunities to practice skills in connected text should enable third-graders to read grade-appropriate text accurately and fluently. A study addressing target rates found in third-grade classrooms and students typically read 79 correct words per minute in the fall and 114 in the spring (Fuchs, 1993). On the average a third grader's weekly reading increases 1.08 words per minute. As students learn to recognize words automatically, they should have opportunities to hear and practice reading text aloud, emphasizing pacing, intonation, and expression. Fluency or facility with print frees up cognitive resources for comprehension (Fuchs, 1993).

Recent research on the efficacy of certain approaches to teaching fluency has led to increased recognition of its importance in the class-room and to changes in instructional practices (National Reading Panel, 2000). Reading practice is generally recognized as an important contributor to fluency. Two instructional approaches, each of which has several variations, have typically been used to teach reading fluency: (1) guided repeated oral reading, encourages students to read passages orally and with systematic and explicit guidance and feed-back from the teacher, (2) independent silent reading encourages students to read silently on their own, inside and outside the classroom, with minimal guidance or feedback (National Reading Panel, 2000).

Guided repeated oral reading has been helpful because the students are reading out loud at least the same material three times orally and each time they read orally they are practicing their oral reading and are becoming more proficient in reading the words in the text. Carnine et al. (2004) suggest that having struggling readers read the text (in most cases at the beginning it is controlled or decodable text) the students will improve in their reading and this will help the students with comprehension and decoding.

Independent silent reading approaches in which students are encouraged to read extensively on their own has not yet been confirmed according to the National Reading Panel (2000) as a means of improving fluency and overall reading achievement. When students read material silently they do not get the correction feedback that is needed if they are having difficulty reading the text they are struggling with in their reading classes. According to the National Reading Panel, the lack of demonstrated effectiveness of strategies encouraging independent silent reading suggests that explicit are more important than implicit instructional approaches for improving reading fluency. It is important to remember that instructional procedures such as guided repeated oral readings do have a positive impact on word recognition and comprehension (Carnine et al., 2004).

COMPREHENSION

According to Carnine et al. (2004) comprehension is defined as the myriad of skills that involve getting meaning from the printed page.

The teaching of comprehension should be approached in the same way as teaching of decoding, systematically and completely, so that high degree of success is accomplished. According to Carnine et al., a comprehension program should have some of the following components: (a) a systematic introduction of vocabulary; (b) a carefully designed sequence for introducing specific comprehension skills as well as structured presentations of strategies, careful example of selection, and cumulative practice and review; and (c) passage reading used as a vehicle for integrating the various specific skills into a meaningful whole.

In order to assist students to develop comprehension skills, the teacher must be aware of various comprehension questions that need to be presented to students so they will learn a variety of questioning strategies. Some of these include the following: literal questions (where students discover answers to questions that are directly noted in the reading material they are reading.) Some examples of literal questions may be what happened in the story, who is the main character, when did the story take place, where is the house located in the story, how did the main character feel about losing her puppy? Another type of question students often encounter in reading material and then discussing it are inference questions. In inference questions the students are not told the answers to the questions explicitly in the story but must try to figure out the answer by putting together clues from the story. These types of questions are often difficult for many students with disabilities and/or those children who are English learners because they have to try to figure out all the clues before they can answer the question(s). The answers are not explicitly stated. Even though these types of questions are difficult for special needs students and those who are English learners, the students will need to be introduced these type of questions. English learners and special needs students are also part of classrooms where they have been included with other students and they must learn these different types of questions if they are going to understand some of the basal reading material that they will be using in the regular classrooms.

Sequencing is another type of question that students will need to learn as part of the comprehension development found in various types of reading material. In this type of question the students are asked to tell the order of what happened first, second, third, or fourth in the story. Again, these types of questions are important for the students to learn so they can be able to summarize in order the various events that happened in the story. The teacher will need to give the students practice on this type of question as he/she would in all the other types of questions. Helping students with visual and verbal cues will help the students better comprehend what event happened first, second, third, or fourth in the story.

Summarization is also needed to be a good comprehender. In summarization, the students are able to give a few sentences of what happened in the story. Again, in order for the students to do well in this type of comprehension activity the students must learn through correction feedback to retell what happened at whatever point they are asked to summarize what they are reading. If the students are unable to retell what they have read the students should read the material again and be asked to summarize after they read smaller chunks of the story.

Another important area needed in comprehension development is prediction. The students need to be able to think about what may happen in the story they are reading or are about to read. This is another very important skill to teach in comprehension development.

Other comprehension skills include compare and contrast, clarifying, classifying and categorizing, and visualizing the information students are trying to recall.

In attempting to give students practice with the different types of comprehension strategies, the teacher can place the different question types in typed format on cards that are laminated. Each card should have printed on it the different types of comprehension that have been mentioned in this section. The students should also get small laminated cards at their desk so they can raise the different cards as they are asking literal questions, visualizing or predicting and utilizing whatever different type of question that they may use or the teacher may use. Such practice on having the students determine each of the different types of comprehension must be modeled by the teacher first so that the students are clear on what each question type means and how to use that question type as they are reading. When students are able to recall the different types of comprehension questions they are using, they are then engaged in the process called metacognition. Metacognition is one of the highest levels of comprehension development where students monitor or self-regulate comprehension while reading, and reflect on the process and content during reading (Carnine et al., 2004).

In order to assist all students including English learners and special needs students to be better comprehenders, it is also important to help build background and preteach vocabulary so that the students can better understand what they will be reading. By helping students build background the students will begin to understand some of the important concepts that are found in the story. Preteaching vocabulary will help the students understand some of the information they will be reading in the story. Pictures, photographs, definitions, synonyms, and defining for students how the vocabulary is used in sentences will be helpful to the students in order for them to understand what they are reading.

WRITING

Another important area in literacy development is writing. From the early grades the students are required to give a brief expository description of a real object, person, place, or event, using sensory details. The students are also asked in the early grades to write and speak in complete, coherent sentences. As part of writing they are also asked to identify and correctly use contractions for example, *isn't, aren't, can't, won't* and singular possessive pronouns for instance, *my, mine, his, hers, yours* in their writing and speaking. Further, they are asked to include the correct punctuation and capitalize the beginning letter of every sentence in their writing.

By third grade, students extend their writing strategies by (1) creating a single paragraph with a topic sentence and supporting details; (2) refining the legibility of their writing; (3) learning to access information from a range of reference materials (for example, thesaurus, encyclopedia); (4) revising drafts to improve coherence and progression of ideas; and (5) progressing through the stages of the writing process (California State Board of Education, 1999). As the students advance through the grades their writing continues to broaden to include different audiences and also include an introductory paragraph with supporting details and a conclusion (California State Board of Education, 1999). The writing requirements continue to increase and become more advanced as students progress through the grades. It is most important to work on developing each of these writing skills through the grades because writing development, like reading, takes years to develop. In order for students to learn to become good writers they must receive practice and correction feedback in order to learn not only to write a sentence and then progress to writing more than one paragraph.

Such writing expectations are often difficult for English learners and special needs students. This author recommends that students who are English learners and those students who have special learning needs first learn descriptive writing then progress to writing as a process or writer's workshop. In descriptive writing the student is shown a picture describing some event. For example, the students may see a man painting a wall. To paint the wall the man will need "paint," a "brush" or "roller," a "ladder," "walls," and a "container" for the paint. Directly under the picture will be the label of each item that is depicted in the picture. The label or name for paint will appear directly below the picture, additionally the words for "ladder," "brush," "roller," "wall," and "container" will also be shown under the picture. The teacher will begin a dialogue with the students and he/she will ask the students what the man is doing? The children will say that the man is painting the wall. The teacher will ask the students what else the man is doing in the picture and the children will respond that the man is on the ladder so he can paint the wall. After the teacher and students have discussed the picture thoroughly, the students will begin writing what they have said as the teacher asked them the questions earlier in the lesson. One sentence the students may write, for instance, would be, "The man is painting the wall." The students will also punctuate the sentence correctly with the help of the teacher.

As the students write their sentences the teacher will have them point to each word that is noted under the picture so they can connect the word with the item in the picture. Other words that may be needed by the children to complete the sentences may be placed on the word wall near the chalkboard. Such a word wall is helpful because it will show the students how to spell common sight words they often miss because they cannot remember how to spell these words. There are several Direct Instruction programs published by SRA (Science Research Associates) which teach descriptive writing which many teachers may find useful in teaching students to become better writers. Once the students can describe pictures and write about the pictures they can be introduced to writing as a process.

Before this writer explains writing as a process, she would like to explain interactive writing which can also be used with younger students, English learners who have learned English, and/or some special needs students who have learned some sight words so they can use these sight words and other words they are learning in their writing. Interactive writing is a writing strategy that combines language and writing. It is a dynamic, collaborative literacy event in which children actively compose together, considering appropriate words, phrases, organization of text, and layout (McCarrier, Pinnell, & Fountas, 2000). At different points the children share the pen with the teacher and bring language and writing together to begin the writing process. As teachers utilize interactive writing with their students, they not only show children how writing works but also invite them to participate, with support, in the act of writing (McCarrier et al., 2000).

In interactive writing, the teacher and the children share the experiences together and collaborate to write information about a shared experience. Also in interactive writing, the children begin to transition to writing as a process. The term "interactive writing" was coined in 1991 by a research group comprised of faculty members from Ohio State University and teachers from Columbus, Ohio. The teachers who worked on interactive writing originally were especially concerned about children who did not have experiences with literacy. The teachers used some of their shared writing techniques and varied the approach with a share-the-pen technique that involved the children contributing individual letters and words to the group writing. When the children have finished composing their story another child can point to each word using a pointer so that the children can chorally read what they have each written on the big chart. This is a very effective strategy because it gives the students practice reading orally and gives them practice reading words they have learned as they composed their story. Once several stories have been collected a child can be selected to write the stories in a smaller booklet and another child can illustrate the cover of the booklet where all the stories have been copied and placed. The teacher can make copies of the booklet and have the children take their book home and read their booklets to different family members. The tasks of writing the stories in the booklet and illustrating the booklet should be given to different students to allow each of them to take turns.

Similarly, writing as a process is also a writing strategy that utilizes language and writing. In this strategy, the students first learn to brainstorm in the prewriting stage. In this prewriting stage the students talk, read, and write to see what they know and what direction they may want to go (Durán et al., 2003). This is often the most neglected stage in the writing process because many children are often encouraged to begin writing without being able to talk about what they are thinking about writing. A large percentage of the children's time should be spent in the **prewriting stage**. Here the students will consider the form, purpose, and audience for whom they will be writing in their paragraph(s). In this stage, the students will also generate and organize ideas for writing. Many times students will have great difficulty choosing a topic to write about; thus, students should be encouraged to talk, draw, read, and write to develop information about their topics. Students may find it helpful to draw semantic maps which will help them cluster their information and details about the topic. For more details on how this is completed see (Durán et al., 2002). Students can additionally read stories and write in their journals after they read to help them focus on what they will be writing about.

Drafting is another important stage the students need to go through in order to get their final product. The students may do a series of drafts. In the beginning drafts, students do not worry too much about spelling, punctuation, and other mechanical errors but, as the final draft is written, students should be encouraged to proof their work by discovering some of the words they are having trouble sounding out. Students should be encouraged to skip every other line to leave space for their revisions. They can use arrows, do cross-out delete sections, and scissors and tape to cut apart and rearrange text, just as adult writers do. If computers are available for the students to work during the week, then some can be encouraged to type their drafts on a computer. Every classroom's circumstance is different, and teachers should attempt to see what can be arranged to assist the students to write their drafts.

Editing and revising are extremely important because it is through these stages where the students will put their writing in final form. Here, the students will refine their ideas in their compositions. The writers add, substitute, delete, and continue rearranging material. Teachers can give feedback to the students and they should revise on the basis of feedback. Students should be encouraged to read their drafts aloud to help them hear if their work makes sense. They can also read to other children who may be listening to them as part of a response group where the children can be paired up with each other to help assist one another in the editing and revising stages of writing. Again, the teacher will need to use his/her judgment to determine if he/she will pair the students to assist one another in their editing. Every classroom situation is different and the teacher will be the best judge of whether his/her students are capable of doing this type of work together. Editing is putting the piece of writing into final form. Mechanics that should be considered in editing are corrected spelling, sentence structure, usage, and correct format information as it relates to the different forms of writing they are completing (Durán et al., 2003).

Publishing is the stage where students make books and share their writing with the class, their parents, brothers and sisters, or another class. The idea of sharing with others what they have written can become a very encouraging process for the students because it is through seeing their work in a published form that they can appreciate the hard work and how long it took them to get to this stage. As the children become more skilled in sharing some of their beginning work, they can share from the author's chair and show the class and other classes their illustrated cover and other pictures of their story before they begin reading their published work. It is important for children to see the connection between reading and writing. Students should also see that listening and speaking are part of the reading and writing processes. Showing students the interrelatedness of reading, writing, listening, and speaking will help them see writing as a process which takes time and work to develop (Durán et al., 2003). Also, nothing is more rewarding than having the students begin to see themselves as authors with their published works. Many students who come from low socioeconomic groups have not had these and other reading and literacy experiences; but if teachers make all of this as a goal for their students, they will achieve these goals which will continue adding to their reading, writing, listening, and speaking skills.

Other types of writing that the students can engage in through the grades are journal writing, where they dialogue with their teachers and buddies, and receive responses from the people with whom they are engaged in a dialog. One of the most effective types of journals are literary response journals where the students write about the story they have read by writing about the characters, setting, plot, and/or what they learned about the story. This type of dialogue will take the form of a literary response journal where the students begin to think and write about whatever they have read. Once students know the teacher will be seeking from the information that relates to the stories they have read, they will begin to write responses in their journals with a purpose because they know that their teacher will be reading and responding to their work.

No matter what forms of writing are used, it is important to connect all of this writing to what the children do in their lives and to what they are reading in their basal readers. Many new and revised basal series have many suggestions to increase writing and make every attempt to help the teacher connect writing with reading, listening, and speaking.

REFERENCES

Adams, M. J. (1990). *Beginning to read: Thinking and learning about print.* Cambridge, MA: MIT Press.

Anglin, J. M. (1993). Vocabulary development: A morphological analysis. *Monographs of the Society for Research in Child Development,* Serial No. 238, 58(10).

Ball, E. W. & Blachman, B. A. (1991). Does phoneme awareness training in kindergarten make a difference in early word recognition and development spelling? *Reading Research Quarterly, 24*(1) 49–66.

Bialystok, E. (1995). Making concepts about print symbolic: Understanding how writing represents language. *First Language, 15,* 135–163.

Brady, S. A. & Shankweiler, O. P. (1991). *Phonological processes in literacy: A tribute to Isabella Y. Liberman,* Hillsdale, NJ: Lawrence Erlbaum.

California State Board of Education (1999). *Reading/language arts framework for California public schools kindergarten through grade twelve.* Sacramento, CA: California Department of Education.

Carnine, D. W., Silbert, J., Kame'enui, E. J. & Tarver, S. G. (2004). *Direct instruction reading* (4th ed.). Upper Saddle River, NJ: Pearson/Merrill Prentice Hall.

Cunningham, P. M. (1998). The multisyllabic meaning, spell, and read big words. *Reading and Writing Quarterly, 14,* 189–218.

Durán, E. (2006). *Teaching sight words to students with reading difficulties.* Lecture given to Language and Literacy I class at California State University Sacramento, Sacramento, CA.

Durán, E. et al. (2003). *Systematic instruction in reading for Spanish-speaking students.* Springfield, IL: Charles C Thomas Publishers, Ltd.

Engelmann, S. & Bruner, E. (1995). *Reading mastery rainbow edition.* Columbus, OH: SRA Publishers.

Fuchs, L. S. (1993). Formative evaluation of academic progress. How much growth can we expect? *School Psychology Review, 22*(1), 27–48.

Fukkink, R. G. & de Glopper, K. (1998). Effects of instruction in deriving word meaning from context: A meta-analysis. *Review of Educational Research, 68*(4).

Lehr, F. et al. (2004). *A focus on vocabulary.* Washington, DC: Pacific Resources for Education, U.S. Department of Education under the regional laboratory program.

Lyon, G. R. (1995). Research initiatives in learning disabilities: Contributions from scientists supported by the National Institute of Child Health and Human Development. *Journal of Child Neurology, 10*, 120–126.

McCarrier, A., Pinnell, G. S., & Fountas, I. C. (2000). *Interactive writing: How language and literacy come together, K-2.* Portsmouth, NH: Heinemann.

National Reading Panel (2000). *Teaching children to read: An evidence-based assessment of the scientific research literature reading and its implications for reading instruction.* Washington, DC: National Institute of Child Health and Human Development.

Shefelbine, J. & Neuman, C. (2003). *SIPPS.* Oakland, CA: Developmental Studies Center.

Smith, S. B., Simmons, D. C. & Kame'enui, E. J. (1995). *Synthesis of research on phonological awareness: Principles and implications for reading acquisitions.* (Tech. Rep. No. 21) Eugene, OR: University of Oregon, National Center to Improve the Tools of Educators.

Snow, C. E. & Ninio, A., (1986). The contracts of literacy: What children learn learning to read books. In W. H. Teale & E Sulzby (Eds.), *Emergent literacy: Writing and reading* (pp. 116–138). Norwood, NJ: Ablex.

White, T. G., Sowell, J. & Yanagihara, A. (1989). Teaching elementary students to use word-part clues. *The Reading Teacher, 42*, 302–309.

Chapter 13

SOCIAL STUDIES CONTENT MADE COMPREHENSIBLE FOR ENGLISH LEARNERS WITH/WITHOUT SPECIAL NEEDS

EUNMI CHO

The intent of this article is to give special and general education teachers a better understanding of why and how sheltered and adapted instruction needs to be developed and implemented to enhance the learning of Social Studies content for English learners with special needs. Since these students need to learn the Social Studies content concurrently with the English language while working with learning issues from disabilities, teachers must deliver Social Studies instruction effectively to this group to increase the level of comprehension.

Currently, Social Studies teachers must take into consideration the pertinent factors from the current trends in their instruction, such as rapidly increasing diversity in the classroom, putting more emphasis on content standards and state framework, strong needs for adaptation of the materials and the learning environment, and selecting research-based effective lesson delivery system. With the teachers' sheltered and adapted instruction, this unique group of students will concurrently learn content material and English so that they can become competent members of our communities who value the divergent perspectives of others and are willing to contribute their knowledge, skills, and values to society.

Understanding the characteristics of Social Studies, English learners with special needs and sheltered and adapted instruction are important. Therefore, the current legal requirements for inclusive Social Studies education, the strong emphasis on the content standards-based instruction, and the urgent need for multicultural education will be included below.

WHAT IS SOCIAL STUDIES?

Ellis (2002) defined Social Studies as "The study of people. In fact, Social Studies is the only curriculum subject with people as its subject matter. Social Studies deals directly with the basic needs of human beings: food, clothing, shelter, belonging, security, and dreams" (p. 7). The curriculum requires us to reflect on people, including our students. The current composition of our students has changed to become more diverse. As Parker (2005) quoted the demographers' estimation, "the white student population will be down to thirty percent by the year 2026 from sixty-three percent in 1992 in the United States" (U.S. Census, 2000). More than ninety percent of recent immigrants are coming from non-English speaking countries (Echevarria, Vogt, & Short, 2004, p. 3), and they are not all alike culturally, ethnically, and socially. With the growing number of English learners in our nation, especially in California, Social Studies needs to be taught to depict our pluralistic and diverse society. As Merryfield (2004) stated "without understanding diverse cultures locally and globally, young people cannot make sense of issues and events that effect their lives" (p. 270).

The National Council for the Social Studies (NCSS) (1994) definition also clearly emphasizes Social Studies as "the integrated study of the social sciences and humanities to promote civic competence. Within the school program, Social Studies provides coordinated, systematic study drawing upon such disciplines as anthropology, archaeology, economics, geography, history, law, philosophy, political science, psychology, religion, and sociology, as well as appropriate contents from the humanities, mathematics, and natural sciences." NCSS also specifies the primary purpose of Social Studies as "to help young people develop the ability to make informed and reasoned decisions for the public good as citizens of a culturally diverse, democratic society in an interdependent world" (NCSS, 1994, p. 3). Simply adding a "multicultural day" or "ethnic food festival" to the curriculum is not enough because it does not allow students to think critically and deeply about the meaning of cultural and linguistic differences (Farr & Trumbeull, 1997).

WHAT IS SHELTERED INSTRUCTION?

Sheltered instruction is an approach to teaching that extends the time that students have for receiving English language support while learning various subject content. Echevarria, Vogt, and Short (2004) stated, "Its ultimate goal is accessibility for English learning students to grade level content standards and concepts while they continue to improve their English language proficiency" (p. 223). It provides academic content to English learners with modified English words and various teaching strategies. Some examples of teaching and assessment strategy can be pictorial presentations, hands-on activities, performance-based assessments for individual students, group tasks or projects, informal class discussions, oral reports, written assignments, portfolios, and more common measures such as paper and pencil tests and quizzes (Echevarria, Vogt, & Short, 2004, p. 14). Teachers need to use instructional language that matches their students' current proficiency level in English so that students can comprehend the Social Studies content material and follow the instruction process. In other words, students need to have intellectually appropriate knowledge of the English language to attain Social Studies content standards. As Lemke (1988) explained, ". . . educators have begun to realize that the mastery of academic subjects is the mastery of their specialized patterns of language use, and that language is the dominant medium in which these subjects are taught and students' mastery of them is tested" (p. 81).

Salend (1998) explained the sequence of the typical sheltered instructional approach. First, teachers preteach the vocabulary needed to understand the lesson content. In the preteaching stage, a variety of instructional strategies can be used (e.g., visual cues, cue cards, word banks) to help students understand the definitions of key vocabulary. Second, teachers select and explain important concepts using a context that is rich with visual aids, objects, physical gestures, facial expressions, hands-on activities, and interactions with peers. Then, teachers must make sure to relate the concepts to students' personal experiences, check each student's understanding of content, and provide necessary feedback. After teaching the lesson, teachers need to offer multiple pathways for students to demonstrate their understanding of the content.

Through the whole process of the sheltered instruction, the unique needs of English learners can be met as well as the needs of students with special needs because the instruction provides academic content with modified English words and a variety of effective teaching strategies, such as visual reinforcements and hands-on activities. The next part of this article will be focused on adaptation and its connection with sheltered instruction to reach students with special needs.

WHAT IS ADAPTED INSTRUCTION?

Adaptations are changes made to help each student learn best and demonstrate what he or she is capable of doing and understanding. Two different types of adaptations exist: accommodation and modification.

Accommodations do not significantly change the instructional level, content, or the performance criteria. They are made to provide a student with equal access to learning and demonstrations. Although accommodations are made, the standards of achievement remain the same. For example, if a student is not able to read an assigned textbook due to reading disabilities, the appropriate accommodation would involve the student listening to a taped version of the reading. After the student has listened to the taped version, he or she must take the required test or complete the assigned work.

Teachers can also meet students' needs by expanding the time limit involved for a project or by reducing the number of social studies terms a student needs to learn at any one time so that their tasks can be manageable. If a student has poor writing and/or spelling skills due to disabilities, he or she may use a tape recorder or word processor instead of using only "pencil and paper" to complete assignments. A student with ADHD (Attention Deficit Hyperactivity Disorder) may sit close to the teacher or in the center of the classroom to prevent distractions by background noise from the windows, the heater, or the air conditioner. Activating background knowledge through primary sources (pictures, outfits, posters, etc.) can be an important accommodation as well.

On the other hand, modifications are significant changes made in the content, delivery, and testing for students with severe disabilities. Those students with modifications are expected to meet reduced standards that are determined to be within their potential to master. An example of a modification would be having a teacher invite an English learner with special needs to hold a globe while the other students locate different geographical locations on the globe in a geography lesson. The teacher may expect the student with disabilities to be able to locate a few states while others learn to locate capitals as well as states. The teacher may allow the student to read a passage at a lower readability level. A student with modifications may classify or categorize photos while his/her typically developing peers write the different characteristics of cities and rural areas.

Without specific adaptations, the standard Social Studies curriculum materials can be inadequate for these students, and too frequently they can find themselves blocked from access to essential aspects of the curriculum (ERIC, 1999). Teachers must develop and implement Social Studies instruction in ways that allow students to engage themselves in a meaningful and comprehensible fashion. Instructional strategies need to be adapted. As an intervention strategy, teachers can preview the lesson, focusing on key concepts and activity processes, using students' primary languages as much as possible.

Using a bilingual instructional assistant would be best, but getting help from parent volunteers, older siblings, or helpers from the community to prepare teaching materials would also be good options. These people can translate key concepts and/or they can even record them onto audiotapes in their primary language for the teacher's repetitive use.

If a bilingual person is not available, the teacher can at least try to present concept cards written in the primary language or picture cards while explaining key vocabulary and important concepts in English. Then the lesson can be given in English. Following the session, English learners should engage in a review of the concept for understanding and for reinforcing targeted skills and knowledge. Using actions and concrete examples to reinforce English learners with special needs is important, too. Teachers should make a balance between direct instruction (e.g., programmed instruction or mastery learning) and indirect instruction (integrated thematic instruction by facilitating students to inquire and discover their learning process). To meet individual needs, modifying or altering assignments is necessary.

In addition, providing more opportunities for cooperative group work will develop students' interdependent life survival skills. By working in small groups, students gain mutual respect for individual differences and practice interpersonal skills. In the following list, additional examples of adapted Social Studies instructional strategies are illustrated.

- Clarify all unfamiliar terms and idioms before delivering the contents.
- Simplify complicated words and use other words with similar meaning.
- Use graphic organizers along with verbal directions.
- Assign a bilingual peer in each small group if possible and arrange English learners with special needs to respond through the bilingual peer.
- Allow a "Reading and/or Writing Partner" for English learners with special needs with bilingual peers whose reading and/or writing skills are higher. If writing is difficult, the partner may take dictation from the English learner with special needs.
- Whenever possible, try to read material as a whole group (whole-group choral reading) right after a teacher's demonstration of reading. Then choose two or three students to read as a small group before choosing an individual student to read. This will reduce the anxiety level of English learners with special needs.
- Use guided and visual imagery.
- Utilize tools (e.g., computers/Internet, realia, TV/VCR set, overhead projector, white board, chalkboard, various colored pencils, markers, etc.) as much as possible.

Teachers should also adapt their classroom environment to illustrate that diverse learning abilities are valued and appreciated as well as cultural and linguistic diversity. The room should show that students of different backgrounds and various abilities are welcome. For example, teachers can create a class library filled with books about cultural diversity and diverse learning abilities, written by minority authors, written in various languages, and/or written for multiability reading levels. Teachers can ask parents and community resource centers to donate suitable reading and learning materials for the multicultural and multiability leveled library in the classroom. Teachers also can put up posters illustrating the beauty of diversity and display the work of all students in the class.

Teachers can plan collaborative activities that promote active interactions among students regardless of different cultural and linguistic backgrounds. At the planning stage, teachers also need to consider the individual student's personality and learning style which often are developed from cultural practices at home and in the community. For example, in general, most students from home cultures in Latin America and Asia work well in small group settings whereas others from European family backgrounds perform better when they work independently.

WHY DOES SHELTERED AND ADAPTED INSTRUCTION NEED TO BE DEVELOPED AND IMPLEMENTED TO ENHANCE SOCIAL STUDIES LEARNING?

First, sheltered and adapted instructions are necessary to meet the needs of English learners with special needs because as part of a very unique population, this group needs very systematic and meaningful instruction. Students with disabilities, whether physical, emotional, or cognitive in nature, respond to the curriculum differently from other students (ERIC, 1999). Teachers should be able to identify and address students' special needs. As Herrell and Jordon (2004) emphasized teachers need to focus on what students already know in order to build on their strengths rather than focusing on the students' academic deficiencies. Providing a nonthreatening learning environment is important as well. English learners with special needs require unique learning practices based on both second language acquisition theories and constructivist theories. Krashen's second language acquisition theory (1982), constructivist perspectives of Scheurman and Yell (1998), and Vygotsky's Zone of Proximal Development (1962) need to be considered.

From Krashen's second language acquisition theory, we learn that second language learners gain knowledge of content while they are exposed to comprehensible input in a low-anxiety environment. Teachers need to modify their instructional methods and teaching materials in a way that allows students to learn the content with low anxiety. Some of the ways that teachers can achieve this include the following: repetition of key words and phrases, checking for understanding during instruction, slowing of their speech, and using simplified vocabulary appropriate to the students' comprehension level. Teachers should also discourage teaching styles that are predominately lectures. Instead of asking questions randomly as a whole group, teachers can encourage English learners with special needs to work as pairs or in small groups. This will reduce the students' anxiety level and cultivate a cooperative learning environment.

Social Studies textbooks are expository with a variety of information. These books often do not provide comprehensible input for English learners with special needs. Thus, some Social Studies teachers may read the text aloud to students or present the material through charts, graphs, illustrations, and/or films. Some teachers rewrite important sections of the textbook in simplified English so that the English language learners have a version to read that they can understand (Zarrillo, 2004).

According to the constructivist perspective of Scheurman and Yell (1998), learning is an active process, whereby knowledge is acquired as learners interact with the environment and modify what they already know. All growth is the result of something new being added to a person's previous knowledge (Zarrillo, 2004). Students process new content by relating it to their previous knowledge and by reconstructing the new ideas actively to store in their pool of knowledge.

Another perspective on Social Studies learning is Vygotsky's *Zone of Proximal Development*. As a psychologist, Vygotsky believed that a gap exists between what children can do independently and what they could do if they had help. In his words, "with assistance every child can do more than he can do by himself" (1962, p. 103). He described the Zone of Proximal Development as "the distance between the actual development level as determined by independent problem solving and the level of potential development as determined through problem solving under adult guidance or in collaboration with more capable peers" (1978, p. 86).

As Krashen's second language acquisition theory and other learning perspectives support, meaningful learning can take place only when the English learners with special needs systematically relate the new learning task to what they already know within in a low-anxiety environment where the affective filter is low. Mistakes are viewed as the stepping-stone for learning. Students can function better if they allow themselves to make mistakes without fear. Teachers need to be able to make mistakes in front of their students to model this type of learning.

Second, using the sheltered and adapted instruction to meet the needs of English learners with special needs is a legislative requirement. The Individuals with Disabilities Education Act (IDEA) Amendments of 1997 require that special education teachers allow their students access to the general education curriculum. In order for English learners with special needs to have access to the Social Studies curriculum, they need sheltered instruction with adaptations.

Furthermore, the No Child Left Behind (NCLB) Act of 2001 also emphasizes the importance of including all children in the process of acquiring equal access to education and assessment. Widespread standardized testing and accountability have become rigorous. Even students in special education are required to participate in standardized testing. Hence, those legislative requirements encourage teachers to create more inclusive classrooms for all students, even students with significant special needs. Teachers need to pay attention to what their students can do, regardless of their disabilities and limited English language skills. Social Studies curriculum materials need to be modified and instructional delivery has to be altered to comply with the legal mandates.

Third, changes in the characteristics and needs of English learners with special needs in current classrooms have required different levels of Social Studies instruction. Students in current classrooms are composed of different linguistic and cultural backgrounds. Not only do students see different ethnic representations in their classrooms daily, but they are also constantly bombarded with information about worldly events. Terrorism, war, and the collapse of communism are not unusual topics around the students' lives anymore due to the impact of public media. Students' personal lives may also be impacted directly or indirectly by the current events like the tragedies of September 11, 2001. The attacks "may be used to stifle dissent and undermine critical thinking" (Thornton, 2002, p. 153). The topic crosses disciplinary boundaries; it is a historical, political, and cultural event for which an understanding of history, geography, and economics is necessary. The crisis of the September 11 attack was a "teachable moment" in Social Studies (Woyshner, 2003, p. 31).

A dominant fundamental issue in Social Studies remains how to best prepare students to become competent and concerned citizens for a democratic society in an increasingly interdependent and culturally diverse world (Martorella & Beal, 2002, p. 6). Teachers must foster a global perspective, ethics, and values with multicultural themes by teaching students how to respect differences.

Setting Social Studies content standards for all learners to raise their academic performance is a good way to keep continuity throughout the nation. However, it is a challenge for English learners with special needs to meet these rather rigorous standards like their peers without similar needs. Thus, Social Studies instruction needs to be sheltered to maintain the similar quality with less, but carefully selected, content for the specific group of students. Often, the greatest difficulty in scaffolding students' learning of Social Studies may be the students' lack of interest due to the disconnect between the topics being covered and students' personal life experiences. When studying Columbus' journeys, teachers cannot assume all students will connect those events with their meaning in history. In addition, English learners with special needs are often not motivated because they are at different levels of academic and language proficiency. They simply may not understand what is going on in the Social Studies classroom. Therefore, Social Studies teachers need to focus on teaching concepts through meaningful activities instead of emphasizing the memorization of facts.

Another noticeable change in today's students is their familiarity with technology. This trend can be an effective tool for Social Studies instruction for English learners with special needs. Utilizing technology enhances the teaching and learning of Social Studies content by reaching out to students' different learning abilities and English language skills. For example, teachers can guide students to take virtual tours on the Internet. English learners with disabilities can experience firsthand being in new places and enjoy the trip without leaving their classrooms. Ferretti and Okolo (1996) found that multimedia design tools promoted students' use of higher-level thinking skills such as critical thinking and problem solving in Social Studies. Virtual tours on the Internet can boost the creativity of all students, especially English learners with special needs.

HOW CAN SHELTERED AND ADAPTED INSTRUCTION BE DEVELOPED AND IMPLEMENTED TO ENHANCE SOCIAL STUDIES LEARNING?

Ways of developing and implementing sheltered and adapted instruction will be explained through examples. The fundamental requirement for any sheltered and adapted instruction is to get to know the students. Teachers must know their students' current strengths and English language competency.

As an example, when teaching a unit on family life at the elementary level, teachers begin by teaching key vocabulary words to students with visual cues. Students are encouraged to think about what each family possesses at home to elicit background knowledge. Students can interview parents about family-owned artifacts and oral stories to enhance the home and school connection. Then those artifacts and traditional family oral stories and songs are brought to class to share. This activity will increase parental involvement as well.

To enrich the process and integrate other subjects, teachers may infuse literature, arts, and music. After a teacher gets to know about her or his students' cultural and linguistic backgrounds, the teacher can choose culturally responsive literature. Introducing children's books and magazines written about and written by authors in students' family backgrounds will boost students' interest. Then the teacher can invite students to participate in a research project that requires an inquiry process about their family history and/or custom. At the elementary level, students can study about their parents or grandparents while the students at the secondary level can focus on a specific time frame from the line of their ancestry. All students can study their own cultural and historical facts, possibly including traditional music and arts, with personal interests. The whole process will motivate students to use higher order thinking and inquiry skills to get the sense out of historical data from a particular historical period.

Teachers can invite family members (e.g., parents, grandparents, cultural brokers in the community, etc.) as guest speakers in the classroom to learn about each family's rich cultural foundation and practices. This will increase awareness of history, including their own, which is the basis for understanding about others' historical and cultural backgrounds. Once students view themselves as researchers of their own family history from a more personal, but professional perspective, they will understand the key concepts of the unit in a meaningful way and eventually transform the skills into exploring other projects.

The second example is a sheltered lesson with adaptations teaching the history of immigration at the secondary level. A teacher promotes students' interest by facilitating a discussion of the key vocabulary words that the teacher presented earlier based on their personal experiences. The teacher also guides students to examine primary resources such as documents and artifacts from the Gilded Age since the greatest wave of U.S. immigration occurred during that period (Pass, 2004). Then the teacher leads the students to explore the Internet for more information about the topic. Here, the teacher can provide graphic organizers to aid the computer information search. On the Internet, many excellent quality resources are available without charge. An example would be the Ellis Island National Museum web site. To make sure that English learners with special needs successfully learn the key concepts, the teacher may want to focus on only one time period for each lesson.

With students at the secondary level, the teacher may assign the students to interview an immigrant whose cultural or racial backgrounds are different from their own so that they can broaden their perspectives. The teacher can demonstrate how to develop relevant interview questions and how to interview respectfully. Students can use a tape recorder and learn how to describe their interaction with their interviewees. As follow-up activities, the teacher may give the option of interviewing more immigrants and comparing their experiences or writing an autobiographical passage based on their learning. During the process, the teacher must accommodate or modify students' project assignments based on individual students' needs. For example, the teacher can provide an alternative project like reading a short book about immigration for the students with low cognitive functioning skills, shorten interview questions, or provide questions in writing for English learners, or have students with physical challenges make an audiotape instead of preparing a written report after the interview.

The third example is a thematic, integrated, and cooperative sheltered approach to teaching the Civil War unit. A teacher may integrate Civil War content and concepts into other subject matters of Science and Mathematics studies, as well as Language Arts in the daily teaching schedule. The teacher makes sure to align their instructional vocabulary to the comprehension level of English learners with special needs and to use teaching strategies to assure that only comprehensible input is provided.

The teacher helps students to incorporate the war and civic participation with Performing and Language Arts. Students develop the scripts to perform a role-play as soldiers representing beliefs of either the South or the North based on their choice. Another role-play may be introduced by assigning students into two groups of either slaves or slave buyers. A short simulation of a slave auction (Furlong & Jacobsen, 1976) might be introduced as needed. Hausfather (1998) shared how he used the *Slave Dancer* by Fox (1973) in his Social Studies class. By incorporating literature about slave issues, he was able to introduce the view of human nature struggling with the realities of the slave trade.

To integrate Mathematics, the teacher may guide students in a business simulation dealing with trade between the North and the South. This may include the business activities of figuring out the cost of slaves, construction calculations, and the meaning of the practices both then and now. The teacher facilitates further discussion about the economic principle of balance, including demand and supply. Songs describing the Civil War and the feelings of people involved in the war can be taught as well. Students may also discuss these concepts after viewing the film *Roots*.

All the learning process of this unit can take place in small groups. Working in small groups, students exchange their prior knowledge of the contents and answer questions. They brainstorm, develop procedures, guide research into further issues, learn how to make decisions with each other, generate plans, and express their understanding within a supportive atmosphere. Using cooperative learning strategies in the process provides English learners with special needs the opportunity to actively communicate their thoughts and ideas in a supportive and nonthreatening environment. By providing thematic, integrated, and cooperative sheltered instruction, the teacher can lower the affective filter for English learners with special needs so that they can effectively utilize their cognitive domain for learning (see Figure 14).

SHELTERED AND ADAPTED SOCIAL STUDIES SAMPLE LESSON

LESSON PLAN
Subject: Social Studies **Grade/Program:** 3rd & 4th grades/Special Day Class for students with mild to moderate disabilities **Date:**   **Teacher:**   **School:**
Lesson Title: Different family styles in the community
CA Content Standards: Contents standard 3.4 Students understand the role of rules and laws in our daily lives, and the basic structure of the United States government, in terms of: 2. the importance of public virtue and the role of citizens, including how to participate in a classroom, community and in civic life.   (What is my students' current performance level?)
Purpose of the Lesson: Students need to know the various family types in their community and they need to respect the differences to be able to participate in the community successfully.   *(Why am I teaching this lesson?)*
Objectives of the Lesson: 1. Students will define community. 2. Students will identify different family types in the community.   *(What will my students know and be able to do as a result of this lesson? Objectives must be stated in observable and measurable terms, e.g., paint a mural, write a poem, draw a picture. Do not use "understand" or "learn" unless it shows how.)*
Materials: pictures of different communities, various family pictures, word banks, a CD player, CD, buttons, colorful markers, white and color papers, hangers, scissors, yarn, and etc.   *(What do I need to use to teach this lesson? e.g., primary sources: photos, diaries, any first-hand accounts, pictures, realia, charts, maps, etc.)*
Special Needs Management Consideration: To meet the needs of English learners with special needs, sheltered and adapted instruction will be implemented.   ➤ First, to shelter and adapt the instruction, multi-modalities approach will be used to consider students' various learning styles and sensory abilities (based on Howard Gardener's multiple intelligence theory).   • For visual learners: lesson outline chart on the wall, computer projector, hand-outs for participants, clearly written directions for small group members will be included.

Figure 14. Sheltered and adapted social studies sample lesson. Lesson plan format source: California State University, Sacramento. MS/Specialist Teaching Credential Lesson Plan, Kathleen Kenfield, Planning for Success, 1993.

Figure 14—*Continued*

- Auditory learners will get step-by-step verbal direction, computer projector, and/or CD player as needed.
- For tactile learners, small group activities will be introduced.
- To meet the needs of musical learners, teacher will have students listen to songs about families and have students come up with family songs.
- Logical learners will learn the content through some activities of numbering families and working with graphics and addition with the numbers.
- Naturalists will also compare/contrast the life conditions for families in cities, suburban areas, and rural areas.
- Small group activities will boost interpersonal skills of students
- Writing self-reflection papers about different family types will meet the needs of intrapersonal students.
➤ Second, the lesson will be students' strength based. The teacher will identify each student's strength to match up with the required skills of small group activities.

Accommodations for English Learners with Special Needs Based on Their Strengths

Students	Strengths	Needs	Suggested Activity
Specific Learning Disabilities (SLD)	Excellent verbal skills - Focus on more oral presentation instead of written report.	Poor writing skills - Just draw without writing or provide more time to write	Activity # 2 (Less writing required)
SLD & Attention Deficit Hyperactivity Disorder	Excellent mobility, strong fine motor skills - Distribute materials to each group, -Make a house instead of drawing, activity 1.	Short attention span - Sharpening pencils for group members, - Sit between positive role models, - Away from stimulating areas, - Break the task into small steps	Activity # 3 (Strong fine motor skills required)
Low Intellectual Function (Mild Mental Retardation)	Some mobility - Pass/collect materials to/from others in his/her group.	Speech & Language delay, poor fine motor, low comprehension - Get a peer help to glue - To be read written directions by a peer	Activity # 1 (Less fine motor skills required)

Figure 14–*Continued*

➤Third, the English learners with special needs will see demonstration by their teacher and peers throughout the lesson.

➤Fourth, the lesson will use an activity-oriented approach. Many activity choices are available to all students to reach the same content standard.

➤Fifth, the teacher will relate the instruction to students' personal life experiences.

➤Sixth, the lesson will incorporate instructional technology by using a computer, a computer projector, and a Compact Disc player.

➤Seventh, the lesson will include various instructional delivery structures, such as whole group instruction, small group activities, and one-on-one instruction.

➤Eighth, different adaptations (accommodations and modifications) will be made throughout the lesson to meet individual needs, such as changing room arrangements, differentiated lesson content, delivery procedures, and assignments.

Anticipatory Set: Show the pictures of different communities. Ask students to identify similarities and differences among different communities. Ask them what the community is. Define the word community as a place where different people live, work, and have fun together. What is the community made of? *(It is usually made by several neighborhoods.)* What do their home communities look like? *(There are many types of families in the community.)* Invite an English learner to sing a family song in the native language from his/her home country if the student is willing. Preteach key vocabulary. If possible, invite a parent volunteer to teach his/her family song to the class.
(How will I motivate my students? How will I promote learner participation early in the lesson? Check prior knowledge, set the stage for learning, engage my students, activate curiosity.)

Lesson Development: After discussion, the class will be divided into three small groups. Each student will participate in an activity based on personal interest and abilities. If possible, students will switch to do other activities. By promoting cooperative group work, the teacher can foster positive interdependent skills. Students gain mutual respect for individual differences and practice interpersonal skills. Teacher explains the activity procedures.

■ ACTIVITY 1: Button Family
(Concept: Buttons may be the same color or have two holes, but should be different shapes and sizes. Families come in all shapes and sizes. We need to respect the differences.)

Directions:
• Find buttons that represent each family member and put him or her together into families.

Figure 14—*Continued*

- Draw a house on construction paper or build a paper house with the construction paper (for higher level of tactile and/or spatial ability).
- Glue buttons in the house.
- Compare your button family members with others.
- Write a written report or give an oral report about your family.

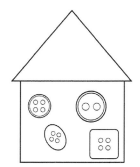

■ **ACTIVITY 2: Family Circle**
(Concept: Many types of families are represented in our class. We need to respect the differences.)

<u>Directions:</u>
- Create a Family Circle picture, with yourself in the center of the circle and other family members on "rays" that stick out.
- Draw faces on construction paper and write their names.
- Or bring in family members' photos to cut out and write their names on each.
- Describe family members by the faces.
- Include whomever you wish (primary and secondary residences as well as those who do not have a traditional family).

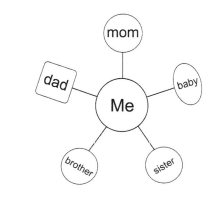

Figure 14—*Continued*

■ **ACTIVITY 3: Mobile Family**
(Concept: Family members are all different in each family. We need to respect the differences.)

Directions:
- Draw and cut out faces of your family members.
- On the reverse side of your drawings, describe each family member positively.
- Attach those drawings to the hanger with yarn in any arrangement you choose. (Provide each student with one coat hanger labeled with his or her name, along with yarn and drawing paper).

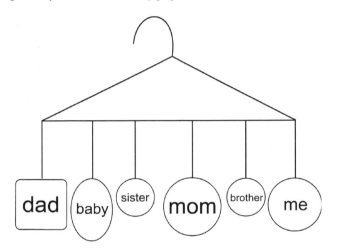

(activity ideas by Dolores Choat,
http://teacher.scholastic.com/lessonrepro/lessonplans)

guided practice, key vocabulary (*student-centered, interactive, stimulates thought, academic*) *How will I organize lesson procedures that are developed in a logical, organized manner which lead my students to successful achievement of the objectives? Do I help my students connect the contents of this lesson to what is familiar or relevant to their lives and/or experiences?* (*strategies, activities, modeling, checking for understanding*)

Lesson Closure: The teacher invites students to reflect on their learning through activities and guides them to focus on the objectives of the lesson. Students know that they are part of a family. They come from many types of families and their families belong to the community. They are proud of their families no matter what kind of family they have. There are many young children that are cared for by extended family members, such as grandparents, uncles, aunts, foster parents, and adoptive parents

Figure 14—*Continued*

independent practice (How will I plan to provide opportunities for my students independently to practice the skills I have introduced? How will I provide closure to ensure my students' comprehension (summarizing, reinforcing ideas, share acquired knowledge, aid retention of knowledge)? Will I give homework? How will I set the stage for the next lesson?)

Extension for higher thinking skill enhancement by integrating Animal Science

The teacher may invite students to think about different animal clans. Students can research various animal clans. They can talk about single-parent families. For example, the male emperor penguins nurture and protect the eggs for about nine weeks. They don't even eat or move during the period. Male sea horses carry the eggs from the females and give birth to the young from special openings in their bellies.

Promote Active Thinking with Guided Questioning

• Teacher (T): Emperor penguins carry their eggs on top of their feet. Why does this make sense?
• Student (S): I don't know.
• T: Well, let's think. What do we know about penguins? For example, where do they live?
• S: In Antarctica.
• T: Good. And what is life like in Antarctica?
• S: Cold, icy, ... frozen.
• T: So, if it is cold and icy in Antarctica, why does it make sense that penguins carry their eggs on their feet?
• S: To keep them from getting frozen?
• T: Good. To keep them warm, to keep them from getting frozen. What else?
(Mastropieri & Scruggs, 2003, The Inclusive Classroom, p 479)

Evaluation of the Lesson: A broad and authentic assessment is needed to check if students have met the objectives. The two objectives were: (1) students will define community and (2) students will identify different family types in the community.

Throughout the lesson process, the teacher uses on-going observations on each student's progress. At the end of the lesson, the teacher checks for students' understanding through their presentations by an oral and/or a written format.

To evaluate their learning effectively, the teacher needs to be aware of students' learning styles, profile, and language proficiency levels (e.g., California English Language Development Test, Language Dominance Tests for assessing English proficiency levels, and Language Assessment Scales for primary language proficiency) through the teacher's observations, portfolio assessment (accumulate selected students' work), based on the rubrics the teacher developed with students' input.

Figure 14–*Continued*

(How will I know that my students learned the lesson objectives? Are there multiple ways for my students to demonstrate their understanding? Is assessment imbedded in the lesson in such a way for me to alter my lesson as I proceed to meet the needs of my students? Checking for understanding becomes on-going assessment?)

Self-Evaluation of the Lesson:
(How did the lesson go, what happened that I was not expecting, what worked very well, what did not, what effect will this have upon the way I plan and teach in the future?)

SOCIAL STUDIES SCOPE (CURRICULUM) AND SEQUENCE (ORDER)

Kindergarten: Living and Learning Together. Students focus upon their immediate environment, and emphasis is placed on individual development and identity through social and civic learning experiences (e.g., interaction with peers and respect for others, learning about myself and classroom community).

Grade One: Families in Our Community. Students learn about changes in their own families and communities while focusing on the rights and responsibilities of citizens as they interact in home, school, and local environments (e.g., families in our community and in other places).

Grade Two: The Local and Regional Community. Students examine local and regional communities in the present and past and how these communities meet peoples' needs (e.g., our community and communities meet our needs and wants).

Grade Three: Culture, People, and Environment. Students learn about changes in the local community and in communities in other states and regions of the world (e.g., Native American past, human and natural resources, interactions with environment, citizens, the government, and civic life of communities).

Grade Four: (Own State) in the Nation and the World. Students study their own state and its relationships to regional, national, and world communities (e.g.; physical and cultural environments on the state's growth and development, the geography, resources, economy, and citizenship of the state).

Grade Five: the United States: The Founding of the Republic. Students learn about the history of the United States to 1800 (e.g., political, geographical, economic, and cultural factors on early development, Native American cultures, exploration, colonization, settlement, the founding period that produced the United States Constitution and Bill of Rights, and independence).

Grade Six: World Geography and Culture: Ancient Pre-history–600. Students learn about the regions and countries of Europe and the Americas (e.g., geographical, historical, economic, political, and cultural relationships).

Grade Seven: Peoples, Places, and Cultures in Africa, Asia, and Australia: World History Emphasis on Western Civilization, BC to 1600. Students study the regions and nations of Africa, Asia, and the Southwest Pacific (e.g., historical geographical, economic, political, and cultural relationships).

Grade Eight: United States History: Growth and Development–U.S. History Review Colonization with Emphasis on 1775–1877. Students learn about national and state development through the Civil War and Reconstruction periods (e.g., principles of the United States and students' own state's Constitutions, the American revolution, the new governments, the federalist era, the Jeffersonian era, the war of 1812, nationalism, industrialism, the Jacksonian era, westward expansion, the civil war, and reconstruction).

HIGH SCHOOL (GRADES 9-12) COURSE FOCUS

Students may study the social studies curriculum of History, Civics and Government, Geography, Economics, and Individuals, Society, and Culture through Psychology, Sociology, and Anthropology.

Grade Nine: United States History (1877 to present). Students learn about the key events, persons, groups, and movements in the period as they relate to life in their State and the United States: economic and geographic expansion and the social and political response, 1877–1920; the great war and a new economic order, 1912-1932; the expanding power of the United States government at home and abroad, 1932–1953, the transformation of modern America, 1950s-present.

Grade Ten: World History/Civilization. Students examine the key concepts of continuity and change, universality and particularity, and unity and diversity among various peoples and cultures from the past to the present (e.g., American government principles, systems; structure, organization, and functions).

Grade Eleven: The Contemporary World And Its Problems. Students learn about the modern world crisis, promises, and paradoxes (e.g., Africa and Asia before 1500, emergence of modern Europe (1300–1815), nationalism, industrialism, and imperialism (1750–1900). Psychology/Sociology.

Grade Twelve: United States Government/ Economics. Students learn about a framework for understanding the purposes, principles, and practices of American government as established by the United States Constitution (e.g., rights and responsibilities of citizens and how to exercise these rights and responsibilities in local, state, and national government, allocation of scarce resources and the economic reasoning used by people as consumers, producers, savers, investors, workers, voters, and as government agencies).

REFERENCES

Choat, D. (2002). *Teacher Made Activities.* Retrieved 2002, from http://teacher.scholastic.com/lessonrepro/lessonplans

Echevarria, J., Vogt, M, & Short, D. (2004). *Making contents comprehensible for English learners: The SIOP model* (2nd Ed.). Boston: Pearson Education, Inc.

Ellis, A. K. (2002). *Teaching and learning elementary Social Studies* (7th Ed.). Boston: Allyn & Bacon.

Farr, B. P., & Trumbeull, E. (1997). *Assessment alternatives for diverse classrooms.* Norwood, MA: Christopher-Gordon Publishers, Inc.

Ferretti, R. P., & Okolo, C. M. (1996). Authenticity in learning: Multimedia design projects in the Social Studies for students with disabilities. *Journal of Learning Disabilities, 29*(5), 45–60.

Furlong, M. S., & Jacobsen, L. W. (1976). *Slave auction: Crisis in human values.* Culver City, CA: Zenger Publications.

Hausfather, S. (1998, July/August). Theme study in elementary-school Social Studies: A different approach to gaining knowledge. *The Social Studies, 89*(4), 171–177.

Herrell, A., & Jordon, M. (2004). *Fifty strategies for teaching English language learners.* Upper Saddle River, NJ: Pearson/Merrill Prentice Hall.

Kenfield, K. (1993). Planning for success for your English learners. Lesson plan.

California State University Sacramento, California.

Krashen, S. D. (1982). *Principles and practice in second language acquisition.* New York: Pergamon Press.

Lemke, J. (1988). Genres, semantics, and classroom education. *Linguistics and Education, 1*(1), 81–99.

Martorella, P. H., & Beal, C. (2002). *Social Studies for elementary school classrooms: Preparing children to be global citizens.* Upper Saddle River, NJ: Pearson Education.

Mastropieri, M. A. & Shruggs, T. E. (2004). *The inclusive classroom: Strategies for effective instruction.* Upper Saddle River, NJ: Prentice Hall.

Merrifield, M. M. (2004. May/June). Elementary students in substantive culture learning. *Social Education, 68*(4), 270–274.

National Council for the Social Studies (NCSS). (1994). *Expectations of excellence: Curriculum standards for Social Studies.* Washington, DC: Author.

Parker, W. (2005). *Social Studies in elementary education,* (12th Ed.). Upper Saddle River, NJ: Pearson Education, Inc.

Pass, S. (2004. May/June). Teaching about immigration, past and present. *Social Education, 68*(4), 2–15.

Salend, S. J. (1998). *Effective mainstreaming: Creating inclusive classrooms* (3rd Ed.). Upper Saddle River, NJ: Merrill.

Scheurman, G., & Yell, M. (1998). Constructing knowledge in Social Studies. Theme issue. *Social Education, 62*(1).

The ERIC Clearinghouse on Disabilities and Gifted Education (1999, July). *Teaching Social Studies to students with learning disabilities.* Arlington, VA: The Council for Exceptional Children.

Thornton, S. J. (2002). Teaching and teacher education in a time of crisis. *Theory and Research in Social Education, 30*(1), 152–154.

U.S. Census (2000). (Title). Retrieved (date), from http://www.census.gov/popest/national.

Vygotsky, L. S. (1962). T*hought and language.* Cambridge, MA: MIT Press.

Vygotsky, L. S. (1978). *Mind in society.* Cambridge, MA: Harvard University Press

Woyshner, C. A. (2003). *Social Studies: A chapter of the curriculum handbook.* Alexandria, VA: The Association for Supervision and Curriculum Development.

Zarrillo, J. J. (2004). *Teaching elementary Social Studies: Principles and applications* (2nd Ed.). Upper Saddle River, NJ: Pearson Education.

Chapter 14

THE CULTURALLY AND LINGUISTICALLY
DIFFERENT STUDENT

ELVA DURÁN

This chapter will define the culturally and linguistically different student and will explain some specific characteristics that distinguish the culturally and linguistically different student. Further, in this chapter this writer will explain some ways that the culturally and linguistically different student, more specifically the Latino student, can be assisted in some areas which have been discussed earlier in this book. Latino is used here as a general term that includes persons of Mexican, Puerto Rican, Cuban, Central or South American, or of other Spanish-speaking origin. It should be recognized that there are differences among and within these groups. In the context of this chapter and other chapters throughout this book (where the term Latino is used), the emphasis is on Mexican American families.

WHO IS THE CULTURALLY AND LINGUISTICALLY
DIFFERENT STUDENT?

The culturally and linguistically different student is defined by Nuttall (1984), Rueda (1984) and Baca and Bransford (1982) as the student who is a native speaker of a language other than English. IDEA 2004 adds to the definition of the limited English proficient student from the No Child Left Behind Act:

An individual, aged 3–21, enrolled or preparing to enroll in an elementary or secondary school (1)(a) who wasn't born in the U.S. or whose native language isn't English; (b) who is a Native American or Alaska Native, or native resident of the outlying areas and comes from an environment where a language other than English has significantly impacted level of English language proficiency; or (c) who is migratory, with a native language other than English, from an environment where a language other than English is dominant; and (2) whose difficulties in speaking, reading, writing, or understanding English may be sufficient to deny the child (a) ability to meet proficient level of achievement on State assessments; (b) ability to successfully achieve in class where instruction is in English, or (c) opportunity to participate fully in society. (Mandlawitz, 2006, p. 5)

The student who is in this category also has a different culture and values than those found among the mainstream of society (Chamot & McKeon, 1984; Rodriquez, 1982). The student, who is culturally and linguistically different and is in special education because he/she additionally has mental retardation, autism spectrum disorders, or another disability as well, presents a special challenge to the teacher/trainer. The student who falls in this category may not be able to speak his/her native language due to his/her severe disability, but has heard it being spoken at home and can understand the language when someone speaks to him/her. If the student has only a moderate intellectual disability, he/she may be able to understand and speak some words in his/her native language.

HISTORICAL INFORMATION

In 1954, the *Brown v. Board of Education* decision that led to the notion that segregation of race is unconstitutional was one of the first decisions that helped refine the concept of equal educational opportunity (Cegelka, 1986; Estrada & Nava, 1976; Henderson, 1980). In other court decisions such as *United States v. Texas* (1972), *Serna v. Portales Municipal Schools* (1974), and *Lau v. Nichols* (1974) the culturally and linguistically different student was also assisted so that this particular type of student could receive a more appropriate education in his/her public school placement. In *United States v. Texas* (1972), it was decided that the failure of school districts in Texas to provide bilingual-bicultural education to Spanish-speaking students violated the constitutional rights of these students (Estrada & Nava, 1976). In *Serna v. Portales Municipal Schools* (1974) and *Lau v. Nichols* (1974), the culturally and linguistically different student was also assisted so that this particular type of student could receive a more appropriate education in his/her public school placement. In *United States v. Texas* (1972), it was decided that the failure of school districts in Texas to provide bilingual-bicultural education to Spanish-speaking students violated the constitutional rights of these students (Estrada & Nava, 1976). *Serna v. Portales Municipal Schools* (1974) revealed discrimination against Mexican American students in the schools and led Portales Public Schools to implement bilingual education programs.

In *Lau v. Nichols* (1974) the United States Supreme Court ruled unanimously that San Francisco Independent School District was in violation of the Civil Rights of 1,800 non-English-speaking Chinese children, since it failed to provide instruction in their native language. The Lau decision had national ramifications, and affected every federally supported school with culturally and linguistically different children (Carpenter, 1983; Estrada & Nava, 1976). Additionally, in *Larry P. v. Riles* (1972), *Covarrubias v. San Diego Unified School District* (1972), and *Spangler v. Board of Education* (1970), the decisions have all resulted in a number of changes in the education of minority students. Most of the changes address identification and placement for special programs (Carpenter, 1983).

Further, P.L. 94-142, the Education for All Handicapped Children's Act of 1975, or more recently the Individuals with Disabilities Education Act (2004) has also been responsible for promoting stronger advocacy and improved services for culturally diverse, exceptional children (Baca, 1980).

With all that has occurred with these laws and court cases to enhance the education of the culturally and linguistically different student, much remains to be done for the student with disabilities who is also culturally and linguistically different. Even more needs to be accomplished for the culturally and linguistically different student who has moderate to severe handicaps and/or autism spectrum disorders. As this writer reviewed the literature, she was unable to locate articles and research which were directly written for the student who falls in this category. This lack of material and information in this particular area has been unfortunate because there are growing numbers of students in special education who have cultural and linguistic difficulties, yet there is a paucity of information that can be used by teachers, parents, and trainers of these particular students.

CULTURAL IMPLICATIONS

When teaching students who also have cultural and linguistic differences, it is important to note some of the characteristics that these students may have due to their particular cultural background. According to Grossman (1984), the Latino culture often emphasizes that the people in the various groups learn by doing. Consequently, Grossman notes that such students, in many cases, learn more by touching, seeing, manipulating, and experiencing concrete objects than by discussing or perhaps reading about ideas. Some of the more direct approaches in teaching Latino students may be seen, for example, when teaching students with moderate to severe handicaps to learn various vocabulary words. The students can be shown concrete objects or pictures to help them grasp the vocabulary concept.

The idea of showing these students everything in a concrete manner is often seen at work when the trainer helps the student with moderate-to-severe handicaps learn how to operate an automatic dishwasher, for instance. Often it is easier for the student to learn how to operate the machine by being guided to actually push the button of the dishwasher several times before the student learns how to do this particular task on his/her own.

In addition to presenting the concept in a concrete means, very often students in various cultural groups need to hear the terms or concept spoken in Spanish or the students' first or native language. In a study done by Durán (1986), it was revealed that students of moderate-to-severe intellectual disabilities did better learning particular vocational tasks when the trainers cued the Mexican American students verbally in Spanish only. The students in the control group cued in Spanish and English were the group that learned second best. The group verbally cued in English only did not do as well as the Spanish only or the Spanish and English mixed groups.

Additionally, it is helpful to present information in a concrete means when students are in a general education classroom or are fully included in the regular classroom with their own age peers. For example, if the students with moderate-to-severe disabilities are not comprehending what the word "volcano" means in a science lesson—showing the students with disabilities a picture of a volcano will be helpful when trying to have them learn the vocabulary word in their science lesson

(Durán, 2005a). This technique is especially helpful when the students are also presented the reading vocabulary on the board. By showing the students the word volcano and immediately showing the students the picture of a volcano, will assist the students to better comprehend the concept being presented to them. Vocabulary learned in isolation will not help the students remember the information in the short- or long-term (Durán, 2005a).

Another cultural implication which needs to be noted is that some Latino students also believe in the supernatural–ghosts, magic, religion, saints, etc.–more than do their Anglo peers (Grossman, 1984). For example, in the Southwest along the Mexican border, students have grown up hearing stories of "*La Llorona,*" (the crying lady) who lost her child in the Rio Grande River and spent her nights walking up and down the river area crying in despair to see if she could see or find her missing child. Teachers or instructional aides can often take some time, if they teach Mexican American students with moderate-to-severe intellectual disabilities, to discover from parents and grandparents some of the *cuentos* or short stories that are present in the particular cultural group. This information could be included as part of the teacher's ecological or environmental inventory (Brown, 1984); asking parents or grandparents questions pertaining to what cuentos or stories the children are familiar with makes it possible for some of this information to be brought to school. Teachers could take a few minutes during the week to teach the students some of these folklore stories which are native to the cultural group. Some time could be allotted for this particular goal during reading, or leisure and recreation types of activities.

Very similar to this idea of the cuentos or stories is the belief that many students coming from various cultural groups are already very familiar with songs which are particular to their culture. Teachers can often discover what some of these students enjoy listening to at home, if they once again ask the families of the students who are in their classes. One popular song among Mexican Americans, for example is the song "*Las Mañanitas.*" This particular song, which is so lively and easy to learn due to the simplicity of the lyrics, is often sung on special occasions like birthdays or for Mother's Day. Very often "Las Mañanitas" is sung for a variety of other occasions. This is a song that makes up an important part of the culture of many Mexican American students, and teachers can have the students with moderate-to-severe handicaps listen and perhaps learn and even attempt to sing some of the verses during leisure and recreation activities. The result may not be of concert quality, but it helps create a positive atmosphere.

Also, what may be important to bring forth in the classroom, or during home training, are some of the particular foods that are also typical of the students' family and cultural groups. Mexican American people, for great part, enjoy *flautas* (rolled crisp tortillas filled with meat), *fajitas* (beef strips which have been marinated in special sauces and grilled and served with tortillas), and *enchiladas*. Students enjoy eating and preparing some of these foods, which some very often have in their homes. Thus, just as some foods and objects from the Anglo culture are often part of the curriculum or teacher-made lessons and materials, some additional materials from the student's culture can easily be integrated into the lessons that are part of the students' education.

City and university libraries often have stories and information about other cultural materials that can be used by teachers who teach students who are culturally and linguistically different. Many libraries have cross-cultural sections or a section entitled, "Chicano Studies" where all kinds of materials and literature can be located for the Mexican American student. Many teachers in El Paso, for example, are aware of this material and often use the "Chicano Studies" portion of the library to help them tie in more closely with their Mexican American students in their classrooms. In addition, there may be storytellers in the community who might be brought to classes for even more enrichment.

CURRICULAR IMPLICATIONS

This section, while mentioning in general terms students of other cultural and linguistic groups, will focus on giving some suggestions for teaching the student of moderate-to-severe intellectual disabilities who comes from the Latino and more specifically the Mexican American group. Some of the ideas presented here have been tried in various classrooms in the Southwest, Texas and California where this writer acts as a consultant. It has been noted in reviewing the literature that no mention has been made concerning the cultural and linguistically different student who also has moderate-to-severe intellectual handicaps. There is little to no literature available of the different cultural groups and students with severe intellectual disabilities. It is vitally important to consider the cultural aspects of different groups when teaching students who have exceptional needs (Durán, 2005b; Gonzáles; 2005; Nuttall, 1984; Ortiz, 1984). More details on how to teach limited English proficient students follows in the next chapter.

FUNCTIONAL READING AND LANGUAGE INTERVENTION

In both of these areas, the teacher or parent and/or other caregivers need to conduct an ecological inventory, and as part of this inventory, there should be some questions or information that the parent or family can generate about particular words, stories or cuentos, etc., that could be presented to the student in class (see Table XXIII). This writer has observed that many Latino parents do not know how to read or write in English and often do not respond to notes and questionnaires the teacher sends home for them to fill out. Putting the questionnaire in the home language of the family will help many parents understand more effectively what they are to do. Often if parents have a phone, or if the neighbor has a phone, then following-up on the questionnaire which was sent home can be done with a phone call; such a practice may be helpful in trying to show parents what to do. This writer has observed in working with parents that they often do not know the importance of giving feedback to teachers, but once they understand that the teacher cares, in many instances they will open up and explain in more detail what it is that the teacher could teach at school pertaining to functional language communication.

Some particular words that may be emphasized in language and reading are those that come from family, foods, and various cultural words that are typical of the Latino group of people. In some programs in Northern California for example, all the words that are taught in reading or language and/or communication to students with moderate-to-severe handicaps and autism and other spectrum disorders are from these groups noted above. The words are presented in Spanish by the teacher along with the actual or concrete object, where possible; for instance, the student learns to say "grape" and is shown a

Table XXIII
ECOLOGICAL INVENTORY

(Inventario de la Casa, la Communindad, y de la Escuela Tocante
a la instrucción de su Hijo o Hija)

Foods *(Comidas)*	Name *(Nombre)*
	_____
	_____
	_____
	_____
	_____
	_____
	_____

Fast Food Restaurants *(Restaurantes)*	What do you purchase most often? *(¿Que compra mas frecuentemente?)*
	_____
	_____
	_____
	_____

Which foods do you most often buy for you family at the grocery store? Please send the names and brands. *(¿Cuáles comidas compra usted en la tienda mas frecuentemente? Mande las nombres y marcas por favor.)* What food do you buy most often in fast food restaurants? *(¿Cuáles comidas compra usted para su familia en los restaurantes y tiendas? Mande las marcas de los platillas por favor.)*

---

real grape. The student is told the same concept in Spanish "*uva*" should they need to hear the word in Spanish. For those Spanish-speaking students who understand the concept and vocabulary word "grape" without utilizing some Spanish then just using English and the picture of grape will be sufficient. The idea behind showing the picture and utilizing their native language is important so that students will comprehend what they are learning.

Also, when presenting reading instruction to students with more moderate intellectual disabilities, students can be shown pictures or objects that are found in their cultural group. For example, photographs of cultural food such as "*tamales*" and "*tacos*" could be shown so that the student could talk about what he/she saw, and later the student would read what he/she dictated orally as he/she told the teacher comments about the pictures or photographs.

This technique could add a little variety to the many other story ideas or pictures that are presented to students in various classes on a daily basis. More advanced students with moderate intellectual disabilities could learn to understand the words said to them in both Spanish and English, and many could learn to spell a few words, at least in their native language. Some simple Spanish words that could be learned along with the English equivalents are "*uva*" (grape), "*taco*" (taco), "*papa*" (potato), and "*caldo*" (soup), etc. If parents and teachers decide to only use the picture of the vocabulary word and not use the Spanish word then this will be fine. The idea behind all of this is to help the students better comprehend what they are being taught.

Parents can also be taught to help their verbal or nonverbal son and/or daughter new words in either or both languages, but caution should be exercised. The teacher should not send home lists of English and Spanish equivalents to the parents; when possible teachers should visit the parents of linguistically and culturally different students, in their homes, in order to teach and to model for the parents what needs to be done if the child is to have his or her learning reinforced at home.

Follow-up needs to be done by the teacher to see if what he/she suggested to the parents is being done at home. Descamps (1987) noted that many Latino parents do not come to school conferences , etc. because they feel alienated and set apart from the big school building and teachers and principals who teach in the schools. Descamps goes on to say that if teachers visit the Latino parents in their homes, or find some way to bring the parents in car pools from their homes, many of them will begin to see what they can do to help their son and/or daughter. Also, Hernandez (1987) adds that it is important for teachers to know some Spanish or have bilingual interpreters present on parents' night; Latino parents would thus feel more at home and like they belong in the public schools. This writer is well aware that many Latino parents do not attend school conferences or school meetings because some do not understand the culture and language of the schools. We have to learn some ways to make people feel comfortable and welcome in the schools. In the entrance of the school lobby a bulletin board could be placed with cultural greetings for example, "*Bienvenidos*" (Welcome) and other greetings could be printed on the bulletin board from other different cultural groups.

In California, Texas, and Illinois, *Fiesta Educativa* has been instrumental in providing many services to Latino families who have children and youth with disabilities (Rueda & Martinez, 1992).

Martinez (personal communication, 1995), who is the founder of Fiesta Educativa in California indicates that Latino parents and families begin to participate more when they become empowered and take leadership to provide each other with information after they have attended mini and major conferences they have helped to organize.

Having been involved directly with Fiesta Educativa in Texas and now in California, this writer feels that it is an excellent way to have Latino parents more actively participate in their son's and/or daughter's education. Where possible, more parents need to be empowered in their neighborhoods so they can become more knowledgeable with their son and/or daughters and contribute toward their education at school and at home.

Thus, in teaching language and reading to students of more moderate-to-severe intellectual disabilities who are also culturally and linguistically different, it is not only important to make sure of familiar cultural materials that are a part of the student's family, but it is also necessary to work closely with the parents. The cooperation thus engendered should include using Spanish (or whatever the language of the home is), but it is also necessary to work closely with the parents so that they can feel that they are part of the school environment. One way of doing this is by empowering the parents, as is done in Fiesta Educativa. Thus, the parents can be made to feel that they have something important to contribute to their son's and/or daughter's education. The strangeness that parents from a nonmainstream culture frequently feel in the "alien" community they face can also be lessened or even dissipated by getting them involved in the educational process as co-equals.

VOCATIONAL AND COMMUNITY TRAINING

Obviously, the areas of functional reading and language are important when dealing with students of moderate-to-severe handicaps, especially when they are of different cultural and linguistic backgrounds from the mainstream around them. But the areas of vocational training and community training are no less vital in their education.

In coordinating several nonsheltered vocational training programs involving various school districts and also directing a post-secondary program on a university campus, this writer has become aware that many Latino parents often do not understand the value of their son's and/or daughter's participation in on-the-job training. Many parents are often reluctant to send their son and/or daughter to learn to do a job in the community because they feel they will be there always to take care of the son and/or daughter, or they feel that the family member has too many disabilities to do the actual work.

This writer has been involved with two districts where the nonsheltered programming was initiated, all parents were telephoned so they could come to an instructional meeting designed to explain to each of them what nonsheltered vocational training would have to offer their son and/or daughter. The principal was asked to speak to the parents concerning the school's involvement in such programming. (It is very important to include principals and other administrators in these inservice meetings because many Latino people tend to follow closely the advice or information of people who represent authority figures in the schools and community.) Once the parents received the explanation in their native language, they were also taken in school buses to be shown the actual setting where their son and/or daughter would participate in on-the-job training. This entire effort proved to be highly successful with the Latino parents because they supported the entire training program once they understood it. Further, once the vocational programming was initiated, the Mexican American students were absent far less often than they had been previously.

The actual training of culturally and linguistically different students should involve some instruction in the students' native language. For instance, if a student is told, "Turn the button on," or "Push the button" in order to start a machine, the trainer should follow this particular cueing with a phrase in the student's native language. In Spanish, the student of moderate-to-severe intellectual disabilities would be cued "*Prenda aquí*" or "*Apriete este boton.*" Cueing the student in Spanish or his/her native language is helpful so that the student can respond more easily and quickly to the trainer's directions. A tape can be made of the most important cueing in vocational training in English and Spanish (or what the "different" language is), so that the college student trainer, teacher, and/or instructional aide can listen to it and follow some of this type of cueing. This material is helpful for those trainers who do not know how to speak the student's particular home language.

Just as the parents must be made a part of the vocational training for their son and/or daughter from the beginning, so too must the parents be made a part of community-based instruction. Parents must be informed by phone or letter, plus an actual meeting and/or conference on the importance of their taking their son and/or daughter to the community. They must have explained to them the importance of their taking their son and/or daughter to the community to shop and buy food. They must also have explained to them the importance of family participating in these same activities in school and in other community environments. Too often it is taken for granted that all parents see and understand the value of their son and/or daughter participating in such activities, but this is not always the case. Many Mexican American parents often do not understand that their son and/or daughter need the exposure to other more normalized peers. Some parents, further, do not understand why their son and/or daughter should learn to use a restaurant or grocery store. All this must be explained to parents initially and be reinforced periodically so their continued support will be there for the teacher and other trainers. This writer has discovered that if parents are not shown some demonstration of how the community training is accomplished, with photographs or cards of the items that they are to have their son and/or daughter purchase, much of the instruction will never be done at home and no generalization training will occur.

Further, teachers or aides will often have to make matching-to-sample cards of the various grocery items and will have to make communication booklets for the student so that parents can use one set of these materials at home with their son and/or daughter. In order to accomplish this goal, the teacher or trainer may need to send some type of questionnaire in the parents' native or home language so they

Table XXIV
FOOD AND RESTAURANT QUESTIONNAIRE
(Inventario de Comidas y Restaurantes)

Home *(La Casa)*	Vocabulary *(Vocabulario o palabras usuales)*	Stories *(Dichos o cuentos)*	Songs *(Canciones particulars)*
	_____	_____	_____
	_____	_____	_____
	_____	_____	_____
	_____	_____	_____
	_____	_____	_____
	_____	_____	_____

Community *(La Communindad)*	Vocabulary *(Vocabulario o palabras usuales)*	Place you and your family visit *(Lugares su familia frecuenta)*	
	_____	_____	_____
	_____	_____	_____
	_____	_____	_____
	_____	_____	_____
	_____	_____	_____
	_____	_____	_____

School *(La Escuela)*	Vocabulary *(Vocabulario o palabras usuales)*		
	_____	_____	_____
	_____	_____	_____
	_____	_____	_____
	_____	_____	_____
	_____	_____	_____

Give us any other suggestions or comments about what you would like us to teach your son and/or daughter. *(Denos otras surgencias acerca de la intrucción a su hijo y hija.)*

can fill it out and return the information to the teacher (see Table XXIV).

When the questionnaire is returned to the teacher, he/she can begin making food cards that the student in his/her class can take home and use while shopping with his/her parents and can even use while shopping independently for his/her parents. The communication booklet can also be developed to include restaurant items. Then communication booklets will have fuller usefulness at home; parents can have their son and/or daughter order what they need in restaurants when they go out to eat as a family, or when the nonverbal student is in the community on his/her own and wants to order something to eat. Thus, parents need not only to be informed of the importance of their son and/or daughter participating in community-based instruction, but they further need to be sent materials at home that they can use with their son and/or daughter in the communication booklets. Additionally, Latino parents who do not understand the value and the techniques of such training need to be given instruction in their home language, so they can understand how to make use of the materials the teacher has made for their son and/or daughter to use at home.

In addition, it does not matter what area of the curriculum one is concerned with in teaching students who are culturally and linguistically different, the teacher must consider not only the student's home language and culture, but the parents of these students as well. Parents must be taught to use the various curricular materials; otherwise, many of these important areas of their child's education will never be used at home as part of the student's education.

DISCUSSION QUESTIONS

1. Define who is a culturally and linguistically different student who may also be a student with moderate to severe handicaps.
2. According to No Child Left Behind, who is the culturally and linguistically different student?
3. What can be done specifically to teach the culturally and linguistically different student in vocational, community training, reading and language?

4. Why are parents important to consider in teaching the culturally and linguistically different student?

5. How can you empower Latino parents to contribute more to their sons and/or daughters with disabilities?

6. What are some cultural implications that should be considered when teaching some Latino students?

REFERENCES

Baca, L. (1980). Issues of the education of culturally diverse exceptional children. *Exceptional Children, 46*(8), 583–605.

Baca, L., & Bransford, L. (1982). *An appropriate education for handicapped children of limited English proficiency*, (pp. 1–22). Reston, VA: The ERIC Clearinghouse on Handicapped and Gifted Children, The Council for Exceptional Children.

Brown, L. (1984). *Functional skills in programs for students with severe handicaps* (pp. 1–6). Unpublished Manuscript in cooperation with University of Wisconsin, Madison and Madison Metropolitan School District.

Carpenter, L. J. (1983). *Bilingual special education. An overview of issues.* Los Alamitos, CA: National Center for Bilingual Research, pp. 3–56.

Cegelka, P. (1986). *Educational services to handicapped students with limited English proficiency: A California statewide study* (pp. 1–121). Reston, VA: The ERIC Clearinghouse on Handicapped and Gifted Children, The Council for Exceptional Children.

Chamot, A., & McKeon, D. (1984). *ESL teaching methodologies educating the minority language student* (pp. 1–51). Reston, VA: National Clearinghouse for Bilingual Education Inter-American Research Associates.

Descamps, J. (1987). The Mexican American student: Cultural implications. Workshop presented at U.T. El Paso during Hispanic Heritage Week.

Durán, E. (1986). Study completed on language development. University of Texas at El Paso.

Durán, E. (2005a, month). *Making vocabulary comprehensible in the content classes.* Lecture presented to Language and Literacy classes at California State University, Sacramento.

Durán, E. (2005b, month). *Cultural implications for all students.* Lecture presented to Teaching English Learners in Inclusive Classrooms, California State University, Sacramento.

Estrada, L. J., & Nava, A. (1976). The long struggle for bilingualism and a consistent language policy: Early Chicano education in California and the Southwest. *Educator, 19*(1), 36–40.

Gonzáles, R. (2005, Fall). *The importance of culture within cross-cultural groups.* Lecture presented to Teaching English Learners in Inclusive Classrooms, California State University, Sacramento.

Grossman, H. (1984). *Educating Hispanic students: Cultural implications for instruction, classroom management, counseling and assessment* (pp. 56–204). Springfield, IL: Charles C Thomas.

Henderson, R. W. (1980). Social and emotional needs of culturally diverse children. *Exceptional Children, 46*(8), 598–604.

Hernández, N. (1987). *The Mexican American student: Cultural implications.* Workshop presented at U.T. El Paso during Hispanic Heritage Week, El Paso, Texas.

Mandlawitz, M. (2006). *What every teacher should know about IDEA 2004.* Boston: Pearson Allyn & Bacon.

Nuttall, E. V. (1984). A critical look at testing and evaluation from a cross-cultural perspective. In P. C. Chinn (Ed.), *Education of culturally and linguistically different children* (pp. 42–63). Reston, VA: The ERIC Clearinghouse on Handicapped and Gifted Children, The Council for Exceptional Children.

Ortiz, A. (1984). Language and curriculum development for exceptional bilingual children. In P. C. Chinn (Ed.), *Education of culturally and linguistically different exceptional children* (pp. 77–100). Reston, VA: The ERIC Clearinghouse on Handicapped and Gifted Children, The Council for Exceptional Children.

Rodriquez, F. (1982). Mainstreaming a multicultural concept into special education: Guidelines for teacher trainers. *Exceptional Children,* 77–100.

Rueda, R. (1984). Cognitive development and learning in mildly handicapped bilingual children. In P. C. Chinn (Ed.), *Education of culturally and linguistically different children* (pp. 63–76). Reston, VA: The ERIC Clearinghouse on Handicapped and Gifted Children, The Council for Exceptional Children.

Rueda, R., & Martinez, I. (1992). Fiesta Educativa: One community's approach to parent training in developmental disabilities for Latino families. *TASH, 17*(2), 93–103.

Chapter 15

STRATEGIES FOR TEACHING
ENGLISH LEARNERS

Elva Durán

The author of this chapter will discuss some second language acquisition theories and strategies which are helpful in teaching English learners or those students whose first language is not English. Also, in this chapter strategies for assisting English learners in general and special education will be discussed. Additionally, the author will share some specific teaching strategies implemented in several classrooms in northern California.

SECOND LANGUAGE ACQUISITION INFORMATION

When students who come from another country or whose primary or first language is not English, it is necessary to keep several ideas in mind when teaching the student whose first language is not English. First, the student whose first language is not English needs to feel no anxiety when learning a new or second language. Students should not be pressured to speak in the new language they are acquiring until they have enough confidence to begin verbalizing in that language on their own. Many students go through a silent period when they are listening and internalizing the new language they are learning, seeing, and possibly tasting. Krashen (1994) who first talked about the affective filter hypothesis to learning a second language gave us extremely important information about creating low anxiety environments so that second language learners could begin listening without feeling they had to speak in the second language immediately. The silent period can last from a few weeks to several months.

It is important for a teacher or parents helping the English learner during this period to be patient and reinforcing. Praise should be given to students as they listen quietly. Praise should be continued as they become further motivated and empowered in order to continue wanting to progress and practice their new skills in the second or new language.

This writer has observed in various classrooms that as teachers are encouraging, warm, and positive with students who are learning English for the first time, students become highly motivated and progress even faster to learn the new language or, in this case, English. One of the greatest characteristics of a truly great teacher is his/her amazing ability to accept the student no matter at what stage or level he/she may be. There is no better way to lower the affective filter or create a low anxiety environment for English learners than by being positive and accepting the student's stage of language learning. Thus, a teacher or parent teaching or helping the second language learner must remember the great progress students make if they are less anxious when learning a new language.

Another important aspect to remember in teaching second language learners is that everything presented to students must be taught to them in comprehensible means. In the comprehensible input hypothesis (Krashen, 1994), the teacher in teaching English learners must remember to present the material so that the students understand the meaning of what they are hearing and seeing. For instance, the teacher needs to remember that English learners need to be shown concrete and visual information in order for them to understand the concept or vocabulary words that they are being presented.

Another important hypothesis that is part of second language acquisition, according to Krashen (1994), is the reading hypothesis. In reading hypothesis, Krashen notes that the more teachers and parents read to children, the more they will hear the language sounds and the more quickly they will begin speaking the language they are learning. Also, the more books that are read to children initially and, later, the more books children read to themselves, the faster the children will learn the second language.

As part of the reading hypothesis, Krashen (1994) also noted that students must be given at least fifteen to twenty minutes daily in order for them to select books they want to see and read. During this time, or sustained silent reading, also called DEAR time, or drop everything and read (Reyes, 1995), the students observe a quiet fifteen minutes as they read their books. It is important to remember that the teacher needs to monitor and follow through as the students are reading or looking at the pictures (for those who are more moderate to severe and can only read a few sight words) because some students may not be holding their books correctly or are unaware of how to use the time appropriately for their independent reading. Thus, giving students this extra monitoring time will help correct any errors that the students may be doing during this independent or sustained silent reading time.

If a student is unable to profit from this independent reading time, it is best to put that student at a station listening and following the book on audiotape. This is another important modification which can be made for different students who may not be at higher levels or reading independently (Durán, 2005).

Ortiz (1994), in her Aim for the Best Program, has noted that developing shared literature units with children and having the teacher prepare reading of various stories and a variety of children's favorite literature will also help increase a child's language development. Ortiz noted that shared literature should take the following suggested format in order to insure success with the language minority student. First, the teacher should be familiar with the story he/she is going to tell or read to the students. If the students are younger, the teacher may choose stories that reflect primary through second-grade focus. These can be stories that follow a simple repetition sequence such as *The Three Bears* or *Brown Bear, Brown Bear*. It is important to note that the teacher may choose simple repetition sequence stories that come from the students' language and culture. There are several publishers and presses that are dedicated to publishing a variety of cross-cultural literature that is appropriate for sharing aloud with students. Many of these publishers will send teachers and/or parents a free catalogue of their holdings if the teacher writes to them. The public libraries also contain several sections where cross-cultural books can be located. These books found in the libraries, like in catalogues of several publishers, are filled with books for different ages and interests.

If these culturally appropriate stories are not selected initially, then the linguistically appropriate stories can be selected later in the month. The teacher should also prepare materials that are age-appropriate for the children to see as he/she is reading the story. The props, the visuals, create a motivation for the children that allow them to be further hooked into listening and chorally reading certain lines of the story.

Following the material or character development, the teacher begins to familiarize the students with the cover of the book. The teacher can ask the children, "What is the title of the story?" "Whose name(s) is on the cover?" "Who is the illustrator?" "Is the cover colorful?" the teacher may go on to ask. Again, the idea is to teach students that there are details in the front of a book as well as the cover. These concepts about print competencies are important for students to learn and the competencies can be introduced to the students as books are being read aloud to them.

The teacher should continue the shared literature lesson by alerting the students to the details of the inside of the book. The children should see the author's and illustrator's names inside the first few pages of the book. The students can chorally read the author's and illustrator's names as the teacher opens the storybook to that particular part of the book.

Continuing with the instruction of the shared literature unit, the teacher begins reading from the book. The teacher carefully shows the children the visual aids he/she has developed for the story and further shows the children the various pictures or special illustrations that he/she wants the children to focus upon. As the teacher reads orally to the children, he/she can ask students questions to help build the drama or suspense of the story such as, "What do you think will happen next?" "Why do you feel the character is acting in such a manner?" These questions along the way help keep the student's motivation high. Questioning the students also helps the children recall details of the story. This interactive type of questioning and the various details of the story will help build oral language which is so important for learning to read and learning vocabulary.

Another part of shared literature or reading aloud to students is to ask the children how many liked or did not like the story and why? Along with this question, the teacher has already prepared a language chart which can be made of large butcher paper or chart material. The chart should be displayed near the students' discussion circle or should be positioned where they can see the titles and wording of the language chart. Some suggested sections of the chart may include: "Title of the Book," "Illustrator," "Names of Characters," and "What I Liked about the Book." The teacher can lead the children in a discussion and he/she can fill in the various columns of the language chart as the students discuss answers with the teacher. The chart should be cumulative so that each of the books that the teacher reads with the students should be part of the language chart information. Keeping such a chart of various books read by the children and teacher will help additionally develop a sense of appreciation for all the various books that they can read together.

In a qualitative study involving language minority students with autism who were in a fully included classroom, Durán (1995) found that language charts and shared literature were very contributing in helping Southeast Asian and Asian American students increase their primary and secondary language. Also, when the students with autism were moved closer to the front of a circle and paired with general education buddies, the more the students with autism who were language minority could cue or pay closer attention to the various details of different storybooks. Durán discovered that the LEP (limited proficient students of English) students with autism came running to the story circle and their attending behaviors increased as the year progressed. Thus, sharing literature and utilizing language charts with students in fully included classroom settings was a significant factor in assisting students to increase their oral language development and appreciation of books they had read during the school year.

In addition to emphasizing second language acquisition information so that students can acquire information presented to them in the classroom and other environments, it is necessary to know various strategies in order to teach English learners. Some of these strategies and other information designed to assist English learners include knowing the levels of English language proficiency, also knowing strategies such as the total physical response approach (Asher, 1981); natural approach (Terrell & Krashen, 1994); cooperative learning (Kagan, 1994); sheltered instruction or specifically designed academic instruction in English (Walqui-vanLier, 1994) and utilizing a combination of reading aloud to students (already discussed previously) and writing strategies to enhance literacy skills in English learners. Also, some of the methodologies that have been found to be useful with English learners include giving students much oral language development (Maldonado-Colón, 2002; Baca, 1989; Ortiz, 1995) as well as increasing their line of reading (Krashen, 1994).

LEVELS OF ENGLISH LANGUAGE PROFICIENCY

Knowing the levels of a student's English language proficiency is very important when trying to determine how to assist the student with instruction in the classroom. In order to assist English learners it is important to assess the student's oral language development by administering a language proficiency test such as the CELDT, California English Language Development Test (California Department of Education, 2002). Each state has various tests they are suggesting are the tests to use for oral language assessment of English learners. It is important to check with the State Departments of each state one lives in order to determine which is the test they are recommending to be used to assess the oral language proficiency of each student whose first language is not English. Once this determination is made it will be important to have a bilingual teacher or bilingual school psychologist assess the English learner in both the native language and in English. These proficiency tests are designed to give information in both languages of the child. The CELDT for example, gives information of the child's languages in English and Spanish. In order to establish proficiency both languages must be assessed.

Some of the levels of language proficiency assessed in these tests include the following levels of proficiency: Beginning, Early Intermediate, Intermediate, Early Advanced, and Advanced. Below will follow a general explanation of each of the levels of English proficiency as defined by various informational material on levels of English proficiency (Dutro et al., 2001). Also, the writer will include a short explanation of the type of instruction that should be completed at each of the different stages.

Beginning Level

In this level the students who are learning English have minimal comprehension of general meaning. The student is beginning to gain familiarity with sounds, rhythms and patterns of English. At the beginning stages there is no verbal response. The students are in a silent period. In the later stages the students may have one or two-word responses for example, "dog, brown." The student responds in single words and phrases and these single words and phrases may be in the form of a subject and predicate, for example. Also, the students in this stage of English development make many basic errors in speech. At this stage of development the student will listen, point to, nod, gesture, act out, manipulate objects/pictures (match, choose, categorize), summarize using objects, gestures, and visuals. When the students are at the beginning stages of English development it is good to have them repeat, tell, say, list, identify people, objects, places, and answer yes/no, who, what, where questions. The students in this stage of development can also practice sound/symbol relationships in known words. In the area of writing the students can draw, circle, label, and match simple sentences with pictures that go with the words (Dutro et al., 2001). The students can also write the letters and sounds they are learning by utilizing dotted line prompts as they are learning to read the beginning sounds in one syllable words (Durán, 2005).

Early Intermediate

In this level there is increased comprehension of general meaning and some specific meaning of words and sentences. The student is beginning to use routine expressions independently and is responding to using phrases and simple sentences, which include a subject and predicate for example, "The dog is brown. He is eating." In this stage of English language development the students are also making some basic errors in speech. When instructing students in this stage of English development, a teacher can have them recite familiar songs and poems. Also, the students begin to ask simple questions, role play, retell and summarize. Using predictable texts such as *Brown Bear, Brown Bear* will be helpful in assisting the students see similar words several times throughout the text. Such review of various vocabularies will help the students hear the vocabulary more than once. If decodable texts (readers that usually present words and letter sounds that have already been taught in the lesson) then the decodables should be a part of a systematic and explicit lesson taught previously or before the decodable is presented to the students. When writing the students can compose simple stories and word banks as they are learning the different vocabulary in this early stage of language development (Dutro et al., 2001).

Intermediate

When the students reach this level they are beginning to have good comprehension of general meaning. They will also have increased comprehension of specific meaning and students also begin to respond to more complex sentences, with more detail using newly acquired vocabulary to experiment and form messages. For instance, they may say a sentence like, "The large dog lived with the other dogs in the family home." Also, at this stage the students make fewer errors in speech. Further, the students can compare and contrast, identify main points of a story and explain, describe, and define using content-related vocabulary (Dutro et al., 2001).

During this stage the students can also read most vocabulary in context and can understand language structures in the text that are familiar and may be predictable. Additionally, in their writing the students can begin to write simple stories from their experience utilizing content word banks and other supports (Dutro et al., 2001).

Early Advanced

In this stage, the students have consistent comprehension of general meaning and also have good understanding of implied meaning. They are able to sustain conversation, respond with detail in compound and complex sentences and they actively participate using more extensive vocabulary. For example, the students may say, "Can bears live in the forest if they find food there?" Also, the students at this stage of English development are beginning to use standard grammar with few random errors. Additionally, in the area of oral language development the students can present, report, identify main ideas, supporting details, and concepts. They can additionally solicit information, analyze, predict, hypothesize, identify antonyms, synonyms, use affixes with known vocabulary and infer word meaning from context. Further, in reading the students can do grade-level text with English language development (vocabulary and structure) support through preteaching of vocabulary. Also, in their writing the students can compose with support utilizing formats and vocabulary webs (Dutro et al., 2001).

Advanced

In this level of English development there is comprehension of general and implied meaning for the students. The students are able to understand idiomatic and figurative language. They will initiate and negotiate using appropriate discourse, varied grammatical structures and vocabulary. For example, they may say, "Would you like me to bring pictures of my dog that I just got?" Many students are able to use the more formal and informal conventions of language for different situations and contexts. In their language development the students who fall in this stage of English development can debate and support their particular point of view, evaluate, persuade, justify, and explain common antonyms and synonyms. The students in this stage of English development can also recognize multiple meanings in texts of familiar topics. Also, the students can understand most idioms and understand and create jokes. In reading the students can understand grade-level text with English language development (vocabulary and structure) support through preteaching. In writing, the students in this level of English development can compose more complex writing using conventions (Dutro et al., 2001).

Once the various levels are determined for the students then the various state standards can be utilized to assist and plan to teach the English learners. In California for example, the students who are English learners have English language development standards that need to be used along with English language arts standards. Teachers should be aware of both standards in order to fully assist the students in their classrooms.

TOTAL PHYSICAL RESPONSE APPROACH

The total physical response approach was a method developed by Asher (1981). In the method the teacher or person presenting to the students gestures and gives them commands so that they follow or try to complete basic directions such as, "stand up," "sit down," "touch your hands, touch your arms." To determine if the students have learned the various commands so the teacher can go on to the new curriculum information, he/she will only indicate the commands verbally and will not do the gestures as he/she is giving the oral commands to the students. If the students can perform the commands the teacher is giving them orally, then Asher suggested that comprehensible input has been achieved and the teacher can present new information to them. Asher does not have a formal curriculum for the total physical response approach, but he suggested that teachers begin with basic vocabulary around the classroom and other environments.

This writer, in assisting a variety of teachers who teach more moderate-to-severe students, suggests that basic vocabulary such as names of objects around the room, school, and other environments such as the home and community be presented to students. The students could further learn to point to their names or addresses, phone numbers, and other personal information. Such information is vital for the students to know, especially if they are attempting to be out in the community.

By utilizing the natural environments in order to learn vocabulary and functional information around the home, school, and community, the teacher is also stressing that the students learn the vocabulary because the students are often unable to generalize or transfer learning from one environment to the next.

When using the Total Physical Response Approach, the teacher should ask the students to demonstrate that they understand by asking them to touch the object or do the action the teacher has named but not physically demonstrated for the children. According to Krashen (1994), true comprehension on the child's part can only come by the teacher giving the word or words orally to the child and not demonstrating the various actions that accompany the vocabulary or commands he/she is presenting to the students.

This writer has successfully used the total physical response approach when teaching university students who know only English by attempting to teach several lessons in Spanish. This is the writer's first language and she presents various demonstrations to the university students in Spanish in order for the English-only students to understand what students of other languages and cultures feel because they do not know English. The university students have told this writer that after experiencing the first vocabulary words in Spanish, they felt more tolerant of their second language learners in their classrooms. It is highly recommended that university students who are preparing to be teachers be taught in a language other than the one they know in order for them to better understand what English learners are experiencing as they attempt to learn new vocabulary or information that is not in their first language.

THE NATURAL APPROACH

Another approach that teachers or instructional aids can successfully use to teach English learners is the Natural Approach. The Natural Approach (Krashen & Terrell, 1981) emphasized that students will continue learning the second language, or in this case English, by having the students practice English in natural everyday talk or conversation. Krashen and Terrell stressed that the time to do the conversations must be planned in the everyday curriculum schedule, otherwise the time that is needed for the students to speak will not occur.

Some suggestions to encourage more conversation may include role-playing introductions, ordering from a menu, and hearing the students answer questions about want ads or other advertisements. The teacher can have the students describe their favorite toys, animals, or events. He/she can have them explain how to get from one point or destination to another. This is a difficult task for many English learners, but practicing pragmatics in learning a second language. Pragmatics, as used here, means the student can explain on a higher level, using their newly acquired language, how to go from one point to another, for example. When presenting lesson demonstrations to students utilizing the Natural Approach, the teacher should demonstrate for the students. He/she may hold up a menu filled with words, fruits, and pictures, and may say, "I will order fruit salad with iced tea." Another person can take the person's order so that a restaurant scene can be depicted for the students. The students can then role-play being the waiter/waitress and another student or students can use menus to order their meals. Utilizing cooperative groups to have them practice ordering meals is an excellent tool in order to give different students opportunities to practice English. After the students have had opportunities to practice their role-playing conversations, as in this case ordering from a menu, the teacher can check their comprehension of the activity by asking them questions about their orders. For example, the teacher may say, "Did you order furniture today, Saul?" If Saul indicates that he does not understand by responding, "Yes, I ordered furniture," the teacher will know to assist the students who were in the cooperative group who made the error in comprehension of the concept. The teacher can sit with the cooperative group where Saul is seated and he/she can participate in ordering various items from the menu. The demonstration will help the students see where they made the mistakes along with Saul.

Krashen (1994) notes that students who are English learners will learn best to speak, read, and write if they are given the direct opportunities to do these activities in various environments. The Natural Approach gives classroom teachers many opportunities to allow English learners the opportunities they need to learn English.

As the students learn more and more English, Krashen (1994) noted that the grammar and all its correct forms are also learned as they begin to get practice in speaking and writing. Grammar should not be emphasized as much in the very beginning stages of learning English as in the later stages because students need to learn to speak in an environment where they will be able to practice learning English initially without being corrected each time they speak, according to Krashen. As the students begin putting more vocabulary together there should be an emphasis in modeling for them the correct grammar forms so they can learn early on how to say various grammatical structures correctly.

This writer has seen many elementary, secondary, and adult second language learners who are at the beginning stages of learning to speak and later write in the second language who do not feel comfortable to continue if someone is constantly reminding them of their oral or written errors. Patience and empowering the English learners are keys in getting these students to learn the new language. The English learner needs to feel empowered to continue learning even if they make a few mistakes. It is a good idea to remember that learning a second language may take up to ten hours and developing oral and written proficiency may take a longer time, but with modeling and correction feedback the students will eventually learn to become more proficient in English grammar. Practice is the key because one does not learn to speak or write, for example, if one does not get the many opportunities to write and speak. This writer is a second language learner herself and has been one all of her life. At the beginning of her first-grade experience this writer struggled to learn so much new vocabulary and would have learned even faster if she had had more positive modeling and experiences as she was learning to speak. What the writer unfortunately experienced were angry remarks from the teacher because she had made a mistake in asking for various items in the classroom. It was this writer's best friend, another student in the class, who acted as a teacher for this writer. The Anglo American student who was also in this writer's first-grade classroom was always acting as a good buddy by modeling for this writer how to say the sentence or phrase in English correctly. This writer's friend made learning possible because she was not judgmental and helped this writer learn English because she was positive and praised this writer as she attempted to speak in English. To this day this writer has never forgotten her first-grade friend who taught her so much English. This writer will never forget that experience learning English so many years ago.

Continuing with this discussion of students learning English, this writer noticed that some students with moderate disabilities or students with Down syndrome who were English learners learned initial words and phrases after thirty-three plus hours using instruction with the students daily for thirty minutes twice a day. This writer, as an English learner, feels that learning a second language is an ongoing process that requires patience and positive teachers who not only understand how English learners learn other languages, but it also helps if the teachers have experienced some difficulty themselves in understanding a foreign language. This writer also feels that teachers should have the highest expectations of their English learners because this will help the students go beyond what they have already learned and they will strive to learn even more new information.

Similarly, the Language Experience Approach can also be utilized effectively with the Natural Approach. In the Language Experience Approach, Van Allen (1985) told us to make use of a student's experiences as someone records their words on a chart or paper. Utilizing this approach as one of several methods will be helpful in teaching the students oral language development. By combining the Natural Approach and Language Experience Approach, students can experience various experiences in their everyday lives and then the teacher can lead them into a discussion and begin recording some of the words and phrases they are saying. The teacher can print the words on the chalkboard or paper and have them read from left to right as he/she teaches each word. Later, the students can read back the words and phrases in a natural speech production so that they can hear the words and phrases read as conversation is naturally spoken. Students can prepare language experience booklets so they can take pride in their work as they are also authors. They can read their language experience booklets to each other or to themselves. The covers of the booklets can be illustrated for more enjoyment of their work. Thus, writing, reading, and speaking are combined with the use of the Natural Approach. All of these strategies work very nicely in fully-included classroom settings.

The study done by Durán (1994, 1995) revealed that five students with moderate disabilities who were also learning English as a second language learned some literacy skills by using a combination of the total physical response approach, natural approach, language experience, and shared literature. These students were also being taught to read utilizing words and picture icons for the various vocabularies they were attempting to learn. Results revealed in this study that the combination of approaches was helpful in teaching the students to learn English and functional reading (Durán, 1995). Data was also collected on five students with autism who were English learners and were fully-included in a general education classroom. The results of this study also indicated that the children with autism who are also English learners learned English because of a combined use of the total physical response approach and the natural approach, which the teachers and the instructional aides also combined with a rich oral language development and shared literature approach (Durán, 1995).

The parents of the children in both general and special education enjoy social skills and language development progress which the students also enjoy in fully-included classroom settings. Everyone has benefited from this class situation.

SHELTERED INSTRUCTION/SPECIFICALLY DESIGNED ACADEMIC INSTRUCTION IN ENGISH (SDAIE)

Sheltered instruction is generally associated with several instructional strategies designed to make academically rigorous subject matter more understandable to English learners at intermediate fluency or above (Schifini, 1991). More recently, some teachers in California

have been using the Sheltered Approach with students at early intermediate stages of fluency and they have also had good success utilizing this approach in lessons with students. This is usually done by
teaching new concepts in context and providing cues to the student.
The teaching techniques geared to provide comprehensible input in
English or the second language the student is learning are now being
used by content teachers (Schifini, 1991). Common cues or context
clues are: gestures, visuals, props, manipulatives, audio visuals, models, charts, graphic organizers, and teacher talk that is appropriate to
the students' English language proficiency (Schifini, 1991).

According to Schifini (1991), a subject matter taught in a sheltered
way usually involves opportunities for careful background related to
the key concepts of the lesson. Texts are used as a tool to help students
develop concepts.

Teachers using sheltered instruction check students' understanding
of the subject matter by observation and questioning of their knowledge of the concepts. Teachers who are strong in content such as science and social studies are usually the instructors of sheltered content
classes.

Students who are the candidates for this type of instruction need to
have intermediate fluency in English. Generally, intermediate speakers are good candidates for sheltered classes because they have acquired many vocabulary words in English and are able to respond to questions that are asked of them orally. Additionally, many are able to
engage in some discussion and would profit from various types of
questions or topic themes that are presented as part of the classroom
information. Students are usually in upper grades and are making a
transition from primary language instruction to English. The primary
language may still be used when the students may be having difficulty understanding additional concepts. At no time should sheltered instruction be considered as watered-down curriculum (Walqui-vanLier,
1994). Also, the primary language may be used when the students' primary language is predominately of one particular cultural and linguistic group.

In California schools where more than seventy different languages
exist in some school districts, it would not be possible to use seventy
different languages in the sheltered classroom unless paraprofessionals
or volunteers could come to the classroom and assist with the majority of linguistic groups which would be found in the classrooms at any

one time. Thus far, this has proven to be quite difficult because there are not enough translators available at any one school to help teachers when more than one or two languages exist in the various classrooms.

In a study conducted by this writer in 1994 until the present, she observed the usefulness of a teacher utilizing sheltered instruction to teach students who were in a third-grade, fully-included classroom in a rural town in northern California. The teacher had her bilingual/ cross-cultural teaching certification and was also certified to teach in general education. She had monolingual English-only speakers and had a student from a self-contained special education classroom attending half a day and additionally had limited English proficient and other students who were at an intermediate fluency and literacy level in English. The teacher had one instructional aide and several student teachers throughout the school year.

Observation data was taken twice weekly for two to two and a half hours on the children who were limited English and those who were on a more advanced English development level. The writer shared results monthly with the classroom teacher. She wanted to know the results and also felt that she could improve the program further by adding any information to her curriculum in the classroom.

After a year, many variables were evident in academic and literacy increases in the five children whom this writer and her assistant took data on each week. One of the variables that was consistently revealed in the results was the teacher's strong use of sheltered instruction. She went out of her way to prepare materials to help all the children who needed the assistance to achieve comprehensible input. Other variables that were in evidence were the effective use of cooperative learning groups, shared literature, and reader's and writer's workshops. Data will be further collected in order to determine if the new teacher at the students' new grade level will utilize any of the variables which proved successful in the former setting. Results of this qualitative study were reported to the principal in a final report. She was able to share the results with the classroom teachers who were involved in the study. Data collection further revealed that the variables which initially proved to be successful continued to show effective results with the students in their literacy skill development.

This writer has noted that once again sheltered instruction, like so many general and multilingual/multicultural strategies, has shown to be quite effective with special education students who are English learners and have moderate-to-severe disabilities. The language and literacy enrichment found in general education classrooms is very helpful to the more moderate-to-severe groups of students who are fully included in these particular classrooms.

Additionally, this writer has already indicated earlier that sheltered instruction when originally developed was designed for intermediate level speakers of English. For several years in California for example, sheltered instruction or SDAIE (Specially Designed Academic Instruction in English) has been used with students as early as the early intermediate levels of English development. One of the reasons this has occurred is because there is such an emphasis for students to learn English at a faster pace due to the many rigorous standards that students must follow in order to learn English and literacy skills.

Further, the term SDAIE is the newer term used to also refer to sheltered instruction in California schools (Walqui-vanLier, 1994). Because there are so many different languages found in California schools, the term SDAIE more closely explains what teachers of sheltered instruction are attempting to do in classrooms.

OTHER STRATEGIES USEFUL IN TEACHING ENGLISH LEARNERS

Cooperative Learning

Cooperative learning consists of student-centered learning activities completed by students in heterogeneous groups of two to six (Cochran, 1989). According to Cochran and Calderón (1990), students benefit from observing learning strategies used by their peers. Further, Cochran noted that English learners benefit from face-to-face verbal interactions, which promote communication that is natural and meaningful.

This writer, in conducting two qualitative studies with limited English proficient students who had autism and five other students in a second study who were at risk for special education, discovered that one of the variables which assisted all students in both studies learn English more effectively was cooperative learning. The students with autism learned more social skills and English because of the inclusive setting they were placed in and also learned more English due to the cooperative learning groups. The students with autism stopped tantruming and were able to attend more due to the various activities scheduled in the fully-included classroom.

In the third-grade classroom where the other study was conducted, the teacher utilized cooperative group work for all her activities where the students needed to discuss and come up with solutions. She rotated the various roles of "leader," "recorder," "observer," and "encourager." This gave all the students an opportunity to be in charge of different activities. She also monitored each group during their discussions and while they were to complete activities. In this way, she could better see which students were not participating in the discussions or other group work.

As an observer and researcher who collected data weekly with these two groups of students, this writer was able to see that students did interact and discuss with one another as a result of the cooperative learning activities. The students with autism were able to seek others in the classroom due to cooperative learning.

It is a good idea when using cooperative learning to teach the students the various roles in which they can participate. Also, it is a good idea to teach them to have respect for each other, especially if one student says or discusses a comment that may be different from the thoughts of others in the group. If respect is not made part of the rules of the cooperative learning activities, the English learners will become fearful of speaking and their progress to learn more English will not be realized.

According to Calderón (1990), in order for students to achieve competence in group work, certain principles must be followed:

1. The teacher models the discourse and processes overtly, explicitly, and concretely in appropriate context of cooperative activities.
2. Strategies for working and learning together and the range and utility of the strategies discussed, and interventions and modifications are attempted by the students.
3. Ineffective strategies and misconceptions about group work and individual participation are confronted.
4. Debriefing activities where thinking is brought out into an open space where students and teacher can see it and learn from it are indicated in the cooperative learning activity.
5. The responsibility for learning to work collaboratively and debriefing of that process should be transferred to the students as soon as they take charge.

The transfer should be gradual, working on one cooperative skill at a time until it is internalized.

6. Students should receive continuous feedback on their improvement.
7. Just as teachers need modeling, rationale, practice, feedback, and coaching, so do students (pp. 11-12).

Thus, just putting students in groups and encouraging them to work together is not enough to produce learning gains according to Calderón (1990). Teachers must be well trained in appropriate teaching strategies and classroom management techniques for organizing critical thinking.

Finally, this writer has seen the use of direct instruction methodologies as noted by Englemann (1978) used very effectively with cooperative learning groups. In direct instruction, the teacher or facilitator uses some signaling, follow-up, and giving the students a business-like atmosphere especially when relaying to them about certain tasks which must be completed. In several classrooms in northern California where the English learners were a part of a fully-included third and fourth-grade class, the teachers initially gave the students rules and explained to them that no one would laugh or not respect a different view from their opinion in the cooperative groups. The teachers would continue to use the direct instruction methodologies to follow-up and ask the students what they had said and further asked them that no one would laugh or not respect a different view from their opinion in the cooperative groups. The teachers would continue to use the direct instruction methodologies to follow-up and ask the students what they had said and further asked them what the rules of respect were for each student in the groups. During this portion of the information giving, direct instruction methodologies were nicely woven in with the cooperative learning group information.

It is this writer's view that no one method is the only answer to improving the students who may need additional help. Using a variety of approaches such as cooperative learning and direct instruction, for instance, at the beginning of setting up rules for the groups to follow, is very helpful. Students who have severe disabilities and who are fully-included in classrooms may also need additional structure that some direct instruction can insure for the learners.

Systematic Explicit Instruction

As has already been mentioned in the section on cooperative learning, direct and/or systematic explicit instruction is very helpful to teach English learners English and literacy skills. In systematic explicit instruction the students can be taught in small and/or large groups and both types of interventions are most effective. One of the reasons systematic and explicit instruction works so well is because the teacher has very specific goals and objectives for each lesson. For example, if the instruction is focused around teaching the students vocabulary, the teacher will say and show a picture of the word being taught and the student will say the name of the object that is represented by the picture the teacher is holding up to the students to see. The lesson might go something like this. Teacher: "Look at this picture. This is a flower." The teacher will ask the students to say the name of the picture once again. The students will say, "Flower." As the students learn more and more vocabulary, the teacher will begin shaping their responses more so that they can say more complete sentences. The dialogue of a lesson where the students have learned more vocabulary and will now say a longer sentence will be done something like this. The teacher will say, "Flower. This is a flower. What is this?" The students will repeat, "This is a flower." Because the lessons are so organized and explicitly tell the teacher when to begin introducing each step of the lesson, the students learn the vocabulary and begin to learn simple sentences in response to the teacher's questions. Later, the students begin learning more complex sentences which are once again modeled for the students by the teacher.

Also, in systematic explicit instruction the students are assessed during each lesson to see if they have learned the information that is presented in the objectives of the various lessons. Students do not go ahead if they have not achieved the mastery level designated by each lesson and the lessons direct the teacher to review the vocabulary for example, that the students may have missed in the lesson.

For thirty-five years (Durán, 2003) this method of instruction has been widely researched and has proven to be most effective in assisting the students to learn many types of lesson objectives. This writer has used this type of instruction for many years and has achieved excellent results with all the subjects she has taught her English learners. This method can also be combined with other methods that have already been noted in this chapter and things can be quite successful for the students and the teacher because the organized atmosphere will create happy students wanting to learn even more information.

This writer has also seen how successful this methodology is when teaching English learners who have special needs and those students with special needs who are in a fully included classroom. Since so many classrooms are utilizing curriculum that follows a systematic explicit approach to teaching, utilizing these various curricular programs fit in nicely with teaching a variety of learners.

More information about this methodology will be discussed in the chapter on literacy development. For now it is important for the audience to realize the power that can be obtained in teaching all students utilizing a systematic and explicit approach.

INCLUSION

Since 1985 we have heard that students with more severe disabilities should be included in general education classrooms. Inclusion in our schools has made some progress since 1985, but according to many school principals much more needs to be done before more students with severe disabilities are placed in general education classrooms for the entire school day. The key is to place students with disabilities in general education classrooms with support from the special education teacher and his/her staff. Inclusion can be major help to students who are English learners and who also have moderate-or-severe disabilities because the enriched curriculum that is seen in general education classrooms is very helpful to the students to learn English or their primary language (Durán, 1995).

Students with autism who are limited English proficient or who are learning English as a second language are enriched by being placed in fully included general education classrooms. In two general education classrooms where students with autism who are also English learners or are attempting to learn English for the first time and other second language learners who were more moderate in their disability were also placed in general education settings, started to increase their English oral language development because the teachers used a variety of approaches and other strong literature and sheltered types of instruction (Durán, 1995).

As more and more students with disabilities are placed in general education settings which have good teacher models who are practicing and implementing a variety of curricular strategies, the more progress students who are English learners and who have disabilities will make.

In conclusion, strategies which can be added to fully-included classrooms, such as cooperative learning, some systematic and explicit instruction methodologies, natural approach, and total physical response approaches, plus a strong program which will increase literacy skills, will help to greatly enhance all students who are in fully- included general education settings. The idea for teachers to use a variety of curricular strategies that are based in research and good sound practice will enhance the learning that language minority students need in order to learn English.

DISCUSSION QUESTIONS

1. What can be done by a teacher to increase comprehensible input among the English learners in the class?
2. How can the Total Physical Response Approach and Natural Approach be used effectively to help English learners who are more moderate-to-severe learn English?
3. Discuss strategies that have been found effective in teaching English learners English?
4. Why is full inclusion effective in assisting English learners to learn English?

REFERENCES

Ada, A. F. (1990). *A magical encounter Spanish-language children's literature in the classroom.* Compton, CA: Santillana Publishing Company.

Ambert, A. M. (1991). B*ilingual education and English as a second language, a research handbook.* New York: Garland.

Asher, J. (1981, January). *Total physical response approach.* Presentation made at San Jose State University, San Jose, CA.

Baca, L. (1989). *The bilingual special education interface* (2nd Ed.). New York: Maxwell Macmillan International.

Calderón, M. (1990). *Cooperative learning for limited English proficient students.* Washington, DC: Center on Effective Schooling for Disadvantaged Students.

California Department of Education. (2002). *CELDT (California English Language Development Test),* Sacramento, CA.

Carnine, D. W., et al., (2004). *Direct instruction reading,* (4th Ed.). Columbus, OH: Pearson Merrill Prentice-Hall.

Chamot, A. U. (1985). *ESL instructional approaches and underlying language learning theories.* Washington, DC: National Clearinghouse for Bilingual Education.

Cochran, C. (1989). *Strategies for involving LEP students in the all-English medium classroom: A cooperative learning approach.* Washington, DC: National Clearinghouse for Bilingual Education.

Crandall, J. (1987). *ESL through content-area instruction mathematics, science, social studies.* Englewood Cliffs, NJ: Regent/Prentice Hall.

Durán, E. (1988). *Teaching the moderately and severely handicapped student and autistic adolescent with particular attention to bilingual special education.* Springfield, IL: Charles C Thomas.

Durán, E. (1992). *Vocational training and employment of the moderately and severely handicapped and autistic adolescent with particular emphasis to bilingual special education.* Springfield, IL: Charles C Thomas.

Durán, E. (1994, April). *How students with moderate to severe disabilities learn English.* Lecture presented to Teaching English Learners class, California State University Sacramento.

Durán, E. (1995, March). *How students with moderate to severe disabilities learn English.* Lecture presented to Teaching English Learners class, California State University Sacramento.

Durán, E. (1995a). *Inclusion and second language acquisition.* Qualitative study report conducted in Sacramento City Unified School District. Report submitted to Sacramento City Unified School District, Sacramento, CA.

Durán, E. (1995b). *Second language acquisition.* Qualitative study report conducted at Valley Oaks Elementary School, submitted to school principal. Galt, CA.

Durán, E. (2003). *Systematic instruction in reading for Spanish-speaking students.* Springfield, IL: Charles C Thomas.

Durán, E. (2005). *Developing independent readers by establishing a child's independent reading level.* Lecture given to Language and Literacy class. California State University, Sacramento.

Dutro, S., et al., (2001). *ELD matrix: Scope and sequence of levels of English language proficiency.* San Diego, CA: California Reading and Literature Project.

Englemann, S. (1978, April). Direct Instruction methodologies. Lecture presented at University of Oregon.

Freeman, Y. S., & Freeman, D. E. (1992). *Whole language for second language learners.* Exeter, NH: Heinemann.

Krashen, S. (1981). Bilingual education and second language acquisition theory. In California State Department of Education (Ed.), *Schooling and language minority students: A theoretical framework* (pp. 51-82). Sacramento, CA: Office of Bilingual Education.

Krashen, S. (1993). *The power of reading insights from the research.* Colorado: Libraries Unlimited, Incorporated.

Krashen, S. D., & Terrell, T. D. (1983). *The natural approach: Language acquisition in the classroom.* Hayward, CA: Alemany Press.

Maldonado-Colón, E. (2003). Developing the foundations of literacy: Oracy. In E. Durán, et al., *Systematic instruction in reading for Spanish-speaking students.* Springfield, IL: Charles C Thomas.

Ortiz, A. (1994). *How bilingual/special education came to be.* Symposium for Second Language Learners in Regular and Special Education. California State University, Sacramento.

Ovando, C. J., & Collier, V. P. (1985). *Bilingual and ESL classrooms teaching in multi-cultural contexts.* New York: McGraw-Hill.

Peregoy. S. F. (1993). *Reading, writing, and learning in ESL: A resource book for K-8 teachers.* New York: Longman.

Pérez, B. & Torres-Guzman, M.E. (1992). *Learning in two worlds: An integrated Spanish/English biliteracy approach.* New York: Longman.

Reyes, R. (1995). *SDAIE as part of literature stories.* Second Language Acquisition Series. Presented at California State University.

Schifini, A. (1991). *Sheltered instruction: The basics.* A training manual, (pp. 1-4) Center for Language Education and Research. University of California, Los Angeles.

Towell, J. (1993). *Strategies for monolingual teachers in multilingual classrooms.* Washington, D.C.: Education Resource.

VanAllen, R. (1985). ESL instructional approaches and underlying language learning theories. Focus. Washington, D.C.: National Clearinghouse for Bilingual Education.

Walqui-vanLier, A. (1994, April). *Providing access to stimulating curriculum through sheltered instruction (SDAIE).* Paper presented at California State University, Sacramento.

Williams, S. J., & Snipper, G. C. (1990). *Literacy and bilingualism.* New York: Longman.

AUTHOR INDEX

SUBJECT INDEX

for Mexican American students, 387
patience and reinforcement in, 401
professionals specializing in, 171
student motivation, 401, 412
universal design application for, 39
English-learning students, social studies
instruction for, 361, 365–366, 370, 372–373
English proficiency limited students. *See*
Limited English proficiency (LEP) students
English-speaking environments, 306
"Enjoying" behavior, 34
Environment
adapting, 366
arranging, 62
assessments, 80
challenges in, 57
communication forms varying by, 153
control over, 184
deficit orientation, 272
exploration, motivation for, 184
language instruction connection to, 62, 151
modifications (for visually impaired), 175
multiple, 62, 63, 65
natural, 81
simulated *versus* real, 133
Environmental inventory (environment-specific vocabulary), 67, 68, 68t, 72, 73, 83, 85, 86, 151, 388
Equal educational opportunities, 385
Equal opportunities, 11
Equitable use, 37t
Error
correction strategies, 75–76, 78, 152
minimizing, 38t
tolerance for, 38t
ESEA (Elementary and Secondary
Education Act), 11, 196. *See also* No Child
Left Behind (NCLB) Act
Essential information, 37t–38t
Ethnic backgrounds, 11
Ethnic differences, 4
Ethnic populations, increase in, 261t
European Americans, 262, 267
Evaluating, 408
Everyday versus academic vocabulary, 255
Evidence-based social support strategies, 30
Exceptional students, 300, 304. *See also*
Disabled students
Exclusion, preventing, 20

Exclusion legislation, 263
Experience, relating concepts to students', 364, 376b
Experience *versus* cultural/situation specific vocabulary, 256
Experiential background, 307–308, 310–311, 312, 313, 318, 319
Experiential profile, 326t
Explicit approaches to reading instruction, 351
Expressions, routine, using, 406
Expressive ability, 67
Expressive language
increasing, 82
learning, 152
Extended families
Asian American, 267, 273
definition of, 198, 199
Korean American, 220
Latino, 177
members, role of, 378b
respecting, 198
External resources, 272–273
Extracurricular activities, participation in, 30
Extra-curriculum activities, 11
Extralinguistic information, 248
Eye contact, 204, 265
Eye-to-eye contact, 75

F

Face, saving, 271
Face to face interactions, opportunities for, 30
Facial expressions, 67, 204, 363
Fail safe features, 38t
Fair Labor Standards Act, 107
Fairness (defined), 26f
Familiarity, 27
Families. *See also* Culturally and linguistically diverse (CLD) families; Transition planning: family involvement in
activities of, 123, 201
beliefs of, 210
of blind and visually impaired, 171, 175, 177
conversations with, 212–213
in crisis, 276
definition and composition of, 194, 198–199

Special educators
  collaborative skills of, 42
  help from, 165, 420
  roles and responsibilities, changing of, 21
Special needs students. *See* Disabled students
Special services, transition without, 93
Specifically designed academic instruction in
  English (SDAIE), 404, 413–416
Speech
  abilities, undeveloped, 61
  errors in, 406, 407
  in hearing impaired, 179t, 181
  as language form, 52
  learning, barriers to, 75
  practicing, 411
  therapy, 100
Spelling, 358
Spelling dictation, 337
Spelling skills, 364
Spoken language, 80
Spontaneous sharing, 34
SPRED, Special Religious Education
  Department in the Diocese of Oakland,
  Calif., 198
SRA (Science Research Associates), 355
Standardized tests, 287
Stanford Achievement Test Hearing
  Impaired Version, 180
Starting school, 10t
State Board of Education, Diana v. (1970), 321
Stigmatization of disabled, 15, 16, 37t, 41, 128
Stimuli, responses to, 183
Stories, 402–404, 406, 407
Stories (cuentos), 388, 390
Storybook reading, 345
Strangers, solicitations by, 134, 155
Strategic planning, proactive, 24
Strengths
  accommodations based on, 375b
  identifying, 110, 117
  and opportunities, focusing on, 41
  and talents, 100, 103f, 104, 105, 128
  valuing, 129
Student achievement. *See* academic achievement
Student assessment. *See also* Standardized tests
  alternative methods of, 314, 320–326
  case law affecting, 321

  challenges of, 301–303
  communication mode selection based on, 80
  comprehensive, 328
  defined, 302
  diagnostic stage of, 320–326, 326t
  impact of, 301
  instruments, modification of, 320
  legislation regarding, 301, 303–305
  during lessons, 319
  modifications stage of, 312–320, 326t
  nonbiased, 274–275, 301–302, 303, 304,
    323, 325
  outcomes, 310, 324
  plan, 314
  prescriptive stage of, 326–327, 326t
  in primary language, 304
  process, 300, 312
  referrals for, 301, 326t
  reports, 204
  specific, 323–326
  tools, 171–174, 172t
Student communities, 214–216, 228, 247,
  294–295, 296
Student Earned Income Exclusion, 139
Student evaluation
  versus assessment, 300, 301, 302
  benefits of, 300
  defined, 302
  impact of, 301
  language ability, determining, 310
  legislation regarding, 303–305
  ongoing, planning, 23
  results, utilizing, 301
  for special education placement, 195
  unbiased, 304
"Student First and Second Language Oral
  and Literacy Skills" (instrument), 313
Student outcomes, collaboration impact on, 24
Student performance. *See* Academic performance
Student placement, 19, 20–21, 30, 195, 203, 326t
Student preferences (in language use), 56
Student presentations, 105–107, 106f
Student progress, evaluating, 271
Student records, 305
Students, demographics of, 294, 362